OSCAR WILDE A PRESENT TIME APPRAISAL

WILDE

by ST. JOHN ERVINE

WILLIAM MORROW & COMPANY
New York 1952

First published in Great Britain 1951.
Published in United States 1952.

L.C. Catalog Card Number: 52-9699
Designed by Merle Armitage

TO FOSTER AND KATHLEEN KENNEDY ■

OSCAR WILDE

A PRESENT TIME APPRAISAL

■

OSCAR WILDE, whose life was spent in the Victorian age, a fact sufficiently paradoxical in itself to satisfy even his passion for absurd conjunctions, has been dead long enough for an opinion of him and his work to be formed without prejudice. He died on 30th November 1900, when he was forty-six. His was a short-lived family. His father, Sir William Robert Wills Wilde, was sixty-one when he died; his mother, Jane Francesca, seventy; his elder brother, William Charles Kingsbury Wills, forty-six; and his only sister, Isola Francesca,

> Lily-white, white as snow
> She hardly knew
> She was a woman, so
> Sweetly she grew,

was nine. The Wildes were a dying fire which shot up one flash of brilliant flame before it faded out.

Wilde's singular career, at once bright and drab, is better understood to-day than it was when misfortune came upon him with such careless speed that it may be called hysterical. Reviled unreasonably, he was stupidly applauded. Rousing in some men, such as Charles Brookfield, a small-part actor in *An Ideal Husband* and son of the lady to whom Thackeray was devoted, a hatred so profound and intense that it became pathological, he roused in others, such as Robert Harborough Sherard, a devotion that was inexplicable; since Sherard had a horror of sodomy as deep as Brookfield's. To be detested by the Marquess of Queensberry, a man with the habits of a demented ox, and admired by William Morris, one of the world's manliest poets, and by Frank Harris, a rapscallion editor, the Ancient Pistol of Fleet Street, who pursued women with mathematical precision, denotes, surely, some extraordinary qualities in one who was so liked and loathed. Morris, as he lay dying, remarked that he would rather be visited by Wilde than any other man;[1] and Harris asserts with transparent sincerity that he "misses no one so much as I miss Oscar Wilde.

I would rather spend an evening with him than with Renan or Carlyle, or Verlaine or Dick Burton or Davidson. I would rather have him back than almost anyone I have ever met. I have known more heroic souls and some deeper souls; souls much more keenly alive to ideas of duty and generosity; but have known no more charming, no more quickening, no more delightful spirit. . . . I do not believe that in all the realms of death there is a more fascinating and delightful companion."

When all is said that can be said in detriment of Frank Harris, and it is a great deal, there remains the surprising fact that he paid this tribute to Wilde who was, in almost every physical respect, antipathetic, and even repellent, to him. If Harris, who may not have been a liar and a blackguard, but behaved as if he were, could write of him in this glowing manner when there was nothing to be gained by false pretence, we may feel confident that the praise was deserved and due.

I

A MAN with his ancestral and medical history would not now be condemned with such severity as Wilde was. It is not a crime, despite the laws of Butler's *Erewhon*, to suffer from congenital disease. Who would escape the lethal chamber if it were? A son

[1] But we must be careful how we believe these allegations. Sir Sydney Cockerell, in a letter which appeared in *The Times Literary Supplement* on the 3rd of February 1950, contradicts them flatly. "I have seen these statements . . . and as they are quite erroneous, it is high time that they should be refuted. Wilde was sentenced to two years' imprisonment on May 25, 1895. Morris's health began to cause uneasiness some months later than this, and he died on October 3, 1896. In the interval he received constant visits from his many friends. I was with him as his secretary all the time he was at Hammersmith (he was sometimes away at Kelmscott) from the end of January 1894, onwards. I never saw Wilde there, though I saw him at a lecture of Morris's, given at the New Gallery in 1893."

of Sir William and Lady Wilde could not, in terms of biology, hope for happiness unless he had an exceptionally large and powerful inheritance of sanctity, and could, therefore, transcend his own nature. Neither of the Wildes had any sanctity to dispense. Their second son, Oscar, was damned on the day he was born, and would have done better to have died in his childhood as his sister, Isola, who followed him, did. No man can choose whether to be born or not born, nor has he any choice in his period or his parents, his country or his condition, his mind or his physique. It is very certain that if any person had been allowed to choose his parents, none would, despite their distinction, have chosen William and Jane Francesca, sometimes spelt Francisca, Wilde. If ever there was a tainted wether of the flock, Oscar Fingal O'Flahertie Wills Wilde was the wether.

His father was an incontinent oculist and aural surgeon in Dublin, eminent in his profession, but notorious for trifling with the virtue of his women patients: one of whom accused him of raping her while she was unconscious from chloroform. This was Miss Mary Josephine Travers, the daughter of Robert Travers, Professor of Jurisprudence at Trinity College, a man of flabby character and woolly wits, who lived apart from his wife. Miss Travers, a pretty girl, combining a cold nature with morbid emotions, was the sort of unsatisfied woman who, if she be not seduced when seduction is her dispassionate desire, asserts, and eventually believes, that rape has been attempted. Potiphar's wife has had many sedulous apes. The circumstances of the action were odd. It was brought, not against Sir William Wilde, though he was, as everybody in Dublin realised, the true defendant, but against his wife; and the charge was not one of rape, but of libel!

About two months after Wilde had been knighted in the spring of 1864, he consented to lecture in the Metropolitan Hall, Abbey Street, Dublin, under the auspices of the Y.M.C.A. His subject was *Ireland: Past and Present; the Land and the People*. The hall was packed, for his reputation as a lecturer and a wit was high. Suddenly a boy, ringing a bell, appeared in the midst of the fashionable assembly, followed by four or five other boys who offered a pamphlet for sale. It was entitled *Florence Boyle Price;*

or A Warning. The name of its author was stated to be "Speranza", which was the pen-name of Wilde's wife. The boys, in addition to selling the pamphlet, distributed free copies of a fly-sheet on which were printed letters written by Sir William. When the nature of the pamphlet was realised by the audience, its sale was swift, in spite of the efforts of some people to stop it and eject the vendors from the hall; and all the rumours that circulated round Wilde's name were instantly revived in volume.

In the street outside the hall was a carriage containing a wild-looking young woman: Mary Josephine Travers, who had become Wilde's patient in 1854, when she was a dark, attractive girl of nineteen. That was the year in which Oscar Wilde was born. She had also become his mistress, a fact of which Lady Wilde was well aware. Lady Wilde, indeed, had, on one occasion, thrown the young person out of her bedroom. There was another occasion when Sir William's two small sons, coming down the stairs of their father's house, saw a grim-looking lady sitting in the hall, where she had been perched for a couple of hours: Miss Travers; to whom their mother forbade them to speak. The young person's pursuit of the great oculist had now become a form of persecution. To escape from this persecution, and to protect her children from it, Lady Wilde went, in May 1864, to live in Bray, a pleasant sea-side place in County Wicklow, and while she was there, incidents occurred which caused her temper to break. Isola, then about six years old, came to her bedroom to tell her that a wretched lad was in the hall, offering to sell a pamphlet about "Speranza" and Lady Wilde. The boy was expelled, and the angry mother wrote a letter to Professor Travers which was the foundation of the libel suit.

Sir [she wrote]:

You may not be aware of the disreputable conduct of your daughter at Bray where she consorts with all the low newspaper boys in the place employing them to disseminate offensive placards in which my name is given, and also tracts in which she makes it appear that she has had an intrigue with Sir William Wilde. If she chooses to disgrace herself, it is not my affair, but as her object in insulting me is in the hope of extorting money for which she has several times applied to Sir William Wilde with threats of more annoyance if not given, I think it right to inform you, as no threat of additional insult shall ever extort money from our hands. The wages of disgrace she has so basely treated for and demanded shall never be given her.

JANE F. WILDE

To Dr. Travers.

This letter fell into the hands of Miss Travers, who promptly started a suit for libel in the Court of Common Pleas, claiming £2000 damages. The trial began on Monday the 12th of December 1864, before Mr. Justice Monahan and a special city jury. There was a heavy array of counsel: three seniors and two juniors on each side.[1]

The jury did not believe that Miss Travers had been seduced under chloroform or against her will, but it did believe that she had been seduced, and many times over a long period. There was even a suggestion that she had borne Sir William a son. The jury's belief in her concubinage was the belief of every person who had any knowledge of Wilde, a man as strongly inclined to beget bastards as Augustus the Strong, who was reputed to have fathered three hundred. Her virginity was valued at a farthing, a valuation which was unjust, and she might, on account of this award, have appeared to many people to have lost her case; but Sir William, a mixture of Caliban and Prospero, who was described by Professor Tyrrell of Trinity as a kind of pithecoid ape, a man excessively violent in his sexual passions and unscrupulous in their satisfaction, had to pay the costs of the action, which were heavy, several thousand pounds. His failure to give evidence in the witness-box told against him. It ought to have told in favour of Miss Travers, and would have done, if she had been less vocal and more veracious in the proclamation of her woes. The deflowered virgin loses sympathy when she becomes a public nuisance, especially if her complicity in her violation is widely suspected.

It is certain that Sir William Wilde suffered from an excess of energy, for which his profession was an inadequate outlet; his pituitary and adrenal glands were over-active. Had he been a navvy, an occupation with which his younger and more brilliant son, under the influence of Ruskin, was to toy very briefly at Oxford,

[1] This account is based on *Victorian Doctor*, a Life of Sir William Wilde, by T. C. Wilson, M.B.

he might have been more restrained in the display of his passions; but his big, loose mouth, contradicting the mental authority of his brow, must have sent him ravishing at regular intervals, whatever his social status or occupation had been. Those thick, bulging, moist and indisciplined lips denoted little likelihood of delicacy in their owner's relations with attractive and nubile girls.

Undersized and ugly, he had the features of a ferret. His forehead was high and narrow, noble even, and full of intellectual authority, but his chin receded into his throat so sharply that it could hardly be called a chin: a mere lapse of flabby flesh into a dirty bush of beard. The mouth which hung above it was long and loose, the sort of mouth that slobbers in old age: a bestial and protruding mouth, especially in its lower lip, which was full of casual lust that can never be sated. His long, sly nose was finely shaped, a prying nose, perhaps, but firm and determined, a nose that might have redeemed the ferrety face but for the lascivious mouth and insignificant chin. He had strong, simian arms that hung heavily down his sides and seemed too long for his body: arms that would be prompt to crush. It was the simian look of him, simian in limbs more than in features, which first impressed those who met him. Yet there was a remarkable mind behind his animal head. The ape he resembled was struggling to become human and escape from the jungle.

He was not a fastidious man, either in his sexual adventures or his habits; and he would bed with a kitchen wench as freely as he would with a lady. Herrick and Dr. Johnson had a foreview of his habits, the first when he wrote:

> Night makes no difference 'twixt the Priest and Clerk;
> Joan as my Lady is as good i' the dark.

the second, when he said, "Were it not for imagination, Sir, a man would be as happy in the arms of a chambermaid as of a Duchess". Sir William Wilde must have been either the least imaginative, or the most catholic-minded man in the world: he enjoyed a rural slut no less than a well-bred woman. He had a bastard, it was said in Dublin, on every farm around the city: and he exercised a peculiar and, apparently, irresistible fascination over the most dissimilar women: a fascination as remarkable in its swift effect as Byron's was reputed to be. His first illegitimate child of whom there is knowledge was born towards the end of 1838, when he was twenty-three, thirteen years before his marriage. Nothing is known of this son's mother, but the boy, who bore, it is said, a remarkable resemblance to Willie and Oscar Wilde, was carefully brought up by his father, to whom he was devoted, and became a capable and popular oculist. He was the author of the first book in English on the ophthalmoscope. His name was Henry Wilson, derived, according to his father's enemies, from "Wil (de') son". Wilson, who was joint heir with Oscar Wilde of part of Sir William's property, died of pneumonia in June 1877, when he was about forty. He was a bachelor, and was, so far as is known, the first of a long succession of unlawful infants begotten by Wilde, a succession which cannot be enumerated. It included two girls who were brought up in maiden-lady seclusion in the Midlands of Ireland and were deeply mourned by their father when they were both burnt to death in a fire at a dance. Wilde was a promiscuous man, careless whether his concubine was coarse or refined; but he did not neglect his offspring.

He was unclean in his person, untidy in his dress, and gross in his eating and drinking. "Why are Dr. Wilde's nails black?" was a popular riddle in Dublin. "Because he scratches himself." And his slovenly habits increased as he grew older, until he became a byword for dirtiness. If he had any hope of redemption from these distresses, his wife extinguished them. A house is certain to be filthy when its mistress lies in bed more than half the morning, thinking about her ego. The expense of his several families, added to the extravagant style of his home, kept him comparatively poor. Earnings were large, but so was expenditure, and when he died he left his widow no more than £7000, a sum insufficient for the needs of a gentlewoman, even if she were a competent housekeeper, which Lady Wilde was not.[1] At the height of his medical vogue, bailiffs were in possession of his big, gaunt mansion at the corner of Lower Merrion Street and Merrion Square North; and

[1] Oscar and Willie and their illegitimate half-brother, Henry Wilson, each received property worth about £4000.

the house always had an air of confusion and uncertainty. All his attributes were those that the readers of Charles Lever and Samuel Lover expect to find in the characters created by these authors. His table groaned with the burden of food and drink it had to bear, but not so loudly as did the tradesmen who applied in vain for payment. Banquets and bastards and bailiffs! . . . Promiscuity is commoner in Ireland than English people, ever prone to sentimentality about the Irish, are willing to believe, or the Irish, even more emotional about themselves than the English, are ready to admit. Yeats told the shocked Senate of Eire that it would once have been impossible to throw a stone over a workhouse wall without hitting one of Dan O'Connell's bastards. Isaac Butt, the first Protestant to lead the Irish Nationalists, was an accomplished begetter of unlawful infants, some of whom, on reaching maturity, embarrassed him at public meetings by claiming him as their daddy. Parnell, long before he met Mrs. O'Shea, was highly irregular in his sex relations, and it is notorious that barmaids had a powerful effect on many pious Papists in the Home Rule Party. The records of bastardy in Roman Catholic Ireland would be far heavier if it were not for the fact that the priests, when a girl is known to be illegitimately pregnant, either compel the father of her child to marry her forthwith, or, if marriage is impossible, hurry her out of the parish so that her infant shall be born elsewhere, preferably in a Protestant place!

Wilde's reputation as an ocular and aural surgeon was very high, although on the single occasion when he came in contact with the Shaw family his skill was inconspicuous. George Carr Shaw, George Bernard's father, suffered from a squint. Sir William operated on it. He shifted the squint from one side of the eye to the other. It is a sobering thought that if he had eliminated the squint, *The Doctor's Dilemma* might never have been written. On such mischances, great literature sometimes turns. In spite of his unfortunate experience with the elder Shaw, however, Sir William was widely renowned in his profession, and was said to be even greater as an otologist than he was as an oculist.

Sherard, in his *Life of Oscar Wilde*, asserts that he was "recognised as one of the greatest surgeons of the last century", and that "the recognition" was "general". He was eulogised in German medical books, Schwartze describing him as "the father of modern otology". His successor at the Royal Victoria Eye and Ear Hospital in Dublin, J. B. Story, declared him to be "one of the most distinguished" ocular and aural "surgeons that Great Britain has yet produced". He was the first medical man in Ireland to be appointed Surgeon Oculist in Ordinary to Queen Victoria, an appointment which did not endanger his sovereign, ocularly or otherwise, since it was entirely honorary; and the King of Sweden gave him the Polar Star. In his spare time he dabbled in archaeology, ethnology, folklore, history, topography, statistics and unfastidious sculduggery. He founded a hospital in Dublin and reclaimed bogs in Mayo; and he wrote a book on the last days of Dean Swift.

Despite his technical victory over Miss Mary Josephine Travers, Wilde was considered in Dublin to have suffered a severe defeat; and both he and his practice became the worse for it. He could have saved the practice, for his skill was great, had he set about its retrieval with some of the zeal he had displayed in the pursuit of women, but the knowledge of Dublin's disapproval took the heart out of him, and he now neglected his patients as much as he had always neglected his appearance. He retreated to his country house, Moytura, above Lough Corrib, a hill outside Cong, where he busied himself, so far as he was busy at all, in archaeological research. In the autumn of 1866 his health began to collapse. Asthma racked his body, and so did senile consumption. The death of his daughter, Isola, the lovely child of nine, distressed him deeply, as it distressed his son, Oscar, but not, it seemed, her mother, who took it very calmly, telling those who condoled with her that it was all for the best. He made some effort to remind his countrymen that he had a notable mind, but it amounted to little; and his abrupt manners and intolerant tongue alienated nearly all those who might have befriended him. He drooped and dwindled, becoming more and more disagreeable and dirtier, until he died on the 19th of April 1876: one in whom the elements were so mixed up that he was neither man nor beast. Lecky, in his *History of European Morals*, makes some odd remarks on happiness.

"Every action, every disposition, every class, every condition of society must take its place on the moral scale precisely in accordance with the degree in which it promotes or diminishes human happiness. Now it is extremely questionable whether some of the most monstrous forms of sensuality which it is scarcely possible to name cause as much unhappiness as some infirmities of temper, or procrastination or hastiness of judgment." He goes on to cite examples which would justify any exhibitionist in the most extravagant outbursts of brutal arrogance and domination, and he leaves his reader wondering whether the effort to be civilised is worth the trouble it costs. But the reader, as he studies the careers of Sir William Wilde and his unfortunate sons, especially Oscar, may feel certain that the wages of sin are death and damnation; for it cannot be said that any of the Wildes, whose forms of sensuality were monstrous, achieved happiness, or that their lack of discipline wrought benefit to the human race or even to themselves.

Justice demands that mention shall be made of the surprising and impressive fact that when Sir William Wilde died an Ulster poet, Sir Samuel Ferguson, a man of unblemished character, who was, until Yeats appeared, regarded as Ireland's greatest poet, composed an elegy in his honour. It mingles admiration, respect and affection; and denotes that this strange man had virtues which Miss Mary Josephine Travers signally failed to discover.

2

LADY WILDE was an affected and ridiculous woman, who might have been the model for Mrs. Jellyby in *Bleak House*, had she not already been better cast as Mrs. Vincent Crummles, who, readers of *Nicholas Nickleby* will remember, first dazzled her future husband by standing on her head on the butt-end of a spear, surrounded by blazing fireworks. That is a posture to which almost all the female exhibitionists who have afflicted Ireland have been too deeply addicted. Parnell's mother and sisters, all of them, in some degree, deranged, were of this sort. Protestant women of the upper class in Ireland, when they go native, develop a fervour of patriotic fanaticism which frightens the fiercest Fenians almost out of their wits. They become minimum poets, breaking out in terrible verse, derived mainly from Thomas Davis at his worst, and are accustomed to robe themselves in Ould Ancient array, as if they were reincarnations of Deirdre or Dervorgilla. Revolutionary politics usually have a deplorable effect on their appearance. They neglect their hair and their finger-nails, and acquire that look of degeneration which is to be seen in women who live on gin and tobacco. They cover their bodies with cairngorm brooches, and wander about in an abstracted manner, as if they were characters in one of the dimmer and more nebulous plays of Yeats. In a short time they begin to resemble the grim and dirty crone in *Cathleen ni Houlihan*, but never the young woman Patrick saw, with the walk of a queen. Yeats, sentimental when he supposed himself to be romantic, shows us the wailing, whimpering and dishevelled hag, but only *tells* us that she is a lovely girl in disguise.

Jane Francesca Elgee had a perfervid and melodramatic mind. Her spiritual home, in a later age, would have been the Queen's Theatre in Dublin, although she would have asserted her right to the Abbey. She had too much Francesca, when it was not Francisca, in her head, and not enough Jane, if, indeed, she had any. This was a mooning and maundering Mary who never dreamt of lending a hand to Martha because her thoughts were full of high-flown fantasies about her genius. She was tall, like her second son, six feet in height, and is said to have been handsome, despite her sallow skin, which seemed always to be bilious and dirty grey; another physical characteristic she shared with Oscar. It was this muddy look which made her plaster her face with paint and powder and sit in darkened rooms in the hope that make-up might be mistaken for the vitality she aped. She is reputed to have been a brilliant conversationalist, but the samples of her wit which have been preserved do not support this reputation; and in her last years she was ridiculous. People went to her salons to see the sights: the faked old woman and her faked sons.

Conversion to revolutionary Irish politics came later in her life than it came to Parnell's sister, Fanny, who was under fourteen when she first perceived the general perfidy of the English and the general rightness of everything Irish. Jane Francesca was comparatively mature, eighteen, when after reading *The Spirit of the Nation*, a tedious work by D'Alton Williams, she saw the light. She began at once to compose rhetorical verse, none of which had much, if any, merit. Where her poems appeared is not apparent from the several biographies of her son, most of them carelessly and emotionally composed, but Sherard asserts that her most famous piece was entitled *A Million a Decade*.

Her first contributions to *The Nation*, the weekly organ of the Young Ireland Party, in which she obtained a small renown, were made, he says, in 1847. Charles Gavan Duffy, to whom Sherard always refers in a contemptuous manner, without, however, offering any excuse for his contempt, was the editor and practically the proprietor of this famous review; and he states, in *Four Years of Irish History, 1845–1849*, that they were in prose. They were signed John Fenshaw Ellis. "I was greatly struck by the first contribution," he writes, "and requested Mr. John Fenshaw Ellis to call at the *Nation* office", but Mr. Ellis was elusive and coy. There were "difficulties" which prevented "him" from accepting Duffy's invitation. These difficulties, it transpired, arose from her reluctance to let her relatives know what she was up to; though who her relatives were is not known, for her father had long been dead and nothing appears in her records at this time about her mother. She continued, therefore, to remain unknown to her editor, to whom, in addition to her pieces of flatulent prose, she now sent even more flatulent pieces of verse. These were signed *Speranza*. Sherard asserts that they were printed in small type in the columns in which correspondents were answered, but that in 1848 she was promoted to larger type and a prominent position; an assertion which is irreconcilable with Duffy's impression of her prose when he first saw it.

The discovery that she was contributing seditious articles and poems to *The Nation* was made, she herself long afterwards alleged, by her nurse, who revealed it to her family. They seem to have behaved very sensibly about it, treating her activities as no more than intellectual spots; and her editor, still importunate, was informed that he might call on Mr. Ellis at 34 Leeson Street, where the Elgees lived. Duffy probably made enquiries about the tenants of this house, and was well aware before his arrival at the front door that nobody named Ellis lived there. He may have learnt that a daughter of the Elgees was named Jane Francesca, and have deduced that John Fenshaw Ellis and she were one and the same person. As he stood on the doorstep, awaiting admission, he says he "was not without a secret suspicion of the transformation I was about to witness".

When he entered the drawing-room, however, he sustained a shock; for awaiting him was, not the handsome girl he suspected he should see, but Mr. George Smith, publisher to the University of Dublin. Could this pillar of political propriety, this fortress of the Ascendancy, be John Fenshaw Ellis and Speranza? His exclamations of surprise were disregarded. Mr. Smith disappeared into the back drawing-room from whence, a moment or two later, he emerged with Miss Jane Francesca Elgee on his arm! . . . None of her relatives was present at this singular performance, nor are we told why Mr. Smith, who seems to have been as silent as Pylades in the *Electra* of Euripides, took part in it.

This drawing-room melodrama was meat and drink to Jane Francesca, who now became one of the quartette of women poets who provided Duffy with weekly verse. It was, no doubt, after the revelation of her identity, that she was promoted to large print. Duffy was an able editor and business man, and he perceived the benefit *The Nation* would derive from the news that one of its regular contributors was a good-looking girl of the Ascendancy, the granddaughter of a renowned Archdeacon of Wexford.

Duffy, an Ulster Roman Catholic, had the innate deference which almost all Irish people of his creed feel for well-placed Protestants; and the more deeply they resent the position these Protestants hold, the more deeply is the deference displayed. He was not indifferent to Miss Jane Francesca Elgee's social status. It caused him, perhaps subconsciously, to give her greater credit as a writer than she deserved. "It will be necessary", he says in *Four Years of Irish History*, "to recur to this new recruit many times in the course of this narrative; for her little scented notes, sealed with wax of a delicate hue and dainty device, represented a substantial force in Irish politics, the vehement will of a woman of genius." The sequence is not obvious, but even if scented notes, sealed with wax of a delicate hue and dainty device, denote political force and genius, Duffy was wrong. She was not a substantial force in anything, nor had she any genius whatever.

Sherard, in a very loose passage, alleges that "the Fenian editor, O'Leary, states that 'Speranza' was one of the four poetesses on *The Nation*, the one who was considered the least talented", and he gives his own opinion of her poetry which, he declares, "had no particular merit of expression or thought". John O'Leary was seventeen when "Speranza" was writing in *The Nation*, and was unlikely then to have had critical faculties of any worth. He may, later in life, have been referring to opinions he had heard from his elders, but he certainly was not delivering an editorial opinion, either his own or any other person's. There was little to choose between *The Nation*'s poetical quartette. None of them was considered by Mr. Lennox Robinson worthy of inclusion in *The Golden Treasury of Irish Verse*. They wrote the kind of poetry which indignant young women, like indignant young men, are accustomed to write. Does any serious and informed man and woman to-day consider Shelley's famous couplet on Castlereagh as otherwise than puerile? It is well to remember that The Famine was still raging in Ireland when Miss Elgee began to write her verse; and men and women were dropping dead in the streets from starvation and fever. Any sensitive boy or girl must have felt deeply stirred by this disaster, even if it was only one of many similar disasters which had afflicted Ireland and, it is seldom remembered, England and Scotland too.

We are not applauding "Speranza's" *poetry* when we feel qualified sympathy with the emotions expressed in this passage from a poem she, then twenty-one, published in *The Nation* in 1847:

> Weary men, what reap ye? Golden corn for the stranger.
> What sow ye? Human corses that wait for the avenger.
> Fainting forms, hunger-stricken, what see you in the offing?
> Stately ships to bear our food away, amid the stranger's scoffing.

There's a proud array of soldiers—what do they round your door?
They guard our master's granaries from the thin hands of the poor.
Pale mothers, wherefore weeping? "Would to God that we were dead—
Our children swoon before us, and we cannot give them bread."

Nor is it deniable that her appeal to people to be careful of their liberty is a familiar one, and such as adolescents and dotards might compose without causing any person to feel conscious of "the vehement will . . . of genius".

> Oh! that I stood upon some lofty tower,
> Before the gathered people face to face,
> That like God's thunder might my words of power
> Roll down the cry of freedom to its base!
> Oh! that my voice, a storm above all storms,
> Could cleave earth, air, and ocean, rend the sky
> With the fierce earthquake-shout, "To arms! to arms!"
> For truth, fame, freedom, vengeance, victory.

Shall we seem cynical if we consider this stuff commonplace?

Duffy, in the passage cited on a previous page, remarks that he will have "to recur to this new recruit many times in the course of this narrative", but, in fact, she is mentioned four times in 780 pages; and two of these references consist exclusively of the quotations from her verse which are cited above. She filled less space in *The Nation* and Irish life than he sentimentally supposed. He does not mention an incident which, Sherard says, "endeared" Jane Francesca "for ever to the Irish nation", although it is said to have occurred during one of Duffy's three trials for sedition. Few people have endeared themselves to any nation, and the Irish, despite their long and bitter memory for grievances, are extraordinarily quick to forget benefactions. Their ingratitude is notorious. It is equalled only by their insistence on thanks. Sherard deceived himself, but can hardly have deceived anyone else, when he stated that this vehement young woman, incorrigibly prone to perform in public, "endeared" herself "for ever", or even for a few weeks, "to the Irish nation" when she participated, if she did, in the scene he describes. What answer, we may wonder, would be returned to the simple English visitor, an easy victim of delusive Irish charm, who should walk into D'Olier Street in Dublin, or the Mall in Cork, or Castle Place in Belfast, or The Crescent in Limerick, or The Diamond in Derry, and ask the first fifty persons he might meet how dear that woman of vehement will and genius, Jane Francesca Elgee, was to them and their country? Would fishermen in the Claddagh or farmers in Mullaghmast or Mallow, or shipwrights in Ballymacarrett, or kelp collectors in Achill Island, or shirt-makers in the Maiden City, feel their pulses stir faster if that name were sounded in their ears? Or would they wonder who on earth Jane Francesca might be? It is doubtful, indeed, if more than a fistful of intellectuals in Ireland would now know that her son had ever existed if he had not been sent to prison.

3

THESE are the circumstances in which Wilde's mother, when she was a young woman of twenty-two, is said to have endeared herself for ever to the Irish nation. The relations between the British and the Irish were steadily deteriorating in that year of revolutions, 1848, chiefly because of the misery which The Famine had caused; and minds which turned too easily to thoughts of insurrection, began to turn that way again. There had been deep and irreconcilable division between Dan O'Connell and the Young Ireland Party. The Liberator, who had become almost a megalomaniac in his last years, would brook no criticism or interference in his Association. It was *his* Association, not Young Ireland's, and he would direct its policy as he pleased. The Young Irelanders, aware of their ability, aware, too, of a serious decline in O'Connell's personal strength—he died in 1847—and animated by a feeling of frustration, had seceded and founded a rival and more bellicose body, the Irish Confederation, whose members did not conceal their intention to bring about revolt. The French revolution which ended the reign of Louis Philippe in February 1848 encouraged the hope of a successful rising in Ireland, although that hope must have seemed dim and delusive to men of sagacity when they contemplated the stricken population, exhausted, first, by The Famine and its following fever, and, second, by the flight of enormous numbers of Ireland's youth across the Atlantic and the Southern Oceans. Rebellion was again the fashion. Articles on elementary warfare were published in subversive sheets, and agricultural labourers were instructed in blowing up bridges and manufacturing arms. It became plain even to Dublin Castle that trouble was a-brewing.

Steps were taken.

In May 1848 John Mitchel, an Ulster Unitarian of violent and vituperative character, hag-ridden by hate and possessed of an outlook on life appallingly like that of Hitler, was arrested on a charge of treason-felony. He was the editor of *The United Irishman*, which he had founded after a breach with Gavan Duffy, who would not allow him to advocate Negro Slavery or denounce religious and civil liberty for the Jews. Mitchel's guilt was not denied. It was, indeed, proclaimed with pride, based on Blackstone and man's undying love of freedom; a love in which, however, no black man nor any Jew was to participate. The sentence he received was savage: fourteen years' transportation, first to Bermuda, second to South Africa, which refused to receive him, and finally to Van Diemen's Land. Little of it was served, for Mitchel escaped to America, where he became prominent on the side of the South in the Civil War. This sentence increased the tension in Ireland, which was excited still further by the news that workmen in Paris had attempted to set up a Communist State in June; an attempt which led directly to the reign of Napoleon the Third, whom Mitchel much admired; the Franco-German War of 1870; and the First and Second World Wars. It was suppressed with every concomitant of brutality, but not before the Archbishop of Paris, seeking to ensue peace, had been shot dead at a barricade. That fact sobered some of the Young Irelanders, and shocked the devout, but it did not quell the rebellious spirit; and even Duffy, a man of peace and addicted to debate, preferring persuasion to slaughter, caught the mood for rising, and published insurrectionary articles in *The Nation*.

He was arrested in the first week of July and lodged in Newgate. The details of his three trials, two of which ended in disagreement among the jury, are irrelevant to our argument and need not, therefore, be discussed. It will be sufficient to say that the third trial ended in his release. The prisoners, despite the customary lies and nonsense which are invariably written and uttered when Irish politicians are imprisoned, were not mistreated. They spent their time very much as it might have been spent in a hospital by "walking cases" under observation. This was the British habit from the days of Daniel O'Connell to the days of de Valera. Almost the single exception to the rule was the harsh treatment awarded to Michael Davitt in an English gaol. Duffy's description of his own imprisonment, as set out in *Four Years of Irish History*, confirms the fact. "The State prisoners", he writes, "were treated with liberality and consideration.

We dined together in my room, our dinner being supplied from a hotel, and a prison servant was appointed to wait on us. Friends whom we desired to see were admitted during the day without restriction; and the conferences of the Confederation were, in effect, held in Newgate from that time forth. The doors of the prison were left as wide open to all comers as the gates of the Phoenix Park; Lord Clarendon perhaps wanted to make sure who were sympathisers with the prisoners. Martin and I wrote for our journals as usual, and continued the political correspondence with friends at a distance by which a party is kept in harmony."

But this luxurious incarceration did not prevent the busy little propagandists from spreading horrific legends of vile usage of the noble and lion-hearted felons of our land by the bloody, base and brutal British.

Insurrection did eventually break out, but it was abortive and absurd. William Smith O'Brien, a Protestant landlord and direct descendant of Brian Boru, led a feeble force of about a hundred men and women, armed with pikes, pitchforks, rusty rifles, sticks and stones, into the Widow McCormick's cabbage-patch at Ballingarry, where after a valiant and picturesque, but futile exhibition of guerrilla warfare, they were overcome by the police. O'Brien was eventually arrested and sentenced to death, but the sentence was commuted to one of transportation to Tasmania. He was pardoned and released in 1854, and, in 1856, allowed to return home to Cahirmoyle. He died in North Wales in 1864.

During this operatic performance, Duffy was endeavouring, in great difficulty, to keep *The Nation* alive and hearten the rebels with exalting counsel. His staff had been dispersed, and the issue for the 29th of July 1848 seemed certain to miss publication. But his sister-in-law, Margaret Callan, undertook to see it through the press, and was in the office when the police arrived to carry off the type and any incriminating documents that might be lying about. "Two of the articles in the unpublished journal were direct incitements to insurrection, and were afterwards included", Duffy states, "in the indictment against me." One was an article by himself, entitled *The Tocsin of Ireland*, which had been smuggled out of Newgate, and the other, entitled *Jacta Alea Est*, was by Jane Francesca Elgee. Margaret Callan and she are described by Duffy as "two women of genius". He was inclined to detect genius in anyone who shared his opinions. *Jacta Alea Est*, which is reproduced in Sherard's *Life of Oscar Wilde*, is a conventional piece of trumpery rhetoric, such as one might expect to be written by an hysterical young woman of twenty-two. It urged the Irish to "war active and passive", and anticipated Parnell's plea for boycott by thirty-two years. "One thing is certain," Jane Francesca wrote, "that if the people do not choose to fight the garrison, they may *starve* them. Adopt the Milan method—let no man sell to them. This passive warfare may be carried on in every village in Ireland, while more active hostilities are proceeding through all the large towns and cities.

But to gain possession of the capital should be the grand object of all efforts. Let every line converge to this point. The Castle is the keystone of English power; take it, destroy it, burn it—at any hazard become masters of it, and on the same ground from whence proceeded all those acts of insult and infamy which aroused the just retribution of a people's vengeance, establish a government in whom the people of all classes can place confidence. . . . Irishmen! this insurrection into a new life depends on you; for we have all lain dead. Hate, distrust, oppression, disunion, selfishness, bigotry—these things are Death. We must crush all vices—annihilate all evil passions—trample on them, as a triumphant Christ with his foot upon the serpent, and then the proud hallelujah of Freedom will rise to heaven from the lips of a pure, a virtuous, a regenerated, a God-blessed people; and this fair land of ours, which now affrights the world with its misery, will be one grand temple, in which we shall all kneel as brothers—one holy, peaceful, loving fraternity—sons of one common country—children of one God—heirs together of those blessings purchased by our blood—a heritage of freedom, justice, independence, prosperity and glory!"

Duffy states that this flyblown stuff is "as lofty and passionate as one of Napoleon's bulletins after a great victory". Napoleon's bulletins were often wide of fact, but even had they always been exact, Miss Jane Francesca Elgee's article in *The Nation* was rhodomontade which would have been called claptrap if it had been composed by a young man; the sort of pestilential trash a Simon Tappertit might have composed on the eve of the Gordon riots. " 'Something will come of this!' said Mr. Tappertit, pausing as if in triumph, and wiping his heated face upon his sleeve. 'Something will come of this. I hope it mayn't be human gore!' "

But did Miss Elgee's heroic assumption of guilt in Duffy's defence come of it? The Attorney-General read extracts from *Jacta Alea Est* to the jury, and said they were sufficient in themselves to convict the prisoner at the bar. The words had scarcely left his lips when, Sherard asserts, a voice from the gallery cried, "I am the culprit, if culprit there be!"

It was Jane Francesca Elgee, who by this fine gesture endeared herself for ever to the Irish nation. The result was to trouble the minds of the jury; they disagreed; and the editor of *The Nation* was discharged to pursue his career more profitably to himself in another hemisphere.

This is dreadful fustian. It suggests that Duffy was discharged because Miss Elgee had disturbed the jury's mind! . . .

But Duffy was arraigned five times between July 1848 and April 1849, and Miss Elgee's cry, if it was ever uttered, must have been made during the first. What happened to the young lady? Was she brought before the judge for brawling in court, or arrested for complicity in treason-felony? Sherard does not say. But, stranger than his silence, is Duffy's. There is not a single word about the incident in *Four Years of Irish History*, although the young girl's chivalrous cry must have stirred emotion in a man of thirty-two who was on trial for his life. His book was published in 1882, thirty-four years after the date of the events it describes, and Duffy, who retained a deep regard for Miss Elgee, as all his remarks about her prove, took considerable pains to give an accurate account of all these transactions. He considered her to be a woman of genius, and compared *Jacta Alea Est* to Napoleon Bonaparte's bulletins after great victories; and she had publicly, and in circumstances of danger to herself, proclaimed her authorship of the article, and of another in the previous issue entitled *The Hour of Destiny*, which, the Attorney-General said, were enough to hang him or justify his transportation. Is it likely that he had forgotten or deliberately omitted to mention an episode which, if it ever occurred, must have made a profound impression upon him, one, too, which had endeared her for ever to the Irish nation? She had been living in London for six years when the book was issued, nor did she die until 1896. Both her sons, and especially the elder, were busy in journalism. It is incredible that none of the three read the book, that none of them, had the incident ever happened, complained of Duffy's omission to mention it; especially if, as Sherard asserts, her sons were prouder of *Jacta Alea Est* than of any other of her writings. May we not believe that the lady invented the tale? Or that it had grown out of a less dramatic incident? Isaac Butt, who defended Duffy, is reported in *Victorian Doctor* to have stated, in his address to the jury, that, "I now hold in my hand a letter from the authoress of these articles, assuring me that Mr. Duffy never saw them before they were published, and that he was not present at the time. I would not be suffered to give pain to the highly-respectable connections of the lady and to herself, by placing her on the table, but I ask the Solicitor-General, as a man of honour, and a man of honour I believe him to be—he knows the lady as well as I do—to contradict my statement if it is not true." Wilson, in his book, repeats the story of "Speranza's" interruption, but gives no authority for it.

That was, it seems, her last appearance in the stricken field of revolutionary Irish politics. The sentences passed on Mitchel and Smith O'Brien and the strain of the long-drawn-out arraignments of Duffy may have frightened her into silence. Where and how she met William Wilde is not stated in any work about her son, but she married him on the 12th of November 1851, when she was, she stated, twenty-five and he was thirty-six. She must have been as hazy about the date of her birth as Oscar, many years later, was about his own; for her father, Charles Elgee, died in India in 1824. She wrote no more poetry, nor did she concern herself any further with the hopes of Young Ireland, though her married life in Dublin lasted for a quarter of a century. She was, at first, no doubt, too busy bearing babies to meddle in revolutions. Two sons and a daughter were born in five years. Her writing now, when there was any, was not incitement to insurrection, but *Driftwood from Scandinavia*, and, after his death, compilations from notes left by her husband on *Ancient Cures, Charms and Usages of Ireland*; in addition to small articles in *The Lady's Pictorial* and in *The Woman's World* when it was edited by Oscar. She developed a languor after the birth of her children, which she transmitted to her second son. It was sometimes mistaken for calm and courage. Her looks began to fade. She lay about on sofas in rooms which were closely shuttered to keep them untainted by the light of day, and were illuminated only by faint beams of candlelight and lamps in pink shades; and her visitors were entertained by recitations from the Greek poets. While the bailiffs were in the ramshackle house, she lay on her sofa declaiming the *Prometheus Vinctus* of Aeschylus to a visitor who had called in sympathy to see her. Her life, after her husband's death, was a steady descent, halted now and then by brief interludes of splendour. In 1886 she removed to Oakley Street, Chelsea, to be near Oscar in Tite Street, and here she lived with her son Willie in a house that was full of dust and dirt. Willie, who had been called to the Bar, but had not practised, was now an unabashed scallywag, a drunken sponger who wrote pornography in the papers and was as hot in pursuit of women as his father had been; with this difference, that he did not maintain them, but was maintained. In 1890 "Speranza" accepted a Civil List Pension of £50 from the Government she had sought to overthrow in 1848; and on the 3rd of February 1896, while her son was in prison, she died. Neither Wilde nor his mother, Wilson says in *Victorian Doctor*, were acromegalics, but they were pituitary types. Her hands, according to Bernard Shaw, were enormous, and he reports that Lady Colin Campbell habitually referred to Oscar as "that great white caterpillar".

Oscar, though he was not his mother's favourite son, was devoted to her in a lazy, inert manner. He gave her flattery, but not service, and he was ready to acclaim her when this could be done without exertion or physical discomfort. There were times, indeed, when his enthusiasm for his father and mother became fantastic, explicable only on the ground of his belief that anyone related to him must, for that reason alone, be remarkable. Referring to his mother's death in *De Profundis*, he tells Douglas that "no one knew better than you how deeply I loved and honoured her:

> Her death was terrible to me: but I, once a lord of language, have no words in which to express my anguish and shame. Never even in the most perfect days of my development as an artist could I have found words fit to bear so august a burden: or to move with sufficient stateliness of music through the purple pageant of my incommunicable woe. She and my father had bequeathed me a name they had made noble and honoured, not merely in literature, art, archaeology, and science, but in the public history of my own country, in its evolution as a nation."

Here, if ever anywhere, was filial piety made extravagant folly. Sir William Wilde was entitled to considerable respect as an oculist, and to a smaller amount of respect as an archaeologist, but he took little or no part in the evolution of Ireland as a nation, an evolution which is still in its primary stages, nor had he substantial claims to respect in literature or art. Lady Wilde's right to renown in any of these matters was so slight that there is scarcely a man or a woman in her country to-day who is aware of any right she ever had. Yet her son, forgetting his critical faculty, informed Douglas in another part of *De Profundis* that she ranks intellectually "with Elizabeth Barrett Browning, and historically with Madame Roland". A more wilful and ridiculous estimate of a parent was never made.

4

THERE is a theory popular in Moscow, that heredity has little or no part in a man's composition, that environment alone has any influence on his character; and it goes hard with a Russian scientist who dares to dispute the theory which the Politburo favours. But men who are under no bondage to Commissars, may justifiably feel that we have swung too far to the left in our beliefs about biology and are over-inclined to think that a man cannot be held accountable for himself or justly be blamed for any of his actions: a doctrine which implies that all condemnation, from remonstrance and rebuke to chastisement and execution, is not only absurd but wicked; and renders missionary effort, from the reform of pedagogues to the redemption of thugs, entirely abortive. This theory makes human association finally impossible. How can we hope to change that which has been irrevocably ordained?

Mankind eventually rejects the extreme Determinist, St. Augustine or Calvin or Karl Marx, those three wicked men, even when he seems to have all the logic and is approved by principalities and powers; for mankind is wisely distrustful of logic: a mental exercise which, according to Lecky in his *History of European Morals*, has been "greatly studied and prized" in "most ages of intellectual poverty". The Churches still deny that the Ulsterman, Pelagius, had any reason in him, but the mass of Christian people, even although they may never have heard of him, are Pelagians, sharing his belief that men, by their own will, can raise themselves. Hamlet, indeed, is willing to follow the predestinationists to their futile conclusions, but Hamlet, when we meet him in Shakespeare, is in a high state of emotional disturbance and scarcely accountable for himself. Why, then, should we expect him to feel that anybody, except, perhaps, his uncle, is accountable for anything? "Oft it chances in particular men," he tells Horatio reasonably enough,

"That for some vicious mole of nature in them,
As, in their birth,—wherein they are not guilty,

Since nature cannot choose his origin,—
By the o'ergrowth of some complexion,
Oft breaking down the pales and forts of reason,
Or by some habit that too much o'er-leavens
The form of plausive manners, that these men,—
Carrying, I say, the stamp of one defect,
Being nature's livery, or fortune's star,—
Their virtues else—be they as pure as grace,
As infinite as man may undergo—
Shall in the general censure take corruption
From that particular fault: the dram of eale
Doth all the noble substance of a doubt
To his own scandal."

The point was continually in the Prince's mind as it was in St. Paul's when he said, "It is no more I that do it, but sin that dwelleth in me". We see this in the end of Shakespeare's play, when Hamlet pleads a variation of it to Laertes before their duel:

"What I have done,
That might your nature, honour and exception
Roughly wake, I here proclaim was madness.
Was't Hamlet wrong'd Laertes? Never Hamlet:
If Hamlet from himself be ta'en away,
And when he's not himself does wrong Laertes,
Then Hamlet does it not, Hamlet denies it.
Who does it then? His madness; if't be so,
Hamlet is of the faction that is wrong'd;
His madness is poor Hamlet's enemy.
Sir, in this audience,
Let my disclaiming from a purposed evil
Free me so far in your most generous thoughts,
That I have shot mine arrow o'er the house,
And hurt my brother."

The argument, we may pardonably fear, is sophistical; for any man with that plea in his mouth can claim pardon for all offences, no matter how many times committed. Cassius and Macbeth, though the latter was less decided than the former, because, no doubt, he had listened, not wisely but too well, to the witches on the blasted heath, would have heard it with impatience. "But in these cases," Macbeth murmured to himself as he meditated Duncan's murder, "we still have judgement here." Macbeth is emphatic in asserting his ability to decide his own affairs. So is his Lady.

> "If chance will have me king, why chance may crown me
> Without my stir."

and he refuses authority to the Witches' proclamation of a destined life when he declares the force of his vaulting ambition. His Lady is sure that her valorous tongue will be more effective than "fate and metaphysical aid". Cassius is fully assured. "Men at some times are masters of their fates," he tells his vacillating comrade in contemplated crime.

> "The fault, dear Brutus, is not in our stars,
> But in ourselves that we are underlings."

Even Iago, that embodiment of evil, is certain of our ability to choose and decide. When Roderigo tells him that it is not in his virtue to amend his folly, Iago rounds on him:

> "Virtue! a fig! 'tis in ourselves that we are thus and thus. Our bodies are gardens; to the which our wills are gardeners: so that if we will plant nettles or sow lettuce, set hyssop and weed up thyme, supply it with one gender of herbs or distract it with many, either to have it sterile with idleness or manured with industry, why, the power and corrigible authority of this lies in our wills. If the balance of our lives had not one scale of reason to poise another of sensuality, the blood and baseness of our natures would conduct us to most preposterous conclusions: but we have reason to cool our raging motions, our carnal stings, our unbitted lusts; whereof I take this, that you call love, to be a sect or scion. It is merely a lust of the blood and a permission of the will."

Shakespeare was accustomed to put the best arguments in favour of personal responsibility for one's own fate in the mouths of unscrupulous men. Iago's argument is equalled in assurance by Edmund the Bastard's in *King Lear*:

> "This is the excellent foppery of the world, that, when we are sick in fortune,—often the surfeit of our own behaviour,—we make guilty of our disasters the sun, the moon, and the stars: as if we were villains by necessity; fools by heavenly compulsion; knaves, thieves, and treachers by spherical predominance; drunkards, liars, and adulterers by an enforced obedience of planetary influence; and all that we are evil in, by a divine thrusting on: an admirable evasion of whoremaster man, to lay his goatish disposition to the charge of a star! My father

compounded with my mother under the dragon's tail, and my nativity was under *ursa major*; so that it follows I am rough and lecherous.—Tut. I should have been that I am, had the maidenliest star in the firmament twinkled on my bastardizing."

These two villains might plausibly have pleaded the doctrine of predestination in excuse of their own evil, but they were manly enough to disdain such a subterfuge and would not shuffle out of their responsibility for it, nor whine for pardon on the plea that the fault was not in them but in their stars. They were not the sort to challenge God's justice by calling Him the final cause of their sins.

Hamlet is not, even in his specious plea to Laertes, surrendering his claim to autonomy. The wound inflicted by the arrow shot o'er the house, was not intended. It was an accident. Hamlet could decide whether or not the arrow should be shot. There was no conspiracy in heaven to compel him to shoot it. Dr. Johnson, customarily sane on such matters as these, puts the point made by Cassius and Macbeth with discretion. "Every man is to take existence on the terms on which it is given to him," he remarks in a curious statement wherein Augustine and Calvin seem to be wrestling with, and overthrowing, their own shadows. "To some men it is given on condition of not taking liberties, which other men may take without much harm. One may drink wine, and be nothing the worse for it; on another, wine may have effects so inflammatory as to injure him both in body and mind, and, perhaps, make him commit something for which he may deserve to be hanged." But he was more downright when, on another occasion, he countered the very logical arguments of Boswell with the masterly riposte, "All theory is against the freedom of the will; all experience for it."

5

THAT, perhaps, is as far as any of us dare venture in a direction where all is dark, and the signposts, if there ever were any, have all been removed. It must be enough to say that if any man was ever ruined by his parents, Oscar Wilde was undoubtedly the man; and that his mother, more, perhaps, than his father, undid him. Her desire, it is said, as she carried him in her womb, was for a daughter, and her disappointment when she delivered a boy was deep. It caused her to dress him in girl's clothes long after the time when a boy is put into pants. His supporters insist that this desire, this habit of clothing, which was not unusual at one time in Ireland, had an evil effect on his character, but the argument is shallow, shallow as the Greek belief that a pregnant woman can make her unborn infant beautiful by gazing at statues of handsome men and lovely women. These are mawkish beliefs, derided by Nature. W. P. Ker, that dry-witted Scot, wrecked them when, hearing that William Sharp donned a woman's dress to write the works of Fiona Macleod, he exclaimed, "Did he, the bitch?"

How much his ruin may be blamed on Wilde himself is hard to say, but he was not guiltless of his fall.

When His disciples asked Jesus, "Master, who did sin, this man, or his parents, that he was born blind?" Our Lord made an irrelevant answer which was almost evasive. "Neither hath this man sinned, nor his parents: but that the works of God should be made manifest in him." It can scarcely be said that the works of God were made manifest in Wilde. This, however, can be said. The punishment was disproportionate to the crime. It is the fashion among his apologists to say that Wilde neither misled nor corrupted the innocent. He was, they protest, the chief sufferer for his sin, almost the sole sufferer; and that he was severely punished for it. These are not the facts. No one can measure the distress endured by other people than Wilde for his sin. It is obvious that his wife's suffering was at least equal to his, and may have been greater. She died of her grief. A study of the evidence given against him at his trial, as it is recorded in H. Montgomery Hyde's *Trials of Oscar Wilde*, amply demonstrates, despite Hyde's allegation that "Wilde was never proved to have corrupted any youthful innocence", that Wilde *did*, in some degree, corrupt innocent lads, and that he hired a degenerate Marlburian, called Alfred Waterhouse Somerset Taylor, who was subsequently charged with him, to procure youths of twenty, who were either innocent or near-innocent, for his unnatural purposes. It is true that Wilde was acquitted of immoral practices with the young clerk, Edward Shelley, who was eighteen when Wilde first took notice of him, but can anybody believe that their association had no debasing effect on the lad? Wilde encountered him in his publisher's office. There was no intervening pimp nor any association with a brothel for male prostitutes. An attempt on the boy's morals was made deliberately by Wilde and in the course of ordinary daily transactions. If Shelley was not corrupted, it was because he resisted Wilde's attempts to corrupt him, and not because no attempts were made. A worse example is that of the newspaper boy, Alphonse Conway, whom Wilde picked up on the pier at Worthing. He will be a very simple-minded person who believes that this lad of eighteen was not somehow corrupted by Wilde, who went so far in his degradation as to introduce him, whom he designed for his unnatural paramour, to Mrs. Wilde and her two young sons, who were then living in Worthing.

There is, perhaps, too much tendency to-day to make light of sodomy, too great a tendency to condemn harshly and without attempt at understanding, those who were most ferocious in their denunciation of Wilde's offence. It is not enough to say that many of them were wicked men, heavily coarse in character. No doubt, they were. We have all sinned and come short of the glory of God. But we must take into account the fact that all men discriminate between natural and unnatural sin. Fornication is natural sin, sodomy is not. The mind of the average sensual man is not outraged by the thought of unlawful copulation with women, no matter how much he may profess to disapprove it; but it *is* outraged by the thought of pederastic relations. Nor is his sense of outrage without reason. Sodomy is a denial of life, a cult of sterility. Life would end, or be disastrously reduced, if it were common. Their sense of dangerous sterility, of barren relations, forces average sensual men to condemn and denounce sodomites, even although they think the seduction of women is no great matter, since it is part of the process of fertility, and in any case, the rules and regulations about sexual relations are made for social convenience, and may be varied according to our need. When Sarah believed herself to be barren, she sent Abraham, who seems not to have thought of her before, to lie with Hagar and get a child, so that Sarah, since she could not conceive herself, should conceive by proxy. Onan sinned in a way that may well seem to us commendable. Is there any woman in Western Europe who would feel that her husband was under a religious obligation to beget a son by his widowed sister-in-law because she had been left childless? The law of levirate was binding on the Jews in Genesis,[1] but who would respect a father to-day who ordered his son to fertilise his sister-in-law as Judah ordered Onan to fertilise Tamar; and what sister-in-law would make bitter complaint that her pregnancy had been prevented by her brother-in-law using the most primitive, as it is still the most popular, form of contraception: *coitus interruptus*? Yet Tamar complained and her complaint was approved, when Onan spilt his seed upon the ground. He was willing to enjoy Tamar, but not to get a child out of her; and for this sin he was put to death.

The whole story of Tamar, as it is told in the thirty-eighth chapter of Genesis, is revolting even to modern minds. When, after the death of Onan, her father-in-law fails to fulfil his promise that she shall be given to his son, Shelah, she devises a plot for her fertilisation by Judah himself. Disguised as a harlot, she tempts him to bed with her. Judah, unaware that she is the seeming harlot with whom he had copulated while on his way to the sheep-shearing at Timnath, vows to have her burnt, when she is found unlawfully pregnant, but she wins his admiration by proving her child to be his. "She has been more righteous than I," he exclaims, and is gratified in due course by the birth of twin sons, Zarah and Pharez.

Moses was a man of several wives, the first of whom, Zipporah, was deserted. There was no whispering behind hands when Solomon, who was said, very strangely, to be the wisest man in the world, took seven hundred wives and three hundred concu-

[1] A French traveller, Charlevoix, who is cited in *The Great Migration*, by J. Fitzgerald Lee (p. 127), says that this law of levirate was upheld by Indians in the northern part of South America.

bines, nor does anyone in her country or in his appear to have been perturbed by his relations with the Queen of Sheba. David's servants felt no sense of immorality when they sought to stimulate his chilling spirit, as he lay dying, by putting the damsel Abishag, a Shunammite, in his bed. How pathetic it is to read in the first chapter of the First Book of Kings that the old man, who had been as valiant with women as he had been in war, was now so far gone in his final throes that, like Parson Abrahams in Fielding's *Joseph Andrews*, he did not realise that a lovely girl was lying by his side, waiting and willing to be cherished. Abishag, the Shunammite, rose from his bed a disappointed virgin.

The Old Testament contains a remarkable record of experiments in marriage; but all of them turn on fertility. Fertility is its whole purpose from the Testament's start to its finish. Saul, seeking his daughter, Michal's, maternity as eagerly as he had sought his father's asses on the day he found a kingdom, does not hesitate in David's absence to give her, although she is David's wife, to Phalti, the son of Laish, which was of Gallim; a gift which David could scarcely resent, since he himself had recently taken Abigail and Ahinoam of Jezreel to be his wives. Nor were they the whole tally; for he took more wives and concubines out of Jerusalem after he was come out of Hebron, and quickly begat sons and daughters by them. How many wives David had we do not know. The names of eight of them appear in the Second Book of Samuel, but he seems to have had about twenty in all, apart from concubines. Fertility is the first fact in Oriental marriage, more than it is now in European, and India teems with infants. It is not for nothing that Diana of the Ephesians is shown to be many-breasted. At the bottom of all outcry against sodomy lies this fact of fertility, the horror men feel at the denial of life, the sin of sterility, graver than Onan's sin when he spilt his seed on the ground, the final refusal to create.

The disaster which befell Sodom and Gomorrah is the first hint of it we get in the Bible, and Sodom gives the sin its name. There was an outbreak of it among Christians in Corinth and elsewhere, which caused great anxiety to St. Jude, and there are hints in St. Paul's epistles that he was disturbed about it too. The prostitutes and pimps who danced outside the Old Bailey when Wilde was sentenced, were no doubt displaying delight at the downfall of one whose habits threatened their livelihood and would, if such habits became common, compel them to take to honest toil, but they were also proving how affronted was their feeling that the way of a man with a maid is the right and natural way. Blake puts the point with the precision of a mystic when he says:

> What is it men in women do require?
> The lineaments of gratified desire.
> What is it women do in men require?
> The lineaments of gratified desire.

As they moved through their dreadful Bacchanalian dance that late Saturday afternoon at the end of May 1895, they were, they would have been exceedingly surprised to learn, in fundamental accord with the Apostles and the Patriarchs.

The will to live overcomes all other wills, and cannot be destroyed. Men, and especially women, are determined to perpetuate their species: a determination which surpasses all legal restrictions in times of war. A curious and implausible illustration of this determination to survive is to be found in the nineteenth chapter of Genesis. When the cities of the plain were destroyed for sodomy, Lot and his two daughters went to live in a cave in a mountain above Zoar, where the young women frightened themselves with the belief that there was no man, except their father, left alive in the world. How could they carry on the race? They resolved to preserve their species by committing incest with their father. Fearing that he would not consent to fertilise them, they filled him with drink two nights in succession, the elder copulating with him on the first night, the younger on the second.

The story is grotesque; it is impossible for a man in a drunken stupor to perform the sexual act, as the Porter well knew when Macduff and Lennox came knocking on Macbeth's gate. Drink, he said, provokes and unprovokes lechery; "it provokes the desire, but it takes away the performance". But the story indicates the strength of the will to live. The elder daughter got a son by her father, and she called him Moab. "And the younger, she also bore a son, and called his name Ben-ammi; the same is the father of the children of Ammon until this day."

All our histories demonstrate this passion for perpetuity. The case for ending life is more reasonable than the case for continuing it. There is no need of profundity to prove that existence is a sorry thing, begun, continued and ended in pain, and that a logical species would accept the advice of the Cathari and put a stop to it. Any person can easily compile a list of common ills and misfortunes, constantly recurring, which prove beyond a shadow of a doubt that existence is delusive. Every creature's life is spent in apprehension. A bird does not dare to peck a crumb from the ground without first glancing in all directions. The hare crouches in its form in fear. A faint scent will send a stag and his hinds flying for their lives. A shadow cast upon a stream makes a fish dive and disappear. We are all prey, from mammoths to mice, yet we long for life, and a man in irremediable agony will cling to it when logic and reason advise him to die. Birds conclude the day with song, hares assemble in the fields for antic dance, and fish lie luxuriating in the flood. Disturb that unlikeable insect, the ant, perfect model for the Communist, and instantly it will seek to save its eggs, struggling to bear its heavy burdens to some safe retreat. Stag battles with stag for the hinds who stand demurely by, ready without a qualm of regret for their defeated lord, to trot at the heels of his victor, the master of their maternity. The first fact of all existence is fertility, the prodigal desire of all animated things to perpetuate themselves, causing the tree to scatter a thousand acorns to get a single oak. Grass seed will find a growing space on the barest ledge of rock, and the plant will thrust the pavement out of place to put its head above the ground. Our most unwelcome visitor is death who takes away our life. Our greatest abhorrence is old age which annuls our power to procreate. It is the will to live, and live abundantly, which turns our minds against the pederast. He is the final atheist, the ultimate blasphemer against existence. Plague, famine and pestilence, persecution and war cannot diminish us, nor will we permit the sodomite to cancel life.

There are, no doubt, people who are naturally deficient in vitality or perverse, and these are not to be held entirely accountable for themselves. The fact that Leonardo da Vinci is said, but on insufficient evidence, to have been a sodomite; that there are some shallow-minded men—Wilde, for example—who were foolish enough to say that Shakespeare, a man particularly aware of feminine attractions, was one; that there are even some who say that Our Lord Himself was a homosexual because he kept the company of men, never married, and did not appoint a single woman to his apostolate, a belief which is made in ignorance or disregard of the fact that He was exceedingly attractive to women, many of whom, Martha and Mary, for example, were obviously in love with him—such suggestions as these must make us wary how we treat men of unusual emotions. The art of a pervert may be sterile, but we cannot deny that it has value, no matter how limited or unfruitful it may be. If Leonardo da Vinci was pederastic, he alone forbids us to misuse his sort of men. We are not so rich in genius that we can afford to dispense with any of it, even when it appears to be revolting and full of sin.

The impulse to perversity is said to be felt by some of the animals, though why this, even if it be true, should be considered to justify perversity in human beings is hard to understand. It is enough, however, to give us pause when we declare, without a qualification, that this is natural and that is unnatural. "Natur'," as Mr. Squeers wisely remarked, "she's a rum' un", and has the malicious trick of imposing oddities on conventional parents, making an exceedingly vital father beget a debilitated or perverse son, and inflicting a Lesbian on parents who do not even know what a Lesbian is. These malicious acts of Nature must be endured with what fortitude we can muster.

We may, however, feel differently about those who deliberately become perverts because they have exhausted the pleasure of connubiality and can no longer delight in women: though even these people should not be denied the justice we extend to all who fall sick and unsound. There is no argument that can excuse the employment of a pederast as a teacher in a school. He may be a superlative teacher, but we shall be criminally culpable if, having discovered his perversity, we permit him to come into frequent and intimate association with boys. The Spartans, the least pleasing of the classic people, when they found a lad unfit for military service, exposed him to wild beasts or sold him to the keepers of male brothels. The fate of the Spartans convinces us that their sins did surely find them out. Our argument here is no more than this, that the problem of perversity is a hard one to solve, but that at least we can draw some distinction between a pederast who has never been anything else and one who has deliberately abandoned the normal sex relation to assume one that is abnormal. Wilde was in the latter class, even if we claim consideration for him on the ground of unwholesome heredity.

6

HE was deliberately sodomistic. He not only practised the vice, but believed that it should be practised. He denied that it was a vice. These are facts to which his friends testify. His mind, bedevilled by over-refined aesthetics, made him revolt against normal relations, and disgusted him with the whole business of birth. A pregnant woman, in his eyes, was a repulsive sight. Her swollen and distorted body made him feel sick. She stirred no tenderness in him, roused no reverence for the vessel in which new life is borne, nor did the pains of her pregnancy excite his compassion or make him feel protective. It never occurred to him that his refinement was fussy as an old maid's, nor did it enter his mind for a moment that he was, in many respects, a vulgar man. His vulgarity will be discussed later in this book. It will be enough now to say that he had more in common with Ouida than he could have believed possible; that there were regions in his nature where the difference between him and a kitchen-maid was so slight that it was imperceptible.

Our immediate purpose, however, is to make clear that homosexuality was not considered unnatural by Wilde, who denied that it was a sin and declined to regard it even as undesirable. Bernard Shaw's testimony to this effect is derived from other people, but the testimony of Frank Harris and Lord Alfred

Douglas comes from Wilde himself and may not be disregarded. Harris is easy prey for anybody. His statements, with some show of reason, can always be dismissed as lies by those to whom they are inconvenient; but his book on Wilde bears a deeper stamp of truth than any of his detractors are willing to admit. Our difficulty with him is that we cannot feel sure he is not telling the truth. His testimony does not differ in substance, but only in detail, from Sherard's or Lord Alfred's. Their complaints of his pornography are false and flimsy. The man was coarse and unscrupulous and difficult to like, but he did not desert Wilde when Wilde was in his worst trouble, and it might have been better for the unhappy man if he had taken his singular friend's advice. His enemies and detractors all overlook the fact that *An Ideal Husband* was dedicated to Harris: "a slight tribute to his power and distinction as an artist, his chivalry and devotion as a friend"; and that he is included in *De Profundis* among those who had given Wilde "help, affection and sympathy".[1] Harris was too fond of hurrying from Wilde's presence to jot down notes of their conversations, and he did not diminish himself in doing so; but he had some chivalry and was not lacking in a coarse kind of courage, even if his defence of Wilde in the *Life* was animated less by liking for its subject than hatred of England, where he had been imprisoned during the First World War. The note-taker has his value. How little we should know of Dr. Johnson without Boswell, how much we wish that Shakespeare, too, had had a friend so notably assiduous.

He does not contradict Sherard in any degree worth discussion, nor does Douglas, despite his emphatic disclaimers, contradict him with facts of substance. He confirms him on many which were furiously denied by Sherard. On the point now under discussion, Wilde's affirmation of his right to be sexually perverse, they are in accord.

In his preface to Harris's *Life*, Shaw says, "I do not believe that he [Wilde] ever condescended to denials except when legal fictions were necessary. Like most similarly afflicted men of culture, he

[1] *De Profundis*. The Complete Text. Edited, with an Introduction, by Vyvyan Holland. Page 122.

was not only unashamed of his reversed sex instinct but proud of it, and of its association with some great names. But he never thrust it upon those of his friends to whom it was repugnant." Pride in perversity seems about as sensible as pride in physical deformity. As well might Little Tich have boasted of five fingers and a thumb on each hand, in addition to double joints, as Wilde have felt proud of sodomy. Little Tich, in fact, was morbidly ashamed of his affliction. Shaw's argument is specious. Wilde was not asked for his personal opinion of pederasty: he was asked if he had broken the law of his country by having sexual relations with men. He denied that he was guilty of this crime, and his denials, as he well knew, were perjury. If he thought it no wrong, why did he not proclaim himself a pederast and demand the right to follow his strange fashion? We should think him perverse had he done so, but we should not think him meanly mendacious.

Shaw's statements, as already stated, are derived from other people's. In the same preface in which they appear, he tells his readers that he "was ordinarily acquainted with Wilde's reputation; but until he prosecuted Queensberry I had never heard a word about his homosexuality"; and he cites "the late Carlos Blacker, an intimate friend of Wilde", who "told me that he also had not the faintest suspicion of anything of the kind, and was as amazed as I was when it came to light". Sherard and Harris, in their *Lives*, assert that they, too, had no knowledge of it. The strange fact is that all these highly intelligent people, who came into frequent contact with Wilde, were ignorant of his pederastic character, although it was obvious and commonly discussed by people whose minds, in their opinion, were beneath contempt. The fact denotes a simplicity in our intellectuals which is almost culpable. What a remarkable man Wilde must have been to prevent Shaw and Sherard and even that knowing card, Frank Harris, from feeling the slightest suspicion of his nature, although it was suspected by lowbrows.

There is a report of a conversation between Harris and Wilde in the *Life* which displays the callous character of Wilde's aesthetic sense, and displays also his creed of life-denial, his passion for sterility. They had been talking about beauty, Wilde asserting,

Harris stoutly denying, that men are more beautiful than women. Suddenly, Wilde made the argument personal.

"When I married, my wife was a beautiful girl, white and slim as a lily, with dancing eyes and gay rippling laughter like music. In a year or so the flower-like grace had all vanished; she became heavy, shapeless, deformed; she dragged herself about the house in uncouth misery with drawn blotched face and hideous body, sick at heart because of our love. I tried to be kind to her; forced myself to touch and kiss her, and—oh! I cannot recall it, it is all loathsome. . . . I used to wash my mouth and open the window to cleanse my lips in the pure air. Oh, nature is disgusting; it takes beauty and defiles it: it defaces the ivory-white body we have adored, with the vile cicatrices of maternity: it befouls the altar of the soul. How can you talk of such intimacy as love? How can you idealise it? Love is not possible to the artist unless it is sterile."

Harris, who might pardonably have felt sick on hearing this nauseating stuff, interrupted him. " 'All her suffering did not endear her to you?' I asked in amazement, 'did not call forth that pity in you which you used to speak of as divine?' "

"Pity, Frank," he exclaimed impatiently; "pity has nothing to do with love. How can one desire what is shapeless, deformed, ugly? Desire is killed by maternity; passion buried in conception," and he flung himself away from the table.

If anyone asserts that Harris invented this conversation, what answer can one make? Those who deny its veracity have no grounds for their denial, other than their reluctance to believe that Wilde was callous and inhuman, and the routine belief that Harris was an incorrigible liar, although liars sometimes tell the truth. Its truth or falsity were known only to Wilde and Harris, both of whom have long been dead; and we can retort, therefore, to those who deny its veracity only the established fact that it is in accordance with Wilde's beliefs. "Ugliness I consider a kind of malady, and illness and suffering always inspire me with repulsion," he remarked to Sherard, who relates, in *The Story of an Unhappy Friendship*, several instances of Wilde's aversion from ugliness and pain which are pathological. "A man with the toothache ought to have my sympathy; he fills me with nothing but aversion. He is tedious, a bore; I cannot stand him. I cannot look at him." This is a commoner attitude towards sickness than is generally supposed, and is, no doubt, part of the primitive inheritance of which we have not yet rid ourselves. Healthy hens will cruelly peck and, if they are not prevented, kill an ailing hen. Animals put disabled and sick creatures of their own species to death. Old and feeble and sickly people were thrown to the crocodiles by savage tribes who could not afford to carry passengers and helpless people. Sick nursing is still, we realise, a task of which only devoted women with a vocation are truly capable. H. G. Wells, a very different author from Wilde, shared this aversion from ill-health. "I can't bear sickness," he said to the writer. "I'm a good nurse for a day or two, but then I can stand no more of it. I just can't bear ill-health." Wilde was not abnormal in this respect, though he was abnormal in the degree of his aversion from sickness, and abnormal in treating a pregnant woman, made pregnant by him, as if she were a repulsive invalid; for it is in the nature of a normal man to feel tender and protective to the woman he has fertilised. Even if Harris were over-stating Wilde's aversion from his wife's swollen womb, he was over-stating an emotion which Wilde certainly possessed, which is felt by other people, not in the least sodomistic, and is a sign of a highly selfish and unworthy nature. His horror of sickness in other people did not prevent him from denouncing those who felt the same aversion. In *De Profundis*,[1] bitter complaint is made of Lord Alfred Douglas who had neglected to attend to Wilde when, in Brighton, he lay sick of influenza. Douglas had said, "the next time you are ill, I will go away at once". "Ah! what coarseness of fibre does that reveal", Wilde writes. "What an entire lack of imagination! How callous, how common had the temperament by that time become! . . . For you to write this to me, when the very illness and fever from which I was suffering I had caught from tending you, was of coarse revolting in its coarseness and crudity; but for any human being in the whole wide world to write thus to another would be a sin for which there is no pardon, were there any sin for which there is none. I confess that when I had finished your letter I felt almost polluted, as if by associating with one of such

[1] Page 37.

a nature I had soiled and shamed my life irretrievably." But were Lord Alfred's behaviour and his remark any worse than Wilde's statement of his feelings when he contemplated Constance in her pregnancy? Was Douglas any coarser in fibre or less imaginative or more callous and common in character than Oscar Wilde? Might not Harris have felt as polluted by Wilde's speech as Wilde felt when he read the remark Douglas made in his inhuman letter?

Alfred Douglas, in *Oscar Wilde*, asserts that Wilde was in love with his wife at the time of their marriage, and Hesketh Pearson in *The Life of Oscar Wilde*, denies, but unconvincingly, that he was a fortune hunter. "It has been said", he writes, "that Oscar married for money. If so, he had a poor financial sense, because Constance could only hope for a moderate income until she came into her grandfather's estate, while many wealthy women would have snatched at the chance of marrying Wilde." How, one wonders, does Pearson, who was still unborn when Wilde went marrying, know this? Several refutals of his statement can be made. The first is that Wilde was unaware of the amount of his wife's fortune, and thought it was larger than it turned out to be. He did not know that any increase was contingent on her grandfather's death. Moreover, her settlement, which was about £800 a year, was a fairly substantial one for the time, and was certainly not to be despised by a young man on the verge of destitution. The excitement he had caused by his peculiar public performance had died down, and he could scarcely draw an audience anywhere in Great Britain to listen to him. He was no catch for any woman then. Constance Lloyd was a considerable catch for him. What attraction had he for the numerous wealthy women who, Pearson alleges, would have snatched at the chance to marry him? His achievements were few and negligible. He had made himself notorious in a manner that was distasteful to many women, and that notoriety was neither profitable nor popular. It seems indisputable, despite his love for her, that Wilde would not have married Miss Lloyd had she been poor. He could not maintain himself. How, then, could he hope to maintain her if she were penniless? We shall see that the single job which was available to him at that time, the editorship of a woman's magazine, brought him no more than six pounds a week. But Miss Lloyd had a settlement of almost three times that sum.

To say that he married her for her fortune is not, however, to say that he felt no love for her. All the testimony proves that he did. "But the truth is", Pearson declares, "that Oscar was very much in love with Constance, who was passionately in love with him." He reports a remark Wilde is said to have confided to a friend. "We telegraph to each other twice a day, and I rush back suddenly from the uttermost parts of the earth to see her for an hour, and do all the foolish things that wise lovers do." This is absurdity, no doubt, but it is the absurdity of a man deeply in love, not the pretence of a man hunting for money. And well might he be in love with her, for she was a beautiful and delightful girl in whom any man might take pride. She was not an intellectual, a fact which appears to have worried Mr. Robert Baldwin Ross, that small, obsequious sodomite, who glided smoothly round corners to whisper that she was sometimes guilty of interrupting Oscar's rehearsed conversations with domestic enquiries. But neither was she a fool. She had her own opinions and she held to them. She thought little of Wilde's first play *Vera*, thus showing her good sense, and she differed deeply from him on the foundation of art. It is true that she was not his mental match, but is it necessary for a wife to be merely her husband's match? May she not possess her own virtues? Constance had hers, and they were plainly pleasing to her husband.

Anna, Comtesse de Brémont, an American who had met Wilde in New York during his first visit to her country, is, despite the mawkishness of her *Oscar Wilde and His Mother*, a valuable witness to the love which existed between him and his wife: for she not only met them both early in their marriage, but makes it clear that she considered herself to be a more suitable mate for Wilde than Constance or, possibly, any other woman: a belief which the reader of her work will have difficulty in sharing. Wilde would have left her in a week. Her testimony to the beauty of the young bride is unequivocal, and she does not doubt that Wilde loved her. "Constance Wilde! As I write a vision of her sweet face and graceful personality seems to arise in the vista of the past. A face whose loveliness was derived more from the expression and exquisite colouring than from any claim to the regular lines that constitute beauty. Sympathy, sensitiveness and shyness were expressed in that charming womanly face, and revealed a character intensely feminine."

She describes a reception at the Wildes' house in Tite Street, where she saw Constance for the first time.

I was attracted by the exceeding beauty of the ceiling, which was all I could perceive of the decorations, as everyone was standing. Oscar spoke of it with much pride as being a masterpiece of design by Whistler. After the ceiling, the next thing that arrested my gaze was a young woman arrayed in an exquisite Greek costume of cowslip yellow and apple leaf green. Her hair, a thick mass of ruddy brown, was wonderfully set off by bands of yellow ribbon, supporting the knot of her hair low on the nape of the neck, and crossing the wavy masses above the brow. The whole arrangement was exceedingly becoming to the youthful, almost boyish face with its clear colouring and full, dark eyes. There was an air of shy self-consciousness and restraint about the wearer of that fantastic yet lovely costume that gave me the impression of what is called stage fright, and I jumped to the conclusion that she was a young actress dressed up for a recital, and somewhat nervous before all the society folk present. Imagine my surprise when she was introduced to me as the hostess.

"My wife," said Oscar Wilde, as we paused before her. Then he whispered, but not too low for me to hear:

"You are looking lovely, Constance—not a bit too tired with all these people."

I saw her sweet face light up, and all the shyness and nervousness melt out of her eyes under those words of approval from her husband and teacher.

But the sense of fear she felt oppressed Anna, Comtesse de Brémont. "I felt that she was bored and overwrought by the part she was playing before all those people—the aesthetic pose that she was not fitted to take." This passage is followed by an account of Oscar taking the floor to give a display of brilliant intellectual fireworks. Constance, who had probably heard it all before, and more than once, immediately subsided into a corner of the room, "completely forgotten and eclipsed by the brilliant glow of her husband's eloquence.

He now occupied the place where she had stood, and posed there in an elegant and graceful attitude. When I looked about for her, she had disappeared, but I soon caught sight of her again beyond the doorway, in the crush of people in the hall, a rapt expression of love and pride on her face, while her eyes were fixed, as one magnetised, on her husband's inspired features. There could be no doubt that, at that period of their married life, Oscar Wilde and his wife were still fondly devoted to one another. A son had been born to them, and the future was all rose-coloured."

That was in July 1886. Anna, Comtesse de Brémont, could not, perhaps, have been expected to know or suspect that Constance Wilde's air of fatigue and lethargy had another and more exhausting cause than nervous agitation at the presence of so many affected people in her drawing-room: the fact that she was five months gone with her second son who was born in the following November, and that the "exquisite Greek costume of cowslip yellow and apple leaf green" was probably devised by her husband to conceal the signs of her impending maternity in its loose and flowing folds.

Alfred Douglas, in the book already cited, testifies that the Wildes were in love, not only at the time of their marriage, but for several years thereafter. If the marriage failed, the fault was not hers: it was his and, in great degree, Mr. Robert Baldwin Ross's. "Honesty", Douglas says, "compels me to say that Oscar, during the time I knew him, was not always very kind to his wife. He certainly had been (as he told me) very much in love with her, and the marriage was purely a love match. At the time when I first met him, he was still fond of her, but he was often impatient with her, and sometimes snubbed her, and he resented, and showed that he resented, the attitude of slight disapproval which she often adopted towards him. Towards the end of the time before the catastrophe (and they never met again after he came out of prison) the relations between them were distinctly strained." And he adds:

While it is true that for a year or two before the final catastrophe there had been a certain amount of estrangement between them, the marriage survived quite as well as nine marriages out of ten do. . . . After the *débâcle*, I never saw her again. The last time I saw her was two nights before the proceedings taken by Oscar Wilde against my father at the Old Bailey, when we all three had dinner in a restaurant and went on to a box at the St. James's Theatre where Oscar's play, *The Importance of Being Earnest*, was running to crowded houses. She was very much agitated, and when I said good-night to her at the door of the theatre she had tears in her eyes. . . .

As, indeed, she well might have.

Fate had dealt harshly with her when it brought Wilde into her life. Those were the days when smart hostesses invited husbands without their wives to parties. Oscar accepted all such invitations; and his bride was left at home while he went out to be brilliant. A man of feeling and fine character would have declined them all. In his acceptance, we discern the full signs of his innately selfish and vulgar disposition. Her income was soon spent by Wilde, and she sometimes had to borrow money where she could, while her husband earned a reputation, but nothing else, as a wit at smart meals. Within a year of their marriage, she was seeking a loan to buy herself a pair of boots! . . . When, eventually, wealth came to him, he squandered most of it outside his home. There was a period when he was living at the Savoy at a cost of £49 a week; a comparatively small expense, as the reproaches in *De Profundis* appear to prove, reproaches that a finer-natured man than Wilde would never have written. "When I tell you that between the autumn of 1892 and the date of my imprisonment," a period of less than three years, "I spent with you and on you more than £5,000 in actual money, irrespective of the bills I incurred, you will have some idea of the sort of life on which you insisted. Do you think I exaggerate? My ordinary expenses with you for any ordinary day in London—for luncheon, dinner, supper, amusements, hansoms and the rest of it—ranged from £12 to £20, and the week's expenses were naturally in proportion and ranged from £80 to £130. For our three months at Goring my expenses (rent of course included) were £1,340." He compares these extravagances, from which he derived no mental stimulus, with a 3 franc 50 c. *table d'hôte* dinner he enjoyed in a Soho restaurant with Ross: a meal which stimulated him to produce "the first and best of all my dialogues".[1] No such sums were spent on Constance and the

[1] *De Profundis*, pp. 19-20.

two little boys in Tite Street. There were no junketings for them! One's sense of disgust on reading these appalling passages in *De Profundis* is increased when we realise that the reproaches were earned when Wilde was nearly forty and Douglas was no more than twenty-five. The fat, middle-aged man, whose success had gone to his silly head, was wasting his money on a wilful and mindless mistress, because the pretty face had excited his lust. The tale is as old as the hills.

It was not much fun to be Mrs. Oscar Wilde. If, as he is said to have told Harris, he felt disgusted by the physical facts of her pregnancies, and allowed her to perceive his disgust, is it not understandable that she, twenty-seven when her first son was born, should begin to feel estranged, and that the nights she spent in solitude while her husband publicly abounded, made a breach between them that grew wider and wider until at last, when calamity came, bringing revelations of evil that must have been unimaginable by her, there was a gulf that could not be bridged? Yet her first thought when, in tears, she heard Mr. Robert Baldwin Ross relating the result of the Queensberry trial, was for Wilde's safety. "I hope Oscar is going away abroad?" she said between her sobs. Her affection and innate kindness were such that when his mother died, while he was in prison, she came from Genoa to England to break the news to him, unwilling that he should receive it from other lips than hers.

She had much to endure from Wilde's friends, reputable and disreputable. Frank Harris, who thought her "a young lady without any particular qualities or beauty", a remark which must seem exceptionally stupid, even for Harris, to anyone who has seen the photograph of her which is reproduced in Hesketh Pearson's book, was unlikely to please a fastidious Irish lady. Mrs. Bernard Shaw refused to have him in her house. Wilde certainly did not share Harris's opinion of his wife's looks, as the passage already cited, in which he refers to her as "a beautiful girl, white and slim as a lily", amply proves. His inscription of a volume of his verse to her, "from a poet to a poem", may have been a piece of lover's flattery, but it indicates his affection for her and his high sense of her beauty. He was not the sort of man who would have married a plain woman unless she had atoned for her plainness by possessing a very great fortune. Sherard and Lord Alfred Douglas liked her, though we may wonder if she liked them,[1] and thought her pretty. Her opinion of Mr. Robert Baldwin Ross would probably be illuminating if we knew what it was. The kind of company Wilde began to keep after her second son was born must have been infinitely boring to her, when it was not disgusting. She was a very unhappy woman. Douglas finds fault with her for failing to stand by Wilde after he came out of prison; and he quotes Shakespeare's sonnet on faithful affection:

Love is not love
Which alters when it alteration finds.

She should, Douglas contends, have "borne it out even to the crack of doom". This is sentimentality. The Church demands, but has no right to demand, that men and women shall marry for better or worse. If "worse" means unmerited misfortune, no one can complain of the demand that there shall be fidelity when it comes; but merited misfortune is another matter.

Constance Mary Lloyd was twenty-six when she married Wilde, and thirty-seven when he was arrested. She died when she was forty. A large part of her married life was spent in trouble and financial anxiety. She was alone oftener than she should have been. Some of her husband's acquaintances and friends puzzled and distressed her. Queer young men, some of them illiterate stable-boys, appeared on the doorstep late at night! . . . There was the brief period of glory and renown, when the plays were performed, but she had less of the pleasure these brought than was her due. And then, almost paralysingly, came the arrest for a crime that could not be named in public prints or even in familiar conversation in mixed company. We cannot doubt that she was ignorant of the nature of sodomy, that even when Wilde was arrested she was unaware of the crime he had committed. What must have been

[1] Douglas, in his *Autobiography*, says, "I was always on the best of terms with Mrs. Wilde. I liked her and she liked me. She told me, about a year after I first met her, that she liked me better than any of Oscar's friends." Wilde contradicts this statement in *De Profundis*, p. 30: "Our friendship had always been a source of distress to her: not merely because she had never liked you personally, but because she saw how your continual companionship altered me, and not for the better".

the effect on her conventional, simply pious, upper middle-class mind when, at last, she realised the nature of her husband's sin?

The shock of Wilde's imprisonment, following on her realisation of what he had done to deserve it, was enough in itself to shatter her love for him, but even these did not destroy it. She was still willing to live with him after he came out of prison, but was not willing that he should resume acquaintance which she had been told and believed to have been his ruin. The breach became complete. They never met again. Wilde was now steadily deteriorating. His end was certain. The unhappy, bewildered woman, overwhelmed by calamity, and compelled to live abroad under an assumed name, could bear no more. She turned her face to the wall and died. Before he condemned her, Douglas should have remembered that there came a time when his own mother could endure her marriage to his father, the Marquess of Queensberry, no longer. He took her side with passion, and did not demand that she should bear it out "even to the crack of doom". A commandment bids us honour our father no less than our mother, but Douglas dishonoured his, as, indeed, he well might, for a more unholy scoundrel never defiled the earth by his presence on it. The Marquess of Queensberry was either the embodiment of evil, who should have been destroyed, or an incurable lunatic, who should have been certified and secluded. Is it not odd that Alfred Douglas, who had every cause in his own experience to feel sympathy for this unhappy lady, should have felt so little? "She was a simple, beautiful woman," Sherard says, "too gentle and good for the part that life called upon her to play. She was a woman of heart whom kindlier gods would never have thrown into the turmoil and stress of an existence which was all a battle."

7

INSISTENCE has been laid on fertility as a supreme law of life, a law which makes sodomy repulsive to normal men and women; but there is another factor in civilised association which must be taken into consideration and is equally adverse to perverts ; the law of family life which has been as prevalent in men's minds as the law of fertility throughout all the chops and changes of marriage. The promiscuity of Abraham and Moses and David and Solomon, their unlimited traffic with wives and concubines, did not debar them from a deep feeling for family life. They did not reject the family; they accepted it too heartily. The patriarchs were not indifferent fathers: they were profoundly paternal. It is immaterial whether we regard Abraham as a man with many children or a social symbol for the head of a tribe with many members. What is material is that these children or members were closely interrelated with one another, a family, not a collection of people casually connected. That curious law of levirate which has already been mentioned, was intended to bind the Israelites more tightly in a family relationship: it was not intended to provide a man with sexual diversions.

Innumerable experiments in marriage have concluded in a widespread and growing belief that monogamy is the most satisfactory form of marriage, although it is tempered everywhere by extramarital relations. The majority of men are probably polygamous, but the majority of women are not polyandrous, though many of them are. The belief that the higher type of man is monogamous is not supported by fact, and in any case it cannot be proved. In a monogamous state, polygamous men are reticent for more reasons than one; and while we find men boasting that they have never been faithless to their wives, a statement which is seldom accepted, we rarely hear men boasting that they have.

Despite extra-marital relations, which are commoner now than they formerly were because of the knowledge of contraceptives unmarried women now possess, the law of the family remains as stable as the law of fertility; and the general ideal is of a husband and a wife and their offspring, even if the offspring are few. Despite the easy manners of our time, we should feel surprised if a man were to introduce us, as Victor Hugo was accustomed to introduce acquaintances, to his wife and his mistress, and even more surprised if we found the wife aware of the relationship and condonative.

Sodomy is a denial of family no less than a denial of life. It splits the family, as Wilde's was split, and divides the man from the woman in a manner that is abhorrent to normal people. Carnal concurrence, as Justin Martyr calls it, between a man and a woman is as natural as breathing. A normal man cannot long associate in any sort of intimacy with a woman without desiring to bed her, nor can she long associate with him without desiring to be bedded. Nature cries out for consummation, and for fruitful consummation. Milton has no puritanical aversions or suppressions about this. "Into their inmost bower", he says of Adam and Eve in *Paradise Lost*,

> Handed they went; and eas'd the putting off
> These troublesome disguises which we wear,
> Strait side by side were laid, nor turned I ween
> Adam from his fair spouse, nor Eve the rites
> Mysterious of connubial love refused:
> Whatever hypocrites austerely talk
> Of purity and place and innocence,
> Defaming as impure what God declares
> Pure, and commands to some, leaves free to all.

There was nothing in Milton of Tom Moore's morbid monk St. Seramus, whose aversion from women was such that he forbade them to land on his island of Scattery, so deep, indeed, that when an angel, led by St. Canara, came to call on him, he declined to see her. Yet angels are sexless, evil angels more certainly than good. Beelzebub is barren, Satan is sterile. The normal man is moved by this fact more than he knows. At the bottom of his mind lies the knowledge that intercourse between men and women is fruitful and natural, while intercourse between men and men or women and women is sterile and unnatural.

It is impossible to say whether or not perversion is increasing. The fact that it is openly practised and tolerantly discussed does not in itself prove increase. There is, however, a belief that it is commoner than it was when Wilde was arrested, and that its increase is real rather than apparent: due, not to rise in population, but to rise in addiction. I remarked to a friend in New York some years ago that the fact about America which had most impressed me was that never once in my two visits to that country had I been accosted by a woman in the street of any city there. My friend, an Englishman long settled in New York and now an American citizen, replied that he, too, had never been accosted by a female prostitute, but, he continued, he had more than once been accosted by male prostitutes. The absence of women whores on the pavements, he cynically suggested, was due to the fact that a living is hard to earn in the streets because of the competition of "amateurs"! But the ease with which a woman can earn a good wage in honest employment is probably the supreme fact.

Homosexuality seems to have increased in Great Britain, though this appearance is not provable. Mr. Chuter Ede, the Home Secretary, replying to a question put to him in the House of Commons by Mr. John Cyril Maude, K.C., said, as reported in *The Times* of Friday 4th November 1949, that "476 persons were charged in the Metropolitan police district with importuning male persons for immoral purposes and 444 were found guilty. In the first nine months of 1949, 415 persons were charged and 392 were found guilty. In 1948, 486 persons were arrested for gross indecency between males, and 211 were arrested in the first nine months of 1949. Of the 89 committed for trial in 1948, 82 were convicted, and of the 94 committed for trial in the first nine months of 1949, 77 were convicted." Another member of Parliament, Frank Medlicott, in a supplementary question, referred to the belief that perversion is increasing and asked the Home Secretary to "consider setting up a committee to enquire into the social, medical, and moral aspects of this grave problem". Mr. Chuter Ede replied that "it is a problem that has been present in my mind for some time, and I am considering whether it is necessary to make any formal enquiries into the possible growth of these practices".

8

OUR study of this strange man, named in a mixture of farce and romance Oscar Fingal O'Flahertie Wills Wilde, has had to start with an examination of his curious ancestry. Other men's parents and upbringing may not abide our question, but Oscar Wilde's are not free. His father and mother were abnormal, and might as easily have produced an idiot as a genius. They very nearly did; for Willie Wilde, Oscar's elder brother, was a singularly foolish fellow, a sponger, a sot and an incorrigible scallywag, who somehow made the *Daily Telegraph* and *The Pink 'Un* meet. Authors, indeed, are such odd fish, so dissimilar from their relations that they may reasonably be regarded as biological "sports", the nearest that human beings achieve in the way of Melchisedec who, St. Paul asserts, if it was he who wrote the Epistle to the Hebrews, was born "without father, without mother, without descendants, having neither beginning of days nor end of life; but made like unto the Son of God; abideth a priest continually". The man of literary genius seems to break all the laws of heredity, so far as there are any laws and so far as we understand them. So rarely is he the child of literary people that it may almost be said he never is; and he seldom leaves sons and daughters who write, or write with force and effect. Perverts might consider this fact as a justification of themselves, were it not that men of literary genius, though they are "sports", are not sterile, even if they are childless. They are immensely fruitful, and their fruit "abideth continually". The literary man of genius sometimes springs from soil so unsuitable to men of his sort that he seems scarcely akin to his relations: a changeling in his family. What had Ibsen in common with his parents or his brothers and sisters? No more than Shakespeare had with his. Dickens and Meredith had so little of the feeling for family which most of us believe to be decent, that they used their relations as raw material. Shelley was profoundly antagonistic to his father and his family, as they were to him. There is little to identify Hardy with the Hardys. Nature cannot easily, it appears, produce two people of literary genius from the same stock, even when she tries; and Wilde's foolish brother, Willie, journalising ineffectively, might be matched with Rossetti's, were it not that Dante Gabriel had a sister, that Alexandre Dumas had a son, and that the three Sitwells exist. These facts are sufficient to make us pause in doubt when we try to speculate on men's beginnings.

Wise people do not emphasise this or that factor in a person's composition, for they realise too well what a long tally of ancestors each of us has, to be willing to feel confident from what near or far-off forefather a man's character comes. But in so far as there is any telling, we have warrant for thinking that Oscar Wilde was unfortunate in his father and mother. They were, perhaps, unfortunate in themselves. Whatever their responsibility for their son may have been, direct or indirect, inherited or personal, their conjunction brought him no good. Wilde, with more warrant than Job, might have cursed the day wherein he was born.

Little is known of his boyhood, and some of that little is suspected to be false; but one requires no profundity of mind or experience to realise that a home governed by a man so physically rapacious as Sir William Wilde and a woman so full of fake emotion and ideas as his wife, was not quite a suitable nursery for an impressionable child. We cannot disregard his origin in measuring Wilde's life, even if we cannot estimate its influence. There is a story of Lady Wilde which has significance in her son's affairs. She was asked during the trial of Miss Travers's case against her why she had not answered that outraged lady's letter. Her reply was exceedingly flippant. "I took no interest in the matter", she said. What sort of a woman is it, one wonders, who takes no interest in a girl's charge of rape against her husband? Had she replied that she thought it inadvisable to correspond with a woman she considered sexually unbalanced, reason would have felt satisfied. But to say in that cynical manner, "I took no interest in the matter", when, in fact, she had been sufficiently stirred by it to write a criminally libellous letter, not to Miss Travers, but to her father, was to create a bad impression on the minds of those who heard it.

It was a flippant remark of that sort which helped to bring Wilde to Reading Gaol. Edward Carson, who had been his contemporary at Trinity College, Dublin, was the senior counsel for Queensberry when Wilde brought his action for criminal libel against him. During his examination of Wilde in the witness-box, Carson put a question to him about his relations with a boy who had been employed in Lord Alfred Douglas's rooms at Oxford.

"Did you ever kiss him?" he said. Wilde answered carelessly, "Oh, dear no. He was a peculiarly plain boy. He was, unfortunately, extremely ugly. I pitied him for it!" The effect on all who heard this answer was frightful for Wilde, and Carson did not fail to make the most of it. It was Lady Wilde's voice repeating, in the Central Criminal Court in London, the flippancies she had uttered in the Court of Common Pleas in Dublin thirty years before. The old lady, now nearly seventy, remembered during her son's trial that she had once been "Speranza" of *The Nation*, a posturing girl who delighted to perform in public, and she began again to strike attitudes and declaim, while her favourite son, Willie, pranced up and down, declaring repeatedly that Oscar was an Irish gentleman and would face the music. "I'll never speak to him again if he doesn't," Speranza said. She was wondering, perhaps, if this would not be a suitable time to put on her paint, and adorn herself with cairngorm brooches, and remember the days of Deirdre and Dervorgilla. The old war-horse began to whinny and neigh! . . .

Would Wilde, had he not been imprisoned, now be remembered? If he were remembered, would his reputation be high? Neither *The Ballad of Reading Gaol* nor *De Profundis* would have been written, and it is almost certain that their author, because of his medical history and his way of life before his arrest, which was resumed after his release, would have died sooner than he did. Remove those two works, the second of which is poor stuff, especially in its entirety, from the body of his writings, and what is left? One remarkable short play, *Salomé*; several witty, humorous and sensible essays and reviews; one interesting, but no more than interesting, novel, *The Picture of Dorian Gray*; and a brilliant farce, *The Importance of Being Earnest*, which fails of genius because its author could not tie up the ends of his acts. Some may say that other plays would have been written, had there been no imprisonment, but such assertions may be doubted on the ground already given, that Wilde was living on the verge of the grave when he was arrested, and that his sentence withdrew him from it for a year or two. There is no truth in the legend that his health declined at Reading. Sherard states that his friends, on his release, noticed "how vastly improved he was in physique, in nerve and muscle, in energy and courage; how his whole being seemed rejuvenated, his whole character sweetened. They attributed it to the prison *régime*", and, despite Sherard's singularly mawkish reflections on this subject, they were right in their attribution.

Harris confirms Sherard. "People have differed a great deal about his mental and physical condition after he came out of prison. All who knew him really, Ross, Turner, More Adey, Lord Alfred Douglas and myself, are agreed that, in spite of a slight deafness, he was never in better health, never indeed so well. But some French friends were determined to make him out a martyr." One of these French friends was André Gide, who wrote that "nothing remained in his shattered life but a mouldy ruin, painful to contemplate, of his former life". Harris makes a sharp comment on this statement. It is "not only untrue when applied to Oscar Wilde, but the reverse of the truth". Even if we had not this testimony, there is the decisive fact that *The Ballad*, which is his best poem, was written after he had been released from Reading, and that *The Sphinx*, which has been highly praised, but is far inferior to *The Ballad*, was written before he was imprisoned.

9

AND here, perhaps, it will be well to return to his beginnings. They are unnotable. When he was nine, he and his brother, who was eleven, were sent to Portora Royal School, Enniskillen, about the time Miss Travers was suing their father through their mother, to get them out of the way, no doubt; and there he remained until he was nearly seventeen. A red chalk drawing of him during this period reveals an ugly-looking lad, with a heavy, animal jowl and an appearance almost of imbecility. This drawing, made by some-one whose name is not divulged in Sherard's *Life*, where it appears, is a poor thing, and probably does the boy injustice; but it was preserved and must, therefore, have given his family and even himself some satisfaction. A badly drawn portrait which defames its subject is hardly likely to have been treasured as a family possession for at least forty years. The face has the same mixture of mind and animality which is to be seen in Sir William Wilde's; and it is significant of the singular blend of brilliance and bestiality which was Wilde himself: the man who could write *Intentions* and *The Importance of Being Earnest* and become the familiar of obscene stable-boys and ostlers.

He was unpopular with his schoolmates, as a large, ungainly boy, with inert habits and an unfortunate fluency in devising apt but acid nicknames, is certain to be. His own, which annoyed him, was Grey Crow. But his unpopularity caused him no distress. He neither shared the recreations of the schoolmates, nor wished to share them. His own company was more congenial to him than theirs. Untidy, inclined to flop about, slovenly both in appearance and dress, with hands and face always in need of washing, and nails showing signs of mourning, he made no deep impression on his fellows; and such impression as he did make was generally unfavourable. He was kind to small boys, to whom he told stories and played the piano. He read much, but was "absolutely incapable of mathematics", which is no crime, though it is a nuisance, and he was exceptionally good in classics. In 1869 he won a prize for Holy Scripture, Butler's *Analogy of Religion*, which is now in the school. It did not, however, occur to his masters or his schoolmates that he was likely to become a writer, for he displayed no gift for composition. It is probable that the lethargy he seems to have inherited from his mother was the most potent element in his nature at this period. Any forecast of distinction that might have been made about him then would probably have been derided. His mother's assertion that he was "a wonderful boy" was, no doubt, regarded as the nonsense of a fond mamma.

From Portora he went, in October 1871, with an Entrance Scholarship, to Trinity College, Dublin, and a Second Entrance prize in Greek Verse Composition. In 1872 he got first class in all the term examinations. In 1873 he concentrated on the Classical Scholarship examinations, and was selected as Scholar in the Trinity term. In the Michaelmas term he got a first-class Honours in examination; and in 1874 he won the Berkeley Gold Medal for

Greek, which had also been won by his grand-uncle, Ralph, and was a prize greatly coveted by Trinity men, although its monetary value was slight. His subject was *Fragments of the Greek Comic Poets*. In the same year he won a demyship at Magdalen College, Oxford, worth £95 a year and tenable for five years. Among his contemporaries at Trinity was a less successful and scholarly student called Edward Carson, whom he was to meet again! . . . He entered Magdalen on 17th October 1874, when he was twenty. There was, it is plain, more scholarship in him then than is usually supposed. In his aesthetic period his detractors denied him any, or much, classical knowledge, but the facts are against them. He was a fairly good classical scholar, and would have been a better one had he possessed the power of sustained study. In mathematics and science he was almost illiterate, but only because he could not take the slightest interest in them. Neither Portora nor Trinity College, Dublin, won his affection. He never returned to them, but neither did he visit Ireland often. Irish authors from the region now known as Eire have seldom shown much affection, even on paper, for their country. They leave it early and promptly, returning to it reluctantly and usually when they are dead. Goldsmith and Sheridan never returned to Ireland, not even in death; nor do they seem to have shown any interest in it. The Irish characters in Sheridan's comedies, such as Sir Lucius O'Trigger, are unpleasing people. O'Trigger is Sheridan's Ancient Pistol, a man who makes Mrs. Malaprop's bitter demand, "Come, come, let's have no honour before ladies!" seem a reasonable request. Goldsmith's Irish atmosphere in his works is entirely family, not more specifically Irish than English, and there is justice in Macaulay's argument that Sweet Auburn describes a village in Kent as faithfully as it is said to describe Lissoy.

Dublin men, when they escape from their native city, take uncommon care to keep out of the trap. Edmund Burke left it when he was twenty-one, and did not return for eleven years; and then only to perform some undefined political duties for Single Speech Hamilton, who was much more garrulous in Parliament than his nickname denotes. He remained in Ireland for two years, and was rewarded for his unknown services by a pension of £300 a year;

a pretty reward for the services, whatever they were. He did not return to his country, although he displayed considerably more interest in it than was ever shown by Goldsmith and Sheridan.

Irish writers from Eire, in our own age, have been almost as indifferent to Ireland as these two. Wilde seems not to have returned to Dublin after his father's death in 1876, until 1885, when he lectured on bustles in the Gaiety Theatre without exciting much enthusiasm. A man is reported to have entered the theatre —it was the period of pantomime—with two boys, and, after listening for a few minutes, to have cried out, "When does the performance start?" He seemed not to have perceived that it had already begun. Wilde's visit to Dublin was not repeated.

Bernard Shaw never set his feet in his native city, not even to attend his father's funeral, for nearly thirty years after he had left it; and he returned then only to please his wife, whom he had recently married, and who had a sentimental feeling for her country which was not strong enough to induce her to live in it. Shaw became a registered citizen of Eire on the 8th of July 1936, and received the freedom of Dublin on the 26th of August 1946, but he declined to repatriate himself. His early life in Dublin appears to have given him a deep distaste for it, distaste so deep that, as Mrs. Shaw herself informed the present writer, he would never enter Ireland by its port, preferring even a sea journey to Cork rather than to land at North Wall.

W. B. Yeats resumed residence in Dublin in his old age, at the suggestion, one suspects, of Mrs. Yeats, who is an Englishwoman, but he tempered his stay by frequent visits to London. George Moore, in an outburst of petulant old-maidery, shook the dust of England off his feet, but retained the lease of his house in Ebury Street, to which he returned when his petulant mood had abated. Stephen McKenna, the translator of Plotinus, was an extreme Republican, but not to the extent of living in Eire. England, despite his rancid political opinions, was more congenial to him. "John Eglinton", the essayist who figures so prominently in Moore's *Hail and Farewell*, had to live in Dublin because his employment kept him there, but as soon as he was pensioned he cleared out of the place and settled in Bournemouth. Sean O'Casey has not lived in Dublin since he left it twenty years ago. He prefers England. So did James Stephens. James Joyce would not live or die or be buried in Dublin. Padraic Colum has lived in America these thirty years and more. George Russell, "A.E.", though he was an Ulsterman, lived in Dublin longer than any of these, but he too, like "John Eglinton", left it when his work there was ended; and he died in Bournemouth. Miss Elizabeth Bowen, Mr. Cecil Day-Lewis and Mr. Denis Johnston could live in their native Eire, if that were their wish, but it is not.[1]

10

WILDE's life may be said to have begun and to have ended at Oxford, which came very frequently into his conversation. Neither Portora nor Trinity College were mentioned by him much, if they were mentioned at all: a fact which was snobbish in origin. Trinity College, Dublin, men will feel more surprised than disgusted by the suggestion that even Wilde could consider the University of Oxford in any degree superior to the University of Dublin; but such was manifestly the fact. He became aware of himself on the Isis as he had never been aware of himself on the Liffey. His delight in Oxford was intense and unbounded.

Sherard, sentimentally and without warrant, asserts that Wilde developed perversion at Magdalen, and asserts, with equal sentimentality and lack of warrant, that he would not have done so if he had remained at Trinity. This assertion disregards the fact that some men at Trinity College, Dublin, have suffered from sodomy, and that the vast majority of Oxford graduates in all ages have been free of it. Classical studies do not, any more than the study of the binomial theorem, produce perverts. We should have to close universities everywhere, or forbid the classics to be studied, if they did. A man who attributes his inverted sex to reading *The Golden Ass* of Apuleius or the *Satyricon* of Petronius, was a pervert before he read it, and must, even if he had never read a classic

[1] But Mr. Johnston, although he was born in Dublin, is the son of Ulster parents.

in his life, sooner or later have revealed his aborted emotions. The number of Lesbians who are classical scholars is not included in any tables of statistics that are generally available, but it will be cause for surprise if they are numerous. If the Greeks were as addicted to sodomy as Wilde imagines they were, what brought about their addiction? What classics did they study to be thus perverted? Do Arabs on their camels debase their minds with Greek and Latin literature?

He did undoubtedly become suspect of peculiar practices at Oxford, but this reputation was founded more on his conversation than his habits. His determination to make himself somehow notorious caused him to hint at scarlet sins which were, in fact, not even pale pink. That he was a pederast at Oxford is almost certainly false. The belief, flimsily held, that he contracted syphilis there is sufficient, if it be true, which may well be doubted, to prove that he was not. Our intent here is to suggest that he was not then a sodomite, and that he was normally interested in women for at least a decade after he had matriculated. If sodomistic tendencies were started in him at all in this period, they are more likely to have been caused by his tour with Dr. John Pentland Mahaffy in Italy and Greece in 1877, although proof that they were cannot be found either in his acts or his words. His first poems included verses about Ellen Terry and Sarah Bernhardt; signs of a normal young man's adoration of women; and it is notorious that he was wildly in love with Lily Langtry who was not in the least in love with him. Remark has already been made about the love he felt for his wife, who quickly bore him two sons. Hesketh Pearson asserts that Sherard, from whose lips Pearson received the tale, was embarrassed in the streets of Paris one morning by a long and detailed account Wilde gave him of the raptures of his bridal night. He had enjoyed Constance immensely. There was no sodomy in Wilde's mind that night. His degeneracy did not, we may feel confident, begin at Oxford, nor did it develop until his unfortunate encounter with Mr. Robert Baldwin Ross. Sherard asperses the University when he states that its atmosphere made Wilde's sodomy inevitable. But Sherard was a man of small, oxlike mind, liable to fall into unreasonable rages and as unreasonable admirations; and deeply addicted to duels. His judgement was as feeble as his literary style. The man was full of commonplace opinions and jejune beliefs and febrile emotion.

Wilde, at Oxford, was deliberately a publicity-hound, an adventurer with a way to make, who plainly perceived that his hope of the success he wished to win lay in notoriety. A man is not a sodomite because he strikes attitudes in public and wears eccentric clothes or makes the heavy jaws of sporting men collapse in awe and wonder by wishing aloud and very intensely that he could live up to his blue china. It is common for clever young men and adolescents to wish to shock their elders: it is even commoner for them to wish to shock other clever young men and adolescents.

The Baptist wore eccentric clothes, a robe made of camel's hair and bound by a leathern girdle. He lived on locusts and wild honey, and behaved in ways that were odd. He spoke his mind very freely about the Royal Family, and lost his head in consequence. It is very likely that respectable people, as they watched him on the banks of the Jordan, assured each other that he was nothing but an exhibitionist. When he spoke about the relations of Herod and Herodias, agreement that his remarks were in very bad taste was probably general.

There is nothing new in seeking to surprise people by startling attire or tactless speech. Wilde, wishing he could live up to his blue china, was living up to his mother who had shocked her neighbours by announcing her intention to found a Society for the Suppression of Virtue, and to his brother, Willie, who, when he was at Trinity, made an impassioned defence of prostitutes in a debate in the University Philosophical Society, over which his father presided. Dublin could scarcely think or speak of anything else for days! . . . Oxford never forgot about the blue china.

Wilde had to live on his wits. The fact was impressed upon him in his second year at Oxford, when his father died leaving his family in comparative penury. The begetting of bastards is an expensive business, and Sir William had begotten many. But the lavish entertainment of the "boosy and boisterous Bohemians" of Dublin, as Sherard describes the sots and spongers of that city, where sots and spongers excessively abound, must have worn a wide hole in Sir William Wilde's ample purse. There is an instruction in The Wisdom, commonly called Ecclesiasticus, of Jesus, son of Sirach, which both Wildes, father and son, could well and wisely have followed:

> Make not merry in much luxury;
> Neither be tied to the expense thereof.
> Be not made a beggar by banqueting upon borrowing,
> When thou hast nothing in thy purse.

There was a house and a plot of unprofitable land for Oscar, but any hope he may have had of leading a leisured life on unearned increment was abolished. The good atin' an' drinkin' in Merrion Square, and the endowment of irregular infants, put a period to that. He would have to earn his living; and he seems, very deliberately, to have made up his mind to earn it by exhibitionism. Consciously clever, but in a way which was uncoinable, so far as he could foresee, he shot his arrow in the air and hoped that it would land by a pot of gold.

We shall not understand his life at this time unless we realise that he was one of a long line of Irish adventurers in England, chancing his luck. Two years after Wilde's birth in Westland Row, another adventurer was born a few hundred yards away—George Bernard Shaw, whose father's squint had been shifted from one side of his eye to the other by Sir William. He, too, was to migrate, but not to Oxford, when he was twenty; and he, too, was to perform in public for a living. These two men, who never met in Ireland, although their homes were only a little distance apart, assailed London in substantially the same way. Their tactics were different, but they used the same strategy. Each donned eccentric clothes; each startled the conventional by paradoxical remarks; each professed Socialism against his nature, though Wilde's had no depth or durability; and each, after misadventures, stormed and over-ran the stage! . . .

Wilde's early years at Oxford were surprisingly conventional. His behaviour and opinions were such as might have been expected in an earnest young man who took himself, perhaps, a little too seriously. He had a vague desire to reform the world, and it flourished for a brief period under the influence of Ruskin who was talking a great deal just then. This impotent prophet, whose mind had been over-lain by his absurd and almost grotesque parents, wasted his own and other people's energy and time by urging undergraduates to become amateur road-menders. They were to reform themselves and the world in general by building highways on Hinksey Marsh. Among those who went was Wilde. The road they made had to be rebuilt by Ruskin's gardener, whose opinion of aesthetic navvies must have been impressive to those who had the luck to hear it. That phase, however, soon ended. Ruskin, having uttered many eloquent and uplifting remarks, departed from Oxford to repeat them somewhere else, and Wilde and his associates ceased to regenerate mankind by manual labour.

He settled down to fairly solid study which won him a First in Classical Moderations in 1876 and a First in Literae Humaniores in 1878. In the latter year he won the Newdigate Prize for a poem, entitled *Ravenna*, which is not good. During this time he spent part of his patrimony on the trip to Italy and Greece, and scattered poems, worse than *Ravenna*, through the pages of Irish magazines such as *The Irish Monthly*, *Kottabos*, *The Month* and *Catholic Review*. They were signed with his name almost in full: Oscar O'F. Wills Wilde. The first poem he had published appeared in the *Dublin University Magazine* in 1875. Its name was *Chorus of Cloud Maidens*, but it is not now included in the collected works. If Wilde received any payment for these poems, he was overpaid. They are almost as bad as his mother's. What a faltering end he puts to his *Sonnet to Liberty*:

> These Christs that die upon the barricades
> God knows that I am with them, in some things.

Tennyson estimating the cost of Enoch Arden's funeral, and Wordsworth addressing Wilkinson's spade, were not more banal; and each had heights that Wilde never saw. Even the death of his sister, Isola, failed to do more than stir up memories of Thomas Hood.

The reader can exercise his critical faculty with profit by comparing Wilde's *Requiescat*, written when he was twenty-three, with Matthew Arnold's *Remembrance*. Milton's *On the Death of a*

Fair Infant was written in his seventeenth year. When he wrote his *Epitaph on the Marchioness of Winchester* he was the age that Wilde was when the *Requiescat* for Isola was written. The great monody on *Lycidas* appeared when he was twenty-nine. Here is a progression of genius nowhere to be found in Wilde's verse. His most notable work when he was twenty-nine was an execrable play, *The Duchess of Padua*, the second of the two terrible melodramas, *Vera* being the first, which he wrote. What was anything he composed in comparison with the work of Keats who died when he was twenty-six? Shelley was twenty-nine when he wrote *Adonais*.

These great names are mentioned in conjunction with Wilde because his admirers have put forth high claims of genius for him. Alfred Douglas, who wrote far better verse than Wilde, declares him to be a major poet, and claims that *The Ballad of Reading Gaol* is equal in rank with *The Ancient Mariner*. "Wilde", he says, "was a minor poet till he wrote *The Ballad of Reading Gaol*... but even before he wrote it, he was a better poet than Yeats. In fact, as I have already said, Wilde can be ranked as a major poet on the strength of that one ballad. Moreover, I would undertake to pick twenty poems out of Wilde's script which are better than any poetry that has been written in England in the last twenty years, with perhaps half a dozen exceptions." The judicious must grieve when they read such statements, and wonder how a man whose work was superior to Wilde's could make them.

They may, perhaps, be explained by the remorse Douglas felt for a ferocious attack he had made on his friend when, smarting from the wounds Wilde had inflicted on him in the suppressed passages of *De Profundis*, he lost his self-control and stormed him with words that were like sticks and stones that break our bones. When he had recovered from his wrath, he tried to make reparation by praising the dead man beyond his desert. This seems to be the only plausible explanation of his extravagance. There was no balance in these people. They shouted at the top of their voices. All their adjectives were superlatives. Wilde was either the best or the worst. He had no place between extremities.

If Wilde had offered his countrymen nothing better than his

Poems, he would have taken a small position among the minimum poets of his period, and would now be known only to industrious anthologists for a few forlorn and pretentious pieces. His was the sort of stuff an undergraduate is liable to compose; and we may estimate his status as a poet when we realise that he wrote verse mainly in his callow years, and that his best piece, the poem which is most widely and deservedly known, *The Ballad*, was written after he had been in prison and been deeply moved by his experience. It was the only product of that emotion and experience.

His mind, in his Oxford period, was much more orthodox than anybody has ever imagined it to be. He was vaguely Liberal, and almost as devoted to Cromwell as Mr. Isaac Foot. Here he differed deeply from his mother, to whom Cromwell was "a soulless iconoclast". It was not laughing Cavaliers in curls who moved him then, but stern-eyed Puritans with lantern jaws and long, unsmiling looks. His taste, like Bernard Shaw's at a later date, was for imperious and dictatorial men; and it was immaterial to him whether they were called Cromwell or Napoleon Bonaparte, to whom he paid tribute when he wrote a lamentation for the third Napoleon's son, the Prince Imperial. "Milton! I think thy spirit hath passed away From these white cliffs and high-embattled towers", he complains; and in *Quantum Mutata* he expresses contempt for an age which has, he declares, fallen from Cromwell's grace and Milton's:

> There was a time in Europe long ago
> When no man died for freedom anywhere
> But England's lion leaping from its lair
> Laid hands on the oppressor! It was so
> While England could a great Republic show.
> Witness the men of Piedmont, chiefest care
> Of Cromwell, when with impotent despair
> The Pontiff in his painted portico
> Trembled before our stern ambassadors.
> How comes it then that from such high estate
> We have thus fallen, save that Luxury
> With barren merchandise piles up the gate
> Where noble thoughts and deeds should enter by:
> Else might we still be Milton's heritors.

That phrase about Luxury must surely have startled the dramatist whose weekly bill at the Savoy was £49, had he read his sonnet then and tried to remember the road Ruskin induced him to build. He was consistent in his antipathy to demagogues and the rule of rude mechanicals and his admiration for dictators, acquired, no doubt, from another of his admirations, Thomas Carlyle, who would have felt considerably surprised had he met his disciple; but he did not make the mistake Shaw made, of imagining that the scrapings of the Bavarian and Roman slums were made in the Cromwellian mould. He was no Red, as he showed in *The Soul of Man Under Socialism*, as he had shown at Oxford in *Libertatis Sacra Fames*:

Albeit nurtured in democracy,
  And liking best that state republican,
  Where every man is Kinglike and no man
Is crowned above his fellows, yet I see
Spite of this modern fret for Liberty,
  Better the rule of One, whom all obey,
  Than to let clamorous demagogues betray
Our freedom with the kiss of anarchy.
Wherefore I love them not whose hands profane
  Plant the red flag upon the piled-up street
  For no right cause, beneath whose ignorant reign
Arts, Culture, Reverence, Honour, all things fade,
  Save Treason and the dagger of her trade,
  Or Murder with his silent bloody feet.

Karl Marx, that envious toad without a jewel in his head, but with a heart full of hate, seems never to have crossed Wilde's mind. How surprised he would have felt if, while dawdling down a London street with a lily in his hand, he had met the scowling and hate-full German Jew hurrying to his studies in the British Museum, and had been told that this shabby sponger was to change the face of Europe, that kings and emperors would tumble in the dust because this malignant bankrupt had wormed his way through stale histories and mouldy manuals on outworn economics. The flowers in his Garden of Eros were Keats and Swinburne and

Morris, our sweet and simple Chaucer's child,
  Dear heritor of Spenser's tuneful reed,

and Dante Gabriel Rossetti. He was alarmed by mechanistic life and the stinks and smells of science, insistent that the world should realise that comfort and convenience are not all, that men lapped in luxury are clad in cerements and graveyard clothes, and that life without beauty is death.

> Ah! there is something more in that bird's flight
> Than could be tested in a crucible!—

This was juvenile emotion, but it was generous enough; and we need not deride the poverty of thought in remembering how very young the young man was. The scientist at his tubes, the engineer in his workshop can claim with cause to have done as much for man as any poet. It is not their fault that men of arbitrary will and dictatorial intent, such as the young Wilde admired, have misapplied their work. It is still there to be used aright.

II

HE was to become more and more dependent on his emotions, to live more and more on sensation, less and less on mind, until at last he could repudiate thought as if it were a cancer of the soul.

> For, sweet, to feel is better than to know,
> And wisdom is a childless heritage,
> One pulse of passion—youth's first fiery glow,
> Are worth the hoarded proverbs of the sage:
> Vex not thy soul with dead philosophy,
> Have we not lips to kiss with, hearts to love and eyes to see?

Any savage could have said as much. Wilde saw the gods sitting at their ease, "strewing with leaves of rose their scented wine", and sleeping.

> Mourning the old glad days before they knew
> What evil things the heart of man could dream, and, dreaming, do.
> And far beneath the brazen floor they see,
> Like swarming flies, the crowd of little men.

The bustles of small lives, then wearily
  Back to their lotus-haunts they turn again.
Kissing each other's mouths, and mix more deep
The poppy-seeded draught which brings soft purple-lidded sleep.

If that is all the gods can do and see, so much the less gods are they, so much the better they should die. Decay has started, is, indeed, advanced. The earnest undergraduate has begun to perish in the arms of the leering and unnatural lord of language who takes no thought for the morrow, but is content to loll on well-appointed sofas while the bum bailiffs of death knock at the door. His work becomes increasingly artificial, bearing a heavy load of over-scented adjectives, until the reader of *The Sphinx* feels that if he does not escape from this airless stuff, he will sicken and faint. The memories of other poets' minds and manners still persist. How false and faked his feelings were at this time appears from Sherard's statement that he badgered his friends in Paris for a "rhyme in *ar*" to fit a verse in *The Sphinx* which he was then writing, and how delighted he was when Sherard, after burrowing in lexicons, found the word *nenuphar*: a word of which, until then, both of them had been sublimely ignorant. Great poetry is not composed by snatching obscure words from their burial-ground in dictionaries: it rises from the poet's mind and heart.

Arthur Ransome endeavours, but vainly, to convince his readers that Wilde's imitations are tributes so true that they are almost original. Wilde, we are to believe, is making crystal-clear what Milton made obscure. "He tries to catch not only the letter but the spirit, and does indeed present a clearer view of Milton than is contained in many academic essays."

But even if this be true, there remains the fact that he never went beyond it, never passed out of his tutor's hands to take possession of himself. We have the imitation of poets. Where is the poet himself? As well might an accomplished actor claim to be Shakespeare because he gives a superb interpretation of Hamlet, as Wilde claim to be a poet because he gives a superb imitation of Swinburne and Milton.

12

WE have now to note the result of Wilde's deliberate decision to perform a Barnum and Bailey act: to call attention to himself by unusual public performances. People were to be induced to walk up and see the sights inside the circus which would, the barker alleged, be even more enthralling than those seen outside. This was to be the most marvellous one-man show on earth. There had been a few desultory performances in Oxford, where a reputation had to be created. It was inevitable that Wilde, in consequence of these performances, should be ragged by hearties. Hearties are people who, in any well-regulated society, would be employed as grooms. Their natural affinity with horses qualifies them for that respectable and inexacting occupation. In civilised states, Sweden, for example, such persons are not admitted to universities at all. Educated men are not expected to waste their time instructing oafs who cannot be instructed, except in the art of chewing straws and making sibilant sounds while they attend their champing steeds. It is otherwise at Oxford and Cambridge, where the lout with means can still take up space he has no right to occupy. It is saddening to reflect that Jude Fawley, in Thomas Hardy's novel, who desired and might have benefited by higher education, could not hope to obtain admission to Christminster, whereas Mr. Henry Foker, in *Pendennis*, who did not desire any education and would have made an excellent hunt servant, had it forced upon him.

Wilde was ragged by Oxford hearties. But Wilde was not supine under ragging, and he is said to have given as good as he got. Opinions on his physique vary very considerably. Bernard Shaw, in his preface to Harris's *Life*, asserts that he was not the sort of man who would dismay a boxer, but Shaw's personal knowledge of him is slight and derived only from his decadence. Wilde was far more robust, according to his school and college contemporaries, than anyone, reading *Intentions* or *The Portrait of Dorian Gray*, could imagine. He had physical and moral courage: statements which will surprise people who fail to realise that even his early extravagances, after he had come down from Oxford, demanded a great deal of that indifference to popular opinion which any man of moral courage must possess.

His first biographer, Sherard, says, "it is on record that while a young man in London, he assisted a man, a friend, to escape from the police, and in the furtherance of this object exerted great physical strength, holding a door against a number of constables, while the fugitive was clambering out of the window to safety and freedom". Lord Alfred Douglas, in *Oscar Wilde*, cites an article by Sir Frank Benson, a famous Shakespearean actor, who, though he was four years younger than Wilde, was his contemporary at Oxford. This article was published in *John o' London's Weekly*, and in it Benson gives an account of a rag:

> Four intruders burst into the victim's room, the others following upstairs as spectators of the game. To the astonishment of the beholders, number one returned into their midst, propelled by a hefty boot-thrust down the stairs; the next received a punch in the wind that doubled him up on the top of his companions below, a third form was lifted bodily and hurled onto the heads of the spectators. Then came the triumphant Wilde, carrying the biggest of the gang, like a baby in his arms. He was about Wilde's size and weight, and hefty at that. But his struggles were useless, and he was borne by Wilde to his own rooms and buried by Wilde underneath a pile of the would-be ragger's fine furniture.

This account of berserker rage almost inclines the reader to believe Lady Wilde's romantic delusion that her son had Viking blood in his veins. Benson, himself an athlete and thought by many to be better at hockey than he was at acting, was not, apparently, present at this rag, and his account of it certainly seems to be fanciful, but it supports the opinions of other people who knew or met Wilde in his youth and young manhood, and is confirmed by the courage, moral and physical, which he displayed during his first visit to the United States. The newspaper men who met him on the *Arizona*'s deck in New York Harbour saw no lily-handed, drooping and effete youth, but a substantial man, despite his comic clothes, "more like an athlete", whose long fingers "when doubled up would form a fist that would hit a hard knock". Nor did he dine on rose leaves and daffodils. His appetite was as vast as Bismarck's, and he could drink stout topers under the table, himself as steady as a rock. When hearties in San Francisco plotted to put "Miss Nancy", as they nicknamed him, into a complete haze with drink, they were astounded to discover that he could out-drink them all and remain sober.

The game began. Soon the Americans were rolling with laughter and as the night wore on, they slumped, one by one, in their cups beneath the table. And still Oscar took all drinks as fast as they came, and still his voice, unhurried, unceasing, went on. Out-drunk, and out-talked, San Francisco was sleeping among the table legs when Wilde looked up at the gray dawn in the windows, arose, put on his great-cloak and sauntered off alone to his rooms at the Palace Hotel. Word of the feat passed over the city during the day. Westerners who had covertly despised anyone who could wear knee pants and talk "woman-talk" suddenly realised that here was "a three-bottle man" indeed.

The miners of Leadville had been expected to treat him very roughly: and attempts were made to subject him to their lawless attentions. But he delivered his lectures and wore his comic clothes in complete disregard of threats or rumours of misuse, maintaining his aplomb with such good humour that those who came to mob, remained to laugh. He went down a mine. "At the bottom of the shaft he was 'met by a dozen miners, each with a bottle. By invariable Western custom, every bottle must make the rounds. Within a few minutes, all have had twelve snorters. The miners without exception are rather dizzy, but Wilde remains cool, steady, and collected. Like Socrates, he could drink any man under the table, and himself remain sober. He is cheered loudly, and is voted a perfect gentleman.' " He had won the respect of miners in the toughest town in the world.

Only a man of unusual courage could have endured that lecture tour with fortitude. Wilde endured it; endured the discomfort and the danger, for there was danger, as good-temperedly as he endured insults and bad manners.

An Ohio newspaper, *The Cincinnati Commercial*, after abusing him in what was then the customary manner, remarked that "if Mr. Wilde will leave the lilies and daffodils and come west to Cincinnati, we will undertake to show him how to deprive thirty hogs of their intestines in one minute". The value of this demonstration as an enhancement of virility was neither mentioned nor proved. Wilde went to Cincinnati, but not to see hogs disembowelled. He told the Cincinnatians, whose bowels, he might pardonably have thought, could more justifiably have been removed than any hog's, that their city was so hideous that he wondered the criminal classes did not make its ugliness an excuse for their crimes. But Cincinnati was in the middle of a religious revival just then, and was less provoked than it ought to have been. Its inhabitants were wallowing in spiritual orgies that were more enthralling than depriving hogs of their guts! . . .

These American passages, which have been taken from a curious compilation entitled *Oscar Wilde Discovers America*, by Lloyd Lewis and Henry Justin Smith, do not denote any cissiness in Wilde. There is not the slightest suggestion of homosexuality in his behaviour in the whole of this odd work. There is, instead, frequent reference to his susceptibility to feminine attractions; and his poem, *Charmides*, which had been included in the volume, presently to be noted, which he had published at his own expense immediately before his voyage to New York, shocked the prudes by its masculine lust. Americans were disappointed in Wilde. They had been told to expect a languishing, niminy-piminy person, even more utterly utter than Bunthorne in *Patience*, but instead there had appeared a robust-looking man, six feet in height, who looked as if he could man-handle anybody who tried to take liberties with him. Mr. Lewis and Mr. Smith mention a Mr. Horace Wilkins who claimed to have been a contemporary of Wilde at Trinity College, Dublin. This gentleman gave an account of him to an audience in Salt Lake City in 1882, which included a description of another exhibition of berserker rage:

> Wilde was a queer, awkward lad . . . who hardly ever made a step he didn't knock something over. He was big, ungainly and clumsy to such a degree that it made him a laughing stock. But those who made fun of Wilde did not know him. He was a big-hearted, liberal fellow,

who never did a mean, underhanded thing, and his last shilling was at anybody's disposal. . . . One day a thing happened which seemed, as it were, to change the current of Wilde's life. He wrote a poem which he read at one of the class symposiums. It struck me as a beautiful thing but when he had finished reading, the bully of the class laughed sneeringly. I never saw a man's face light up with such savagery of hate as Wilde's. He strode across the room and, standing in front of the man, asked him by what right he sneered at his poetry. The man laughed again, and Wilde slapped him across the face. The class interfered, but inside of an hour the crowd was out behind the college, arranging for a fight. Wilde, in a towering rage, was ready to fight with howitzers if necessary, but the bully wanted to fight with nature's weapons. No one supposed that Wilde had a ghost of a show, but when he led out with his right, it was like a pile-driver. He followed the surprised bully up with half a dozen crushers, and that ended it. Talk about that man being "a pallid young man"! When I see these allusions in the newspapers, I always think of his fighting qualities. I think he would make an ox shake his head and blink.

No other record of this affair is to be found anywhere, and Mr. Wilkins may have been drawing on his imagination; but he told his tale in 1882 when Wilde was twenty-eight, with no renown that would warrant a sycophant in currying favour with him. There is, indeed, no record that Wilkins met Wilde during this tour in America. He could gain nothing from his tribute, apart, perhaps, from a small and fleeting notoriety in Salt Lake City. We may, therefore, believe that the statement was sincerely made and that it had some foundation in fact, despite our scepticism about the poem. No record of such a work, composed while he was at Trinity, appears anywhere else.

But the evidence of physical strength and courage is too widespread to be doubted. Lord Alfred Douglas, after citing Sir Frank Benson, adds his own testimony:

The fact is that Oscar Wilde was a very powerful man, and he was also, then, and all his life, completely fearless. Twenty years after this exploit in his rooms at Magdalen when he routed the "raggers" he turned my father out of his house in Tite Street, although the "screaming scarlet Marquis", as Wilde, paraphrasing a phrase in his own poem "*The Sphinx*", used to call him, was an ex-amateur light-weight champion and although his lordship had taken the precaution to bring along a prize fighter to keep him company. . . . When he had listened to what Queensberry had to say, Wilde rang the bell and said to the butler, "this man is the Marquis of Queensberry, the most infamous brute in London; never admit him to this house again". He then opened the door and said, "Get out", and the screaming scarlet marquis went like a lamb. Had my father attempted to attack him, Wilde could and would have picked him up and thrown him down the front-door steps. He was about five inches taller and four stones heavier than Q., and though he may not have been in quite first-class condition, I wouldn't have given my father a dog's chance with him in a "rough-and-tumble", while as for the poor pugilist, he was far too well behaved (as is the habit with pugilists except when they are drunk) to interfere in an argument between two gentlemen. Oscar was as strong as a horse. . . .

The purpose in drawing all these passages together in advance of the theme's course, is to dispel the legend of flabby physique and flabbier spirit in Wilde's young manhood. After his downfall, people asserted that they had known all along what sort of a man he was ever since his stay at Magdalen; but they were exaggerating the extent of their knowledge. There is no proof that Wilde was a homosexual at Oxford. His well-furnished rooms and his aesthetic utterances and his flippant remarks about his blue china prove only that he had some taste, some indisciplined ideas about beauty, and a good deal of juvenile desire to shock the stupid. Ransome asserts that Wilde "first experimented with the vice" of sodomy "in 1886", two years after his marriage, and in the year his second son was born, and "it became a habit in 1889". This, according to Douglas, is probably correct, and he implies that Wilde contracted the vice from Mr. Robert Baldwin Ross, "who was an active homosexualist long before Wilde was and who knew him intimately several years before I met him. I met Wilde in 1891." Douglas, customarily careless, overstates the facts. Ross was seventeen in 1886, and can scarcely have been "an active homosexualist *long* before" that year, although he must have been perverse for some period when he and Wilde first met. The testimony to Ross's seduction of Wilde is confirmed by Frank Harris who remarks that Ross boasted to him that he "was the first boy Oscar had". It may seem hard to believe that a man of thirty-two was perverted by a boy of seventeen, but Wilde was, in many respects, less adult than his years denoted; and he was easily influenced by wilful and determined youths. Wilde himself, in the full edition of *De Profundis*, confesses an abjection before the wiles of Alfred Douglas, with a lack of reserve which would embarrass even a Grouper, when he was almost ten years older than he had been when he first met Ross. We know that elderly and even wise men can be made drivelling idiots by mindless but physically satisfying girls; and we never cease to marvel at the women some men marry when abler women, more suitable to be wives and mothers, are left unsought. Why, then, should we feel astonished that a boy of seventeen should be able to seduce a man of thirty-two? Ross, a sly, intriguing, suave and timorous little fellow, possessive as a maiden aunt, will, we may surmise, receive a dusty answer when he comes smirking into the courts of God with that claim to immortality on his lips. What hell will be deep enough and dark enough to hold him when he is violently hurled from heaven for corrupting and debauching a brilliant mind?

13

WILDE was a young man of modest and diminishing means. His income was about £200 a year, enough, and more than enough, for a bank clerk of studious habits, but insufficient for a man of fashion. Plentiful money was essential to the style of life he meant to follow, if he was to move in high circles without embarrassment. Wilde had no illusions about poverty. Young gentlemen of leisure, sons of rich men and amply provided with unearned increment, such as St. Francis of Assisi, may embrace poverty and deprive themselves of sufficient food in the delusion that the Almighty likes to see His creatures emaciated and dirty, but they forget that it is one thing to go without boots because you like being barefoot, and another and very different thing to go barefoot because you cannot afford to buy boots. The hunger of an anchorite is self-indulgence. The hunger of a pauper is starvation. The shabby stringencies which succeeded the gross liberalities of

Merrion Square were unpleasant recollections for Wilde. The bum bailiffs and the boosy Bohemians who frequented his prodigal father's house were equally distasteful to him. Money was an urgent necessity of his design for life. The passion for notoriety was equally strong. It would not be enough if he were rich: he must also be renowned. The life of a Rockefeller, no less than the life of a Tennyson or Hardy, would have seemed unutterably dull to Wilde. He wanted money to spend, not to hoard; and he desired celebrity in good company, not in splendid isolation.

Like the majority of Eirean authors, he had a calculating mind. The simple spendthrift, Oliver Goldsmith, is not their model, nor indeed is the more complicated spendthrift, Sheridan, to whom Wilde in his extravagance seemed, but only superficially, to bear resemblance. George Moore was mean about money, a man with the mind of a penurious pawnbroker. Yeats took uncommon care of any coins that came his way: an acute business man and a very able advertising agent, who contrived to make the best of several worlds, and, while applauding every slum patriot who shot a peeler in the back for the honour and glory of Ireland, arranged his affairs so well that he, like Oscar's mother, was pensioned by the British. Bernard Shaw was a generous-minded man in all respects: a gay, unrancorous soldier of fortune who had never been heard to moan or whimper or even admit a wound. But he, too, remembering a home where shabby shifts were normal, had no taste for rollicking Irish poverty, with guests eating and drinking their fill while the broker's man sat like a seedy vulture in the hall; and he took great care that his pence should become pounds.

All these authors from the Eirean area calculated very cunningly how they should get on, and decided that England was the place for them. They shook the Irish dust off their shoes and departed for the alien shore, where they performed the tricks the English expect from the Irish. They seldom met in Ireland, meeting not at all in their early manhood, and they disliked each other. Moore, as a schoolboy, had heard of Oscar and Willie Wilde of Cong, but his encounters with them were so few and brief that they can scarcely be called encounters. When, in London, they met as men of some celebrity, they fell foul of one another almost at once. Shaw, it has already been noted, was born within a few hundred yards of Wilde's home in Dublin, where both the young men must often and for long spells have lived simultaneously. But they never met there, and they rarely met in London, to which they both migrated, Wilde from Oxford in 1878, Shaw from Dublin in 1876. They were uncongenial companions. The author of *Back to Methuselah* could neither have written nor ever have liked *The Importance of Being Earnest*, nor, fresh from *Widowers' Houses*, have felt impressed by *Lady Windermere's Fan*. It is equally certain that Wilde would have been bored by *Heartbreak House* and could never have written *Saint Joan*. Had he ever thought of a play about the Maid, he would have made her look like Mrs. Langtry.

Even odder than the fact that these Eireans seldom or never met in Ireland, and were all antipathetic to each other, is the fact that the single notable Irish author who spent the greater part of his life in Dublin, meeting there all of them except Wilde, was the Ulster poet, "A. E." Russell was regarded with affection and respect by Moore and Yeats who detested each other. Yet it will take a miracle to remove from the English mind the grotesque superstition that Eireans are affable men and congenial companions, likeable and witty, whereas Ulstermen are dour and unlikeable, without wit or humour, and accustomed to spend their spare time in offensive aspirations about the Pope's eternal home.

14

THERE is some interest to be derived from the dates of their birth which are here tabulated:

George Augustus Moore was born at Moore Hall, Lough Carra, Co. Mayo, on the 24th of February 1852.

Oscar Fingal O'Flahertie Wills Wilde was born at 21 Westland Row, Dublin, on the 16th of October 1854.

George Bernard Shaw was born at 3, now numbered 33, Synge Street, Dublin, on the 26th of July 1856.

William Butler Yeats was born at Sandymount, near Dublin, on the 13th of June 1865.
George William Russell was born at Lurgan, Co. Armagh, on the 10th of April 1867.

15

ONE of the prime differences between Wilde and Shaw is that Shaw was exceedingly shy and that Wilde was always at his ease. Wilde entered the most exclusive house as if he had a right to be there, whereas Shaw, he himself says, as recorded by Archibald Henderson, "suffered such agonies of shyness that I sometimes walked up and down the Chelsea Embankment for twenty minutes or more before venturing to knock at the door" of the Lawsons' house in Cheyne Walk. The Lawsons were friends of his mother. "Indeed," Shaw adds, "I should have funked it altogether, and hurried home asking myself what was the use of torturing myself when it was easy to run away, if I had not been instinctively aware that I must never let myself off in this manner if I ever meant to do anything in the world." It was about this time that Shaw first met Wilde, at one of Lady Wilde's absurd receptions, and they manifestly failed to be congenial. Shaw, according to Archibald Henderson, suggests that he owed his invitation to "a passing fancy" Wilde had taken to Lucy Shaw, G. B. S.'s elder sister, who was a singer with a very pleasing voice: a suggestion which supports the theory advanced on a previous page that Wilde's mind on sex was normal at Oxford, and remained so for several years after he had come down. The two men did not meet again for a long time after this encounter, did not, Harris says, meet more than ten times in their lives.

Their uncongeniality had many causes, the main one being the total disparity between their highly marked characters. Shaw was a Puritan: Wilde was a Pagan. There was a tautness of nature and mind in Shaw which was not only alien, but incomprehensible, to Wilde. It will not do merely to say that Wilde was a Romantic and that Shaw was a Realist. Shaw, too, was a Romantic, although he was unaware of the fact. Wilde's mind was less athletic than Shaw's. He ran to fat in mind as well as in body, but Shaw's mind was, and had always been, lean and energetic. Shaw was solitary: Wilde was gregarious. Shaw had never needed anybody. He was sufficient unto himself. But Wilde was in continual need of companions. Solitude made him miserable. Wilde became a man of fashion. Shaw was always a man of unfashion.

The differences between them were differences not only of personality, but of upbringing and environment. The Shaws, father and mother, were as different from the Wildes, father and mother, as George Bernard and Oscar were. Never in this world could Shaw's mother have felt friendship for Lady Wilde. Sir William Wilde was an open and even boisterous booser: George Carr Shaw was a secret and furtive drunkard, who deluded himself with the belief that he was practically a teetotaller. The Shaws and Wildes, as has been stated, lived only a short distance from each other in Dublin, but they might have lived five thousand miles apart, so little were they alike. Had Shaw's mother entered Lady Wilde's drawing-room on the day when her son met Oscar for the first time, she must have felt derisive when she gazed upon that painted hulk of a woman and observed her grotesque pretensions.

But there was another cause of uncongeniality between the two men, of which, perhaps, neither of them was aware. It was, nevertheless, influential. Oscar, who was rising on the crest of the wave, was inclined to patronise Shaw, who was almost unknown. Shaw was a proud man, much prouder than Wilde ever was. Wilde, indeed, could not be called proud in the sense that Shaw could. He was a vain man, a conceited man, as Shaw was too, but he had none of that severe and inflexible self-respect and fastidious objection to patronage which Shaw had in full measure. Nor had he any of the fierce humility which makes a proud man refuse favours. Shaw was too proud to demand indulgence. If his fellows conceded places to him, he accepted them, for he was not a churl who declined acts of grace; but he did not ask for special attention. It must be given to him.

Shaw would not endure patronage from anybody. He certainly

did not endure it from Wilde who was, he knew in his bones and blood, his intellectual and moral inferior. Wilde suspected a rival in Shaw. He feared a superior. And he was justified in his fear and his suspicion. But at that moment of first encounter he was almost a risen star. Shaw had scarcely appeared on the horizon and he was hidden in cloud. So Wilde was a little condescending to him. It was not in the nature of these two men to feel drawn together; but if there had been any inclination in Shaw to become friendly with Wilde, Wilde that day destroyed it.

Wilde's formal education was, in conventional language, better than Shaw's, although Shaw's informal education was manifestly superior to Wilde's. Shaw left school before he was fifteen, as if he were the son of a working-man, attending a National School, and he began to earn his living as a junior clerk in a land agent's office. Wilde was then leaving Portora, preparatory to entering Trinity College, Dublin. Two years before Shaw left Dublin, Wilde went to Oxford. A year after Shaw had arrived in London, to live in genteel poverty, Wilde took his long tour in Italy and Greece. He seemed, in comparison with Shaw, a fortunate young man; but Shaw had a learning in music that Wilde never had, and a knowledge of people, gained in places of which Wilde was unaware, which served him better, perhaps, than Wilde's good education, though that, indeed, was of a quality which cannot be despised. Association with sharp-witted, eager youths of one's own age is, in itself, a good and stimulating thing, and contact with older and richer minds, even if those minds have become overset, is also good and stimulating. It is arguable that Wilde's tour with Mahaffy, though it was not a product of university education, was as stimulating to him as his mother's musical parties were to Shaw. Douglas surmises that it did him harm, that Mahaffy's influence was "perhaps" an unfortunate one, but Douglas, in thus surmising, betrays the enthusiasm a convert to Roman Catholicism feels for his new faith and his aversion from the faith he has abandoned. Mahaffy, who was an ordained minister of the Episcopal Church of Ireland and became Provost of Trinity College, is alleged to have precipitated Wilde from Christianity to Paganism by teaching him Greek and inducing him to take a trip on the Continent! Ought travel in Greece to be forbidden? And the study of Greek abandoned? Has Professor Gilbert Murray's long life been misspent? Browning suggested that the Grammarian who "gave us the doctrine of the enclitic *De*" was "dead from the waist down", but he did not ask us to believe that thought about *Hoti* and *Oun* and *De* had made him a pervert.

16

THERE was a larger difference than these between Wilde and Shaw, an odd one when we remember that they both set out to conquer their world in substantially the same way: Wilde was successful at once; Shaw suffered almost a decade of severe failure. That, perhaps, was because Wilde went West, whereas Shaw went East End. But Wilde went West in another and more dismal sense when Shaw was rising like the sun and warming the world with his beams.

Wilde was renowned on two continents before he had done anything to deserve renown. He was sufficiently well known in America when he was twenty-seven to be invited there to lecture. *Invited* is, perhaps, the wrong word. It was not certain whether he was asked to go to America by a lecture agent or by Mr. D'Oyly Carte, who saw possibilities in him as an advertising agent for *Patience*, or was chancing his luck in New York as he had chanced it in London.

We shall refer to the point again: but must note now with insistence that this young man, new from Oxford, without social influence or money, had imposed himself not only on the smart set, which is easily imposed upon since its appetite for sensation makes it the natural prey of charlatans, but on the general attention. To have done this for a month or two would, no doubt, have been easy, but Wilde did it for several years. Yet if anyone in 1881 had enquired what he had done to justify *Punch* in satirising and deriding him almost weekly, no one could have given a satisfactory reply.

Was it because of his advocacy of aestheticism? But this advocacy had been advanced long before Wilde appeared in London. The Pre-Raphaelites had been assailed even more ferociously as "the Fleshly School". Walter Pater had published an essay on Aesthetic Poetry in *The Fortnightly Review* in 1868, when Wilde was still at Portora, and was presently to gather round him aesthetic undergraduates, Wilde among them, at Oxford. George du Maurier had been guying affected people in *Punch* in 1877 when Wilde, not long returned from his tour with Mahaffy, was preparing his Newdigate Prize Poem. And there was an art-for-art's-sake movement in France before the time of the Pre-Raphaelites and Pater.

"The love of poets and artists for flowers as designs for art decoration had begun in the paintings of Millais and Poynter long before Wilde joined the aesthetic group, and lilies were being ridiculed as an accepted badge of the cult in September 1878, months before Wilde carried them to Lily Langtry." So those industrious researchers, Lewis and Smith, assert in *Oscar Wilde Discovers America*. Their discoveries have yielded other information to the same effect:

> "Nincompoopiana", a series of drawings satirising the aesthetic geniuses and poseurs, had been a Du Maurier series in the summer of 1879, and London had laughed hard and loud at the long-haired idlers drooling of "cultah", flowers, china, beauty, and "intensity". It was not until February 4, 1880, that Du Maurier recognised Wilde as a leader in the new cult.

Wilde, who was not yet twenty-six at that date, was, it appears, unoriginal even in this respect. All he did was to follow a fashion.

But he followed it with astonishing skill. The vulgar strain in him, the Barnum and Bailey manner, was, perhaps, excessively developed, but when a man goes into the advertising business at a fair, especially when he is barker to himself, he cannot be blamed for using all his abilities, even though they are vulgar, to secure his object. The purpose of Colman was to sell mustard, as the purpose of Beecham was to sell pills, as the purpose of Guinness to-day is to sell stout. If they are a little blatant in their methods, declaring that their wares are worth a guinea a box and that Guinness is good for you, we cannot condemn them morally, though we may deplore their taste. Wilde's purpose was to sell Wilde; and he sold him with immense verve. There was more notoriety than money in the traffic, and he was presently to find his lack of funds embarrassing; but the notoriety brought him some financial profit. His deficiency in mathematical skill did not prevent him from earning an income, any more than a lack of letters has prevented illiterates from acquiring wealth. Wilde, as Douglas surmises, must have been in receipt of more money at this time, from anonymous journalism, than Sherard supposes. He could not have lived as he did on his meagre unearned increment. But these earnings were not enough.

Whatever his income may have been, he imposed himself on the knowledge of the general public to such an extent that Gilbert, searching for a theme, was glad to use him as a figure in *Patience*, which was produced at the Opéra-Comique on April 23, 1881. While still short of twenty-seven, Wilde had achieved a height of notoriety which is attained only by fraudulent financiers operating on a very large scale, and murderers who mix their crimes with sex appeal. His notoriety, indeed, was more widespread and lasting than theirs: for who, apart from criminologists, remembers yesterday's defaulting director or the poisoner of the week before? As a notorious person Wilde was a great success. He never failed to win notoriety in large measure; and is to-day, fifty years after his death, as notorious as he was when *Punch* was caricaturing and deriding him in almost every number. There were some people indeed, Whistler, for example, who believed that du Maurier was his colleague in advertisement. Coming upon them in conversation, he remarked a little acidly, "Which of you two discovered the other?" Whistler disliked rivals in notoriety. "Why drag in Velasquez?" he said, when someone assured him that he and the Spaniard were the greatest of artists.

Burnand, the editor of *Punch*, may have aroused Wilde's resentment, but not, we may feel certain, by his attack. It was the poverty of the puns he resented, and he must often have felt inclined to offer to do the job himself, so badly was it done. To publish a picture of Wilde as the centre of a drooping sunflower, and print the following verse under it, was a poor performance:

> Aesthete of Aesthetes!
> What's in a name?
> The poet is Wilde,
> But his poetry's tame.

A satirist in a manuscript magazine compiled by the boys in a preparatory school could have done better than that. Wilde seldom made puns, but when he did make them, they were witty. Hesketh Pearson cites several. One was made in a review of *The Chronicle of Mites*, "a mock-heroic poem about the inhabitants of a decaying cheese who speculate about the origin of species". Wilde, describing it, wrote, "This cheese-epic is a rather unsavoury production and the style is at times so monstrous and so realistic that the author should be called the Gorgon-Zola of literature". He could be far wittier than that, but compared with Burnand's stuff, Wilde's pun is a brilliant electric light in comparison with a farthing dip.

Wilde displayed no resentment against du Maurier, nor was he offended by his portrait as Bunthorne in *Patience*. It pleased him almost as much as Mr. Punch's pictures. He had set out to call attention to himself, and all who gave his attention, even if only in paltry puns, were doing him a service.

But the notoriety, great though it was, was far from being sufficient. It buttered no parsnips, or, if it did, it buttered them thinly. Funds were sinking. The small property in Ireland was in danger of disappearing. Unless money could be made quickly and substantially, the career which had opened with so much success in notoriety, might close abruptly in debt. All he had in stock was a small collection of poems, snatched from the pages of obscure magazines in Ireland. The hope of profit from them must have seemed singularly forlorn. The poet, as he himself was to remark much later, is born, but not paid; and the minimum poet is not published, except at his own expense. But Wilde was not dismayed by these unpromising facts. He resolved to publish his poems, and to make them pay. As he did, despite the discouragement not only of general experience in publishing poetry, but of his own experience in the publication of his Prize Poem, *Ravenna*, which appeared in Oxford, with the sanction of the University, under the imprint of Shrimpton, in 1878. It is possible that Wilde bought more copies of it than were sold to the public.

In addition to his fugitive verse, there was a mindless melodrama, *Vera, or The Nihilists*, which would have caused the author of *The Worst Woman in London* to blush for himself had he, in a time of mental aberration, written it. Alfred Douglas describes it as "preposterous rubbish", which is an exact account of it. Wilde was so simple when he wrote this piece that he made the Czar jokingly threaten to banish some of his officers because they had cracked foolish jests. "If you value your lives you will catch the first train to Paris!" The period of the play is 1800, when there were no trains, in Russia or anywhere else, to be caught.

17

WE may profitably pause for a moment to note that when Dr. Mahaffy and Wilde were passing through Paris on their way to Italy and Greece, a young, yellow-haired, slump-shouldered Irish landlord, with a sheeplike face characteristic of his family, was about to leave it for London to seek his fortune much in the same fashion in which Wilde was to seek his two or three years later. This was George Moore, a singular mixture of fop and gifted fool, who was almost illiterate and seemed to be half-witted, and became a vain and envious and mean and quarrelsome old man. The French thought him very droll, but did not take him seriously. Moore, indeed, was never taken seriously by anybody until he met Charles Morgan, whose veneration discomposed him so much that he exhausted his strength in striving to live up to it, and died at the physical age of eighty-one and the mental age of eighteen. It is impossible to read Moore's letters to his mother—they may be found in J. M. Hone's *The Life of George Moore*—without feeling that their author suffered severely from arrested mental development. But he had the fixed ideas which simpletons commonly possess; and among these ideas was the belief that he was supremely an artist. By dint of industry and frequent revision, he produced what he called his style; and he persuaded a number of persons who hung about the fringes of the literary world to believe that it was great; forgetting that style is only the third element in works of genius, the first two being character and theme.

Moore, too, was an adventurer, seeking whom he might exploit; but he had chosen Paris as the scene of his bandit's business. If he were to frequent a Parisian studio, he must, he imagined, become a painter; as if the power to paint were acquired by suction. In a moment of awful clarity, however, he realised that he had deceived himself, and he dropped his palette and seized a pen. He would become a poet and dramatist. His first play, a comedy in three acts called *Worldliness*, was written after he had taken a course "of Congreve and other Restoration dramatists", but, although it was published, it was never performed; and Hone asserts that not a single copy of it is now known to exist. He then collaborated with a Frenchman, named Lopez, in a five-act tragedy entitled *Martin Luther*, in which, although Moore was a Roman Catholic, he displayed an ultra-Protestant point of view. He read Baudelaire's *Les Fleurs du mal*, and immediately began to write verse in the Baudelairean manner. His first poem was entitled *Ode to a Dead Body*.

It was these poems which Moore, in the summer of 1877, carried to London while Mahaffy and Wilde went paganising in Italy and Greece. They were issued by Provost, with the title of *Flowers of Passion*, under a cover which bore a skull, cross-bones and a lyre stamped in gold. He had developed aestheticism ineffectively before it was developed sensationally by Wilde, who seems not to have known anything of Moore or his work at this period. Moore, like Wilde, was influenced by Walter Pater. He was not an exuberant undergraduate, but a man of thirty-four, when, entering Mrs. Robinson's drawing-room in Earl's Terrace, Kensington, he looked around and said, "I like this room. The wall paper sets off my yellow hair." Yet no one accused him of unnameable vice for that remark, as Wilde was accused, when he was half Moore's age, because of a remark, no sillier, about living up to blue china. In his second volume of verse, *Pagan Poems*, he told his admirers terrible lies about himself. This man with dull eyes, a futile face, a lapsing chin, shoulders that almost slid off his body, and small, soapy hands that felt like dead fish, asserted that

> I am filled with carnivorous lust, like a tiger
> I crouch and feed on my beautiful prey.

But such stuff as that was flyblown then, and *Pagan Poems* was sold by its publishers for waste paper.

He, too, dressed up a part and gave a performance. Returning to Mayo from Paris, he appeared at a shooting-party wearing a French top-hat on the side of his head, high-heeled boots and very wide trousers, and pretended that he had become so Frenchified that he could scarcely speak English. For a short time, he treated London to views of himself in this rig-out. Then, having made his effect, he dressed in conventional clothes, as Wilde did, as Shaw did. Like Wilde, he pretended to a knowledge of music which he did not possess. The Irish are not musical. Gaels seldom are. They play the bagpipes instead.

How *Flowers of Passion* escaped Wilde's notice is difficult to understand. It was denounced by Edmund Yates in *The World*, under the headline *A Bestial Bard*, and Yates was friendly to Wilde, whose brother Willie was employed on the paper and used it to boost Oscar. Moore, Yates wrote, ought to be whipped at the cart's tail, and his book burnt by the common hangman!...

Wilde's descent on London and his first visit to America were made much in the manner of Moore's return to London from Paris: with a volume of bad poems and a wretched play in his pocket; and he, too, was severely manhandled by the critics. But Wilde was a better business man than Moore. Moore withdrew his *Flowers of Passion*: Wilde sent his *Poems* into four editions in as many weeks.

18

FOR three years Wilde toiled at his notoriety, years more terrible, if less numerous, than those during which Jacob toiled for Rachel; although he must have felt at the end of them as foiled as Jacob felt when he was fobbed off with Leah by Laban: he had his notoriety, but that was all he had. Wearing "a velvet-coat, knee-breeches, a loose shirt with a turned-down collar, and a floating tie of some unusual shade, fastened in a *Lavallière* knot", he sauntered down Piccadilly, "carrying in his hand a lily or a sun-flower, which he used to contemplate with an expression of the greatest admiration". He could not have foreseen the time, seventy years later, when men of all ages and classes would appear in the streets, and especially on seaside promenades, arrayed more deplorably than he was: exposing their thrawny throats in crumpled and dirty turned-down collars, and their knobbly knees in boy scout shorts. He would have abandoned his eccentric garb had he suspected that a race would one day arise which would walk about the pavements of the town, not only clad in this repulsive fashion, but accompanied by fucated women in bloody talons, bloody toes and bloodier trousers! . . . To such base usage our aesthetes brought us.

It seems odd that his appearance in this get-up aroused anything but derisive laughter. That was aroused. The street urchins, our most effective social censors, guffawed and ululated and guyed and split their sides, without, however, deterring Wilde from fulfilling his intent. Cabmen appealed to heaven to tell them if it had ever seen the like. Wilde passed by unabashed. Bus-drivers flicked their whips and announced apocalypse. So that was what the world was a-comin' to! . . . But Wilde flourished his lily or gazed seraphically at his sunflower, feeling certain that there would be many paragraphs in the next day's papers. None but a man of audacious will and courage could thus have dared and defined the derision of the street. Why there should have been rage and rancour over this performance is difficult to understand. Wilde's purpose was surely transparent? Self-advertisement. His antics would have ended if there had been no paragraphs. But the paragraphs did not cease. They became more numerous and angrier. It is a saddening thought that humourists seldom have a sense of humour. A grain of Attic salt might have saved Wilde from making himself so ridiculous. It would certainly have saved Burnand from filling *Punch* with bitter poems of the feeblest sort.

Wilde's pluck and determination were apparent in this public parade. Excuse ourselves from such exhibitions as we may, there remains the fact that few would have the nerve, to put it no higher, to flout the habits of the time by such behaviour. Once, perhaps, and for a large wager, but not many times and in full view of multitudes and for no wager. Insult and derision did not deter Wilde. He went his foolish but intended way, and all the people whose acquaintance he desired, presently sought him out. He was, they told each other, *so* amusing. That is the Irishman's curse: that he is *so* amusing. He will never reach the measure and the stature of an adult man until other men cease to think him funny, and he no longer behaves as if he were. In a few years, an unknown undergraduate from a provincial city, for Dublin was, and is still, a provincial city, had become an habitué of fashionable houses in London and was the subject of wide and remarkably diverse conversation.

But there was no money in it; and Wilde, more than most men, needed money.

There is, plainly, no question of aestheticism here. Wilde was as commercially minded as any pawnbroker or pork butcher or stockbroker or banker. He had some poems to sell, just as a greengrocer has some cabbages to sell, and he determined to sell them at a high profit. Moore had felt the same need of money, and he, too, had a few poems to sell. But Moore, being a fool, had bungled his business. His raw head and bloody cross-bones volume had failed calamitously, causing him to take to his bed and cover his head with the sheet and moan like a sick cow. Wilde was made of sterner stuff than Moore. No moaning under the sheet for him—not then, anyhow. There would be plenty of moaning later on, but not in 1880. He had kept himself by devious methods: sponging a little on his mother, mortgaging some of his small property in Ireland, selling some of it, incurring debt, scribbling in the newspapers: but he was near the end of all that. Another means of raising the wind must be found, and the wind must be ampler and steadier.

He ransacked the little magazines of Ireland for his juvenile poems, and assembled a book. A nondescript publisher, David Bogue, was found willing to publish them at Wilde's expense: and a very pretty book was made of it "bound in white vellum, decorated in gold and beautifully printed", according to Ransome, and highly priced, half a guinea, high for the time; the sort of ornate tomb in which precious and pretentious young men are accustomed to bury their first poems. Four editions were sold in four weeks. Wilde was a good business man. He was his own advertising agent and his own commercial traveller. He did very well with it, but, as Bogue had pointed out, there was no money, not big money, in poetry, and it was big money that Wilde wanted. He had written a play! . . . Mrs. Bernard Beere had toyed, but not very seriously, with the notion of producing *Vera* for a single morning performance on Saturday the 17th of December 1881, at the Adelphi Theatre in London. Three weeks before that date, however, she decided not to perform it, and a paragraph appeared in the press announcing that Wilde had postponed its production owing to "the present state of political feeling in England". Nihilism had fallen out of favour: the assassination of a Czar and the fact that the new Czarina was the sister of the Princess of Wales robbed *Vera* of its academic or literary air and brought it perilously near to being diplomatically offensive—apart from its own inherent defect. It was then that he thought of America, the natural stage for melodrama. Was not every American a character in a melodrama? Where could he hope to find a more suitable audience for his play than in New York? The decision to go to America was primarily, and perhaps exclusively, Wilde's. The matter is unimportant, but it has been so bedevilled by legends invented by his admirers, that it will be well to set out the known facts and supplement them with reasonable assumptions, even if in doing so the risk is run of seeming to attach importance to what is insignificant. The legend is that Wilde, because of the success of his poems and also because of the interest his aestheticism had aroused, was invited to lecture in America. A variation of the legend is that Richard D'Oyly Carte, the impresario who produced the Gilbert and Sullivan operas, thought that a visit by Wilde to New York about the time *Patience* was to be produced there, might be good publicity for the opera, particularly if Wilde could be persuaded to walk about the streets of the city, carrying a lily or sunflower, and wearing his aesthetic clothes. Lord Alfred Douglas, in *Oscar Wilde*, asserts with an appearance of precision which does not survive examination, that Wilde, whose "financial prospects were far from rosy and when he really seemed to have got into an *impasse* . . . suddenly received a cable dated 30th September 1881, from New York from Colonel W. F. Morse, business manager of Richard D'Oyly Carte, which was as follows:

> Responsible agent asks me to enquire if you will consider offer he makes for fifty readings beginning November 1st. This is confidential. Answer."

Wilde's reply was, "Yes, if offer is good", and, according to Douglas, he "shortly afterwards sailed for New York and began his series of lectures throughout the United States". The tour "brought" Wilde "quite a lot of money, and enabled him to start an epoch of material prosperity which never declined, and ultimately enormously increased, right up to the time of his crash in 1895". This last statement is false. Douglas, who was eleven years old when the cablegram was received by Wilde, but writes almost as if he had been present when it was delivered, lifted this information, without acknowledgement, from *Oscar Wilde Discovers America* by Lloyd Lewis and Henry Justin Smith.[1] His evidence, therefore, is second or third hand and has no value, especially as the statements with which he supplements it are either inaccurate or so loose that they are practically inaccurate. Wilde was unlikely to have gone to New York "shortly after" receiving this cablegram when there was a possibility of Mrs. Beere producing *Vera* at the Adelphi.

[1] His book was published in 1940: theirs in 1936.

Lloyd Lewis and Justin Smith give as detailed an account of the transaction as we are ever likely to obtain, from which it appears that D'Oyly Carte and his agent, Morse, feared that American ignorance of the aesthetic craze satirised in *Patience* would prevent the comic opera from becoming popular. They sought, therefore, for some means of making the subject familiar to the public before the first performance. There was in New York then a well-to-do widow, Mrs. Frank Leslie, who owned and edited a paper called the *Illustrated Newspaper*. Mrs. Leslie, who subsequently married Wilde's brother, Willie, an act which she promptly rued, had some knowledge of Oscar's performances, although she had no personal acquaintance with him, and it was she, it is surmised, who suggested to Morse that Wilde should be hired as a sort of superior sandwich-board man. If he could be persuaded to repeat in New York his comic clothes and sunflower and lily performances, Bunthorne in *Patience* would cease to be incomprehensible to the playgoing public. Mrs. Leslie is said to have made her suggestion in September, and, after it had been cabled to D'Oyly Carte in London and been, presumably, sanctioned by him, Morse then sent his oddly-worded cablegram to Wilde. Its oddity lies in the fact that Morse himself was a lecture agent. A rival agent was unlikely to ask him to make enquiries about a potential lecturer, and we may believe, therefore, that he was covering himself, so that if any hitch in the negotiations should develop, he could evade responsibility for the whole business.

There is no information about the negotiations after the dispatch of Wilde's reply to Morse. Frank Harris bluntly states that the tale of an invitation to New York was invented by Willie Wilde, who published a paragraph about it in *The World*, alleging that the success of the *Poems* in England had created American interest in Oscar. This assertion is supported by Sherard in the *Life*, where the date on which the paragraph was published is stated to be the 9th of November 1881, about the date when Mrs. Beere had decided not to do *Vera*. The probability is that the negotiations with Morse were broken off, and that Wilde, after Mrs. Beere's defection, chanced his luck in America and paid for his passage to New York himself. Sherard states that Wilde had no arrangement with any impresario when he left England. There is no proof that he received a penny from D'Oyly Carte or from anyone on Carte's behalf. Lewis and Smith assert that Carte agreed to pay Wilde's expenses in America and to give him one-third of the gross proceeds of his lectures, but there is ample cause to think that no such arrangement was made, and that Wilde was hired by Morse in the common course of lecture engagements after he had arrived in New York. The principal reason for believing this is that *Patience* had been very successfully produced in September 1881, before Wilde's arrival in January 1882, and that there was, therefore, no need for the publicity Wilde was to have provided. By the time Wilde reached America it was well set for a long and prosperous run. D'Oyly Carte did not arrive until two days after Wilde had delivered his first lecture in New York. When press reporters asked him what he had to say about "Bunthorne in the flesh", he replied, "A very clever young man. I don't think it was out of the way bringing him here. I think I shall take him around the country." This intention, if it was ever realised by Carte, which is uncertain, involved him in little or no responsibility. Sherard says in the *Life* that the long tour, lasting about a year, was arranged by a famous American lecture agent, Major Pond, after he had heard the first lecture in New York, and that Pond said he had lost money on it, but Stuart Mason, in *Bibliography of Oscar Wilde*, publishes letters written by Wilde to Colonel Morse which prove that Morse arranged some of the lectures—those delivered early in 1882. Wilde complains that he is expected to deliver six a week for three weeks, and wonders if he will be able to stand the strain. "However, I will do my best—and if I feel Titan-like, will do matinées." Pond's allegation that the lecture tour was a financial failure is contradicted by a statement of receipts published by Harris in *Oscar Wilde*, to which reference will presently be made. This contradiction is mentioned now to stress the difficulty there is in ascertaining the simplest facts about Wilde. One almost believes that his friends published the first thought that came into their heads, without making the slightest attempt to verify it. The letters published by Mason include two written by Wilde to D'Oyly Carte, from which it appears that that astute Jew was willing to help him to obtain a production for *Vera* in New York. Miss Clara Morris, who was known to be difficult, was to play the eponymous part, but if her difficult character proved unendurable, Miss Rose Coghlan should be engaged. Wilde hoped that Kyrle Bellew or Johnston Forbes-Robertson would be secured for the part of the Czarevitch. But nothing came of any negotiations with Miss Morris or anybody else that Carte may have made, and the negotiations with Miss Marie Prescott, who eventually produced the play, were made by Wilde himself.

D'Oyly Carte's concern with Wilde in America, therefore, seems to have been slight. *Patience* was sailing very comfortably under its own steam. The value of knee-breeches and lilies and velvet coats and sunflowers as an advertisement for a comic opera was not great. Wilde went to New York, sailing in the *Arizona* on the 24th of December 1881, primarily to secure, if he could, production for *Vera*. He thought that this singularly footling piece had fine quality, and felt as certain as Moore felt about *Martin Luther*, that it would make his fortune. But he hoped, no doubt, to make a little money on the side, as Americans say, and so he packed his comic clothes and took them with him. They were part of his few assets. We must admire the superb audacity of this young man who, with nothing to justify his claim to consideration but an over-elaborately bound volume of minimum poetry, an unperformed melodrama, and a spurious renown as an eccentric comedian, set out on a voyage of discovery almost as vague as that of Christopher Columbus. Columbus was the vaguer of the two: he never realised that he had found America; he thought he had landed in the East, a mistake which a traveller might pardonably make in Fifth Avenue to-day, for New York is the largest Oriental city in the world.

Arrayed in a bottle-green and frogged fur coat and knee-breeches, with his long hair dangling down almost to his shoulders in the fashion now cultivated by unwanted women who sell cigarettes, Wilde, on his arrival in New York, looked remarkably like a quack dentist or the proprietor of a cheap circus, and not at all like the delicate-minded aesthete America had been told to expect. Sarony's photographs of him reveal a vulgar-looking man: a ham actor, if ever there was one. It was not easy to believe that *he* had ever walked down Piccadilly with a sunflower or a lily in his medieval hand. The meals he avidly ate repudiated du Maurier's picture of him dining on a glance at a lily in a glass of water. He liked his food, and he liked it in abundance. We have already noted his powers of endurance with drink.

The captain told American reporters how heartily he disliked Wilde. "I wish I had that man lashed to the bowsprit on the windward side," he said to one of them. Fellow-passengers on the *Arizona* had been unimpressed by him. His famous remark, that he was disappointed in the Atlantic, was, it is suggested by Lewis and Smith, an invention of the reporters, who devised it from accounts of his boredom with the ocean given by some of the passengers. Why this reasonable remark, if it was made by Wilde, should have been considered an example of perversity, is hard to understand. A wide waste of water is insufferably tedious, especially in calm weather, and Wilde was expressing a feeling which many people have felt. The sight of another ship, even if it were only a fishing-smack, would have broken the monotony of that measureless liquid.

19

ASKED by the Customs officers what he had to declare, Wilde replied "Nothing but my genius", which was a good crack for a start. It looked well in the next morning's papers. The reply made by the Customs officer is less well known, although it was equal in wit to Wilde's remark. "That, sir," he is reported to have said, "is a commodity which does not require protection in the United States." The first lecture was delivered at the Chickering Hall on Monday the 9th of January. Its subject was *The English Renaissance*. Wilde, wearing his comic clothes, but not carrying a sunflower, as every member of his audience had expected him to do, came on to the platform accompanied by his chairman, Colonel

Morse, who briefly announced him and retired. The fact that Morse was his chairman seems to support the belief that D'Oyly Carte had some arrangement with Wilde, but its nature, if there was one, must remain a matter for assumption and surmise, since there is no proof of one, nor likely to be any. Morse may have been making an arrangement of his own.

The sight of the notorious knee-breeches caused titters in the audience, and the titters are alleged to have made Wilde blush. He read his lecture in a monotonous manner. He had not yet learnt how to use his fine tenor voice in public speech, and he was embarrassed by the titters. But it was a tolerably good lecture, and impressed many of those who heard it far more than they had expected to be impressed. Wilde was not merely a circus man: he was also an artist. "It is not increased moral sense your literature needs. Indeed, we should never talk of a moral or an immoral poem. Poems are either well written or badly written. That is all. A good work aims at the purely artistic effect. Love art for its own sake, and all things that you need will be added to it." This is stale stuff now, and there is an answer to it, but it was a revolutionary statement then, and very shocking to some who heard it for the first time. He jibbed at nothing. He mentioned *Patience*, and admitted that Bunthorne was intended for a satire on himself. Satire, he said, was the tribute paid by mediocrity to genius. "You must not judge our aestheticism by the satire of Mr. Gilbert any more than you can judge of the strength and splendour of the sun by the dust that dances in the beam or the bubble that breaks upon the wave." He won applause and laughter by smiling benignly as he referred to the legends of the lily and sunflower:

"You have heard, I think, a few of you, of two flowers, called erroneously, I assure you, the food of aesthetic young men. Well, let me tell you that the reason we love the lily and the sunflower is not, in spite of what Mr. Gilbert may tell you, for any vegetable fashion at all. It is because these two lovely flowers are, in England, the two most perfect models of design. They are the most naturally adopted for decorative art. The gaudy, leonine beauty of the one, the precious loveliness of the other, give to the artist the most nearly perfect joy. . . ."

We need not allow our sense of the cissiness in these remarks to blind us to their point in that time and in that place. Wilde's taste was far from being good. He had little or no knowledge of music, and probably, like Yeats, no ear for it. His architectural sense was feeble, and the style in dress and decoration which he admired would make angels weep. His literary judgements were sometimes deplorable when they were sincere, and irritating when they were perverse; and a great deal of his wit, when it was not stolen, was mechanical.

But he maintained a belief about life at a time when the majority of men had only a convention about it. In an age of the worst taste in the history of civilisation, Wilde proclaimed the need for beauty of mind and behaviour and environment; and he was not afraid to make a fool of himself for his faith. It is not absurd to suggest that the architects who are making Chicago one of the loveliest cities in the world may have been stimulated by Wilde's demand for seemly civic life. Those who are sympathetic to his cause often wish that the charlatan in him, the man in need of easy money, the vulgar notoriety hunter, had been less evident; but we must take men as we find them, and make the best of what they have. Wilde had much that was worth possessing. His lecture in the Chickering Hall was undoubtedly a failure, if by success we mean the receipt of rapturous applause. His audience began to feel bored. Americans, like infants, easily feel bored, and, again like infants, must have immediate success. That is why so many of their marriages quickly crash. They had come to see this guy, Wilde, but the guy declined to remain a guy, and insisted on discussing seriously a subject of importance. "Beauty is the only thing we cannot harm", he said, a statement which meant nothing at all to them and was not what they had come to hear. When was the guy going to gnaw a daffodil and fondle a sunflower and lie down before a lily . . .? Knee-breeches were not enough. The audience had paid good dollars to be entertained by the guy, but the guy was not entertaining enough. Why couldn't the guy act like a guy? All this stuff about beauty! . . .

"There can be no sculpture, no great drama, without a noble national life. The commercial spirit of England has killed that . . ."

a statement which was interrupted by loud cheers from "pathriotic" Irishmen, who would have cheered Judas Iscariot himself, as he counted his thirty pieces of silver, if only he had made a derogatory remark about the English. But, apart from the frenzied Broths of Boys, there was only boredom; and the audience began to depart. Even his compliments to America failed to hold them in their seats. "It is perhaps to you that we turn to perfect this great movement of ours.

There is something Hellenic in your air, something that has a quicker breath of the joy and power of Elizabeth's England about it than our ancient civilisation can give us. You are young. No hungry generations tread you down. . . . The past does not mock you with the ruins of a beauty the secret of whose creation you have lost! . . ."

Wilde could utter this stuff in the ears of stupefied Americans, although he was well aware that the Victorian era had produced a host of great men of every sort, far surpassing the host produced in the age of Elizabeth; but it was useless to utter it there, for the Americans were folding their tents and stealing, but not silently, away. He should have made a few more "pathriotic" remarks to the Broths of Boys in the gallery. They would have cheered.

The receipts were good, a thousand dollars, but the press was bad. On the other hand, it was widespread, and any publicity, Morse thought, and Wilde agreed, was better than no publicity. *The Boston Transcript* had, so to speak, burst into song:

A lily by the river's brim,
An advertising dodge to him
It was, and nothing more.

a poor parody for so high-toned a paper, but good enough for the box-office. A voice here and a voice there were respectful enough, and better-mannered than the majority. *The Cincinnati Commercial*, as we have noted already, invited Wilde to its city to see what honest-to-God-he-men could do in depriving hogs of their bowels, but *The Cincinnati Inquirer* complained of rudeness and imperception. "The stranger among us", George Alfred

Townsend wrote, "is a young apostle of beauty against a decaying age of trade and swap", and he protested vigorously against "the little jackals who make smart newspaper paragraphs about subjects they neither reverence nor understand".

20

IT is not our purpose to follow Wilde up and down the United States. His experience was often unpleasant, but it was far from being entirely unpleasant, and, despite the gross insults he received from gutter reporters, he made a deeper impression on many minds than was imagined in London. His remarks were occasionally banal—whose are not?—and he discussed matters, such as women's bustles, that a more practised speaker would not have mentioned, since they excite easy laughter in the empty-minded. But even in such references he was strictly within the scope of his argument. He was deploring ugly fashions and observing how a woman can disfigure herself in the belief that she is adding to her beauty. He praised Whitman in the *Philadelphia Press* at a time when some courage was needed to mention him, except in contempt and denunciation. He told a pardonable lie to the reporter who interviewed him for this paper, saying that he and Dante Gabriel Rossetti, Swinburne and William Morris often discussed Whitman. Wilde was not yet twenty-seven, and he had achieved nothing but a book of negligible verse and a good deal of notoriety that he would have been better without, and it was unlikely, therefore, that he and the poets named were intimate enough, if they were intimate at all at that date, to have frequent arguments on any subject. But that's a small matter. We all brag and boast and claim exalted acquaintance without warrant.

There was, however, a passage in his interview with the *Philadelphia Press* reporter which may be cited as a proof that he was not always posing in public or uttering flippant remarks or being banal about lilies and sunflowers, though there is a good deal about them in the interview. "Poets, you know, are always ahead of science", he said:

> all the discoveries of science have been stated in poetry. So far as science comes in contact with our school, we love its practical side; but we think it absurd to seek to make the material include the spiritual, to make the body mean the soul, to say that one emotion is only a secretion of sugar, and another nothing but a contraction of the spine. Why does not science, instead of troubling itself about sunspots, which nobody ever saw, or, if they did, ought not to speak about—why does not science busy itself with drainage and sanitary engineering? Why does it not clean the streets and free the rivers from pollution? Why, in England, there is scarcely a river which at some point is not polluted; and the flowers are all withering on the banks.

There is some nonsense in this passage, but there is also good sense. Sense prevailed in his remarks to the reporter from the *Philadelphia Inquirer*, who was assured that the Aesthetes, whose fugleman he claimed to be, "believe that the people of the artisan class have toiled long enough on unloved labour amid unlovely, hard, repulsive surroundings. Hence you see the politico-economical importance of aesthetics. The toiling thousands of Great Britain are growing more and more dissatisfied every year with their dreary lives filled only with incessant, unattractive toil. . . . The problem of controlling them is only to be solved by making them happy in their labour." He had not listened in vain to Ruskin, but he might have been drawing his belief from *Hard Times* by Dickens, who drew his from Carlyle. The succession is almost apostolic.

That was not the aptest time for Wilde's handicraft beliefs. America had maddened itself with mass-production, and a plea for joy in labour was unlikely to be heard with favour in a country where people boasted with unabateable pride in their ability to deprive thirty hogs of their bowels in sixty seconds. Philadelphia paid little heed to the guy in the comic clothes, who showed the sort of man he was by going out to Camden to call on Walt Whitman! *Leaves of Grass* was still being assailed as filth. "Yes, Mr. Wilde came to see me this afternoon," Whitman, then sixty-three, told a reporter. "I think him genuine, honest and manly.

I was glad to have him with me, for his youthful health, enthusiasm and buoyancy are refreshing. He was in his best mood, and I imagine that he laid aside any affectation he is said to have, and that I saw behind the scenes."

Whitman's appreciation must have fortified Wilde when, at Harvard, shortly after he and the poet had met, he was insulted by beefy students, dressed up in "aesthetic" fashion, who sat in the front rows of the hall, gazing at sunflowers in affected ecstasy. But their intention to turn him to ridicule was foiled by the fact that Wilde appeared on the platform, not in his comic clothes, but in ordinary dress. . . . It was the students who looked foolish, and they were properly trounced by the Boston papers on the following morning. A little later, in Rochester, he was insulted in the same fashion by students there, but the Rochester sophomores fared no better than their superiors at Harvard; and Wilde overwhelmed a simple soldier man who had sought, anonymously, to insult him and condone the students' behaviour, by referring to him as "a scribbling anonymuncule". The letter in which this taunt appeared—it was written to Joaquin Miller, an American exhibitionist of the same sort as Wilde, who had defended him in *The New York World*—was, perhaps, too shrill. The simple soldier man scarcely deserved all that follows:

> Who, after all, that I should write of him is this scribbling anonymuncule in grand old Massachusetts who scrawls and screams so glibly about what he cannot understand? This apostle of inhospitality, who delights to defile, to desecrate, and to defame the gracious courtesies he is unworthy to enjoy? Who are these scribes who, passing with purposeless alacrity from the police news to the Parthenon, and from crime to criticism, sway with such serene incapacity the office which they so lately swept. "Narcissuses of imbecility", what should they see in the clear waters of Beauty and in the well undefiled of Truth but the shifting and shadowy image of their own substantial stupidity? Secure of that oblivion for which they toil so laboriously and, I must acknowledge, with such success, let them peer at us through their telescopes and report what they like of us. But, my dear Joaquin, should we put them under the microscope there would be really nothing to be seen.

After this onslaught, the abashed warrior went into retreat and was heard no more. His punishment was excessive, but it proved, at least, that Wilde could defend himself with vigour, and that those who provoked him beyond endurance must expect to be smitten. They insulted him at their peril.

But it was not insult all the way. He was civilly and courteously treated by distinguished Americans, who were quick to perceive the talent behind his exhibitionist fripperies. The well-bred American then, like the well-bred American to-day, had charm and distinction. His manners were, and are, generally better than those of many of his English contemporaries; and his hospitality was and is abundant and generous. Uncouth Americans surpass uncouth people of almost all countries by their appalling *gaffes*, ill-breeding and misbehaviour. But we shall do ourselves disservice if we submit to the fallacy that all Americans somehow are inferior to all Europeans. It is a simple fact that in many respects they are superior to Europeans. This age is the Renaissance in the United States, where, the world will presently have to confess, there is an immense outpouring of mind and spirit as great as, if not greater than, any the world has hitherto seen.

Wilde saw the best and the worst of America. He did not deceive himself, despite some good-natured chaff of the Americans, by thinking that the best of them were little better than the worst. He was not flattering them when he foresaw rich opportunities of superb living in their country. It did not require unusual insight to perceive that plain fact, but such insight as was required, Wilde displayed. He belonged in every respect to the Old World, but he was not blind to the existence and power of the New, nor did he underrate its importance or fail to observe its potentialities.

There were, of course, absurdities in his reception, among those who admired him as well as among those who did not: and Anna, Comtesse de Brémont, herself rather ridiculous, gives an account of a dinner-party in Madison Square, which leaves the reader wondering who were the more absurd, Wilde or his fellow-guests. The host, unnamed, was, it is alleged, "an old friend and former pupil of Sir William Wilde", but whether he practised ocular surgery in New York is not stated. All the guests, twenty in number, except for the innominate host and Oscar Wilde, were women, some of whom were aesthetically dressed. "He sat, or rather posed, in a large, high-backed chair, while directly opposite to him the host occupied a chair of more modest dimensions. The two prettiest women of the company were seated on the right and left of the guest of honour." They were expensively but aesthetically clad. "Tall crystal glasses supported exquisite white lilies: the display of the famous sunflower being a privilege accorded only to Oscar Wilde", who had put on all his war paint: "black velvet coat and knee-breeches, black silk stockings, low shoes with glittering buckles", and seemed, in the beauty-decked dining-room, more in accordance with his surroundings than he seemed on platforms. "Had I not known the fame of the wearer of that bizarre costume for wit and artistic genius I could have fancied I was in the midst of a party of merry masqueraders, gathered round a medieval banquet presided over by a disguised mummer." *Mummer* seems the right word for the occasion.

Wilde, Anna, Comtesse de Brémont declares, caught sight of her sympathetic eyes and instantly perceived his soul mate, though nothing very much seems to have come of this sympathetic conjunction:

> and, with a return of that frivolous pose, he raised one of the roses lying on the table beside him, and pressed it to his lips, as he said dreamily, as though in answer to my thought: "What is the soul? It is the essence of perfect beauty. I would inhale the soul of beauty as I do the fragrance of this perfect rose—and die upon it if need be!" A murmur of admiration floated round the table, as his melodious voice chanted this significant phrase. My attention was riveted by that coincidence of our thoughts on the soul. I have never forgotten those words. "The soul of woman is beauty," he continued, "as the soul of man is strength. If the two could be combined in one being we should have the perfection sought by art since art began. But art cannot create a real rose though it can improve it." He smiled upon the company, and assumed a Bunthornian pose, a pose decidedly more graceful and fascinating than ever the puppet of Gilbert's wit creation could assume.

This party would have been meat and drink to George du Maurier. It ended with a scene out of a musical comedy. Wilde had made a small pun. "America," he said, "reminds me of one of Edgar Allan Poe's exquisite poems, because it is full of belles!"

We were duly impressed by the wit of this happy compliment, and one of our number enthusiastically cried: "Behold the tribute of the belles!" as she caught up the roses lying on the table before her and cast them towards him. Roses rained upon him from every side. And I am sure there was not a thorn in all that shower of roses to judge from the smile that illumined his face as he bowed under our fragrant ovation.

Who could not feel flattered on being pelted with roses by beautiful girls, but might not an onlooker at this performance have reasonably expected the young ladies to burst into song, like the flowers that bloom in the spring, tra la?

21

THE purpose which had taken him to America was not fulfilled. No one would produce *Vera*. So Wilde, on the 27th December 1882, sailed from New York to Liverpool on the *Bothnia*, almost exactly a year after the date on which he had sailed from Liverpool to New York. He had earned enough dollars to support him for a few months at home. Harris professes precision on the point. Wilde, he declares, received £1200 for his year's work, which "left him with a few hundreds above his expenses". But *Vera* was unproduced, and he was still insecure. He *must* get money. It was plain to him that his comic clothes and his dangling locks were no longer an asset. They had become a liability. So he dropped the clothes overboard, it has been said; and when he went to Paris he had his hair cut. Henceforth he would be a man of fashion. While he was in Paris, he wrote his second play, *The Duchess of Padua*, which Mary Anderson, he hoped, would produce. She had paid him a thousand dollars for the privilege of reading it, and had promised to pay him a further sum of four thousand dollars on account of royalties if the play were acceptable. Pearson thinks she ought to have paid him this sum although the play was trash. Life would be very agreeable to incompetent authors were the Pearson principle in general operation. But Mary Anderson, when she had read it, decided that it would not do, and Wilde was instantly confronted with a grave financial crisis. It never has done, despite several productions. It is dreadful rubbish, almost as bad as *Vera*: a fact which is admitted by his most devoted admirers.

Yet there were people who thought well of it. William Archer, a man of high integrity but small imagination, praised it, although he denounces Elizabethan and Caroline plays of far greater merit in his book, *The Old Drama and the New*. It was Archer who publicly appealed to Bernard Shaw to give up his attempt to storm the stage since he had no talent for writing plays! Ibsen, too, was told by the chief dramatic critic of Copenhagen that he had no talent for the theatre, and Chekhov was advised by his friends, all experts in the drama, to stick to his pills and potions and leave plays to those who could write them. Chekhov, indeed, was so discouraged by the knowledgeable ones in the theatre that he contemplated suicide. If the writing of *The Cherry Orchard*, *The Wild Duck* and *Heartbreak House* had depended on the encouragement given to their authors by knowing people, they would never have been written.

Archer was a most likeable man, the only person in the world who could tell a man to his face how little he thought of his play without hurting his feelings. He had immense knowledge of the theatre. Discussing drama with him, one had to begin with the fact that Archer had read the plays on which he generalised and that if he did not bring much imagination to their criticism, he certainly brought knowledge of their material parts. But he was deficient in discernment, and was poorly provided with humour, although he had more than was generally believed. He denounced Ben Jonson's *Volpone* for improbability, on the ground that while "men of reputed wealth have doubtless lived more or less comfortably on their relatives' 'lively sense of favours to come' ", they could never have "coined it to the tune of millions and lived riotously upon it. The case of *Volpone*, in short," he concluded, "does not exist in nature. It is a figment of crude cynicism." When he was reminded that Madame Humbert in our own time had lived a long time in considerable comfort on the lively sense other people felt of the wealth contained in her unopened safe, he denied that there was any similarity between the two cases! . . . As if cheats and frauds have not lived on simpletons in every age. But Archer, up to the eve of disaster, remained hopeful of Wilde and never ceased to show him his generous spirit. Writing to his brother Charles,[1] on the 1st of May 1895, he referred to Wilde's trial at the Old Bailey:

Things are jogging on much as usual here, except for this infernal Oscar Wilde business, which by the way will be over to-day. I'm afraid Oscar hasn't the ghost of a chance, and of course even if the jury acquitted him he's practically a dead man on his own admissions in the previous trial. It's a loathsome and unthinkable business, but certainly Oscar's madness is not inconsistent with an extraordinary courage and nerve. It appears that yesterday he made a sort of speech of such beauty and power that the people in court applauded loudly,[2] though of course the feeling is intense against him. Really the luck is against the poor British drama—the man who has more brains in his little finger than all the rest of them in their whole body goes and commits worse than suicide in this way. However, it shows that what I had hoped for in Oscar could never have come about—I thought he might get rid of his tomfoolery and affectation and do something really fine, but . . .

The Duchess of Padua will be discussed in the next section. Our immediate concern is with Wilde's monetary distresses which were becoming acute, since he had spent most of his American dollars in Paris and was now rapidly getting rid of the money he had raised on what was left of his property in Mayo. The visit to Paris had been intended to create a reputation which would allow him to live down the spurious renown he had achieved in London, but it was a failure. The French were amused by him—they, too, found him *so* droll—but were not otherwise impressed. He had tricks, rather than manners or even mannerisms, and they were tricks which the French despise. The schoolboy wish to shock the middle-classes seems to them, as it should seem to everybody, infantile, and one which should not be held after the age of twenty. He wore long hair—for he clung to his curls for a short

[1] *William Archer*, by Charles Archer, p. 215.

[2] This was the famous speech, on the love that dare not speak its name, existing between an elder man and a youth. It will be found on page 236 of *Trials of Oscar Wilde*, by H. Montgomery Hyde. The case was not, as Archer expected, ended on the day he wrote to his brother. The jury disagreed, and a new trial began on the 20th of May.

time after his arrival in Paris—and, even worse, he wore fur coats with frogs, a habit which appeared particularly vulgar in France, and he was accustomed to talk smart twaddle.

The French like their men of letters and their wits to be serious people, in the sense that they will not talk trivially or fatuously about matters of importance. This may be a fault in the French, though few sensible people will agree that it is, but we are discussing, not its value, but its fact. It made them regard Wilde as considerably less than he thought himself. He never became, in their eyes, a serious artist. It was all very well for him to model himself on Balzac, who gave eccentric performances in public, but he forgot, if, indeed, he ever knew, that Balzac's eccentricities were not assumed: they were part of his nature. Balzac was as florid as a Jew, not because he thought his extravagance would gain him as few paragraphs in the papers, but because he liked Oriental display. Wilde had thought out his odd behaviour in the way of an advertising agent, but Balzac's eccentricities were as natural as the circulation of his blood. Even if Balzac, whose genius was indisputable, had been a poseur, was that a reason why Wilde should pose? A man who behaves like Balzac should first take care to be Balzac.

Wilde, always sensitive to his surroundings, soon realised that he was making far less headway in France than he had hoped to make, and that the headway he was making was worthless. So he promptly had his hair cut, still keeping it, however, in curl, which, the French thought, was worse than wearing it long: although there would seem to be worse folly in making a principle of life out of such matters as long or short hair, curled or straight. Our Lord is commonly portrayed with His hair down His back. He followed the fashion of His time. The Cavaliers had curls surging round their shoulders, but they were not less manly than the Roundheads whose hair was closely cropped. We make too much fuss about these hirsute matters, and Wilde was among the most offensive of the fussers. Whatever our opinions on such trifles may be, the fact stands, that the French thought Wilde a lightweight, a bubble of a man, a literary *flâneur*, who, though he was entertaining enough for an evening, was unlikely to last out a season. There was something extremely absurd, they thought, in Wilde's daring to present himself to Victor Hugo. The young man had done nothing, but behaved as if he had done all. The great French authors did not bother themselves with him. They met him, perhaps once, and found that once enough.

The "third period" of Wilde's life, as he liked to call it, therefore opened very badly. There was no sensational capture of public attention in Paris as there had been in London and New York, nor was there any appreciation of him as a poet, despite the care with which he had distributed his beautifully bound book in the best circles. Things were beginning to look uncommonly black. Something must soon be done.

His biographers are not to be trusted about his movements at this period. Harris, who seems to be confused about them, asserts that Wilde returned to New York in August 1883 to see the production of *Vera* at the Union Square Theatre on the 20th of that month; and that on his return from America in September, he *then* went to Paris, where he wrote *The Duchess of Padua*. But Wilde went to Paris in the spring of 1883. The evidence is clear and conclusive. Harris was no pedant about facts, and despised anyone who was. Hesketh Pearson is more precise, however, and he tells his readers that Wilde, having arranged a lecture tour in Great Britain and Ireland for the autumn, sailed on the 2nd of August for New York, where he "received an ovation" on the first night of *Vera*: a delusive reception, as it turned out, since the play lasted no longer than a week. Authors in America, when they are called at all, appear on the stage at the end of the second act. Unluckily for those concerned in it, there was more to follow, and what followed, two acts of it, was more than the audience could bear. Marie Prescott played the eponymous part, and Wilde induced her to don "a flaming vermilion gown", which started cat-calls in the audience and brought the play to a rowdy end. Critical opinion on it was remarkably divided. *The New York Mirror* fell into an ecstasy and became incoherent with delight. After an attack on the vulgarians who had assailed "Mr. Wilde with every manner of coarse, cheap and indecent indignity", as if they were "unable or unwilling to understand, much less appreciate, the nobility of character that prompted him to devote his remarkable talents to the development of a taste for all that is beautiful on earth", the indignant scribe informed his readers that "it is not the first instance in history of the crucifixion of a good man on the cross of popular prejudice and disbelief. . . . From a literary, as well as a dramatic point of view, *Vera* is a work that takes rank among the highest order of plays." "The plot, the dialogue, the spirit of the drama are all of that exalted character which entitle it to take place with the first. The subject is masterly, and it demanded masterly treatment. This the author has given it. . . . Just as it stands . . . *Vera* is the noblest contribution to literature the stage has received in many years." But *The New York Tribune*, *The New York Times* and *The New York Herald* dared to differ from *The New York Mirror*. The first declared the play to be "a foolish, highly-peppered story of love, intrigue and politics. . . . It was little better than fizzle", while the second called it "unreal, long-winded and wearisome". The third boldly denounced it as "long-drawn, dramatic rot, a series of disconnected essays and sickening rant, with a coarse and common kind of cleverness". *The Pilot*, however, denied that it was silly or stupid or weak. "We have read *Vera*, and we believe that if well acted, it would be a great success. Mr. Wilde has entrusted his play to an inferior actress, who can only scold on the stage and off it." But the Noes had it, and at the end of the first week *Vera* folded up, and, except for a few performances "on the road", was never seen or heard again. Miss Prescott, who seems to have been as fertile in ideas as she was buoyant in belief, suggested that Wilde should join the cast of the play on tour, but Wilde decided that a lecture tour at home would probably be more profitable, and in September he sailed for England. He did not visit America again.

The lecture tour, which began at Prince's Hall in Piccadilly, was, however, almost as calamitous a failure as *Vera*. A year's absence in the United States, followed by a long sojourn in France, had given the general public ample time in which to forget about sunflowers and lilies and the need for beauty in civic life; and the interest that might have been evoked eighteen months earlier, could not now be stirred. Aestheticism was a stale joke, and no posturing on platforms could make it attractive. Even if Wilde had snatched his comic clothes from the Atlantic in which he was alleged to have buried them, and had displayed himself in a bower of daffodils and lilies, the English would have done no more than yawn at his lectures on a subject which had become boring, if, indeed, they had troubled to attend them. A joke's a joke for a limited period. But his suit, during this tour, was the conventional evening dress of the time. He did, indeed, tuck a large red silk handkerchief in his waistcoat, leaving a portion of it visible against his white shirt; an adornment which, one would have imagined, was used even then only by second-rate conjurers and ballad-singers. Had he worn a waxed moustache, the appearance of routine mediocrity would have been complete. The reporters jeered at him, and the public, in great numbers, stayed away. The money he earned scarcely sufficed to keep him alive. There would be nothing left for expensive existence in London. His penury became so deep that he had to pawn his Berkeley Gold Medal! . . .

It was then that he met again Miss Constance Mary Lloyd, the daughter of a successful barrister and the granddaughter of a wealthy man whose sole heiress she was reputed to be. Remarkably little is known about Wilde's acquaintance with this lady. Sherard, a very gullible author, asserts that Wilde had "been paying attentions" to her "for some time past". "It was during the course of his lecture tour that he was able to visit Dublin and ask her to become his wife." This statement is singularly unconvincing. The attentions he is said to have paid her cannot have been ardent or recent. He had not been in Dublin, until he went to fulfil his lecture engagement, for a considerable period. It is doubtful, indeed, if he had visited his native city since the death of his father in 1876. The opportunities for paying attentions to Miss Lloyd cannot, therefore, have been numerous or regular; for Lady Wilde, soon after the death of her husband, had left her house in Merrion Square and settled in London.

There is no certainty about this matter, so far as published books are concerned; and the view here expressed is no more than surmise. It is likely that Wilde met Miss Lloyd in Dublin, after a long interval, and that he made himself amiable to a pretty woman with fine financial prospects, who was willing to give so clever and audacious a young man her utmost admiration. The young girl's veneration of public people, especially those who are superbly insolent, is a very odd and even moving thing. It unbalances her mind, and makes her susceptible to men who should, as Ulster people say, be "lifted by the peelers". Miss Lloyd soon fell under Wilde's spell. Life with this daring and audacious person must, she felt, be a continual succession of excitements. Not for a second did she suspect the boredom an author's wife must often feel at hearing him frequently repeat himself, nor how hard it is for her to forbear from screaming at the grasshopper noises he makes as he polishes his spontaneous wit on his wife so that it may leap lightly from his lips when he goes out to dine. Wilde was an industrious rehearser of epigrams, and adroit in directing the conversation to the point at which they could be sprung upon his audience, who, unaware that gallons of midnight oil had been burnt in their preparation, applauded his readiness and assured each other that Mrs. Wilde, who listened apathetically to her husband's bright remarks, must be a dull companion for so brilliant a man. It is only by knitting hard and not listening that the celebrated writer's long-suffering spouse keeps herself sane. Very early in her married life, she learns the use of well-timed and indefinite ejaculations of a monosyllabic character. No more, she realises, need be said. More, indeed, would be resented, since it must interrupt the flow of the master's all-too-familiar epigrams and deep remarks. There was, however, no perception of this almost tragic fact in Constance Mary Lloyd's mind when she listened to Oscar Wilde murmuring words that were now well worn, about beauty.

His reaction to her admiration was, we believe, very prompt. Here was the source of the income he greatly needed, for which he had sought so keenly on two continents.

The marriage was celebrated at St. James's Church, Paddington, on the 29th of May 1884, and they spent their honeymoon at the Hôtel Wagram in the rue de Rivoli in Paris, where Wilde wasted a good deal of her money: and on their return to London, they took a house at 16 Tite Street, Chelsea. It was decorated for them under the supervision of Whistler who lived near by. The wedding, which was said to be somewhat "aesthetic" in style, brought immediate disappointment. His wife's fortune was considerably less than Wilde had imagined it to be. He himself, during his examination in bankruptcy on the 12th of November 1895, said it was "about £800 per year",[1] a fairly substantial sum in an age when a sovereign was a sovereign and income tax was only a few pence in the pound. His own unearned income, derived from what remained of his estate in Ireland, was "between £100 and £150 a year". The newly-married couple had, therefore, the best part of a thousand pounds a year, apart from any moneys Wilde might earn from his writing. This does not denote wealth, but neither does it denote poverty; and they should have been able to live well and to keep themselves free from debt. But Wilde, whose income at the height of his prosperity was never anything like the sum his sycophants alleged it was, would have lived in debt if he had enjoyed a million a year. He was that sort of incontinent person. His wife's fortune would eventually be larger, but increase would not come until after her grandfather's death; and the old gentleman, who could hardly be expected to impoverish himself for Wilde's benefit by transferring any more of his property to his granddaughter, seemed likely to live a long time. Wilde was therefore faced, at a time when he had incurred heavy liabilities, with the need to earn a living. He took to journalism and returned to the platform. But his hopes, which had been deferred, but not abandoned, by the failure of *Vera* in New York, still clung to *The Duchess of Padua*, despite Mary Anderson's defection, though these, too, proved delusive.

22

THE DUCHESS OF PADUA is a poor, pretentious piece, little, if any, better than *Vera*; a paltry melodrama which is dismissed

[1] See *Trials of Oscar Wilde*, p. 355. Edited by H. Montgomery Hyde.

by Alfred Douglas as Wilde's "other 'dud' play", the first, of course, being the miserable *Vera*. It is full of fainting echoes. Its author took Molière's remark about literary thefts, *Je prends mon bien où je le trouve*, too much to heart. Seventeenth-century dramatists had a different opinion of plagiarism from that prevailing in Wilde's day, but even if this were not true, men of quality do not steal from each other if they can make better stuff themselves. Plagiarism is a confession, not of crime, but of incompetence or idleness. An author who steals a phrase from another acknowledges his inferiority to the author he robs; and the fact that men of genius have sometimes lazily yielded to temptation does not justify the theft, though its offence is mitigated if the stolen sentence is improved. Wilde was an incorrigible pilferer, unable, it seemed, to keep his hands from picking and stealing, confessing only after detection that the stolen property was not his own. Even the celebrated knee-breeches were no novelty. Postmen and dustmen were still wearing them in Wilde's infancy.

He stole too often and too obviously, but he did worse than that: he stole inefficiently. That very tedious gentleman, Lord Henry Wotton, in *The Portrait of Dorian Gray*, does not improve upon Tertullian when he remarks, "And as for believing things, I can believe anything provided it is incredible". John the Baptist, or Jokannan, as Wilde, surprisingly pedantic and even priggish, prefers to call him in *Salomé*, is less happy in his phrasing than John Bright when he says, "I hear in the palace the beating of the wings of the angel of death". Rochefoucauld, in his *Maxims*, anticipated Wilde's epigram on the fortitude with which we bear other people's misfortunes. "*Nous avons tous assez de force pour supporter les maux d'autrui.*"

But if he did not improve on others, he certainly improved on himself. Lord Darlington, when he defined a cynic to Mr. Cecil Graham in *Lady Windermere's Fan*, expressed himself more deftly than Lord Henry Wotton; and Lady Bracknell, too, was defter in *The Importance of Being Earnest* than Sybil Vane's mother in *Dorian Gray*, when a scornful remark had to be made about solicitors at dinner-parties in great houses. Epigrams are often no more than verbal tricks, performed by merely inverting a familiar phrase. Wilde became very slick at this performance, and could perform it for hours, almost without thinking, like a drill-sergeant doing a bit of arm drill. It made him seem shallower than he was, and it caused him to deal too often in easy wit, such as Lord Henry Wotton's banal remark that "Beer, the Bible and the seven deadly virtues have made our England what it is": a remark which might be permitted in an auctioneer's clerk who is having a larky night in the local pub. Even Bernard Shaw, a finer and more fastidious wit than Wilde, descended to the seven deadly virtues. It was a witticism that could have been taught to a correspondence class by a down-at-heel pedagogue.

The pages of *The Duchess of Padua* are strewn with stolen sentences, proving that Wilde's gravest defect was a good memory; and the thief has not improved any of them by his rearrangement. How poor a passage is this, spoken by the Duke in the first act:

> "As for conscience,
> Conscience is but the name which cowardice,
> Fleeing from battle, scrawls upon its shield."

Hamlet put the point with terser truth: "Thus conscience doth make cowards of us all": and the Second Murderer in *Richard III* expressed it with greater wit:

> "I'll not meddle with it,—it makes a man a coward; a man cannot steal, but it accuseth him; a man cannot lie with his neighbour's wife, but it detects him; 'tis a blushing shame-faced spirit that mutinies in a man's bosom; it fills one full of obstacles; it made me once restore a purse of gold that by chance I had found; it beggars any man that keeps it; it is turned out of all towns and cities for a dangerous thing; and every man that means to live well, endeavours to trust himself and live without it."

When the Duchess pleads with her husband for remission of the people's taxes, and tells him that the water they drink is stagnant and muddy, the Duke, anticipating Marie Antoinette, remarks, "They should drink wine; water is unwholesome". We feel little surprise when the Duchess, almost snatching the words out of Hamlet's mouth, remarks:

> "The cold meats of my husband's funeral feast
> Are set for you; this is a wedding feast."

The play concludes with the Duchess dying in great pain after she has swallowed a poison. She "leaps up in the dreadful spasm of death, tears in agony at her dress, and, finally, with a face twisted and distorted with pain, falls back dead in a chair. Guido, seizing her dagger from her belt, kills himself; and, as he falls across her knees, clutches at her cloak which is on the back of the chair, and throws it entirely over her." A moment or two later, the cloak so surprisingly pulled across the lady's face, is withdrawn, and her features which, a few seconds earlier, were "twisted and distorted with pain", are "now the marble image of peace, the sign of God's forgiveness". The terms in which these stage directions are written indicate sufficiently the style of the whole play. Wilde had a deep strain of violence in him, and it appears in almost all his work, especially in the plays, the majority of which are crudely melodramatic. They live on their wit. Had their survival depended on character or theme, they would long ago have perished.

Opinions on *The Duchess of Padua* differ as remarkably as did American opinion on *Vera*. Alfred Douglas, in an appreciation of its author, *Oscar Wilde*, which was published in 1940, damns it outright as "a dud play", but Robert Sherard, Wilde's first biographer, a man whose literary judgements were worthless, proclaims it "great", and asserts that some of its admirers rank it "with the Elizabethan masterpieces". Wilde himself, as he lay dying in Paris, passed sentence upon it. "It is unworthy of me", he said. It was performed for the first time at the Broadway Theatre, New York, on the 26th of January 1891, under the title of *Guido Ferranti*, the name of its principal boy, a pantomime term one is encouraged to use by the play's vapidity. Lawrence Barrett was the Guido; Minna K. Gale, the Beatrice. It ran for three calamitous weeks, and has never been revived in America, nor has it ever been publicly performed in Great Britain.[1] An industrious German, one Dr. Max Meyerfeld, made a translation of it which was performed in Hamburg in December 1904. On the third night, the actor who took the part of the Cardinal went out

[1] I am indebted to Mr. John Parker, the Secretary of the Critics' Circle, for this information and for that about the production of *Vera*. A copyright performance of *The Duchess of Padua* was given at the St. James's Theatre, London, on the 18th of March 1907. See *Bibliography of Oscar Wilde*, by Stuart Mason, p. 331.

of his mind, as, indeed, he had every excuse for doing, and was carried off to the nearest asylum. The play was then withdrawn. But the industrious Meyerfeld was not discouraged. He secured a revival in Berlin in 1906. It, too, was a total failure. The history of the play since that year, so far as the stage is concerned, is one of silence.

A letter, hitherto unpublished,[1] which was, it is supposed, addressed to Lawrence Barrett early in 1891, reveals Wilde's simple-minded vanity at this time. If, as we may justifiably surmise, he was impecunious at the time it was written, its sophomoric insolence will seem excusable when we consider what disappointment he must have felt when he saw his returns.

Dear Sir [he wrote]:

I have to acknowledge the receipt of two drafts, for £20 each, for eight performances of the Duchess of Padua.

As I understand that my play was to be the principal feature of Miss Gale's tour, the amount of performances has both surprised and annoyed me. It was in order to have my play played, not in order to have my play suppressed, that I assigned my American rights to Miss Gale. This, however, I suppose is not a matter that lies within your province. I have written to Miss Gale on the subject.

I hear my play was played on a Saturday night at Harlem lately. No doubt you have already forwarded what is due. My play should be the opening production in each important city. To keep it for the last night is to show a want of recognition of the value and importance of the play.

Wilde was thirty-seven when he wrote that letter, in which there is neither wit nor style, but he might have been nineteen and still at Oxford. Miss Gale would have done him great service if she had suppressed *The Duchess of Padua*. Nine years later, when he lay dying in Paris, he knew it for the wretched stuff it is.

There is not a single credible person, except, perhaps, the Cardinal, among its chief characters. Neither the Duchess nor her lover, Guido, bears any resemblance to rational men and women; and people who are devoid of any reason, common or fantastic,

[1] Now in the possession of Mr. Montgomery Hyde, to whom I am indebted for a copy of it. I am also indebted to Mr. Vyvyan Holland, the owner of Wilde's copyrights, for permission to publish it here.

are unfit for treatment in any play. There is no *sense* in *The Duchess of Padua*, nor does its author attempt to make it plausible. When the avenger, Moranzone, appears out of the blue to Guido, demanding that he shall slay his father's murderer, the Duke of Padua, Guido, who until that moment has had no knowledge of his father or of Moranzone, accepts his orders without question or enquiry. He is forbidden to speak again to his lifelong friend, and without the slightest hesitation, obeys the arbitrary command. He is told to delay the execution of the criminal Duke until some unspecified moment when Moranzone shall be pleased to permit it. Why? Because, presumably, there would be no play if the Duke were instantly dispatched. But a play which turns on mindless decisions such as Moranzone's is not a play, certainly not a tragedy: it is an arrangement of unnatural events, intended to excite febrile emotions. Wilde wishes the Duchess and Guido to fall in love; and, therefore, wilfully and out of all reason, he makes Moranzone behave whimsically about the Duke's assassination. It is a matter, perhaps, for smaller speculation why Moranzone himself did not execute the Duke: he may have wished to have the murderer punished by the son of the murdered man. But the calculation is too cool and long-deferred for a man so hot with hate.

The twists and turns of this singularly silly play are explicable only in terms of that berserker rage which periodically possessed Wilde in his youth and young manhood: transpontine violence appealed to a mind which was liable to leap out of all control in sudden bursts of rage. One feels, on reading it, that Wilde has shaken *Hamlet* and *The Cenci* into a bloody mess, and is himself in very much the same state of ungovernable wrath in which Maldonado wrecks the furniture at the end of Pinero's play, *Letty*: but that the reason which is in all three plays is nowhere to be found in his. This addiction to strained language and overstated emotion is apparent in nearly all Wilde's work, late as well as early, and is proof, if any be needed, of the fatal bequest made to him by overwrought parents whose blood pressure must have been appalling. If we are told to remember that *The Duchess of Padua* is an early work, we shall reply, first, that Wilde was twenty-nine when he wrote it, an age at which a writer, unless he is incurable, may well be expected to have recovered from violent adolescence; second, that genius has long been claimed for him, and that we may, therefore, fairly compare his early work with that of other men of genius, a comparison which leaves him looking uncommonly foolish; and, third, that some of his later work, for example *The Ideal Husband*, is not less stupid than *The Duchess of Padua*. It is the fashion to deride Pinero, but the fashion is puerile. In no play that Pinero wrote, not even in farces, where probability is unimportant, did he descend to such depths of silliness, implausibility and unnatural violence as Wilde did in *The Duchess of Padua*: and he had a sense of craft which was beyond Wilde's understanding.

23

THE discovery that his wife's means were less ample than he had supposed them to be, made it imperative for him to find employment. He lectured and wrote articles and reviews of books, and dramatic criticism, and composed fairy tales, in addition to doing a great deal of miscellaneous hack work. The quality of his occasional contributions to *The World* and *The Pall Mall Gazette* has been belittled by some of his friends, but it was excellent, informed and witty and well written, and of such quality that any editor, however exacting, would have been glad to have had more of it in his paper. Wilde was not, as some of his critics, even those who admired him, have suggested, a haphazard author whose knowledge, especially of the classics, was shallow. He was, as his record at Portora, Trinity College, Dublin, and Oxford amply proves, a considerable classical scholar, and his knowledge was strengthened by travel in classical countries and by contact with the richly-stored mine of Dr. Mahaffy. Mahaffy had many faults, but only an ignoramus would deny that he was a man of great classical learning. But even if this evidence were not available to prove the point, the reviews and miscellanies which are reprinted in several volumes, and especially in *A Critic in Pall Mall*, are sufficient in themselves to demonstrate his scholarship. Wilde, during his days of free-lance journalism, acquired a discipline that would have been invaluable to him when he was writing *Vera* and *The Duchess of Padua*, a discipline which might have saved him from shipwreck had he maintained it for the rest of his life. He displays in these fugitive pieces wit, humour and sense, and a well-furnished and exceptionally various mind.

His *Fairy Tales* have been over-praised, particularly by his tepid admirers, such as Walter Pater and Vincent O'Sullivan, who profess to find in them richer qualities than he displays in the rest of his work. But has anyone ever read Wilde's fairy-tales to children? If anyone has, did the children listen? They are full of sentimental pessimism and disappointment and cynical despair of people. *The Happy Prince*, the best known and most highly praised, is a sour and bitter piece which might well cause any child to lose its faith, not only in its elders, which is easy enough, but in itself, which is almost impossible. O'Sullivan asserts that Wilde had a poor opinion of his fairy-tales. He was entitled to it.

But all this activity, though profitable enough—for Wilde, despite his fits of lethargy, could be as suddenly industrious as Hitler—was still insufficiently remunerative, even when eked out by his wife's income, for his needs, which grew with his increase of fortune and responsibilities. The latter included two sons: Cyril, who was born in June 1885 and was killed in the First World War, and Vyvyan, who was born in November 1886. When, therefore, in October 1887, he was offered the editorship of *The Woman's World* by the publishing house of Cassell & Company at a salary of six pounds a week, he accepted it gladly; and held it for almost exactly two years, until September 1889, doing his duties ably and steadily.

The years 1884 to 1891, from his thirtieth to his thirty-seventh, were, however, barren of any major achievement. It was during this period that he became intoxicated with words, a drunkenness which is plainly to be noticed in *The Picture of Dorian Gray*. He was no longer interested in their meaning, but only in their look and sound. Appearance had become more important to him than reality; and he took up the habit, often attributed to Anatole

France, of "mugging up" articles in encyclopaedias and translating them into his own style. The eleventh chapter of *The Picture of Dorian Gray* is an example of this literary loafing. His catchword, too, had changed. Formerly it had been *charming*, but now it was *tedious*.

Something had happened to Wilde. He had met Mr. Robert Baldwin Ross.

The effect of this unfortunate encounter is to be seen in Wilde's work during the period under discussion. Ross and he met for the first time about 1886, when Ross was seventeen and Wilde was thirty-two. *The Happy Prince* appeared in 1888; and was followed up to the year 1891, when Wilde made his second unfortunate friendship, with Lord Alfred Douglas, by *The House of Pomegranates*, *The Soul of Man Under Socialism*, *Intentions*, *The Picture of Dorian Gray* and *Lord Arthur Savile's Crime*. There's nothing here for exultation.

His admirers are accustomed to refer to *Dorian Gray* in terms that would be fulsome if they were applied to Cervantes, Fielding, Dickens, Victor Hugo or Tolstoy, but this novel, which is better described as a long short story, is no more than a competently composed tale on a familiar theme: the influence of evil on those who yield to it. It contains some good writing, but more that is terrible. Wilde, who sometimes wrote in the manner of an author of servant girls' novelettes, also cultivated a euphuistic style which occasionally descended to the level of Mrs. Amanda McKittrick Ros. What are we to make of the following passage from *The Picture of Dorian Gray*?

> A fit of passionate sobbing choked her. She crouched on the floor like a wounded thing, and Dorian Gray, with his beautiful eyes, looked down at her, and his chiselled lips curled in exquisite disdain.

Miss Corelli, sorrowing for Satan, could not have been more subservient to the scullery. One may, having regard to Wilde's subsequent history, detect in this story some apprehensive forecast of his own fate. The theme, though familiar, is one that a man of genius is entitled to work over again, and the *idea* of the story, once its fantastic character is accepted, is able enough. But the execution of the story is poor, especially in the passage referring to the young actress. Wilde is here trying to depict a life of which he was not only ignorant but imaginatively incapable. The novel excited suspicions, suspicions which were justifiably excited, of perversity in its author, although it is almost tractlike in its general morality. The mark of Mr. Robert Baldwin Ross had now been made on Wilde's mind.

24

THIS small, bunched-up sodomite was born in Tours on 25th May 1869, the son of the Hon. John Ross, Q.C., Attorney-General for Upper Canada. His mother was the daughter of the Hon. Robert Baldwin, Prime Minister of that Province. He was educated privately and at King's College, Cambridge, which he left without taking a degree. He then did desultory journalism in various papers, and was for a period on the staff of *The Morning Post*. But his main business was the buying and selling of pictures. He was considered to be a good judge of paintings, and was appointed Assessor of Picture Valuations to the Board of Trade by Mr. Asquith, a post which he held from 1912 to 1914. On 5th December 1918, his valet, entering his bedroom in Half Moon Street to wake him, found him dead from trouble of the heart. Ross was as devoted to Wilde as Engels was to Karl Marx, and he spent a large part of his life in retrieving his ruined friend's fortune. The care of Wilde's sons devolved on him to a considerable extent, and he behaved to them, as one of them said, like a second father. He had many of the virtues of an excellent Norland nurse. There can be no dispute about the steadfast devotion he showed for Wilde at a time when even to be casually acquainted with him was to incur contempt and enmity. But neither can there be any doubt that he was, more than any other single person, directly responsible for Wilde's moral degeneracy and physical disintegration. It was after Wilde met this little nervous, insinuating, rather writhing young man, with all the mannerisms of a satyr and a devoted maiden aunt, that the taint of perversion appeared in his work and in his own life.

If anything is plain in *The Picture of Dorian Gray*, it is that Basil Hallward, the painter of the portrait; its subject; and Lord Arthur Wotton are all pederasts. The unwarrantable rumours about Wilde's life at Oxford were now revived, and the vice of which he was then falsely accused was now a true indictment. There is a sense in which Dorian Gray is Oscar Wilde, though he had the physical features of Lord Alfred Douglas, and Lord Arthur Wotton, whom many of his detractors have identified with Wilde, was Mr. Robert Baldwin Ross.

25

WE may glance at some of the works Wilde produced in this period, particularly at *The Soul of Man Under Socialism*, a work which was once popular with proletarian politicians, and was praised by H. G. Wells. It was written, someone has asserted, after Wilde had heard Bernard Shaw lecturing on Socialism. Shaw's rendering of the gospel according to Sidney Webb created such disgust in Wilde, the legend runs, that he went home and wrote *The Soul of Man Under Socialism* almost in a sitting. There never was a work less proletarian in character than this book, which must have excited fury in Marx had he lived to read it. As a contribution to social science it is unimportant, but it is an excellent discussion of Socialism, and especially of its dangers, and is the most sensible work its author wrote in the period under review. Lord Alfred Douglas, who seems not to have read it with much understanding, dismisses it with contempt. "Frankly," he writes in *Oscar Wilde*, "I think it is the worst thing Oscar ever wrote with the exception of *Vera*. It seems to me the most feeble and paltry and insincere stuff." This is unjust, and Douglas has here allowed his hatred of Socialism to cloud his judgement. Wilde like Shaw was not a Socialist: he was an intensified Individualist, a fastidious, aristocratically-minded man, to whom the ugly excrescences of life, whatever their origin might be, were repulsive. He demanded a Socialist state, not because he had an overwhelming desire to hobnob with coal-heavers and stevedores, but because it would relieve him of the obnoxious necessity to live for others. He desired to live only for himself. His Irish Protestant percipience enabled him to detect the danger which we now know to be inherent in totalitarian communities, and he was careful to proclaim it. Individualism, he declared, was essential to the "full development of life to its highest mode of perfection". "If the Socialism is Authoritarian; if there are Governments armed with economic power as they are now with political power; if, in a word, we are to have industrial Tyrannies, then the last state of man will be worse than the first." A few sentences later, he makes the profound statement that

> disobedience, in the eyes of anyone who has read history, is man's original virtue. It is through disobedience that progress has been made, through disobedience and through rebellion.

But how can there be hope of disobedience and rebellion or even of simple enquiry in a totalitarian society, where all power, economic, military, social and political, is concentrated in a single group, whose members hang together lest, should they disintegrate even slightly, they should hang separately. If progress is dependent upon a man's power to criticise and enquire, to question and alter, to rebel and disobey, then there can be no such thing as progress in Russia. "It is to be regretted", Wilde says in this remarkable essay, "that a portion of our community should be practically in slavery, but to propose to solve the problem by enslaving the entire community is childish." The single value of Socialism for him was that it seemed likely to lead to greater Individualism. If greater Individualism were not its result, then it must lead to death and damnation.

> Man is made for something better than distributing dirt. All work of that kind should be done by a machine.

So he remarks without much thought. But children, those incorrigible and determined Individualists, delight in distributing dirt.

What man can make a garden if he does not. Kipling has wiser words than any of Wilde's on this subject:

> Our England is a garden, and such gardens are not made
> By singing: "Oh, how beautiful!" and sitting in the shade,
> While better men than we go out and start their working lives,
> At grubbing weeds from gravel paths with broken dinner-knives.

Did Wilde imagine that machines operate themselves or that the life of a machine-minder, pushing a button here or pulling a lever there, is ampler than that of a man who performs his labour mainly with his hands? Is there, indeed, anything inherently disgusting in what is called "dirty work"? Does it matter much if the miner is blackened in the pit, provided he has ample and easy means of washing himself when he comes out of it? Has any sensible man ever felt degraded by soiling his hands with his labour? Are we not more likely to feel sickened by the sight of bloody talons on a woman's finger-tips and toes than we are by the sight of labour stains on a man's fists? Wilde, despite his aestheticism and his perpetual *blah* about beauty, when it was faked, for he detested natural beauty, was not foolish enough to join the mindless people who demand that machines shall be scrapped. But he confused his own inertia with his sense of aesthetic values, and believed himself to be denouncing undignified labour when he was only indulging his idleness. It never occurred to him that one result of a highly mechanised society will be a great increase of handicraft, because men cannot endure the boredom of mass-production and universal similarity. Nevertheless, he did not fall into the error of the arty-and-crafty person who vapours about the man who digs a field with a spade and complains when the spade is discarded for a tractor. Any instrument we use to lighten our labour is a machine, just as all cultivation is unnatural. The crops we grow in our fields are as artificial as the bloom a woman paints on her cheeks. Nature could not have produced them without man's help and ingenuity, and they would revert to jungle growth if we were careless in selecting seeds. Wilde would have scoffed at those who detect something uplifting in a quill, but are appalled by fountain-pens. He did not imagine that George Herbert was applauding besoms and denouncing vacuum-cleaners when he wrote his verse:

> A servant with this clause
> Makes drudgery divine;
> Who sweeps a room as for Thy laws
> Makes that and the action fine.

though he might, perhaps, have remarked that it is unnecessary for the parlour-maid to remove crumbs from the table as if she had taken vows of perpetual chastity. He might profess art-for-art's-sake, but he was not arty-and-crafty.

Nor was he one who cried peace when there is no peace. He did not deny that physical force is a fact, or imagine, like Tolstoy, that a man enters into the emotions of a peasant by donning a smock and toying on Saturday afternoons with a spade. He dissented from the view of those infatuates who say that force has never settled anything and never can settle anything. Are we to believe that inertness settles all? "Many of the most important problems of the last few centuries, such as the continuance of personal government in England or of feudalism in France," he says in *The Soul of Man Under Socialism*, "have been solved entirely by means of physical force"; a view in which Bertrand Russell would concur. "There have been wars that have done good", Russell remarks in *Which Way to Peace?* and he cites the American War of Independence, a dubious example, when he had better have cited the Civil War which, more than any other war, was fought almost entirely on a moral issue. Another example he gives is Caesar's conquest of Gaul. Religious wars, he states, were characterised by so much persecution "that, in most European countries, the dominant religion at the present day is that which was held by the Government in the early seventeenth century.

> Nor can it be said that either party could have succeeded as well if it, but not the other party, had practised non-resistance. If the German Protestants had not taken up arms, there would soon have been no Protestants in Germany; and if the German Catholics had avoided war, there would have been no Catholics. As it was, they fought until Germany was devastated and neither side gained anything; but if one side and not the other, had been willing to fight, the peaceable side would have lost everything."

That was the lesson which was learnt in bitterness and sorrow by the Hebrews who obstinately kept the law when they were assailed by the Gentiles on the sabbath. The Hebrews would not profane the day by labour of any sort, and they answered "their enemies not, neither cast they a stone at them, nor stopped up the secret places", saying, as the First Book of the Maccabees records, "Let us all die in our innocency: heaven and earth witness over us, that ye put us to death without trial. And they rose up against them in battle on the sabbath, and they died, they and their wives and their children, and their cattle, to the number of a thousand souls." Here was fanaticism become mania. The Gentiles had only to attack them on the sabbath to be assured of victory that would be bloodless for themselves, but horribly bloody for Israelites. Wisdom broke in on such lunacy as this.

And Mattathias and his friends knew it, and they mourned over them exceedingly. And one said to another, If we all do as our brethren have done, and fight not against the Gentiles for our lives and our ordinances, they will now quickly destroy us from off the earth. And they took counsel on that day, saying, Whosoever shall come against us to do battle on the sabbath day, let us fight against him and we shall in no wise all die, as our brethren died in the secret places. Then were gathered together unto them a company of Hasideans, mighty men of Israel, every one that offered himself willingly for the law. And all they that fled from the evils were added to them, and became a stay unto them. And they mustered a host, and smote sinners in their anger, and lawless men in their wrath: and the rest fled to the Gentiles for safety. And Mattathias and his friends went round about, and pulled down the altars; and they circumcised by force the children that were uncircumcised, as many as they found in the coasts of Israel. And they pursued after the sons of pride, and the work prospered in their hands. And they rescued the law out of the hands of the Gentiles, and out of the hand of the kings, neither suffered they the sinner to triumph.

The First World War, had it not been fought by the Allies, might have saved mankind from the Second, but at the price of fixing it in slavery from which there could have been little hope of escape for a long time.

Wilde had no truck with this Tolstoyan trash. There are worse things than war, and life in servitude is worse than death in battle.

It is better to die on your feet than to live on your hands and knees. If good survives in this world, it survives because men were willing to fight and die for it. It is false to say that war had never brought any benefit to mankind, and Wilde, in a time when intellectuals were uttering the lie loudly amid applause, courageously refuted it.

There is much in *The Soul of Man Under Socialism* which is flatulent stuff, but the reader dare not skip a page lest he should miss a piece of wisdom; for Wilde had a trick of concealing a fine thought in a heap of rubbish. At the end of a long passage of twaddle on the futility of those who pity people in pain, he suddenly writes, "Anybody can sympathise with the sufferings of a friend, but it requires a very fine nature to sympathise with a friend's success". That was a sympathy Wilde never felt or received.

26

THE SOUL OF MAN UNDER SOCIALISM is Wilde's most important work in this period, but it is not a major work. Nothing that he wrote then is a major work. *Salomé* is an impressive short play, but it would have been a far better work if, in writing it, he had not aped so sedulously the style of Maurice Maeterlinck. Although it was written about a month after *Lady Windermere's Fan* was finished, it was conceived long before that play was thought of, and belongs, in every respect, more to the period under review than to the period in which it was written. I have, therefore, ignored its physical time, preferring to treat it in terms of its intellectual time and to place it here.

Biblical themes had a peculiar attraction for Wilde, and his mind in his last years, when it was capable of sustained thought about work, dallied with the notion of a play on a Pharaoh and another on Ahab and Jezebel. He studied the Bible closely while he was in prison, and its influence is apparent in *De Profundis*.

But his mind seems to have been attracted more, dramatically at all events, by minor episodes and small people. Great figures such as Moses and David and Isaiah and Ezekiel and Jeremiah, had no effect on his imagination; nor did he display any interest in so gracious a character as Amos. St. Paul eluded him. He might have been expected to feel drawn to men like Esau, one of the noblest characters in the Old Testament, and to have been scornful of Jacob, who was, surely, the first pawnbroker, the complete and irredeemable Sheeny as distinct from the Jew; but Esau, the great Israelite, drew no admiration from him, nor did he condemn Jacob. Ishmael, in comparison with whom Sarah's colourless son, Isaac, was dust and ashes, the sort of dull and dispirited prig who would have been perfectly placed as one of Mr. Attlee's Under-Secretaries, inspired no feeling in Wilde, although that magnificent outcast would have seemed certain of his sympathy. Our Lord seldom fails to capture any imagination which is capable of perceiving untainted beauty and undefiled grace. H. G. Wells, indeed, succeeded, almost alone among men of distinction, in evading him; but Wells, who had the street urchin's irresistible tendency to cock snooks at high character and lofty spirit, and was almost incapable of recognising supreme nobility, was quick to thumb his nose and shout "Yah!" and slow to fall on his knees and thank God. Perfection made manifest in flesh did not fail to waken respect and reverence in Oscar Wilde. It gave him comfort in a time when the whole world must have seemed bare and destitute.

Dramatically, however, he was interested only in small and even ignominious Bible characters. Salomé and Herod and Herodias stirred his imagination as John the Baptist failed to do. The evil people, polluting the very air of night in which they lived, roused emotion in him that was not moved at all by the bedouin nature of the lonely prophet, who was so secure in his sanctity and moral courage that he never felt a qualm about consequences.

The history of *Salomé* is fairly familiar. Wilde wrote it at Torquay,[1] in 1891, in French which, despite his detractors who were over-eager to find fault with him, was good, if formal; and,

[1] So Ross asserts. Pearson says it was written in Paris.

it was translated into English by Lord Alfred Douglas.[1] His decision to write it in French was, in part no doubt, a piece of exhibitionism, but it was, in much larger part, a piece of calculation as deliberate as his antics in aesthetic clothes. Wilde desired recognition in France, and he sought it by writing a play in the French language. How careful he was in composing *Salomé* is proved by his solicitation of help from Marcel Schwob, Adolph Retté and Pierre Louÿs, to the last of whom the play is inscribed. Each of them made a few revisions of parts of speech, but none of them made many, since, as Schwob informed Ross, there was a wish not to interfere extensively with Wilde's style, even although this restraint meant that some faults were not corrected. It was a considerable feat for a foreigner to have written a play in French at all. To have written one with so few mistakes was much more than that.

Salomé was *not* written for Sarah Bernhardt, but was already written when, Ross informs us, she casually suggested to Wilde that he should write a play for her. Wilde himself, in a letter published in *The Times* on the 2nd of March 1893, denied the statement, which had appeared in a review of the play in that journal on the 23rd of February. "But my play was in no sense of the words written for that great actress. I have never written a play for any actor or actress, nor shall I ever do so. Such work is for the artisan in literature,—not for the artist." Bernhardt was eager to produce it during her visit to the Palace Theatre, London, in 1892, but was unable to do so because of a rule made by the Lord Chamberlain against the performance in public of plays on Biblical subjects. Under this rule, Stephen Phillips, who had written *The Sin of David* round the relations of David and Bethsheba, had to remove the scene of his play from Israel to Cromwellian England, and make a Roundhead of the Psalmist who was not in the least like one of the Protector's Major-Generals. The Censor's ban on *Salomé* threw Wilde into one of his humourless rages, and he threatened, in *Le Gaulois*, to renounce his British nationality

[1] Wilde, unjustly, accuses Douglas, in *De Profundis*, of clumsy and inaccurate translation, but we may believe that the charge was an afterthought and would not have been made if Wilde had not been in a mood of bitter resentment when he wrote it.

and become a Frenchman: a threat which he was careful not to fulfil, although, perhaps, his fate would have been happier if he had. Pearson asserts that this petulant threat caused him, for the first time in his life, to lose his sense of humour. Pearson gravely over-estimates Wilde's sense of humour. He hadn't any, and was liable in times of irritation to reveal his lack. Their readers will search the works of Wilde, Moore, Shaw and Yeats in vain if it is a sense of humour for which they are looking. Wit, yes, in abundance, but humour, not a scrap.

The play was published, first, in French in 1892, and, second, in English in 1893. The English translation was disfigured and made repellent by sixteen illustrations, drawn by Aubrey Beardsley, which insidiously increased Wilde's reputation as a moral degenerate. Beardsley greatly disliked, and was as greatly disliked by, Wilde, who is, Ross asserts, caricatured in two of the drawings, *The Woman in the Moon* and *Enter Herodias*; and it is difficult to avoid the belief that Beardsley deliberately made pictures of malodorous life with the intention of inflicting injury on Wilde. Dissent can, of course, be made to that statement by replying that all Beardsley's drawings were in the same style, a statement which is not quite true, and that the figures in the *Salomé* pictures are no more malodorous than the rest of his work. That may be substantially the fact, but when two antipathetic elements, each of them harmless apart from the other, are brought into contact, an explosion may follow. Beardsley had a higher sense of pure line than almost any other artist. His drawing is singularly clear and delicate. The lines do not waver though they seem as fragile as a spider's web. He handles black and white as if they were brilliant colours, and can draw red blood in black. The smallest dot in one of his lines is significant. The man had genius, but it was diabolical, and his mind, which was tuberculous, turned as promptly to evil as saints turn to sanctity. He drew men and women in the shape of mirthless imps and cretins. There is not a single smile in one of the sixteen illustrations to *Salomé*. Evil leers in all of them, or stands about in a mindless state, dusty with degeneration. One looks with horror on hydrocephalous dwarfs, with their curled lips and crimped hair, those of them who have any, and feels afraid.

There is no joy in Beardsley's drawings, nothing but unsatisfied and cheerless lust and evil, the perpetual frustration of people doomed to seek, but never to find. His women are all on the verge of nervous collapse. His men are embodied sin.

Inevitably, the play's publication drew upon its author severe censure. If Wilde had had any hope of applause for *Salomé*, Beardsley's drawings would have destroyed it. They seemed to exude the stench of stale corruption. The stews had poured their foul inhabitants into them. No one, in attempting to explain the vehemence with which *Salomé* was denounced on its first publication in English, seems to have realised how much of the storm was raised by Beardsley. It was Mr. Robert Baldwin Ross who persuaded Wilde, greatly against his will, to permit Beardsley to make the drawings. This was another disservice Ross rendered him.

The play itself is full of evil, although it is a moral piece, in the sense in which the strict and superficial moralist uses that word. The author of the Revelation of St. John the Divine would not have found fault with it. Its atmosphere is mephitic as the air of a charnel-house, and full of foul exhalations, but the evil is not denied, nor are the evil-doers acclaimed. Wilde, indeed, punishes the evil-doer as sensationally as any revivalist could wish to do: Salomé is violently and suddenly slain for her sin. Nevertheless, the play, powerful as no other play by Wilde is powerful, reeks with unrelieved wickedness. Its characters have passed beyond the pale of humanity, and are hellish creatures in whom there is no human emotion. The old lecher, Herod, finding Herodias sexually dissatisfying, lusts after her daughter, who, in her turn, lusts after the Baptist because he seems likely to provide her with a new sensation. Herodias moves through the play like a superannuated whore, destined to become the madam of an expensive brothel. Death lurks in every line. The atmosphere is full of decay. The pseudo-Biblical language in which the play is written, with its Maeterlinckian repetitions and irrelevant remarks, creates an appearance of monotonous evil, an evil which has lost its mind and retains only its impulse. It excites no compassion in the reader, who scarcely observes the suicide of the young Syrian captain who kills himself because his passion for Salomé is unrequited and hopeless.

It is the lack of humanity in the play which annuls its strength and skill. Salomé, intent on the Baptist's body, does not notice the dead Syrian lying between them. She does not utter a word to show that she is aware of him or his violent end. Even the Page of Herodias, who loves the Syrian, babbles like an imbecile when his friend destroys himself. "The young Syrian has slain himself! The young captain has slain himself! He has slain himself who was my friend! I gave him a little box of perfumes and ear-rings wrought in silver, and now he has killed himself...." The banality of that speech makes us realise how little sense of humour Wilde had.

The Baptist is a lifeless figure, a mere machine for uttering recorded sounds, but Herod is alive from the crown of his head to the soles of his feet, and there is dusty life in Herodias. How sharp is the impression we receive of a disillusioned woman when, after Herod has been babbling about the moon, she confounds his drunken noise with a single realistic speech:

> HEROD: The moon has a strange look to-night. Has she not a strange look? She is like a mad woman, a mad woman who is seeking everywhere for lovers. She is naked too. She is quite naked. The clouds are seeking to clothe her nakedness, but she will not let them. She reels through the clouds like a drunken woman.... I am sure she is looking for lovers.... Does she not reel like a drunken woman? She is like a mad woman, is she not?
>
> HERODIAS: No. The moon is like the moon, that is all. Let us go within....

The end of the play is less impressive than the beginning and middle. It is garrulous and over-mannered, and the final scene is abrupt, as if Wilde had not known how to finish his play and, in despair, had suddenly decided to slay Salomé. The story does not follow the Bible with any fidelity. Both Matthew and Mark state that Herodias instructed her daughter to ask for the Baptist's head on a charger, but in Wilde's play Salomé herself conceives the idea, because she has been repelled by John and is still lusting for him. If she cannot have him alive, she will have him dead. As the

Negro Executioner lifts up the shield on which the Baptist's head is lying she cries:

"Ah! thou wouldst not suffer me to kiss thy mouth, Jokanaan. Well! I will kiss it now. I will bite it with my teeth as one bites a ripe fruit. Yes, I will kiss thy mouth, Jokanaan. I said it; did I not say it? I said it. Ah! I will kiss it now. . . . Oh, how I loved thee! I love thee yet, Jokanaan. I love thee only. . . . I am athirst for thy beauty: I am hungry for thy body; and neither wine nor fruits can appease my desire. What shall I do now, Jokanaan? Neither the floods nor the great waters can quench my passion."

The passion seems to have been as swift as it was violent, for there is no suggestion either in *Salomé* or in the Synoptic Gospels that she had ever set eyes on him before the night of the dance. Indeed, Matthew and Mark give no hint that she ever saw him alive.

The play is full of mannered nonsense and banalities, especially when the moon is mentioned, and the repetitions exhaust the reader's patience; as Salomé's do when she describes Jokanaan's eyes:

"It is his eyes above all that are terrible. They are like black holes burned by torches in a Tyrian tapestry. . . ."

a description which is pure affectation.

"They are like black caverns where dragons dwell. They are like the black caverns of Egypt in which the dragons make their lairs. They are like black lakes troubled by fantastic moons. . . ."

There seems no reason why Salomé should cease from finding resemblance to the Baptist's eyes. And very little reason why she should have started. But the play, despite its numerous defects, has power, and is among the few works Wilde wrote which are worth preserving.

Its fate at first was unfortunate. In publication, it was savagely denounced by practically all the critics in Britain; the "one exception", according to Ross, being William Archer, who gave it high praise, finding it superior to Maeterlinck's work. "There is", he wrote in *Black and White* on 11th March 1893, "far more depth and body in Mr. Wilde's work than in Maeterlinck's. His characters are men and women, not filmy shapes of mist and moonshine.

His properties are more various and less conventional. His . . . palette is infinitely richer. Maeterlinck paints in washes of water-colour. Mr. Wilde attains to depth and brilliancy of oils. *Salomé* has all the qualities of a great historical picture, pedantry and conventionality excepted." It was, perhaps, the rationalist, rather than the Scottish puritan, in Archer who wrote that review. Ross was more emphatically enthusiastic about it than Archer. *Salomé*, he declares, is "the most powerful and perfect of all Oscar's dramas", a statement which bewilders Frank Harris, to whom the play's cold lust is repulsive.

It was not publicly performed until the 11th of February 1896, when Wilde was in Reading Gaol. Lugné-Poë produced it at the Théâtre de l'Œuvre in Paris. The reception, according to Ross, was cold, but the fact that it was performed at all gave the unhappy prisoner some pleasure. There was no other performance in Wilde's lifetime. Two years after his death, it was produced, by Reinhardt, on 15th November 1902, at the Kleines Theater in Berlin, where it ran for two hundred nights, "an unprecedented run for the Prussian capital". The play has been popular in Germany ever since; a fact which, perhaps, the history of that country in the two World Wars, and especially in the Second, helps to explain. The strain of morbid sadism in *Salomé* must have been congenial to the German nature. In May 1905 it was performed twice in London by a society, now defunct, called the New Stage Club at the Bijou Theatre, Archer Street; and in June 1906 further performances were given at the National Sporting Club by the Literary Theatre Society: performances which were decorated by Charles Ricketts. In 1911 a private performance of the original version was given at the Court Theatre, in Sloane Square, where it was revived in April 1918. It was performed at the Gate Theatre in May 1931, and in that year a full licence to perform it was granted. The play was then produced in October at the Savoy. The majority of these performances, it will be noticed, were given in private, that is to say, without the sanction of the Lord Chamberlain. They were not open to the general paying public, but only to subscribing members of the societies which gave them. These audiences, being eclectic and few, were no indication of popular favour. The play has not been done in the normal course of theatrical production since 1931, and its chances of survival on the stage seem slight.

Two operas have been composed on Salomé: one by Richard Strauss, which has been performed all over the world; the second by "a young French naval officer, Lieutenant Mariotte, a native of Lyons". The German opera was performed for the first time at Dresden in 1905, the French at Paris in 1911; and on 8th December 1910 the Strauss was produced at Covent Garden, Sir Thomas Beecham conducting. It was produced in New York in January 1907, but further performances were forbidden for many years. Such is the history of this singular play, which brought no profit to its author, who never saw it performed.

27

ONE other work of this period in Wilde's life remains to be noticed: the volume of essays, entitled *Intentions*. It contains four essays, one of which is in two parts. These are *The Decay of Lying*; *Pen, Pencil and Poison*; *The Critic as Artist*, Parts I and II; and *The Truth of Masks*. They are excellent entertainment, but no more than that. A grain or two of wisdom is buried in a heap of chaff.

If we are to take *Intentions* as seriously as it is taken by Wilde's admirers, then we must refuse it the place they claim for it. *The Decay of Lying* is full of fallacies and wit and graceful writing. There is a disturbing hint in the first page of the author's changing moral character. It appears in the complaint against Nature, the praise given to Art. "My own experience", says Vivian—the essay is in the form of a duologue—who may be regarded as Wilde, "is that the more we study Art, the less we care for Nature", a statement with which none of the world's supreme artists would have agreed. "What Art really reveals to us is Nature's lack of design, her curious crudities, her extraordinary monotony, her absolutely unfinished condition. . . . Art is our spirited protest, our gallant attempt to teach Nature her proper place." Such is the specious stuff with which Vivian starts his long harangue of superficialities. He ends his opening with a remark which could not have been made by a man with any powers of observation. "As for the infinite variety of Nature, that is pure myth. It is not to be found in Nature herself. It resides in the imagination, or fancy, or cultivated blindness of the man who looks at her." Apart from the flat silliness of this statement, might we not, accepting for the moment Wilde's argument, retort to him that the "monotony" which he finds in Nature also "resides in the imagination, or fancy, or cultivated blindness of the man who looks at her"? We may go metaphysically mad and deny that Nature exists, that all we describe as Nature resides in our imagination and is a myth.

But what an amazing myth it is which persuades almost the whole of humanity of its reality. Nor is it only mankind which is deceived. All living creatures appear to live in this delusion. Are the cattle in the fields deceiving themselves with mythical grass or living on a lie when they prefer one field to another? How infinitely various Nature is! There is not one shade of green, but many shades: green that is almost blue, green that is almost black, green that is almost yellow, light green and dark green, the green of pine trees and larches, the green of grass and apples and primrose leaves and falling water. If a man who had been born blind were suddenly to receive his sight, he would feel afraid of the variety of Nature. How, he might cry in distress, am I to learn all these varieties of one thing? I shall never remember all the sorts of green there are in this bewildering world! . . .

Wilde's references to Nature are few and almost invariably false. They are such as we might expect from an incorrigibly urban-minded man who has seen some pictures of it, but has seldom or never directly observed it. His affectations were inclined to shrivel before natural facts. Therefore, he disregarded or denied natural facts. In *De Profundis* he imagines Jesus advising men not to trouble themselves about their affairs, and seeks to enforce his surmise by saying, "The birds don't, so why should man!" This is ornithological, as well as economic, nonsense. Birds, whose variety should have cured him of his heresy about Nature's monotony, bother a great deal about their affairs. Their lives are a long, unending preoccupation, and their determination to perpetuate their species amounts almost to mania. The whole business of nesting, apart from the constant search for food for their young, is exhaustive effort. Their variety is amazing, even in a single species. How various in size and colour are ducks and geese. There is not one kind of hawk or tit, but many kinds. Nature is not only various, but whimsical. Why did she put that dab of red on the sea-gull's yellow beak and four white spots on its black tail? Why did she make puffins look like the White-eyed Kaffir, Chirgwin? For the fun of it, perhaps.

The Decay of Lying contains Wilde's celebrated paradox that Nature imitates Art. Nature had no idea that her mists and fogs were beautiful until James McNeill Whistler arrived in London to tell her so, nor had it ever occurred to her that girls with long ivory throats and strange square-cut jaws and loosened shadowy hair were lovely until Dante Gabriel Rossetti painted them.

> A great artist invents a type, and Life tries to copy it, to reproduce it in a popular form, like an enterprising publisher. Neither Holbein nor Vandyck found in England what they have given us. They brought their types with them, and Life with her keen imitative faculty set herself to supply the master with models. . . .

We may interrupt him here to enquire whether Nature had made Henry the Eighth before or after Holbein's arrival in England, to enquire, too, *where* Holbein and Vandyck found the types they are said to have brought with them to England? Wilde follows this amusing stuff with an assertion which might have impressed Betsy Prig and Mrs. Gamp, but leaves the rest of us jeering and derisive. Here it is in all its simple fatuity:

> The Greeks, with their quick artistic instinct, understood this, and set in the bride's chamber the statue of Hermes or of Apollo, that she might bear children as lovely as the works of art that she looked at in her rapture or her pain. They knew that Life gains from Art not merely spirituality, depth of thought and feeling, soul-turmoil or soul-peace, but that she can form herself on the very lines and colours of Art, and can reproduce the dignity of Phidias as well as the grace of Praxiteles. Hence came their objection to realism. They disliked it on purely social

grounds, and they were perfectly right. We try to improve the conditions of the race by means of good air, free sunlight, wholesome water, and hideous bare buildings for the better housing of the lower orders. But these things merely produce health, they do not produce beauty. . . .

The mother of Socrates must have omitted to order a statue of Hermes or Apollo for her bridal-chamber on the night she conceived her son. Were there no ugly men and plain women in ancient Greece? How is it that there are so many unsightly people if we can get beautiful men and women by placing fine statuary in conspicuous positions by our beds before we start our marital ardours? The bride about to be fertilised, has only to gaze in rapture at the reproduction of a marble effigy, to get herself with beautiful child! . . . This is the nonsense chattered by midwives. Its banality is evident in the statement that a well-directed community produces, not beauty, but health. As if health were not vital to beauty.

The wit of the essay is not ample enough to conceal its shallowness. The argument about fogs could be supported if it were confined to the statement that artists call our attention to beauty which we have overlooked, make us aware of beauty that we have failed to recognise; but Wilde is not content with that sensible, if obvious assertion; he must indulge in a bout of bad paradox.

There may have been fogs for centuries in London. I daresay there were. But no one saw them, and so we do not know anything about them. They did not exist until Art had invented them. Now, it must be admitted, fogs are carried to excess. They have become the mere mannerism of a clique, and the exaggerated realism of their method gives dull people bronchitis. Where the cultured catch an effect, the uncultured catch cold.

The wit in the final sentences is not enhanced by the gaseous folly in the first. Wilde was cutting Nature, and, like the snob he was, had to find a paradoxical excuse for his unmannerly behaviour. He was capable even of vulgar surrender to conventional disapproval of rebellious and innovating people. What, apart from the wit, is there in the passage towards the end of the essay in which Vivian makes remarks that would be received with ringing cheers at a meeting of fundamentalists? "As for the Church", he says:

"I cannot conceive anything better for the culture of a country than the presence in it of a body of men whose duty it is to believe in the supernatural, to perform daily miracles, and to keep alive that mythopoetic faculty which is so essential for the imagination. But in the English Church a man succeeds, not through his capacity for belief, but through his capacity for disbelief. Ours is the only Church where the sceptic stands at the altar, and where St. Thomas is regarded as the ideal apostle. Many a worthy clergyman, who passes his life in admirable works of kindly charity, lives and dies unnoticed and unknown; but it is sufficient, for some shallow uneducated passman out of either University to get up in his pulpit and express doubts about Noah's Ark, or Balaam's ass, or Jonah and the Whale, for half London to flock to hear him, and to sit open-mouthed in rapt admiration of his superb intellect. The growth of common sense in the English Church is a thing very much to be regretted."

One can hear the nuns and deaconesses and district visitors and emotional curates and routine rectors smiting their hands together in fierce approval of these puerile phrases. We need only a reference to the worthy clergyman's white hairs to feel that the play to the gallery is complete.

Pen, Pencil and Poison requires no consideration. It is pestilential stuff if it is taken as any other than a squib in doubtful taste. It may, perhaps, be enjoyed as a parody of a chapter in Samuel Smile's *Self-Help*, but such jokes are wry: murder is not amusing. The life of a light-hearted poisoner, such as Wainewright, is unsuitable matter for light-hearted essays. Strychnine and banter do not go well together. The reader of *Pen, Pencil and Poison* suddenly feels appalled by Wilde's bright remarks on the fun of being murdered by a callous scoundrel, as appalled as he would feel if a clown were to perform his antics at a funeral. But Wilde was not a man of much feeling, and he was dropping down the drain. His Witches' Sabbaths had begun.

The third essay, *The Critic as Artist*, is the most important piece in the book. It is a *tour de force*, marred in places by long bursts of empty eloquence. Wilde's mania for words and phrases occasionally overpowers him, and he submerges his meaning in a flood of waste water. But the argument, on the whole, is good, and it is sustained with wit and learning. Wilde was not, it must again be said, a man deficient in scholarship. He was, in some degree, over-educated. He could not control his scholarship, but must always parade it. But he possessed it—or ought we to say was possessed by it? He exhibits it in *The Critic as Artist* to excess. The midnight oil stinks, so that we feel like crying out with Pope in complaint of

> The bookful blockhead, ignorantly read,
> With loads of learned rubbish in his head.

Too often, Wilde whirls his knowledge about. The reader becomes impatient and either turns the page in haste or puts down the book. But when he curbs his undisciplined fancy and gives it athletic exercise, attention is held.

This is the essay in which Wilde makes a reference to Browning which has long been widely misunderstood. "Meredith is a prose Browning, and so is Browning." That is as much as the majority of people know of the matter, and they conclude that Wilde was belittling Browning. But such is far from the fact. The statement occurs in a long passage which is, for the most part, a panegyric of Browning, for whom Wilde felt a deep, but qualified, respect. Some of his adverse remarks are unconvincing. He appreciated the poet, but did not appreciate him sufficiently. "Taken as a whole," he says in that superior manner which earned him many enemies, "the man was great. He did not belong to the Olympians, and had all the incompleteness of the Titan. He did not survey, and it was but rarely that he could sing. His work is marred by struggle, violence and effort, and he passed not from emotion to form, but from thought to chaos. Still, he was great." The greater part of that impertinent passage, a passage almost insolent and certainly offensive when written by a minimum poet about a poet of genius, is plain punk. Luckily, the rest of the reference is, on the whole, free from such impertinence, and is a sincere tribute to Browning.

> Yes, he was great: and though he turned language into ignoble clay, he made from it men and women that live. He is the most Shakespearian creature since Shakespeare. If Shakespeare could sing with

myriad lips, Browning could stammer through a thousand mouths. Even now, as I am speaking, and speaking not against him but for him, there glides through the room the pageant of his persons. There, creeps Fra Lippo Lippi with his cheeks still burning from some girl's hot kiss. There, stands dread Saul with the lordly male-sapphires gleaming in his turban. Mildred Tresham is there, and the Spanish monk, yellow with hatred, and Blougram, and Ben Ezra, and the Bishop of St. Praxted's. The spawn of Setebos gibbers in the corner, and Sebald, hearing Pippa pass by, looks on Ottima's haggard face, and loathes her and his own sin, and himself. Pale as the white satin of his doublet, the melancholy king watches with dreamy treacherous eyes too loyal Strafford pass forth to his doom, and Andrea shudders as he hears his cousin's whistle in the garden, and bids his perfect wife go down. Yes, Browning was great. And as what will he be remembered? As a poet? Ah, not as a poet! He will be remembered as a writer of fiction, as the most supreme writer of fiction, it may be, that we have ever had. His sense of dramatic situation was unrivalled, and, if he could not answer his own problems, he could at least put problems forth, and what more should an artist do? Considered from the point of view of a creator of character he ranks next to him who made Hamlet. Had he been articulate, he might have sat beside him. The only man who can touch the hem of his garment is George Meredith. Meredith is a prose Browning, and so is Browning. He used poetry as a medium for writing in prose.

There can be no doubt of the respect, amounting almost to veneration, in this passage, but there can be very considerable doubt of the critical faculty. Why is it, we may well enquire, that Browning, if he was an unrivalled master of dramatic situation, a creator of character second only to Shakespeare, failed to write an actable play? It was not for want of trying. Browning desired to be a dramatist as ardently as Henry James, and went so far in his desire as to describe himself, in *A Light Woman*, as "Robert Browning, you writer of plays", but like James he was baulked of his desire. Neither of them had the sense of the stage which a dramatist must possess. James was a hopeless candidate for the theatre. A man with so unwieldy a mind as his, full of involved words that could not easily be disentangled from his laborious style, had no hope of subduing the stage to his will. It was as much as he could do to gain a hold on the novel. Browning, indeed, had a sense of dramatic situation, and he might have become a dramatist if he had applied himself more closely to the technique of the play. His words leap from life. His people are alive and definite. He seizes the essential points. But he failed utterly to make himself a master of the stage, as anyone may perceive by reading that broken-backed piece, *King Victor and King Charles.*

He was supremely a poet, full of lyric, a man so possessed of lovely words that he could make a simple statement of fact, *Beautiful Evelyn Hope is dead,* sound like a song.

Wilde is so pleased with his trick of assembling a poet's characters in a purple passage that he repeats it several times in *The Critic as Artist,* as when he sees Helen in Troy, re-living her life and loves, or walks through the Inferno with Dante. His tricks are so often employed that we are irritated by them, and tempted to discredit the substance because the tricks are tedious. We pounce too eagerly on his baseless beliefs. When he makes Gilbert, another name for himself, assert that "no poet sings because he must sing. At least, no great poet does. A great poet sings because he chooses to sing", our impulse is to deride him with the question, "But why does the poet *choose* to sing?" Are not *choose* and *must* here the same? We feel equally derisive when we are told that the artist, like the critic, "does not even require for the perfection of his art the finest materials. Anything will serve his purpose." Why, then, does the sculptor prefer marble to clay, clay to putty? Why does the poet prefer this word to that word? Why does the painter prefer oil to water, and choose colours when black and white would serve? Is there no difference between the violin and the Jew's harp? Is a barrel-organ as good as a Bechstein or an Erard grand? Is an orchestra of two fiddles, a piano and a fife equal to the Philadelphia Orchestra? Are Toscanini and Beecham no more than a conductor on a pier?

Such shallow utterances as these forbid us to look on Wilde with as much favour in these essays as we should; for, indeed, there is wisdom here, although he tries to hide it under a flippant manner. His main argument, on the necessity of great criticism to the production of great art, is profoundly true, though he overstates it. "The higher criticism", he says, "is the record of one's own soul", and the reader likes to believe that he, so frequently and so justly accused of stealing other men's thoughts and passing them off as his own, was the original begetter of that epigram, and that Anatole France filched it from him. It is plain to the most superficial student of the drama that it was at its worst in times when criticism was feeble and ineffective, just as monarchs are on the point of deposal or decapitation when courtiers are most flattering and complaints are scarcely heard. It is not the strong kings who lose their thrones, but the weak ones, nor is it the kings who caused the wrongs who suffer for them: it is the bewildered and well-meaning, but indecisive and helpless sovereigns who lose their heads.

Gilbert has scarcely uttered his nonsense about poets not singing because they must, when he delivers this wisdom:

> The longer one studies life and literature, the more strongly one feels that behind everything that is wonderful stands the individual, and that it is not the moment that makes the man, but the man who creates the age.

A few sentences before his shallow pronouncement that an artist is indifferent to his materials, that "anything will serve his purpose", he delivers a profound speech on progress and materialism. "Men are the slaves of words", he says. "They rage against Materialism, as they call it, forgetting that there has been no material improvement that has not spiritualised the world", a statement which contradicts his outcry against a mechanised society, "and that there have been few, if any, spiritual awakenings that have not wasted the world's faculties in barren hopes, and fruitless aspirations, and empty or trammelling creeds". Would Jesus, we may well wonder, have sought His death on the cross had he foreseen the Bishop of Hippo or the Church of Rome in the age of the Borgian Popes or Calvin or Saint Bartholomew's Eve or the Inquisition or Smithfield's fires? Wilde follows this statement with a profound passage in which there is not a false or flippant note:

> What is termed Sin is an essential element of progress. Without it the world would stagnate, or grow old, or become colourless. By its curiosity, Sin increases the experience of the race. Through its intensified assertion of individualism, it saves us from monotony of types. In its rejection of the current notions of morality, it is one with the higher

ethics. And as for virtues! What are the virtues? Nature, M. Renan tells us, cares very little about chastity, and it may be that it is to the shame of the Magdalen, and not to their own purity, that the Lucretias of modern life owe their freedom from stain. . . .

as, indeed, Lecky, a very different sort of Trinity College, Dublin, man from Wilde, has pointed out. Our virgins walk about in safety and with little fear of rape because they are protected by the harlots at the corner of the street.

When we consider how the world has been enriched by bastards can we feel certain that rigid regularity is worth the trouble it costs, or that a child coldly conceived in lawful marriage is more likely to be fine than one conceived in unpremeditated passion? Unscrupulous Edmund, in *King Lear*, is not, perhaps, the best authority on this point, although his ability is superior to that of his legitimate brother, but his opinion is worth consideration since his character, as he himself asserted, was not dependent upon the date of his conception.

"Why bastard? Wherefore base?
When my dimensions are as well compact,
My mind as generous, and my shape as true
As honest madam's issue? Why brand they us
With base? with baseness? bastardy? base, base?
Who, in the lusty stealth of nature, take
More composition and fierce quality
Than doth, within a dull, stale, tired bed,
Go to the creating a whole tribe of fops
Got 'tween asleep and wake?"

Bastardy has not proved a barrier to advancement in any age, and a surprising number of eminent people, especially in royal circles, have been by-blows. The prejudice against illegitimate birth is, indeed, a comparatively recent one. The people of the Middle Ages did not feel it. They regarded it as slightly irregular, but no more than that; and a bastard, broadly speaking, was at few disadvantages in comparison with a legitimate child. The Emperor Constantine the Great, who first established Christianity politically, was the bastard son of a barmaid. William the Conqueror was a bastard. So was the Empress Elizabeth of Russia. Charles Martel, who saved France for Christendom by defeating the

Moors between Tours and Poitiers in 732 and driving the Saracens out of Burgundy and Languedoc in 737, was "the natural son", to use the quaint expression with which we soften the word *bastard*, as if all other sons were unnatural, of the mayor of the palace of the later Merovingian kings. Charlemagne, who is himself said to have been illegitimate, was the father of several bastards by several concubines, as well as begetting children by four wives. He was a devoted father, loving his daughters so dearly that he would not permit them to marry. They, therefore, contracted irregular unions, fortified by their father's example. Rotrud had a son by Count Roderic of Maine, and Bertha bedded with a holy man of God, the Abbot Angilbert of St. Riquier, and bore him two boys. No one seems to have thought a penny the worse of them for that. Alcuin, indeed, praised Rotrud for her virtue. Genseric, the King of the Vandals, and Manfred, the King of Sicily, and Zwentibold, the King of Lorraine, and Don John of Austria, and Jean Dunois, the French Commander who was the friend of Jeanne d'Arc, were all bastards. So were Boccaccio, who wrote *The Decameron*; Erasmus—his father was a priest—whose part in the Reformation must have exceeded Luther's, for he had more mind than Luther, if he had had as stout a heart; Patrick Hamilton, a martyr whose influence in reforming the religion of Scotland was profound; Alexandre Dumas *fils*, the novelist; Alexander Hamilton, one of America's greatest statesmen; Field-Marshal Sir John Burgoyne, whose father was a celebrated British General in the War of Independence; Jerome Cardan, a notable Italian philosopher and mathematician; d'Alembert, a great French mathematician; Viscount Beresford, who won a peerage for successful soldiering; Jacques Delille, the greatest French poet of his age; Bernard O'Higgins, the first President of Chili; Sir Henry Stanley, the explorer who found Livingstone; William Elphinstone, Bishop of Aberdeen, and Dr. Alexander, Archbishop of St. Andrews; James Macie Smithson, a distinguished English chemist and mineralogist who founded the Smithsonian Institution at Washington; Henry Casey, the poet and musician, who wrote *Sally in Our Alley*; James Ramsay MacDonald, the first Labour Prime Minister of Great Britain; and two popular novelists, Marie Corelli and Edgar Wallace. Abraham Lincoln boasted that his mother was a bastard. Saint Augustine dearly loved his concubine, and was devoted to her son. He is human only when he remembers her, and almost makes us like him when he cries to God:

> "*Da mihi castitatem et continentiam, sed noli modo.*"
> "Give me chastity and continency, but not yet."

Shakespeare had to marry in haste; Descartes, the founder of modern philosophy, never married, but, although he was neither amorous nor physically very potent, begot a daughter without benefit of clergy, whose death, when she was five, deeply distressed him. He was a good father to his bastard. The same cannot be said for Henrik Ibsen, who, when he was an apothecary's assistant at Grimstad, got an illegitimate son by a servant girl, who was his senior by ten years. The fact that he had to maintain this child for fourteen years galled him so much that he moaned bitterly about it in *Peer Gynt*; and he ceased, as soon as the fourteen years had ended, to take the slightest interest in the boy who is said to have borne a remarkable physical resemblance to his father. His intellectual parts, however, were unnotable, and he became the keeper of a lighthouse. Tolstoy, too, a man of extraordinary vigour and virility, fathered a son on the wife of one of his serfs. This pretty young peasant, Aksinya Bazykin, won his love for a long time, but it did not make any difference to her social position: she continued to be a charwoman at Yasnaya Polyana, where, indeed, she was seen scrubbing a floor by Tolstoy's eighteen-year-old wife, Sonya. For Tolstoy, who had a morbid desire for confession, had noted his frequent copulations with Aksinya in his diary, and had given it to his bride to read! Aksinya's son, Timofei, was employed as a coachman to one of Tolstoy's sons by Sonya. Tolstoy seems to have been as indifferent to his bastards as Ibsen was to his. Russian feeling about adultery was easy. Professor Ernest J. Simmons in his remarkable work, *Leo Tolstoy*, informs his readers that Tolstoy's Aunt Pelageya, a religiously-minded woman and "herself one of the purest of beings . . . strongly urged him to have relations with a married woman, on the principle that nothing so forms a young man as intimacy with a woman of good breeding!"

But perhaps the most remarkable proof that bastardy is no bar to success is to be found in the history of Marshal Saxe, the French soldier and illegitimate son of Augustus the Strong, Elector of Saxony and King of Poland, who is alleged to have had only one legitimate child among his three hundred offspring. Bastardy may almost be said to have been regularised by Saxe and his descendants. His illegitimate daughter married Count Horn, a natural son of Louis XV. The son of this marriage, Maurice Dupin de Francueil, married only just in time to save his daughter, Amandine, from being bastardised. She was born a month after her parents' marriage, and she became world-renowned as "George Sand". Her marriage was a failure, and she became the mistress of several celebrated men, including Chopin and Alfred de Musset. All her children, however, were legitimate: she conceived none by her lovers.

In citing these names, chosen for their diversity, we are not contradicting our faith in family life or our belief that monogamy, if mitigated by extra-marital relations, is likely to prove the most convenient form of sexual relationship; though it is well to remember that some thinkers, Bertrand Russell, for example, do not share this belief. Russell, in *The Scientific Outlook*, foresees a time when one man will serve five women: a prospect which recalls the verse in Isaiah iv. 1, foretelling the day when "seven women shall take hold of one man, saying, We will eat our own bread, and wear our own apparel: only let us be called by thy name, to take away our reproach".

But even Russell, bleak though his foresight seems to be, admires the monogamous ideal, of a man and a woman maturing together in the love of their children.

Our purpose in this recital of famous bastards is only to point our moral, that marriage, throughout the ages, has been a series of experiments in search of a happy way of living and begetting; and that no one can assert dogmatically that we have yet found the best system. The conditions of contemporary life exclude large numbers of women not only from sexual experience, although this exclusion is steadily declining, but, more importantly, from maternal experience; and many of these women are of a quality which makes them highly suitable to be mothers. Mankind will not long continue to allow an arbitrary rule of marriage to sterilise women who will themselves, as their economic independence becomes more assured, insist on their right to carnal concurrence which is fruitful. It is, surely, better that four million women should each have two children, than that two million women should each have four, and the remaining two million have none? The contraction of fathers and mothers to a small number of breeders, if the views of Russell should be fulfilled, must increase enormously the inbreeding from which the world still suffers; and since it is evident from all history that people have no desire to disappear from the earth, we may believe that they will resort to any system of sexual relationship which will secure the healthiest race. The age of the virgin is ending: the age of the mother, married or unmarried, is beginning. Barrenness satisfies nobody, nor do we now believe that many people are naturally sterile, since the fact is that many childless couples have, on separating and making fresh marriages, conceived and begotten babies. The concubine may yet become as honoured a member of the family as she was in the days of Sarah and Hagar and Abraham; and a naturally barren woman will find maternal satisfaction in tending children her husband has begotten on another woman's body. But not, we may surmise, until she feels sure, after diverse experiments, that she is sterile. The Spartans, indeed, encouraged a childless married woman to take a lover in the hope that he would be more successful than her husband in fertilising her. She was not to consider herself barren until she had established the fact by several experiments in mates. Polygamy has fallen into disfavour, partly for economic reasons and partly because it has hitherto degraded women; but when women are able to support themselves and their infants, and are no longer dependent on keepers, it may revive.

Wilde puts wise words into his Gilbert's mouth on the necessity of experiment and revolt against rancid conventions. "Charity," he says, continuing the passage cited on pages 148-9, "as even those of whose religion it makes a formal part have been compelled to acknowledge, creates a multitude of evils.

The mere existence of conscience, that faculty of which people prate so much nowadays, and are so ignorantly proud, is a sign of our imperfect development. It must be merged in instinct before we become fine. Self-denial is simply a method by which man arrests his progress, and self-sacrifice a survival of the mutilation of the savage part of that old worship of pain which is so terrible a factor in the history of the world, and which even now makes its victims day by day, and has its altars in the land. Virtues! Who knows what virtues are? Not you. Not I. Not anyone. It is well for our vanity that we slay the criminal, for if we suffered him to live he might show us what we had gained by his crime. It is well for his peace that the saint goes to his martyrdom. He is spared the sight of the horror of his harvest."

Is he here not dealing in that speculation which has vexed the minds of centuries of theologians: the question whether Judas Iscariot is to be canonised or condemned, whether Pontius Pilate and Caiaphas are entitled to haloes or the hangman's noose? If there had been no betrayal, would there have been any redemption? There could not have been a crucifixion if there had been no condemnation. Was it the will of God that His son should die in agony and shame? If it was, then Iscariot and Caiaphas and Pontius Pilate were the instruments of the almighty will and deserve neither reproach nor praise. It is when Wilde speaks in such accents as these, that our sense of deprivation when he went down the drain becomes acute. There was a high belief in his mind, belief which was cancelled by his surrender to the decadence of his period. We have caught glimpses of it in *The Soul of Man Under Socialism*, and in these passages from *The Critic as Artist* we can catch further glimpses. Why did this mind become depraved? Was it his fault or his parents'? Were they, too, victims of parents that were capriciously imposed upon them? There was a mind in Wilde which he deliberately debased. It was not a great mind, as the mind of Socrates and the mind of Shakespeare were great, but it had elements of greatness and it was stimulating to thought, especially the thought of disagreement and dissent. How deplorable it is that the man who could write this provocative passage in the second part of *The Critic as Artist* was preparing to throw himself into the sewer, to become the companion of stable-boys and unemployable clerks and degenerate public schoolboy pimps in foul adventures in unlawful sex:

> That the desire to do good to others produced a plentiful crop of prigs is the least of the evils of which it is the cause. The prig is a very interesting psychological study, and though of all poses a moral pose is the most offensive, still to have a pose at all is something. It is a formal recognition of the importance of treating life from a definite and reasoned standpoint. That Humanitarian Sympathy wars against Nature, by securing the survival of the failure, may make the man of science loathe its facile virtues. The political economist may cry out against it for putting the improvident on the same level as the provident, and so robbing life of its strongest, because most sordid, incentive to industry. But, in the eyes of the thinker, the real harm that emotional sympathy does is that it limits knowledge, and so prevents us from solving any single social problem. We are trying to stave off the coming crisis, the coming revolution as my friends the Fabians call it, by means of doles and alms. Well, when the revolution or crisis arrives, we shall be powerless because we shall know nothing. . . . What we want are unpractical people who see beyond the moment, and think beyond the day. Those who try to lead the people can only do so by following the mob. It is through the voice of one crying in the wilderness that the way of the gods must be prepared.

He becomes too brilliantly paradoxical, perhaps, in the remainder of the passage, but how shrewd he is, how closely he comes to the essential point.

> It takes a thoroughly selfish age, like our own, to deify self-sacrifice. It takes a thoroughly grasping age, such as that in which we live, to set above the fine intellectual virtues, those shallow and emotional virtues that are an immediate practical benefit to itself. They miss their aim, too, these philanthropists and sentimentalists of our day, who are always chattering to one about one's duty to one's neighbour. For the development of the race depends on the development of the individual, and where self-culture has ceased to be the ideal, the intellectual standard is instantly lowered, and, often, ultimately lost. If you meet a man at dinner who has spent his life in educating himself—a rare type in our time, I admit, but still occasionally to be met with—you rise from the table richer, and conscious that a high ideal has for a moment touched and sanctified your days. But oh, my dear Ernest, to sit next to a man who has spent his life trying to educate others! What a dread-

ful experience that is! How appalling is that ignorance which is the inevitable result of the fatal habit of imparting opinions! How limited in range the creature's mind proves to be! How it wearies us, and must weary himself, with its endless repetitions and sickly reiteration! How lacking it is in any element of intellectual growth! In what a vicious circle it moves. . . . People say that the schoolmaster is abroad. I wish to goodness he were. But the type of which, after all, he is only one, and certainly the least important of the representatives, seems to me to be really dominating our lives; and just as the philanthropist is the nuisance of the ethical sphere, so the nuisance of the intellectual sphere is the man who is so occupied in trying to educate others, that he has never had time to educate himself. No, Ernest, self-culture is the true ideal of man.

That interesting and diverting statement is far from being the entire truth, but it is enough of it to give every pedagogue occasion for pause. "It is so easy for people to have sympathy with suffering. It is so difficult for them to have sympathy with thought." How wittily he discourses on the need for bias and passion in opinion. "It is only an auctioneer who can equally and impartially admire all schools of Art." The great artist cannot criticise other artists, cannot criticise himself, because he is conscious only of an urgent ambition, whose origin he does not know, to put down what he sees or wishes to see. Few people are so indifferent to great work by other people as great artists, nor are many men so lacking in discernment about their brothers' work as all the eminent. The mountains do not nod to each other over the heads of the little hills: they are so wrapt about by their mists that they cannot even see each other. Tolstoy esteemed Guy de Maupassant far beyond Shakespeare, whom, indeed, he did not esteem at all. He thought Ibsen was mad, and Ibsen called him a fool. The gods do not tolerate each other; for I the Lord Thy God am a jealous god, having no other gods before me.

It is because the artist cannot criticise himself or others that the critic must appear: he is the artist who finds the point of contact between the creative artists and discovers the unity of the arts.

Wilde demands intensive critical culture. It is idle to demand creative ability, since that cometh like the wind which bloweth where it listeth. No Government can supply the world with a single Milton or Michelangelo or Molière or Mozart. These are like Melchisidec, without father or mother, without ancestors or descendants. But it is possible to make a world in which minds may increase themselves without avoidable impediments, in which every individual is encouraged to exercise his faculty of perception to its uttermost power. We cannot provide people with brains, but we can prevent the stultification of the brains they possess by adverse conditions. The enemy of our mental development is emotional debauch. "They have their Peace Societies, so dear to the sentimentalists, and their proposals for unarmed International Arbitration so popular among those who have never read history." How keenly that sentence strikes our thoughts when we recall the luckless League of Nations! "But mere emotional sympathy will not do. It is too variable, and too closely connected with the passions; and a board of arbitrators who, for the general welfare of the race, are to be deprived of the power of putting their decisions into execution, will not be of much avail. There is only one worse thing than Injustice, and that is Justice without her sword in her hand. When Right is not Might, it is Evil."

Criticism will annihilate race-prejudice, by insisting upon the unity of the human mind in the variety of its forms. If we are tempted to make war upon another nation, we shall remember that we are seeking to destroy an element of our own culture, and possibly its most important element. As long as war is regarded as wicked, it will always have its fascination. When it is looked upon as vulgar, it will cease to be popular. The change will, of course, be slow, and people will not be conscious of it. They will not say, "We will not war against France because her prose is perfect", but because the prose of France is perfect they will not hate the land. Intellectual criticism will bind Europe together in bonds far closer than those that can be forged by shopman or sentimentalist. It will give us the peace that springs from understanding.

The foolish lie, that he had no scholarship, with which his enemies aspersed him, requires no further refutal than is provided in *The Truth of Masks*, the final essay of *Intentions*, where his scholarship is easily and gracefully made manifest. Wilde had the Irishman's love of Shakespeare, a love which, despite his sharp complaints of the plays, Bernard Shaw felt as deeply as any other Irishman: a love which springs from the fact that the speech which loiters on Irish lips is not, as pedants aver, Gaelic translated into English, but the remains of Elizabethan English, and is to be heard most beautifully on the islands of its western shores. You may hear in common use in Ulster, and no doubt elsewhere in Ireland, locutions that are to be found in Tyndale's translation of the Bible, spelt as the Ulsterman pronounces them to-day: locutions that are probably as old as Chaucer. Here are a few examples:

Consayte for conceit.
Dissaytefulness for deceitfulness.
Heed for head.
Honde for hand.
Wemen for women.
Kaye for key.
Bet for beat.
Powred for poured.
Platted for plaited.
Fowrtene for fourteen.
Deef for deaf.

One of Tyndale's locutions is a typical Ulster turn of speech: *heerd tell* for *heard of* in the last verse of the sixth chapter of St. Mark's Gospel. He spells the word *winds* as it is still pronounced in Northern Ireland: *wyndes*. It is not the short-*i*'d winds that blow in Ulster, but winds with long *i*'s. Sir E. K. Chambers, in *The Elizabethan Stage* (vol. iii, page 22), notes an edition, dated 1630, of Thomas Dekker's play, *The Honest Whore*, in which the last word of the title is spelt *Hoore*, exactly as it is commonly pronounced in Ulster to-day.

Those who belittled Wilde's learning would have had ample cause for self-appreciation had they possessed a quarter of the knowledge, apart from the felicity of style and the wit, which appears in *The Truth of Masks*.

28

THESE works, however, as well as the poem entitled *The Sphinx* and the charming and extremely entertaining short stories which are contained in the volume, *Lord Arthur Savile's Crime*, are not major works. Had Wilde died before 1892, when he was thirty-eight, it is improbable that any but a few people to-day would know that he had ever existed. The sum of his work would be one short play, *Salomé*, and one comedy, *Lady Windermere's Fan*, both of moderate quality; two deplorable melodramas; two or three excellent essays; less than half a dozen entertaining short tales; a volume of inferior verse; and one mediocre novel. His place would be among the eccentrics: a footnote to *Patience*.

The Sphinx is a heavily-laboured piece of synthetic verse. Sherard, whose critical faculty, if he ever possessed one, disappears from page after page of his biography of Wilde, refers to this piece with comparative coolness. After informing his readers that "there were not more than three men in the Paris literary world" at the time *The Duchess of Padua* and *The Sphinx* were written, "who were" Wilde's "equals", and describing the verse Wilde wrote about this time as "some of his finest", he calms down sufficiently to be able to state that *The Sphinx* "is a masterpiece of the poetry which is not spontaneous. The inspiration came from Poe through Baudelaire." "Because of *Salomé* Oscar Wilde has been placed high in Germany's Walhalla", this abject admirer of Wilde declares. "In Italy, his success is no less startling. The Italians do not resent the comparison of him to the divine Alighieri." He does not state by whom the comparison was made, but in his artless simplicity and infantile devotion, he says, "It may be very foolish, very wrong, but it is simply so". *The Sphinx* was published in 1894 by Elkin Matthews and John Lane, in whose office, while he was arranging the publication, Wilde met the overwrought young clerk, Edward Shelley. Wilde, by this time, was a complete pederast, almost to the point of madness. The main interest this poem has for the dispassionate student of his work is to be found in the final verses where we may, without straining the fact, find him asking himself the question posed on a previous page: why did this man with his intellectual potentialities descend to the stews?

What songless ghost of sin crept through the curtains of the night
And saw my taper burning bright, and knocked, and bade you enter in?

Are there not others more accursed, whiter with leprosies than I?
Are Abana and Pharphar dry that you come here to slake your thirst?
Get hence, you loathsome mystery! Hideous animal, get hence!
You wake in me each bestial sense, you make me what I would not be.

You make my creed a barren sham, you wake foul dream of sensual
  life,
And Atys with his blood-stained knife were better than the thing I am.
False Sphinx! False Sphinx! By reedy Styx old Charon, leaning on
  his oar,
Waits for my coin. Go thou before, and leave me to my crucifix.

Was he here complaining that Mr. Robert Baldwin Ross was creeping round the corner?

29

HESKETH PEARSON makes a strange remark in *The Life of Oscar Wilde*. "It must", he says, "have been mainly due to his perennial boyishness that Wilde never experienced a day's unhappiness until he was forty years old." The statement excites incredulity. Any person who has lived for four decades, including the difficult and disappointing period of adolescence when ambition greatly exceeds ability, without feeling even a day's unhappiness, must either be mentally deficient or so shallow or egotistical that trouble is not felt for more than a moment or is used as fuel for the fires of self-esteem. Pearson himself reports the impression made on the doctor who attended her that the death of Wilde's sister, Isola, filled him with "lonely and inconsolable grief". A mindless man might make the claim Pearson attributes to Wilde, but are we to regard the experience of mindless men as enviable or to believe that Wilde was one? It is evident even to the most casual thinker that genius is not possessed by people who have never suffered in the slightest degree. The capacity to feel deeply is one of the signs of genius. Inability to feel unhappy in any circumstances is the mark of an idiot. If Wilde's admirers insist that he was able to live for forty years without enduring a day's distress of mind, they must abandon the claim to genius which they make in his behalf. Inert people may cast trouble aside because they are too lazy or flabby in spirit to feel a wound or sympathise with sorrow, and imbeciles may never know a single pang, but such people are for ever excluded from the company of genius.

When he married Constance Mary Lloyd, the daughter of a Dublin barrister, Horatio Lloyd, a Queen's Counsellor who had died while she was still a child, Wilde was almost destitute. The excitement he had aroused by his peculiar public performances had died down, and he could scarcely draw an audience anywhere in Great Britain or Ireland. There must have been some times in this period of his life when he felt doubts about himself. Was he merely a clown? Had he great talent, or was he another of that large crowd of clever men and women who make a brief blaze and then go out? The great happiness he felt in the first two years of his marriage seems to prove that he had felt some unhappiness before he married. Constance was starving for affection. Her mother had remarried, but this marriage had made the girl unhappy, and she had removed herself from her mother's house to her paternal grandfather's. This was John Horatio Lloyd, a wealthy man who is said to have been a solicitor, but was now living in retirement in a handsome house in Ely Place, Dublin: a cul-de-sac which was later on to become notorious as the temporary abiding place of George Moore. Where she first met Wilde is not known, but it is said to have been in 1881. She was then twenty-three. He was four years older. It is obvious that the young, evangelically-minded and emotionally-deprived girl found the prospects of life with the flashing Oscar more alluring than the life she was leading in her grandfather's house, far more attractive than the life she would have to lead in her stepfather's, if she were to return to it, and that she accepted him eagerly as much to escape from her dull existence as to enjoy his devotion. She should have married a sedate young professor from Trinity College, Dublin, who was well set on the road to episcopacy. As the wife of a cautious bishop of the Church of Ireland, she would have been successful and happy. That was the world she liked and understood. Innumerable meetings of the Dorcas Society could not have daunted her, nor would she have flinched from opening bazaar after bazaar in aid of the Additional Curates' Fund. To preside over missionary meetings would have been meat and drink to Constance, who felt miserable and out of place in Tite Street, where Oscar insisted on dressing her up in ancient Greek and medieval gowns and making her pose before his ecstatic friends, of whom the males seemed to be even more ecstatic than the females. These twain never became one flesh in any serious sense. They were essentially incompatible. All she had for him was adoration, and adoration soon becomes dissatisfying fare for intelligent people. A husband who is incessantly subject to mindless devotion quickly develops a roving eye. It is not in human nature to endure excess of love.

Wilde, then, was in a mood for divagation when he met that suave little fellow, Mr. Robert Baldwin Ross, who caught him when his wife's adoration was beginning to pall and cloy, and she herself was big with child. Ross was not the sort of man Constance Wilde liked. These small, smooth, effeminate men are attractive only to women who need someone to carry parcels for them and is unlikely to become a nuisance by displaying robust masculine desire. Constance preferred to have her parcels delivered by the tradesmen's vans, which came and immediately went. But Mr. Robert Baldwin Ross was always coming to lunch! . . .

It is not our purpose here to dwell at length on the fatal change in Wilde's life, although it manifestly cannot be disregarded. The subject has been sufficiently discussed elsewhere, and we shall not conduct our readers through the stews of Westminster where Wilde became too frequent a visitor. It must suffice to say that when he stepped up to the swill-tub, full of the husks that the swine do eat, and started on the road to Reading Gaol, it was Mr. Robert Baldwin Ross who showed him the way. That neat, unobtrusive person, who never thrust himself forward, yet was always there, began the devil's dance which brought irretrievable ruin on a man of talent and turned him into a drunken sponger in the back streets of Paris. The writer, a good Pelagian, as becomes an Ulsterman and a compatriot of Pelagius, declines to believe the boneless doctrine of the sadistic and evil Arab, St. Augustine, that men have no decision in their own destiny and become elect or unelect according to a capricious principle of grace, if, indeed, it can be called a principle, exercised in undiscerning whim by a God who cannot have much discretion or knowledge of character if we may judge by the quality of the elect we have encountered in history or our own experience. Pelagius, holding that men have the power to lift themselves up and are capable of choice between good and evil, was more in tune with the hearts of men than the Bishop of Hippo who, were he the referee of eternal life, would fill heaven with the most unpleasing members of the human race: the impotent and sour and disappointed, the ill-natured and meanly cruel and rancorous; and make it a paradise of baffled and frustrated parasites, all gloating at the agonies in hell of those who surpassed them on earth and crowned their lives with great achievements.

But even Augustine had his moments of lucidity. *De vitiis nostris scalam nobis facimus, si vitia ipsa calcamus*, he said: "we make a ladder of our vices, if we trample those same vices underfoot", an assertion which seems to suggest that we have some decision in whether we shall tread them down or be trodden by them. Ladders may be used for ascent and descent. Ross made the ladder which Wilde deliberately descended. It led him down to deep and irredeemable disaster. This elegant wit and man of almost foppish fashion stole into the sties to make himself an intimate associate with slime. Claiming to be a lord of language, he chose for his companions creatures whose speech came from the gutter and the slum. He turned away from the slim lily he had married and made a mother, and sought the society of degenerate stable-boys and painted pimps. This, surely, is the sin against the Holy Ghost, that a man endowed with a brilliant talent should cast it in the mud and defile the gift of God.

30

BUT he had his hours of shining glory. Suddenly, when poverty seemed as if it must overwhelm him and Constance and their two sons, great fortune came upon him. How deep his financial distress was before this fortune came, is apparent when we learn that he sought employment as an inspector of schools. Matthew Arnold was not incongruous in that position, although it was uncongenial to him, for he came of a scholastic family and was himself interested in education, but what a figure Wilde would have cut had he received the appointment. He was saved from this incongruity by George Alexander, a popular and exceedingly successful actor-manager who made a fortune of £90,000 at St. James's Theatre. Alexander, unlike modern managers, sought authors and incited them to write plays. His judgement was acute and his spirit enterprising. He detected talent almost before its possessor was aware that he had it, and he was not afraid of adventure. Pinero's play, *The Second Mrs. Tanqueray*, is a subject for derisory remarks among half-highbrows now, but to produce it in 1893 required courage. Alexander had the courage. He not only produced a play which seemed certain to be unpopular, but chose for his leading lady, on Pinero's suggestion, an actress who was almost unknown, although she was widely renowned after the first performance. This was Mrs. Patrick Campbell.

George Alexander, whose full name was George Alexander Gibb Samson, was an actor-manager, and it became the fashion long before the First World War slew them, as an organisation, to deride and denounce actor-managers. There was no half-highbrow so ineffective that he did not feel entitled to jeer at these distinguished men, who had faults, it appeared, which was scarcely surprising, since God made them, and nothing made by Him is faultless. It is a disturbing thought, with which, however, we need not here concern ourselves, that the perfect God seems incapable of creating a perfect creature, that all His handiwork is frail and unendurable. But although the actor-managers had faults, which were loudly and frequently proclaimed, they also had virtues, though these were either ignored or mentioned only in low tones and whispers. Henry Irving, Charles Wyndham, Herbert Beerbohm Tree, George Alexander, John Hare, Frank Benson, Johnston Forbes-Robertson and Harley Granville-Barker are names which redound both to the stage and the drama. They were supported by subsidiary actor-managers who won, and well deserved, credit and renown: Lewis Waller, Cyril Maude, Arthur Bourchier, John Martin Harvey, Fred Terry, Oscar Asche, Dion Boucicault, Charles Hawtrey, H. B. and Lawrence Irving, Sir Henry's sons, Seymour Hicks, Dennis Eadie, Matheson Lang, Nigel Playfair, Robert Loraine and Gerald du Maurier; and by non-acting managers, such as D'Oyly Carte, George Edwardes, Frederick Harrison, Charles Frohman, Herbert Trench, Bronson Albery, Alec Rea, Basil Dean and C. B. Cochran. There were actress-managers: Ellen Terry, Mary Moore and Lena Ashwell, and non-acting manageresses: Annie E. F. Horniman and Lilian Baylis. Each of them, in his or her sphere, added to the status of the stage.

It was D'Oyly Carte who brought Gilbert and Sullivan together and gave us a superb succession of great comic operas. Tree's record, first at the Haymarket, and then at Her Majesty's, was as notable in the West End as Nigel Playfair's was in the suburb of Hammersmith. Charles Cochran is styled a commercial manager, as if it were a crime to earn a living, but whose career has been more audacious in enterprise, more resplendent in production, more various in plays? Is the history of Alec Rea and Bronson Albery ignoble? What rich entertainment memory recalls when the name of Charles Frohman is mentioned! There was high enterprise at the Haymarket when Herbert Trench was there. High over all these notable names hangs the unmatched Irving: a name that still excites enthusiasm even among those who never saw him act. The stage everywhere is starred with great names of actor-managers and managers who never acted; all of whom took pride in their profession and were eager to enrich it in all respects. They sought new players and new authors, and were ready at all times to speculate with new methods and ideas.

Alexander was one of the three most prominent actor-managers in the English theatre after the death of Henry Irving. He made the St. James's, which had not been prosperous when he took possession of it, the most fashionable theatre in London. It lost that position after his death, at the age of fifty-nine, on the 16th March 1918, and has not since recovered it. *Fashion* is the word which most truly denotes him. He had not the depth and genius of Irving, nor the fantastic and sometimes bizarre adventure of Tree, nor the wise and gracious ease of Wyndham, but he had a high sense of formality. He was urbane, kindly and correct, inclined, in a phrase which has been attributed to Wilde and Pinero, to behave rather than act. But he was also a shrewd business man, and he did not permit his sense of social style, his obligation to do whatever was done by the correct people, to hamper his success. He was quick to detect changes of wind and turns of tide. If he saw a prospect of advantage for his handsome theatre, he promptly seized it. At all times Alexander encouraged authors, those who had arrived and those who had not, and his behaviour, except on one lamentable occasion, was generous and even courageous. It was his servitude to fashion which sent him in pursuit of Wilde: for Wilde, too, despite his trips to the stews, was a man of fashion, moving exclusively, it seemed to Alexander, in the same parish as himself, the parish of St. James.

How formal and fashionable Alexander was is shown by his behaviour when, walking one morning in Bond Street, he encountered two young members of his company: Lilian Braithwaite and Henry Ainley, who were carelessly arrayed. Ainley's hat was impossible. His garments were suitable for Bognor on a Bank Holiday. Lilian Braithwaite would not have been out of place that morning at a village fête, but she was certainly out of place in Bond Street. She wore a "costume" made of tweed. Alexander could not believe his eyes, and, in his doubt, passed by; but he could not evade the horrid truth. Two members of his company were in Bond Street in the season, very carelessly clad! . . . He turned back and courteously called them to attention. "I ask you to remember that this is Bond Street," he said, "and that you are members of the St. James's Theatre company. That requires social obligations in dress. I am sure I need not say more." The rebuke thus civilly delivered, Alexander, glorious in a shining silk hat, a morning coat superbly cut, and trousers creased according to the higher mathematics, bowed and departed, leaving Ainley deeply abashed and Lilian Braithwaite blushing and almost in tears of shame. Those were the days, as Irene Vanbrugh tells the readers of her reminiscences, when a man might be ostracised if he were found informally garbed in Piccadilly. His friends, encountering him thus barbarously clad, would avert their eyes from the unseemly sight and hurry away in dread lest he should speak to them and they should be caught in his company.

This pride in formal attire seems foolish now, but when we contemplate the slovenly and crumpled clothes in which men and women array themselves to-day, do we not sometimes wish for some of the style we have lost? Beauty may be found in formal movements and formal garments, but is there any beauty whatever in the graceless movements and reach-me-down stuff we affected before the deprivations of war reduced us to utility clothes? George Alexander, well tailored and courteous, was a more pleasing person at a rehearsal than a film producer, who slops about in flabby flannel trousers and a dirty jumper, muttering inaudibly, because his mouth is full of gum, "Say, kid, can't you be lusher'n that? You gotta make the li'l girls in the factories feel they're missin' somepin when they're doin' piece-work for kepitalists. Well, show 'em what they're missin', sister! . . ."

31

ALEXANDER, who was nearly four years younger than Wilde, had been in management for about eighteen months when he commissioned Wilde to write a play for production at St. James's. He had begun his managerial life at the Avenue, now the Playhouse, with moderate success. His first production was successful, but his business manager decamped to Mexico with most of the profit, some £700, which was a large amount then and sufficient to sink a young actor-manager at the beginning of his career, especially as the second production, an adaptation from the French, was a failure. The third production just paid its way. Older and more experienced men might pardonably have felt discouraged by these misfortunes, and it must have seemed to the young man of thirty-two that he would be wise to accept the offer

Henry Irving had made, of re-employment at the Lyceum if, at the end of six months of management, he found himself in trouble. A salary of £45 a week, with extra money for matinées, waited him at the Lyceum. But Alexander, in addition to Scottish caution, possessed Scottish courage and enterprise. He was not daunted by disaster: he was stimulated by it: and he boldly rented an unfortunate and unfashionable theatre in a side street at a fair distance from the regular theatrical area, which he managed with audacity, distinction and success for twenty-eight years, despite the fact that about half the total number of the plays he produced either were financial failures or did no more than cover their cost.

Let us give an actor-manager his due. Alexander not only sought a play from Wilde who, at that time, had written little or nothing of note, but paid him £100 on account of royalties, although he had no proof that Wilde could, or ever would, write anything that was fit for performance. Had Alexander known of *Vera* and *The Duchess of Padua*, he might have been charier with his money. His instinct, however, was sound. All drama is talk, and a man who could talk as well as Wilde habitually talked—the testimony to his conversational skill is unanimous—must be able to write plays. So Alexander argued, and argued very sensibly. Wilde usually told stories in dialogue rather than in narrative. This is the method of the dramatist: the method of dynamic conversation. If a comparison is drawn between the dialogue of a novelist and that of a dramatist, a remarkable difference between them will soon be detected. The novelist's dialogue is almost always unspeakable, the stuff that is composed by a man who does not utter his dialogue aloud as he writes it. Henry James, whose ambition to become a dramatist was as persistent as it was unsuccessful, wrote speech which lacked that quality, and lacked, too, another essential quality of dramatic conversation: power of progression. Henry James's dialogue is static, as still as a sheltered pool, but dramatic dialogue must move, carrying the theme and the characters along with it. The play turns on speech. It cannot turn on anything else.

Alexander, being an accomplished actor, knew what was essential in a play; and his knowledge of Wilde persuaded him to believe that he could write brilliant comedy. That was not absolutely certain. Wits are of two kinds: those whose wit is entirely spontaneous, and those whose wit is considered. The first are witty without thought, saying what comes into their heads without being aware that wit is about to be uttered. The second concoct their wit, intending it to be wit. The spontaneous wit is usually excellent company, holding the attention of the table, and setting his companions in a roar. The thoughtful wit can be conversationally disappointing, and duller at a dinner-table than people with half his brains. But the latter's wit is the more lasting. Put a pen in the fingers of a spontaneous wit and he will falter and fumble and write you stuff that is about as tasty as a crab apple that has been bitten by frost. There was a dramatist called Joseph Comyns Carr whose reputation for ready wit still survives in the Garrick Club, although he died in 1916. His spontaneous witticisms are repeated by those who had the felicity of hearing them uttered, and they convinced the listener that Carr had a wit of uncommon quality. Yet his plays were almost witless. A pen was the ruin of his tongue. Seymour Hicks was another one of the same sort: spontaneously brilliant, but deliberately dull. I have myself met men in Dublin whose conversation sparkled like a sunlit stream, and have been dazed by the dullness of the words they wrote. How could so much dead stuff issue from minds seemingly fresh and gay? Nature is niggardly when we expect her to be lavish, and lavish when we are sick of surfeit. She seldom offers both her hands, preferring to keep one behind her back.

It was possible, therefore, that Wilde's readiness of tongue might be delusive, and that his wit would fall dead on the point of a pen. There was the disturbing fact of his age and the still more disturbing fact of his slight volume of work. He was thirty-seven when Alexander approached him with his hundred pounds in his hand. At that age, a man should surely have done far more substantial work than Wilde had then achieved. Irishmen are clever with their tongues, but are they clever with anything else? Alexander might well have wondered. There was that odd fellow with the straggling red beard who wore hygienic clothes and was alleged to have trodden the sacred pavements of Bond Street in sandals and to spend his time haranguing coal-heavers in public parks—people were beginning to talk about him as a great Irish wit, but what had he done, apart from spouting at street corners? Bernard Shaw, at the age of thirty-five, as he was when Alexander asked Wilde for a comedy, had written five novels that had been declined by almost every publisher in London. When, at last, they came out in holes and corners, their sales were comic. In 1889 the royalties were two shillings and tenpence. In 1891, when Alexander was flourishing cheques in front of Wilde, they had risen to seven shillings and tenpence. A hundred pounds would have seemed incredible wealth then to Shaw. That was the sum of Shaw as a writer at the age of thirty-five. He had not yet begun to criticise the drama for *The Saturday Review*. Compared with him, Wilde was prolific! . . . He was also fashionable, a frequenter of important mansions, delighting the guests at grand dinners with his enchanting conversation. Wilde had, indeed, been incorrect in his salad days, but he was incorrect no longer . . . so Alexander thought . . . and he moved in the best circles. His hats and ties, the cut of his coat and the crease in his trousers, could not affront the eyes of Bond Street's most devoted denizen. He was impeccably clad and correct as Alexander himself. More could not be said in favour of anyone.

The actor-manager's instinct did not betray him. The chance he took turned out to be a certainty. But there were times, spread over several months, when he wondered if he had not misjudged Wilde and wasted his money. For Wilde, like many authors, was a lazy man, liable to sudden fits of industry, but more liable to long bouts of idleness. He was slow in starting on the comedy he had agreed to write. But when he began, he worked quickly, and finished it in about a month. In the summer of 1891 he rented a cottage in the neighbourhood of Windermere—the lake provided him with the title of his principal characters—and there he composed the comedy which changed the style of the English stage at that period, reviving the careless raptures of Sheridan and causing the more solid manner of Henry Arthur Jones and Arthur Pinero to seem heavy in comparison.

Writing *Lady Windermere's Fan* and, a month or so later,

Salomé was not all that Wilde did that summer. He made the acquaintance of Lord Alfred Douglas, who was introduced to him in Tite Street by Lionel Johnson, a poet whose promise of distinction was prevented from fulfilment by drink and early death. This encounter with Douglas was the second major disaster of Wilde's life. The first was his meeting with Mr. Robert Baldwin Ross.

32

ALFRED BRUCE DOUGLAS was the third son and child of the ninth Marquess of Queensberry and descended from one of the most ancient and romantic families in Scotland: a family with a verifiable pedigree stretching back to the ninth century. Nearly a hundred and twenty pages of the *Dictionary of National Biography* are filled with the records of this astounding family. One of its members, "Old Q.", the sixth marquess, was the original of the Marquis of Steyne in Thackeray's *Vanity Fair*. A family as old and rich and undisciplined as this one must include some very queer people; and the Douglases had more than their fair share of oddities and eccentrics. None of them was so queer as the ninth marquess, Lord Alfred's singular father: a man of such peculiar character that it is almost a compliment to call him a lunatic. He was, undoubtedly, demented. His insanity developed into a violent hatred of his wife, a very beautiful and fine-natured woman, and five children. His second son, Percy, grossly insulted by him in public, disturbed the decorum of Bond Street by punching his head in broad daylight. Father and son were summoned before a magistrate and bound over to keep the peace. In 1887 Lady Queensberry divorced her husband, who promptly married a girl of nineteen and was again divorced in a remarkably short time. In 1900, when he was fifty-five, he died in the belief that he had lived in dire poverty. His rent roll was over £20,000 a year.

The ninth Marquess of Queensberry could not have been conceived in fiction. Imagination is incapable of such conception. He was a sportsman—the prize ring owed its fourteen famous rules to him—but he contradicted and denied all the legends of fair behaviour and generous dealing which have unaccountably gathered round those who spend the greater part of their lives in playing or watching games. Ability to hit, slap, smack, push and shove balls of varying sizes about does not, in itself, seem sufficient to justify a reputation of superlative integrity in those who possess it; nor does association with horses and dogs develop almost automatically in those who frequent race-courses, stables, dog-tracks and kennels a nobility of mind and spirit which puts the rest of us to shame. But if there were a vestige of truth in the myth that sport-addicts are God's finest creatures, all sporting men and women would be hard put to it to find any traces of nobility in the ninth Marquess of Queensberry. Fitful and violent, he took umbrage at imaginary offences and pursued the innocent people he accused of committing them with extraordinary venom and persistence. Lord Rosebery, when he was Foreign Secretary, was among those who, without the slightest justification, incurred his hatred. Sportsmen are usually inclined to simple piety when they are inclined to religion at all, and are easily moved by banal hymns. In this respect, Queensberry was untrue to type. He was a notorious atheist, and he roused the wrath of Queen Victoria by stating in public that the oath of allegiance was "religious tomfoolery". That venerable lady did not forgive easily. Queensberry was never forgiven.

He had the courage and determination which are often to be found in nervous degenerates who are self-willed and arrogant; and he was implacable in pursuit of his quarry. There must be a kill. It was this man who was the immediate means by which Oscar Wilde was brought to ruin that could never be repaired. On that afternoon in the autumn of 1891 when Lionel Johnson brought Lord Alfred Douglas to tea with Wilde in Tite Street, a long feud was started which ended in irretrievable disaster. But the beginning seemed pretty enough.

Wilde was nearly thirty-seven when he met Douglas, who was born on the 22nd of October 1870, and was still short of his majority. Wilde has been accused of snobbery, especially by Harris, because he delighted in this encounter with Douglas and sought to make him his close friend. Irishmen, more than other men, dearly love lords, even when they are seeking to found republics, but it is false to think that Wilde was attracted to Douglas by the paltry feeling that impresses suburban minds. He was inordinately romantic. Ancient lineage, more almost than anything else, evoked emotion in Wilde. As he looked at the beautiful boy —for Douglas was indisputably beautiful in appearance—he saw the history of Scotland unrolling itself before his eyes. Ten centuries of Scottish romance were sitting in his house drinking tea. That thought enthralled Wilde, who did not stop to wonder if ten centuries of tainted blood were also sitting there. The history of Scotland was embodied in the exquisite young man who was listening enraptured to the flow of brilliant talk which poured from Oscar's lips: for Wilde was inspired by his romantic reverie. He could almost hear the cries of contending clans, those that had descended from the mountains to murder and to ravish, and those who had risen up from the glens to revenge their slaughtered kin and recover their pillaged flocks. The berserker strain which, his mother had averred, was strong in his blood, was stirred by the very name of Douglas. A thousand years of Douglases had been concentrated in this incredibly good-looking youth. Here were myths mouldy with age, and heroic legends and gallous deeds and picturesque crimes, and vehement love and revenge, and wild men and wilder women, all the elements of high romance, drinking tea in Tite Street.

Enough stress has not been laid on Wilde's romantic side. He loved the roll of syllables he heard when he spoke the names of his principal characters in the comedy he had written in the Lakes: Lord and Lady Windermere. He was so pleased with fine-sounding syllables that he forgot how dull the people owning them could be. The banalities they uttered, the stupid opinions they held, the puerile habits they had—all these were forgotten in the rich sonority of their titles. Wilde, despite his toyings with sentimental socialism and his abortive attempts to build roads on Hinksey Marsh, was essentially royal-minded, a man of aristocratic outlook on life, as any poet, even if he be only a minimum poet, must be. Men like William Morris are not socialists in the sense that Aneurin Bevan and Emanuel Shinwell are socialists. Morris wanted an aristocratic world; they want a proletarian world. The fact that their desires sometimes make them wish for the same thing does not alter the profound difference in their views of life. Bevan and Shinwell, in their essence, are repellent to Morris. They have back-street minds, but he had the mind of a creative artist, a man so pervaded with aristocratic thoughts that even wallpaper had to change before he felt satisfied.

No men were more different in character and nature than Wilde and Shaw. Yet they were at one in this, that their whole outlook on life, even when Shaw was asserting himself to be a communist, was aristocratic. They had that ease with working-men which is felt only by the man of high origin and high belief. It was difficult for Wilde, as it was for Shaw, to talk to routine middle-class men and women, but he had no difficulty in talking to working-men, and could, as we have already noted, win their regard and admiration even when they were American toughs and determined to "razz" him. Ugly-minded people have ugly religions and ugly politics and ugly ambitions. No one but a man with an incurably ugly mind could have written *Das Kapital.* Marx was fundamentally base, and could only devise a base belief. It was inevitable that he should draw unto him all the ugly-minded, warped and twisted, hate-ridden men and women of the world: men and women whose very names, by some irony of nature, are as ugly as their views.

On the ground of high romance, Oscar Wilde and the kitchen-maid were one. The girl sitting among cinders and dreaming of princes was in precisely the same state of mind as Wilde when Lionel Johnson brought Lord Alfred Douglas to tea in Tite Street that autumn afternoon. He felt so much elation as he saw his romantic dream come true, that he took Douglas upstairs to the drawing-room which Whistler had decorated, to introduce him to Constance. The boy was ushered into her presence as if he were an anointed king.

33

THE stage, we now observe, is being set with great care for the performance of a strange tragedy in which there is not a single noble character, in which comedians are suddenly called to take tragic parts for which they are unfitted both by temperament and appearance. Touchstone is alien for ever as Hamlet. Neither Beatrice nor Portia can play Volumnia or Lady Macbeth. Who would cast Helen of Troy for the part of Cassandra? Neither Wilde, the man of fashion, nor Wilde, the prowler in back-street stews, was a fitting figure in a tragic theme. There is a frightful photograph of him and Douglas in 1894. It appears in Hesketh Pearson's *Life*, and shows Wilde looking like an overblown bookie with a pretty barmaid at Epsom. The fat and prosperous commission agent has had a good day, and is looking forward to a good night! . . . That man, bulging out of his tightly-buttoned striped suit, was not designed for tragedy. There was not enough nobility in him for that. Intended for a farce, he was miscast in tragedy.

Nearly all the principal players are now present, and the plot is planned. The scene-shifters are already building the set. The secondary actors and the supers are loitering in the wings, waiting to be called. Only the villain, the most ludicrous figure in the play, is absent, unaware, as yet, that he has been cast for any part or that his will turn out to be nearly the most important. The ninth Marquess of Queensberry at this moment is busy with boxers and oblivious of the company his third son is keeping in Tite Street, nor would he have cared had he known: for he hated Alfred as heartily as Alfred hated him. This son, the most indulged of her five children, is dear to his mother and, therefore, loathed by his father. Orestean tragedy seems here to be topsy-turvy, with Agamemnon playing the part of Clytemnestra. Thersites cast for Hector would not have been more absurd than Queensberry playing the part of an avenging Fury and outraged father. Wilde may have heard of him in 1891, just as a man, even in Tierra del Fuego, may have heard of Hitler in 1931, but it is unlikely that Queensberry, the boon companion of pugilists and jockeys, had heard of Wilde. Nothing in their lives, it seemed, could make them aware of each other. A prophecy that these two would one day become the leading actors in a tragic farce that would bring irreparable ruin on Wilde would have seemed to those who heard it utterly grotesque.

Inconspicuous in the wings, among the secondary players and the supers, were Mr. Robert Baldwin Ross and Charles Brookfield, the latter of whom was to develop a pathological hatred of Wilde as intense as the hatred the Marquess felt for everybody. Brookfield was to lose every friend he had because of his incontinently bitter tongue, but not before he had entertained Lord Alfred's father at a banquet with wine to celebrate the downfall of Wilde. Ross had a curious part to play, that of the superseded mistress. What was a devoted and quite intelligent, but insignificant and rather kittenish, small young man from Upper Canada in comparison with this superb and dazzling descendant of all the Douglases who had flourished through the history of Scotland for a thousand years? Enumeration of their titles alone was a stupendous task. They had held four dukedoms, one in England, one in Scotland and two in France, and could discard earldoms and baronies as if they were pieces of paper, they had so many. They had made kings and tumbled kings. They had fought their way from Scotland, through England and France, to Spain, and had snatched a bride from under the nose of her sovereign lord the king. There was no war in Scotland, and few in England, in which they had not fought. They thought themselves the equals of any monarch, and held a Scottish earl of greater rank than an English duke; a proud, rapacious race, disdainful of death and not afraid of life: picturesque and brave, cruel, greedy and desperately wicked. The heir to all this history had a natural right to supplant the heir of two generations of attorneys, even although he was a connoisseur of pictures and a man of creditable taste.

The preparations for the play were pleasant, holding no hint of its dismal end. Constance, indeed, was uneasy, even, at times, unhappy. Oscar had developed odd habits, and was inclined to lose his temper at the slightest sign of disapproval. He went out very often, leaving her alone, and returned at all hours of the night. His social success, in which she had no share, was making him unbearably arrogant. There were times when she wondered if he were quite right in his head. His odd ways were becoming odder! . . . It all began when that Ross started to visit the house. That Ross was always somewhere about, listening for the bricks she dropped, so that he might run tee-heeing to his tee-heeing companions to tell them how she had interrupted Oscar's brilliant talk to ask if he had remembered to call at the cobbler's shop to enquire about Cyril's shoes. That Ross! . . .

But even her shadows lifted a little then. Oscar had written his comedy, and kind Mr. Alexander was delighted with it. Oscar felt immensely elated, and swore that he could write plays as good as *Lady Windermere's Fan* with ease and celerity. Half a dozen a year, if he felt inclined! . . . Perhaps, now that Lord Alfred Douglas, third son of the ninth Marquess of Queensberry, had become their friend, life with Oscar would brighten again. Perhaps that Ross would not come to lunch so often! . . .

Rehearsals were less satisfying than they should have been. Wilde, despite his natural sense of the stage, had no practical knowledge of it. Natural sense is not enough. A man, no matter how much of that he possesses, must learn the limitations of the stage and of audiences from experience of both. He cannot derive them from intuitions. Wilde entered St. James's Theatre for the rehearsals of *Lady Windermere's Fan* with no more knowledge of theatrical technique than he had acquired as the author of *Vera* and *The Duchess of Padua*, and as an occasional critic of the drama. He was, in effect, an ignorant apprentice, but he behaved as if he were a highly skilled craftsman, and he had the presumption to try to teach Alexander, who was a skilled craftsman, how to do his job.

There is a belief that a dramatic critic, because he has seen many plays performed, must know more about the technicalities of drama than the majority of people. Some heretics hold that he must be better informed about them than anybody because he sees far more plays than any actor or producer or theatrical manager.

A critic, during the theatre year, is present, on an average, at three or four first performances of plays a week. The average, indeed, may be higher than that. He sees every sort of play, good, bad and indifferent, the failures as well as the successes. Actors in employment see few plays. Actors out of employment may see more, but are likely to be given admission only to failures. (In these times, indeed, they have to pay for admission like ordinary playgoers. High costs of production do not permit managers to scatter free tickets like confetti. An author is given a box for the first performance of his play, but if he wants other seats, he must pay for them, which is right and proper.)

It might, then, be thought that dramatic critics, because of their frequent attendance at every kind of theatrical production, must acquire a familiarity with the technique of the stage beyond that of any other person. The fact is otherwise. The dramatic critic sees only finished productions, and sees them before the specialised first-night audience. He does not see them as unproduced scripts or as performances before ordinary audiences innocent of all interest in drama except as an evening's entertainment. C. E. Montague, who criticised plays for *The Manchester Guardian* and wrote a work, entitled *Dramatic Values*, which has been highly extolled by other dramatic critics, but is almost unknown to players and producers, attempted, at least once in his life, to write a play: a dramatisation of his novel, *A Hind Let Loose*. It is easily the worst play I have ever read. James Agate, whose arrogance about the stage was as vast as his ignorance, wrote several plays which his friends have tried to hush up. A rumour persists in America that George Jean Nathan, in collaboration with H. L. Mencken, wrote a play called *Heliogabalus*, but neither Nathan nor Mencken ever mentions it, and both discourage enquiry. William Archer, a seasoned critic and author of "a manual of craftmanship", entitled *Play-Making*, wrote six or seven plays which, although they are composed on the highest principles, failed to find producers. He then abandoned reason and took to dreaming. He dreamt *The Green Goddess*, and it became a great success both in London and New York. Aristotle, who had the hardihood to lay down laws about the drama, never, so far as anyone knows, wrote a play in his life. It would almost certainly have been the flop of flops, if he had.

Bernard Shaw and other dramatic critics who became successful dramatists, achieved their success, not because they had been critics, but because they had a natural talent for writing plays and would have written them if they had never criticised a play in their lives. Shaw's work has been composed in revolt against the style of plays he was paid to review, and he may be said to have learnt nothing from his experience as a critic, except that he must not write such plays as he was accustomed to see. Professor G. P. Baker wrote a book on the technique of the drama, and conducted a school at Yale to teach people how to write it. His most successful students were those who, like Eugene O'Neill, broke every rule he taught them. O'Neill learnt his craft in little theatres in back streets and villages. The greatest dramatists, Shakespeare, Molière, Sheridan, Ibsen and Chekhov, for example, acquired their skill, not from text-books, but from acting or producing plays in the theatre. Wilde had no technical knowledge of the playhouse, but he behaved as if he knew all there was to know. Shaw, when he entered the theatre, listened to his betters and cut his scripts to pieces. Page after page was torn up, and rightly torn up. He could have improved several plays if he had torn up more pages! . . .

The truly incompetent author is one who behaves as if he had heard a voice from heaven saying, Write, and treats any suggestion of cuts as if it were blasphemy. Wilde, luckily, learnt sense, but he was reluctant to learn it when he began to rehearse his first comedy. He refused to listen to Alexander, who told him that it was a fundamental mistake to conceal the knowledge of Mrs. Erlynne's relationship to Lady Windermere until the last act, and it was not until the fact forced itself upon him after the first performance that he consented to make the revelation in the second act. His play would have been ruined if he had not listened to good advice.

An author in the mood Wilde was in during the rehearsals of *Lady Windermere's Fan* is a thorn in the flesh of the producer and the cast; and there were occasions when Alexander felt that he had had more than he could bear. But he did not allow his natural and reasonable impatience with an arrogant and even insolent novice to overcome his admiration for the play. Wilde was Irish, and the world knew how obstinate the Irish are! . . . Thus Alexander reasoned with himself when he came near to breaking point. His submission to the dramatist was heroic, for he must have felt fearful that Wilde, by his obstinate persistence in foolish opinions, was endangering an enterprise which had already cost Alexander a large sum of money. Mr. Montgomery Hyde possesses a long letter which was addressed to Alexander by Wilde from the Hotel Albemarle, Piccadilly, in February 1892. Some extracts from it appear in A. E. W. Mason's *Sir George Alexander and the St. James's Theatre*, but they did not adequately present the unimpressive character of Wilde's argument, although they give the substance of it. The letter is full of the folly of the half-baked intellectual whose head is stuffed with untested theories, but innocent of all practical knowledge of his subject, and it proves, if proof be required, that Wilde did not know what he was talking about. He begins with a complaint of illness almost as if he were accusing Alexander of having caused it, and then rehearses his singular reasons for deferring the revelation that Mrs. Erlynne is Lady Windermere's mother until the last act.

. . . Had I intended to let out the secret, which is the element of suspense and curiosity, quality so essentially dramatic, I would have written the play on entirely different lines. I would have made Mrs. Erlynne a vulgar horrid woman and struck out the incident of the fan. The audience must not know until the last act that the woman Lady Windermere proposed to strike with her fan was her own mother. The note would be too harsh, too horrible. When they learn it, it is after Lady Windermere has left her husband's house to seek the protection of another man, and their interest is concentrated on Mrs. Erlynne to whom, dramatically speaking, belongs the last act. Also it would destroy the dramatic wonder excited by the incident of Mrs. Erlynne taking the letter and opening it and sacrificing herself in the third act. If they knew Mrs. Erlynne was the mother, there would be no surprise in her sacrifice—it would be expected. But in my play the sacrifice is dramatic and unexpected. The cry with which Mrs. Erlynne flies into the other room on hearing Lord Augustus' voice, the wild pathetic cry of self-preservation, "Then it is I who am lost!", would be repulsive coming from the lips of one known to be the mother by the audience. It seems natural and is very dramatic coming from one who seems to be an adventuress, and who, while anxious to save Lady Windermere, thinks of her own safety when a crisis comes. Also it would destroy the last act; and the chief merit of my last act is to me the fact that it does not contain, as most plays do, the explanation of what the audience knows already, but that it is the sudden explanation of what the audience desires to know, followed immediately by the revelation of a character as yet untouched by literature.

This is the sort of stuff that makes a deep impression in Bloomsbury back-rooms, but nowhere else. Wilde asserts that if the audience were acquainted with the fact that Mrs. Erlynne is Lady Windermere's mother "there would be no surprise in her sacrifice", but seems not to have realised that without the knowledge there would not appear to be any reason for it. It would seem no more than a momentary impulse by a woman who might as suddenly repent of it. Why should Mrs. Erlynne sacrifice herself for Lady Windermere? That is the question the audience would have asked itself if its members had not known that she was Lady Windermere's mother; and when an audience begins to ask questions about unexplained matters, illusion is lost and the play is ruined, as must have been plain to any person who heard the murmurs of enquiry throughout the performances of James Bridie's *The Sleeping Clergyman*. "But what's the clergyman got to do with the play?" was almost incessantly whispered by the bewildered audience, which was thus prevented from becoming a fused body and compelled to remain a confused group of individuals. Bridie, in brief, was too clever by half. He sent his audience out of the theatre muttering, "But I still don't see what the clergyman has to do with the play! . . ."

Wilde's letter concludes with a forcible-feeble assertion and declaration. "I have built my house on a certain foundation, and this foundation cannot be altered. I can say no more."

Fortunately for all concerned in the production, he could say more. The foundation of his house was not only alterable, but altered. He himself decided on the alteration, justifying Alexander in making it, but it was not made until after the first performance, and Alexander must have suffered a good deal of anxiety until it was made. His was the money being risked in the production, and it was being risked by a wilful and inexperienced dramatist at a time when Alexander's commitments were many and his finances shaky. We shall refer to the decision to alter the play in its proper place, and will deal now only with the comparatively minor point about the end of the second act.

This act, according to Mason, ended, as Wilde wrote it, with Mrs. Erlynne's speech in which she commands Lord Augustus Lorton to take Windermere to his club and keep him there.

> "Don't let Windermere out of your sight to-night. If you do, I will never forgive you. I will never speak to you again. I'll have nothing to do with you. Remember you are to keep Windermere at your club, and don't let him come back to-night."

That said, she sweeps out of the room in a "tornado" and the curtain falls like a thunder-clap. But Alexander thought that a quiet comedy scene would be more effective, and he besought Wilde to provide it, and Wilde, very reluctantly, added the eleven-word speech for Lord Augustus which ends the act. Mrs. Erlynne has had her shouting scene, and has swept out of the room, leaving Lorton alone. He stands ruminating for a moment or two, and then exclaims, "Well, really, I might be her husband already. Positively I might", and follows her out. No one with a sense of the stage can fail to perceive the superiority of this humorous curtain over Wilde's original end. The entire temper of the scene is altered, and altered for the better. Wilde felt annoyed when the new ending proved better than the first, but he had the grace to confess that he was wrong and Alexander right.

Alexander was to incur odium because he had Wilde's name blotted off the play-bills and the programmes after his arrest; and perhaps those of us who were not in his shoes then may feel inclined to join in the reproaches. The excuse offered in his behalf, that he was trying to save *The Importance of Being Earnest* from collapse at a time when Wilde was in desperate need of money for his defence, is, perhaps, unconvincing. There cannot have been many people in London or, indeed, in Britain who were likely to go to St. James's Theatre in ignorance of the fact that the play had been written by Wilde.[1] There was, then, some culpability on Alexander's part, but not much, and he atoned for it very handsomely. Frank Harris, in *Oscar Wilde*, relates a story which, he states, was told to him by Wilde. While reading Vergil by the roadside on the way to Cannes, Wilde, on looking up, saw George Alexander on a bicycle. "I had known him intimately in the old days"—this was in 1898, about a year after Wilde had been released from prison—"and naturally I got up delighted to see him, and went towards him. But he turned his head aside and pedalled past me deliberately. He meant to cut me.... Think of Alexander, who made all his money out of my work, cutting me! Alexander! It is too ignoble." Mason makes several suggestions about this improbable tale: the first being that it was invented by Harris: the second, that Wilde may have imagined that Alexander saw him when, in fact, he did not, and that he told the story without any thought that it would ever appear in a book professing to be biography. He does not suggest that the tale might have been invented by Wilde who was then in a state of almost chronic self-pity and had never in his life been scrupulous in telling the truth. Mason successfully refutes part of the tale alleged to have been told by Wilde, and he states a highly plausible case for believing that the rest of it is false. He proves from Alexander's carefully-kept accounts that the total sum made out of Wilde's plays up to the year 1898 was £5280 : 12 : 7. The first production of *The Importance of Being Earnest* resulted in a loss of £289 : 8 : 4. It was far from the fact that Alexander had "made all his money out of" Wilde's works. In terms of the theatre, he had made a relatively small sum, less than half the sum he had made out of *The Second Mrs. Tanqueray* and *The Prisoner of Zenda*, and far, far less than he made out of *His House in Order*.

Hesketh Pearson, in *The Life of Oscar Wilde*, proves that Harris was not in or near La Napoule when Wilde was living there at the time of the alleged cut from Alexander; and that he could

[1] But Alexander was not the only sinner in this respect, although he is always treated as if he were. *An Ideal Husband* was in performance at the Lyceum Theatre, New York, when Wilde was arrested. The management, according to the *London American* of the 10th of April 1895, removed his name from the playbills and programmes. See *Bibliography of Oscar Wilde*, p. 438.

not have been informed of the slight immediately after it is said to have been received. This fact, however, may mean only that Harris, who had a passion for dramatising himself, misdated the time. It does not prove that Wilde did not tell him the story. Pearson, indeed, believes that the cut was given; for he says that Alexander confessed to Mr. Robert Baldwin Ross, that he felt ashamed of his behaviour at La Napoule. There is no direct evidence that this assertion is true. Alexander had been dead for twenty-eight years when Pearson's book was published and could neither affirm nor deny the story. The argument against its veracity is powerfully supported by a letter Wilde wrote to Alexander from the Hôtel d'Alsace, Paris, in July 1900, two years after Alexander is supposed to have cut him. Wilde, after his arrest, had been made a bankrupt by his creditors, and Alexander had bought "for next to nothing", Pearson says, "the acting rights of *Lady Windermere's Fan* and *The Importance of Being Earnest*", neither of which, Pearson omits to mention, seemed likely then or for a long time to be producible. Plays, even by popular authors under no stigma, fall out of favour, cease, even to obtain any revival. Few dramatists have enjoyed so much success as Barrie, but how many of his plays have been performed since his death in 1937? Has any play by John Galsworthy been revived in London since his death in 1933? Alexander had an interest in the two Wilde comedies he bought, and he was entitled to protect that interest. If Wilde could not retain them, who had a better right to buy them than Alexander? But he cannot have had much hope of immediate return from his purchase, and the hope of remote return was as likely as not to prove delusive. *Lady Windermere's Fan* was revived for the first time four years after Wilde's death, nine years after the rights in it had been bought by Alexander. It was not a success. It was revived again in 1911 without much, if any, profit to its producer. *The Importance of Being Earnest* was first revived on the 7th of January 1902, seven years after Alexander acquired the rights, and a little more than a year after Wilde's death. It, too, was a financial failure. It was revived again, in 1909, when it was immensely successful, receiving 324 performances. Other revivals were made in 1911 and

1913.[1] *An Ideal Husband* was not originally produced by Alexander, but he acquired the right to produce it in May 1914, and lost £2000 on the production.

These facts, which are lifted from Mason, prove that Alexander was not, as Pearson seems to suggest, greedily snatching at a deeply distressed bankrupt's property when he bought the rights of the two comedies he had commissioned and produced. But they do not tell the whole story which, in full, reveals Alexander in a highly honourable light. What follows is also taken from Mason.

In July 1900 Alexander, while driving in a cab in Paris, saw Wilde slouching along the street. That was about four months before Wilde died, and he was not then usually in a state when even unfastidious people would seek his company. Had Alexander wished to avoid meeting him, he could easily have done so. But he stopped his cab and greeted the unhappy man with warmth and fervour. Overcome by Wilde's miserable plight, he voluntarily made him a monthly allowance of £20 and entered into an arrangement with Ross, who was Wilde's trustee, to pay a royalty to the estate on any performances of the two plays he might give. Wilde himself derived little benefit from the arrangement, for he died in the following November, but his sons were greatly benefited by it. Nor was that the end of Alexander's beneficence. He bequeathed the rights in both the plays to Wilde's younger son, Vyvyan Holland—the elder boy, Cyril, had been killed in the First World War—who drew a handsome income from them. Can we credit the story that Alexander, who sprang from his cab in a conspicuous place in Paris to greet the shabby drunkard he saw on the pavement, had cut him two years earlier on a secluded part of the road to Cannes? The first meeting, if it ever occurred, was accidental: the second, so far as Alexander was concerned, was deliberately sought.

What Wilde thought of Alexander's action in Paris appears in a letter he wrote to him from the Hôtel d'Alsace a day or two after their meeting. It appears in full in Mason's book, and it will, therefore, be enough to cite its opening here:

[1] I am here referring only to revivals made by Alexander or with his permission. There have been several very profitable revivals since his death.

My dear Aleck, It was really a great pleasure to see you again, and to receive your friendly grasp of the hand after so many years, nor shall I forget your dear wife's charming and affectionate greeting of me. I know now the value of things like that. With regard to your proposal to spread the payment for the plays over a certain time, I know it was dictated by sheer kindness and the thoughtfulness of an old friend. . . .

34

In spite of quarrels and fatuous adherence to theories that had no relation to practical experience, *Lady Windermere's Fan* was produced on the 20th of February 1892. The parts of Lord and Lady Windermere and Mrs. Erlynne were played by Alexander, Lily Hanbury and Marion Terry. The run lasted for twenty-three weeks, until the 29th of July. The play was then taken on tour for ten weeks, from the 22nd of August until the 29th of October. Two days later, on the 31st of October, it was revived in London, but unsuccessfully, the run lasting only for a month, until the 30th of November. It was taken on tour again, with three other plays, including *The Second Mrs. Tanqueray*, in 1893, but was not revived thereafter until 1904. Wilde is reputed by his friends to have received about £7000 in royalties from it. The legend is that all his plays had long and profitable runs, that he earned vast sums of money from them, and that Alexander made a large fortune out of them. The runs were respectable but not long, and the earnings, though substantial, were not large. *A Woman of No Importance*, the next play to be produced, was performed for seventeen weeks. The third play, *An Ideal Husband*, ran for thirteen weeks. Its withdrawal was not due to Wilde's arrest, for the play was under notice before it was made. The fourth and last play, *The Importance of Being Earnest*, was performed for sixteen weeks, surviving the arrest by a month.

These first runs were good, but not notably good. They would be regarded with equanimity, at their best, to-day, but some of them would cause misgiving to the manager responsible for them. In 1891, however, a run of twenty-three weeks was considered to be excellent, though not remarkable, and it denoted a financial success. Alexander was liberal to dramatists, but even with his liberality it is doubtful if Wilde earned as much as his admirers said he earned. The average weekly takings during a successful run at St. James's Theatre were £200 at each performance. Even if Wilde received a straight 10 per cent of the gross proceeds, which is improbable, he could not have made anything like £7000 out of the first production of *Lady Windermere's Fan*—and there was no other production in his lifetime. Sherard, whose assertions are almost invariably to be distrusted, states in *Oscar Wilde: The Story of an Unhappy Friendship* that Wilde's income, before the crash came, "exceeded £8000". This loosely worded statement seems to suggest that he earned this sum regularly during the brief period of his prosperity: but the facts do not support this assertion. A dramatist does not draw £150 a week for three or four years from runs as short as those enjoyed by Wilde. Insistence on this fact is laid because of the false air of glory and popularity with which his sycophantic followers have enveloped his memory. The legend is that a man who combined great genius with exceptional popularity, and was able, almost casually, to write plays that earned vast sums of money, was capriciously ruined by a stupid and sadistic people. No other legend was ever further from fact.

But it is true to say that Wilde had skill in the composition of unimportant plays which must have made him a fairly rich man had he been normal in mind and habits. That, however, is all that can be said.

It was at the end of the first performance of *Lady Windermere's Fan* that Wilde infuriated the critics by taking a call with a lighted cigarette in his fingers. The critics were very willing to take offence at anything Wilde did, but they were, surely, over-ready to feel offended by this small incident? Wilde was an addict of tobacco, the sort of person, usually a woman, who is nowadays called a chain-smoker. He probably suffered that night, as nearly every dramatist does at a first performance, from nervous agitation. It is reasonable to suppose that he carried his cigarette on to the stage, unaware that it was still in his fingers, but even if this were not the fact, had the critics reasonable cause for complaint? The speech he made to the cheering audience—it is reported by Hesketh Pearson—gave no one with any sense of humour grounds for grievance. This is what he said:

"Ladies and Gentlemen: I have enjoyed this evening *immensely*. The actors have given us a *charming* rendering of a *delightful* play, and your appreciation has been *most* intelligent. I congratulate you on the *great* success of your performance, which persuades me that you think *almost* as highly of the play as I do myself."

To fling oneself into a rage over this amusing piece of impertinence was surely to betray infantility. The critics were entitled to belittle the play which is poor stuff—even Wilde's brother, Willie, denounced it in his notice—but they were foolish to resent the cigarette and the speech. It is probable that tales of Wilde's peculiar adventures in the purlieus of Westminster were circulating in the town, and that robustly male people like Clement Scott were rendered uncritical by them: but the value of a play does not depend on its author's habits or manners. It is the business of a critic to ignore irrelevant matters in passing his judgements.

35

LADY WINDERMERE'S FAN contains all the elements that are characteristic of Wilde's work, elements that we may find in his own life. There is a beautiful, austerely virtuous, but not very intelligent wife; and there is a husband who, like Byron's Manfred, has a secret which he dare not divulge. How far Wilde was consciously drawing Lady Windermere from Constance, Lord Windermere from himself, is, of course, conjecture and may be fanciful and false. But it is notable that this situation of the beautiful and good and rather stupid wife, and the distinguished husband with a secret, recurs in *An Ideal Husband*. It is varied in *A Woman of No Importance* where the austere woman, who has yielded to a distinguished, but essentially stupid, lover, has the secret to keep. There is one even in *The Importance of Being Earnest*: the mystery of Worthing's birth. All authors reveal themselves in their work, however detached they seem to be; and some reveal themselves without realising what they are doing. It is easy, when all the facts of an author's life, so far as they are discoverable, are before us, to read into casual sentences intentions or apprehensions which were not in his mind when they were composed. We may believe that Wilde was referring to himself in that passage from *The Sphinx* which is cited in section 28; but shall we be riding a theory to death if we suspect him of a personal reference when he puts this speech into Lord Windermere's mouth?

"Misfortunes one can endure—they come from outside, they are accidents. But to suffer for one's own faults—ah!—there is the sting of life."

In estimating any dramatist's plays, the critic must constantly keep in mind the fact that he is examining, not the play which the author delivered to the producer and the cast, but the play which was subjected to the hard discipline of rehearsal. All plays, in their final form, are the result of collaboration between the dramatist and the producer and the cast and, occasionally, the audience. Cuts and additions and transpositions of dialogue and even of incident are made in rehearsal which have an important influence on the play, but they are not apparent to readers or audience who take for granted that what they read or see is the unaided work of the author. We know that Alexander induced Wilde to change the end of the second act. "I want Mrs. Erlynne's whole scene with Lord Augustus to be a 'tornado' scene", Wilde wrote to him in the letter already referred to, "and the thing to go as quickly as possible. However, I will think over the speech, and talk it over with Miss Terry." We know now that Wilde, having first refused to reveal Mrs. Erlynne's relationship to Lady Windermere until the last act, agreed after the first performance, to do what Alexander had advised: make the revelation in the second act. Wilde, in a letter to the *St. James's Gazette*, acknowledges the fact in repudiating a statement that he had altered the play in deference to the dramatic critics. At a first-night party, he said:

"All of my friends without exception were of the opinion that the psychological interest of the second act would be greatly increased by the disclosure of the actual relationship existing between Lady Windermere and Mrs. Erlynne—an opinion, I may add, that had previously been strongly held and urged by Mr. Alexander. . . . I determined, consequently, to make a change in the precise moment of revelation."

Other suggestions may have been made by members of the cast. An author who disregards them proves himself to be inexperienced as well as stupidly obstinate.

Superficially considered, Wilde's four plays seem to be well made. He belonged to the school of Scribe and Sardou, not to that of Chekhov and Shaw. His hand was lighter than Pinero's, but it lacked Pinero's constructive power. Essentially, however, they were akin. *Lady Windermere's Fan*, *A Woman of No Importance* and *An Ideal Husband* are each in four acts—*The Importance of Being Earnest* has only three—and the action takes place within twenty-four hours. Wilde, more than the majority of dramatists, observes the law of unities which is alleged to have been laid down by Aristotle: though why Aristotle, who knew very little about drama and was probably incapable of writing a play, should be considered an authority on this subject, surpasses understanding. There is no originality of form in Wilde's work. He follows a familiar pattern. Nor is his use of this pattern notably skilful. It would be easy to name a score of authors who handle their material more skilfully. The cunning with which Shakespeare manipulates a puerile plot in *The Merchant of Venice* is unmatchable. The third act of *Lady Windermere's Fan* is similar to the screen scene in *The School for Scandal*, but how much more masterly is Sheridan's craft than Wilde's. Sheridan was twenty-seven when he wrote his comedy, but Wilde was ten years older when he wrote his. Any play by Pinero, whether it be one of the early farces or one of the later problem pieces, reveals a more accomplished craftsman than Wilde. Henry Arthur Jones is generally derided to-day, but there is nothing in a play by Wilde which is comparable in dexterity to the cross-examination scene in *Mrs. Dane's Defence*. J. M. Barrie and Somerset Maugham knew all that Wilde knew, and far more.

Nevertheless, there is skill in Wilde's work, despite the habit he has of calling attention, over loudly, to his points. Half a minute after the curtain rises on the first act of *Lady Windermere's Fan*, Lord Darlington is exclaiming in ecstasy at the sight of the fan lying on a table. The title of the play sufficiently indicates the fan's importance. An adroiter dramatist would have called attention to it later in the act and less obviously. But Wilde is always over-emphatic. Not only must Lord Darlington hint to Lady Windermere that her husband is unfaithful, but hot on his heels, the Duchess of Berwick, almost before he has left the room, must blurt out her suspicions crudely and coarsely. These are the devices of a jejune author. They reveal neither skill nor delicate perception. Wilde's sense of character is uncommonly slight. It is frequently false. He fails, for instance, to distinguish between Lady Windermere and her author, putting words into her mouth more fitting for his when he was in a moralising or cynical mood: what the French would call *un mot de caractère* or *situation* in contrast with *un mot d'auteur*. Wilde makes Lady Windermere express sentiments which, at her age and with her mind and experience of life, she is plainly incapable of holding or uttering. Examples will be cited in a later section. Lord Windermere is a dummy. Nothing that he does, and little that he says, is what we expect from an adult man who, without being exceptionally able, is tolerably intelligent. If the play be stripped of its irrelevant epigrams and her grace of Berwick's inconsequent and mindless chatter, the residue is seen to be commonplace melodrama.

36

THE comedy opens in Lord Windermere's morning-room in Carlton House Terrace. Lady Windermere's twenty-first birthday is to be celebrated that night by a small and early dance which she considers to be very select, although we meet some very queer fish at it. A corrupt and malignant gossip, the Duchess of Berwick, is there, in hot pursuit of a wealthy Australian for her dull daughter, Agatha. Her brother, Lord Augustus Lorton, who cannot remember whether he has been twice married and once divorced, or twice divorced and once married, is also there. So are Lady Plymdale and her present lover, Mr. Cecil Dumby. Lord Darlington, a renowned rip, and rampant with desire for Lady Windermere herself, is another guest. If these are the people who are to be found in morally select and exclusive houses, what sort of people might have been found in carelessly-conducted houses? Lady Windermere is, we suspect, either culpably ignorant of the character of some of her guests or an unconscionable hypocrite. At her small and early parties, no one less virtuous than an archimandrite or an abbess of an enclosed order should have been present. Her avowals of strict Puritanism and high discrimination about people's characters seem inconsistent with the company she keeps, but as the woman is a fool, that perhaps is not surprising. She has no doubt about her own austere and incorruptible integrity. She accepts no excuse and makes no allowance for lapse. All breaches of the convention are unpardonable, and the question of their cause has no bearing on the matter. When Lord Darlington asks her if she "thinks seriously that women who have committed what the world calls a fault should never be forgiven", she replies, with downright and vicious virtue, "I think they should never be forgiven". Her teeth clash, we feel certain, as in the act of biting, and her lips compress into hard inflexible lines as she speaks. This must be Torquemada's daughter! . . .

No time is wasted in the first short and hustled act, and we are quickly made aware of the essential facts of the play. Lady Windermere is arranging roses in a blue bowl when the curtain rises. A moment or two later, Lord Darlington enters, spots the fan, pays Lady Windermere routine compliments, is told that she is twenty-one that very day, and declares himself to be in love with her. He is then informed of her moral attitude:

LADY WINDERMERE: . . . You think I am a Puritan, I suppose? Well, I have something of the Puritan in me. I was brought up like that, I am glad of it. My mother died when I was a mere child. I lived always with Lady Julia, my father's elder sister, you know. She was stern to me, but she taught me what the world is forgetting, the difference that there is between what is right and what is wrong. *She* allowed of no compromise. *I* allow of none.

LORD DARLINGTON: My dear Lady Windermere!

LADY WINDERMERE (*leaning back on the sofa*): You look on me as being behind the age. Well, I am! I should be sorry to be on the same level as an age like this.

LORD DARLINGTON: You think the age very bad?

LADY WINDERMERE: Yes. Nowadays people seem to look on life as a speculation. It is not a speculation. It is a sacrament. Its purification is sacrifice.

LORD DARLINGTON (*smiling*): Oh, anything is better than being sacrificed!

LADY WINDERMERE (*leaning forward*): Don't say that.

LORD DARLINGTON: I do say it. I feel it—I know it.

At this point they are interrupted for a few moments by the butler. Wilde avoids long uninterrupted conversations, even if he has to make a trivial interruption to break them. Or was this useful interruption, lasting only a few moments, suggested by Alexander, who knew how impatient audiences were during long speeches, until Bernard Shaw taught them how to listen to argument? After the butler's withdrawal, the conversation on Lady Windermere's severe moral code is resumed, and resumed, so far as Darlington is concerned, with the intention of advancing his suit for her seduction:

LORD DARLINGTON (*still seated*): Do you think then—of course I am only putting an imaginary instance—do you think that in the case of a young married couple, say about two years married, if the husband suddenly becomes the intimate friend of a woman of—well, more than doubtful character—is always calling upon her, lunching with her, and probably paying her bills—do you think that the wife should not console herself?

LADY WINDERMERE (*frowning*): Console herself?

LORD DARLINGTON: Yes. I think she should—I think she has the right.

LADY WINDERMERE: Because the husband is vile—should the wife be vile also?

LORD DARLINGTON: Vileness is a terrible word, Lady Windermere.

LADY WINDERMERE: It is a terrible thing, Lord Darlington.

Lord Darlington then delivers as much as he can remember of Wilde's *Intentions*. "Do you know," he says, "I am afraid that good people do a great deal of harm in this world. Certainly the greatest harm they do is that they make badness of such extraordinary importance. It is absurd to divide people into good and bad. People are either charming or tedious. I take the side of the charming, and you, Lady Windermere, can't help belonging to them." Soon after this speech is made, comes the question from Lord Darlington to which Lady Windermere, as stated earlier in this section, replies that women who have fallen into fault should never be forgiven.

Lord Darlington is not a pretty fellow. He may fairly be described as an unscrupulous cad. That speech in which an "imaginary instance" is cited, must seem poisonous even to those who are neither squeamish nor particular. As a sample of charm, it is poor stuff. But Lady Windermere, despite his reference to two years of marriage in his "imaginary instance", does not suspect that he is referring to her husband and herself. It is not until the Duchess of Berwick, a few minutes later, tells her, almost brutally, the gossip of the town, that she perceives his point. This mischievous and detestable old woman is amusing enough as a mindless chatterbox, but she becomes appalling when she is accepted as a human being. "And now I must tell you how sorry I am for you, dear Margaret", she says to Lady Windermere after the door has closed behind Lord Darlington, so soon afterwards that one is tempted to think of her as his procuress. "But, really, I am so sorry for you, Margaret."

LADY WINDERMERE (*smiling*): Why, Duchess?

DUCHESS OF BERWICK: Oh, on account of that horrid woman. She dresses so well, too, which makes it much worse, sets such a dreadful example. Augustus—you know my disreputable brother—such a trial to us all—well, Augustus is completely infatuated by her. It is quite scandalous, for she is absolutely inadmissible to society. Many a woman has a past, but I'm told that she has at least a dozen, and that they all fit.

LADY WINDERMERE: Whom are you talking about, Duchess?

DUCHESS OF BERWICK: About Mrs. Erlynne.

LADY WINDERMERE: Mrs. Erlynne? I never heard of her, Duchess. And what *has* she to do with me?

DUCHESS OF BERWICK: My poor child!

Then the Duchess makes her revelation. Windermere, she tells his wife, "goes to see" Mrs. Erlynne "continually, and stops for hours at a time, and while he is there she is not at home to anyone". Mrs. Erlynne "has taken a house in Curzon Street . . . and they tell me that Windermere goes there four or five times a week. . . . And the worst of it is that I have been told that this woman has got a great deal of money out of somebody, for it seems that she came to London six months ago without anything at all to speak of, and now she has this charming house in Mayfair, drives her ponies in the Park every afternoon, and all—well, all—since she has known poor dear Windermere."

This revelation distresses Lady Windermere terribly. "We are only married two years", she cries. "Our child is but two months old."

Her behaviour thereafter is entirely fatuous, but no more so than her husband's both before and after the revelation. Wilde gives no hint that he realises either Lady Windermere's folly or her husband's. An author is entitled, if he so desires, to make fools the principal figures in his play, but he is not entitled to treat them as if they were wise. To do so, is to become as culpable as he would be were he to claim our sympathy for cruel or cowardly characters by treating them as if they were kind and courageous. It is permissible, it is, indeed, desirable that an author should account for the cowardice of a character, but it is neither permissible nor desirable to pretend that he is uncommonly brave. Shakespeare does not present Macbeth as a man of noble spirit, nor does he ask us to overlook the murder of Duncan in remembering Lady Macbeth's cleverness and charm.

There is no escape from the fact that Lady Windermere, as Wilde portrays her, is an exceptionally stupid and narrow-minded woman, with a strong strain of sadism in her nature, and that when she is set upon her own comfort and convenience, she is utterly unscrupulous. How quickly her unbending morality collapses when her life is troubled. She repudiates Lord Darlington's suggestion that a wife should return infidelity for infidelity, and proclaims her inflexible conviction that a woman who breaks the conventional code should never be forgiven nor expect to be forgiven; yet her first thought, on discovering what appears to be infidelity in her husband, is to fly to Darlington's rooms to become his mistress. She is not consistent with herself, and her inconsistency is due, not to the contradictions we find in Nature, which is not interested in chastity, but to the simple fact that her creator did not take enough thought over his character. It was Wilde's job to know intimately the woman he had conceived, but he neglected his duty as if he had been the lover in Swinburne's poem:

I remember the way we parted,
The day and the way we met;
You hoped we were both broken-hearted,
And knew we should both forget.

And the best and the worst of that is
That neither is most to blame,
If you have forgotten my kisses
And I have forgotten your name.

Lady Windermere's conduct after she has become convinced that her husband is unfaithful to her is entirely stupid. Her ignorance of Mrs. Erlynne's existence is incredible in view of the lively discussion that lady causes among Lady Windermere's friends and acquaintances. Was no mention of Mrs. Erlynne ever made in Lady Windermere's presence during the whole of the six months which preceded the revelation? Was the Duchess of Berwick, who was so plainspoken on the day of the dance, unwontedly mum for the whole of that time? Did Lord Darlington never insinuate a remark to his own advantage until that afternoon? Had Lady Windermere never met Mrs. Erlynne at any of the parties and receptions they both frequented? To be oblivious to that extent is surely to be exceptionally obtuse?

There are many mysteries of this sort, especially in connexion with Mrs. Erlynne, to which reference will presently be made. Our concern now is the reaction of Lady Windermere to her discovery, as she believes, of Lord Windermere's adultery. It is not such as we should expect in a woman as morally rigid as she professes to be. Her stern Aunt Julia, she tells Lord Darlington, had taught her the difference between right and wrong, and had allowed no compromise between them, although we may warrantably wonder whether her stern Aunt Julia knew very much about the difference, and imagined herself to be virtuous when she was merely repressive. Is it probable that an inflexible Puritan, as certain of her uprightness and sound judgement as Aunt Julia herself, would, on hearing of her husband's infidelity, instantly behave in a way which her stern Aunt Julia would certainly have condemned and reprobated? To show disapproval of Mrs. Erlynne by behaving like Mrs. Erlynne is, surely, a senseless proceeding? She could have demanded a break with Mrs. Erlynne as a condition of her remaining in her husband's house or, if she were too deeply revolted by her discovery even to contemplate that action, she could have flown, not to Darlington, but to stern Aunt Julia for shelter.

But the first thought that enters her head is that she must elope with the lover whose tenders of affection she had, only an hour earlier, repelled with every appearance of scorn and disgust.

Insistence is laid on this cardinal point—the whole comedy turns on it—to support the argument that Wilde did not *think out* his people. He dashed the play off in less than a month, flipping his irrelevant epigrams about as if they alone mattered, and omitted to understand the nature of his characters or to make their actions plausible.

37

IMMEDIATELY after the departure of the damnable duchess, Lady Windermere, protesting in a highly rhetorical soliloquy, her disbelief in a single word of that lady's accusations, runs to her husband's desk to rifle it. She finds a sealed bank pass-book and slits it open. There she finds entries of payments made to Mrs. Erlynne: one of £600, another of £700, a third of £400. There appear to be others. While she is scanning them in deep distress, Windermere enters. In reply to her reproaches, he first complains of her action in opening his pass-book; then insists that she has no ground for grievance against him; and finally denies that he is or ever was or ever will be Mrs. Erlynne's lover. Until six months earlier, he had never heard of her, a lady who, he remarks, has "conducted herself well" since he has known her, a statement which is manifestly false, as we soon discover, for it transpires that she has been blackmailing him—the word *blackmailing* is his—by threatening to reveal her relationship to his wife unless he keeps her well supplied with funds. As he himself says to Mrs. Erlynne in the fourth act, "rather than my wife should know—that the mother she was taught to consider as dead, the mother she had mourned as dead, is living—a divorced woman, going about under an assumed name, a bad woman preying upon life, as I know you now to be—rather than that, I was ready to supply you with money to pay bill after bill, extravagance after extravagance, to risk what occurred yesterday, the first quarrel I have ever had with my wife". Yet he concluded this speech, which amounts to a grave accusation, with the statement that he "used to think that with all your faults you were frank and honest". How could he have thought that when she had made it perfectly plain to him that she was not, when, as he tells her a few moments later:

"For twenty years of your life you lived without your child, without a thought of your child. One day you read in the papers that she had married a rich man. You saw your hideous chance. You knew that to spare her the ignominy of learning that a woman like you was her mother, I would endure anything. You began your blackmailing."

She is still blackmailing him in the second act, demanding a settlement of £2000 or, "better still", £2500 a year so that she may not go empty-handed to Lord Augustus Lorton who contemplates marrying her. His ignorance of Mrs. Erlynne's existence and history seems to be general. Lord Augustus Lorton is as ignorant as Windermere, and, apparently, everybody else. "What I want to know is this. Who is she?" Lord Augustus asks his host during the dance. "Where does she come from? Why hasn't she got any demmed relations?"

Is not Wilde here making a demand on our credulity which no author has any right to make? The Victorian era has received some hard knocks, especially from people who never lived in it, but were the Victorians as mindless as Wilde, himself a Victorian, here tries to persuade us they were? Mrs. Erlynne's elopement caused excitement at the time it took place, and there must have been many people in the society to which she sought to return, who remembered it and her, despite the lapse of twenty years. Was there *nobody* in London acquainted with her? She had been deserted by the lover with whom she eloped, but had lived not uncomfortably through the subsequent years. The source of her income must have been known to somebody. It is not possible for a woman of her origin and history, living in the style in which presumably she did live, to move about Europe without ever encountering countrymen who had some knowledge of her career. A woman does not suddenly turn up in London and create a furore in exclusive society when not a soul has the slightest idea of her history. Yet Lord Windermere is able to tell his wife that although people "chatter about her, they don't know anything against her". But the fact that they do not know anything *for* her is surely graver? A mysterious woman, obviously "damaged goods" in Brieux' sense of that term, cannot turn up, almost destitute, in any society and establish a right of entrance to what are called exclusive houses merely because that is her wish; and the general ignorance of her history must have made the satisfaction of her desire impossible. Mrs. Erlynne is devoid of any quality other than a fading beauty and some skill in handling unparticular men. She seems not to have the slightest interest in her daughter, apart from her value as a social lever, and there is no hint in the whole play that the sight of the daughter she deserted in her infancy stirs even mild affection in her. The effort she makes to save Lady Windermere from disaster is no more than she might have made for any young girl whom she had found on the brink of calamity—an impulse such as stirred Dick Dudgeon in *The Devil's Disciple* and having little or no relation to natural love.

Lady Windermere's ignorance of her mother's existence and history is hard to believe. Even a narrow-minded young woman who had been strictly brought up by a sternly moral aunt who knew the difference between right and wrong and was intimately informed of the Almighty's intentions about His universe, must, some time and somewhere, have heard whispers about her mother. Were there no servants in Aunt Julia's house to tittle-tattle? Did no one, when the abandoned child had become a woman and a wife, enquire, "Do you ever hear of your mother?" or remark, "I saw your mother in Vienna last week"?

To maintain his fantastic tale, Wilde has to create a fantastic world, inhabited by fantastic people who never mention disturbing facts. Yet the Duchess of Berwick is sufficiently insensitive to make remarks without the slightest concern about the wounds she inflicts.

The legend that Victorians were morbidly diffident about such matters, and habitually treated young women, even when they were matrons, as if they were liable to be flung into fits and convulsions if anyone so much as mentioned unsanctified relations, does not bear examination. Lord Windermere's age is not revealed in the play, but he is, presumably, six to ten years older than his wife. His part could hardly have been taken by Alexander if he were not. Adult men do not behave in the way Windermere behaved. Even if he had been as eager to hide the fact of Mrs. Erlynne's existence from her daughter, his wife, he would, surely, have had the common sense to ask his solicitors to make any arrangements with the importunate lady he was willing to make? Why must he visit her in Curzon Street so frequently that, even if the Duchess of Berwick is exaggerating, he seems to be there almost every day? Was it wise to make money gifts to Mrs. Erlynne amounting, in less than six months, to at least £1700? "If Men were wise," William Blake wrote, "the Most arbitrary Princes could not hurt them. If they are not Wise, the Freest Government is compell'd to be a tyranny." Windermere was not wise, it appears, but whose was the fault for his folly: his or his author's? Wilde, surely, was the culprit, since he created a character out of all nature and reason.

Even if Windermere's stupidity before his wife's discovery of the peccant entries in his pass-book were credible, a man must be nearly imbecile to be guilty of the folly he commits after it has been made? His wife believes him to be Mrs. Erlynne's lover. She has been told, obliquely by Darlington, directly by the Duchess of Berwick, that her husband has become notorious through his association, almost ostentatious, with a woman who is a notorious demi-rep, and has learnt with horror that he is paying her large sums of money. She believes that Mrs. Erlynne, as the phrase goes, is his kept woman. Three minutes after the discovery of the pass-book, Windermere requests her to invite Mrs. Erlynne to the dance she is giving that very evening to celebrate her twenty-first birthday! . . .

"Margaret," he says with extraordinary ineptitude, "you could save this woman. She wants to get back into society, and she wants you to help her. . . . I want you to send her an invitation to our party to-night."

This is a monstrous suggestion, whatever view of Lady Windermere we may take, and its monstrosity is increased when Windermere, receiving her refusal, asserts that he will send an invitation to Mrs. Erlynne: which, despite his wife's protests, he does. Is it conceivable that an adult man, not mentally deficient, would behave as Wilde makes Windermere behave? A mindless and arbitrary man, or a man who had ceased to feel any affection for his wife and was eager to humiliate her in public, or a drink-sodden sadist might so behave; but there is nothing in the play to indicate that any of these descriptions apply to Windermere, who is shown as deeply devoted to his wife and anxious to spare her distress, even if he suffers misunderstanding for it. What a paltry excuse he offers in defence of his demand. Mrs. Erlynne, of whose existence six months before he had been ignorant, wishes to "get back into society"! The banality of Windermere's excuse for a demand which must cause public, as well as private, humiliation to his wife, is almost unbelievable. Is he under any obligation to restore Mrs. Erlynne to the society she has deserted? Is she, in his knowledge of her as a blackmailer, fit to be restored to any society? He has made grave efforts to conceal the knowledge that Mrs. Erlynne is Lady Windermere's mother, yet proposes to make her a frequenter of his house—for we cannot suppose that the invitation to the dance will be the last she will expect to receive—and thus expose his wife to the constant risk that the revelation will, accidentally or deliberately, be made by somebody.

Lady Windermere has no duty of which she is aware to help Mrs. Erlynne in any way. Even if she had known that Mrs. Erlynne was her mother, would the fact have given Mrs. Erlynne a claim on the duty of the daughter she had deserted in her infancy? Lord Windermere's demand on his wife's generosity of spirit is not one which any man who loves his wife can possibly make. Wilde sacrifices probability to sensation. He is determined, even at the cost of distorting the nature of his characters, to devise a "strong" scene, a scene, that is to say, in which not only reasonable, but natural, behaviour is abandoned by seemingly sensible people.

The demand that Mrs. Erlynne shall be invited to the dance is followed by a swift and skilfully contrived "curtain". Wilde was essentially melodramatic, but he was skilful in stunning his audience with a "strong" scene and depriving it of its powers of discrimination. Lord Windermere, having written out the card of invitation, rings for Parker, his butler, and instructs him to have it sent to Mrs. Erlynne at once. The butler retires, and Lady Windermere immediately exclaims, "Arthur, if that woman comes here, I shall insult her".

LORD WINDERMERE: Margaret, don't say that.

LADY WINDERMERE: I mean it.

LORD WINDERMERE: Child, if you did such a thing, there's not a woman in London who wouldn't pity you.

LADY WINDERMERE: There is not a *good* woman in London who would not applaud me. We have been too lax. We must make an example. I propose to begin to-night. (*Picking up fan*) Yes, you gave me this fan to-day; it was your birthday present. If that woman crosses my threshold, I shall strike her across the face with it.

LORD WINDERMERE: Margaret, you couldn't do such a thing.

LADY WINDERMERE: You don't know me! (*Moves away.*)

Enter PARKER.

LADY WINDERMERE: Parker!

PARKER: Yes, my lady.

LADY WINDERMERE: I shall dine in my own room. I don't want dinner, in fact. See that everything is ready by half-past ten. And, Parker, be sure you pronounce the names of the guests very distinctly to-night. Sometimes you speak so fast that I miss them. I am particularly anxious to hear the names quite clearly, so as to make no mistake. You understand, Parker.

Parker: Yes, my lady.

Lady Windermere: That will do!

Parker *goes out.*

Lady Windermere (*speaking to* Lord Windermere): Arthur, if that woman comes here—I warn you—

Lord Windermere: Margaret, you'll ruin us!

Lady Windermere: Us! From this moment my life is separate from yours. But if you wish to avoid a public scandal, write at once to this woman, and tell her that I forbid her to come here!

Lord Windermere: I will not—I cannot—she must come!

Lady Windermere: Then I shall do exactly as I have said. (*Goes to leave.*) You leave me no choice. (*She goes out.*)

Lord Windermere (*calling after her*): Margaret! Margaret! (*A pause.*) My God! What shall I do? I dare not tell her who this woman really is. The shame would kill her. (*Sinks down into a chair and buries his face in his hands.*)

CURTAIN

It would be foolish, as well as ungenerous, to deny that this is good melodramatic stuff: a highly effective end to a scene, though we must not forget that the final speech was suggested by Alexander and eventually forced upon Wilde by some of his friends. William Archer, in *Play-Making*, describes its effect on the first-night audience and on himself. Admitting that "there is no plausible excuse for Lord Windermere's obstinacy in forcing Mrs. Erlynne upon his wife, and risking a violent scandal in order to postpone an explanation which he must know to be ultimately inevitable", he declares, first, that "interest is largely independent of critical judgement", which is, unfortunately, a fact, and then states that, "for my own part, I can aver that, when the curtain fell on the first act, a five-pound note would not have bribed me to leave the theatre without assisting at Lady Windermere's reception in the second act. The dramatist has higher functions than mere story-telling; but this is fundamental, and the true artist is the last to despise it."

It is not true, as Lady Windermere asserts, that her husband's refusal to cancel Mrs. Erlynne's invitation leaves her no choice. She could have asked him a question: why do you insist that Mrs. Erlynne shall be invited here? That is what any sensible woman would have enquired, but if Lady Windermere had asked her husband that question, a very exciting curtain would have been ruined. Many plays and many novels would end abruptly or require a very different development if one intelligent question were asked in the first act! We may well enquire if sense is to be sacrificed to "curtains", but we cannot deny that it often is with immense melodramatic effect. If a single lawyer in Venice had known what Portia, who was not a native of Venice, knew, that it was against the Venetian law for an alien to conspire against the life of a citizen, one of the most skilfully-contrived acts in the whole history of dramatic literature would have been rendered impossible. But was Shakespeare entitled to ask his audience to surrender its intelligence for the sake of a good bit of melodrama? A mindless woman of violent temper might not enquire why her husband is eager to make a notorious woman an habituée of his house, but Lady Windermere is not intended by Wilde to be regarded as such a woman. That speech by Lord Windermere—"I will not—I cannot—she must come!"—must surely have stirred some enquiry in Lady Windermere's mind. Why *must* Mrs. Erlynne come? What is behind all this mystery? But Lady Windermere, so strictly brought up by stern Aunt Julia, asks no questions. She sweeps out of the room, clutching her fan.

38

FROM this point to the end of the play, improbability is the prevailing characteristic, with occasional outbursts of puerility. Wilde, having worked his audience up to the point at which it wonders whether there is to be another "strong" scene in the second act when Lady Windermere will give Mrs. Erlynne a resounding smack in the face with her fan, disappoints its expectations. Mrs. Erlynne is announced, but "*Lady Windermere clutches at her fan, then lets it drop on the floor. She bows coldly to Mrs. Erlynne, who bows sweetly in turn, and sails into the room.*" This is anti-climax. A determined melodramatist would have compelled Lady Windermere to commit the assault; and a highly diverting conclusion could have been constructed from its result. Shaw, in an impish mood, would have made Lady Windermere hit the wrong woman: a Serene Highness, perhaps, or the wife of the Archbishop of Canterbury. A reasonable author, however, would have forced Lord Windermere to tell his wife the truth in the first act or, if melodrama was desired, in the second act, as Mrs. Erlynne was approaching Lady Windermere and Lady Windermere was about to raise her fan. Windermere had only to say to his wife, "She's your mother!" and the fan would have fallen on the floor with a terrific crash. That, indeed, is what Wilde at the penultimate moment almost does. The dance has begun. Mrs. Erlynne's arrival is imminent.

LORD WINDERMERE: Margaret! I must speak to you.

LADY WINDERMERE: Will you hold my fan for me, Lord Darlington? Thanks. (*Comes towards him.*)

LORD WINDERMERE (*crossing to her*): Margaret, what you said before dinner is, of course, impossible?

LADY WINDERMERE: That woman is not coming here to-night!

LORD WINDERMERE: Mrs. Erlynne is coming here, and if you in any way annoy or wound her, you will bring shame and sorrow on us both. Remember that! Ah, Margaret, only trust me! A wife should trust her husband!

to which Lady Windermere rejoins, in one of several speeches which spring, not from her lips, but from Wilde's:

London is full of women who trust their husbands. One can always recognise them. They look so thoroughly unhappy. I am not going to be one of them. (*Moves away.*) Lord Darlington, will you give me back my fan, please? Thanks. . . . A useful thing a fan, isn't it? . . . I want a friend to-night, Lord Darlington: I didn't know I would want one so soon.

LORD DARLINGTON: Lady Windermere! I knew the time would come some day; but why to-night?

LORD WINDERMERE: I *will* tell her. I must. It would be terrible if there were a scene. Margaret . . .

PARKER: Mrs. Erlynne!

LORD WINDERMERE *starts.* MRS. ERLYNNE *enters, very beautifully dressed and very dignified.* LADY WINDERMERE *clutches at her fan, then lets it drop on the floor. She bows coldly to* Mrs. Erlynne, *who bows sweetly in turn, and sails into the room.*

Lord Darlington: You have dropped your fan, Lady Windermere. (*Picks it up and hands it to her.*)

Mrs. Erlynne: How do you do, again, Lord Windermere? How charming your sweet wife looks! Quite a picture!

Lord Windermere (*in a low voice*): It was terribly rash of you to come!

Mrs. Erlynne (*smiling*): The wisest thing I ever did in my life. And, by the way, you must pay me a good deal of attention this evening. I am afraid of the women. You must introduce me to some of them. The men I can always manage.

Windermere had time, after Parker's announcement of Mrs. Erlynne, to whisper to his wife, "She's your mother!" a revelation which would have been more sensational than any other that is made in the play and would have had an effect on his wife and on the audience far beyond any that Wilde achieved. Objection may, perhaps, be raised to this suggestion on the ground that the play would then and there have ended. But would it? Is there not a very interesting play to be made out of the discovery by such a woman as Lady Windermere, who believes herself to be an orphan, that such a woman as Mrs. Erlynne is her mother?

Wilde having surrendered his theme to commonplace melodrama, must devise even more commonplace devices to keep the play, now beginning to creak, alive. But before we consider them, let us here note a peculiar change in Lady Windermere, as revealed in her conversation, which follows on her discovery of what she believes to be her husband's relation to Mrs. Erlynne: the cynical turn it takes. Our argument here is not that a change could not have occurred, but that the change made by Wilde is out of character, that he puts words into her mouth which she is incapable of using, words which come from his lips, not from hers; and that by making her speak as he would have spoken, he reduced her to the level of a ventriloquist's doll.

The first words to denote the cynicism she now begins to display are spoken in the first act immediately after she has refused her husband's request that she shall send Mrs. Erlynne an invitation to the dance. "How hard good women are!" Lord Windermere exclaims. His wife retorts, "How weak bad men are!" From what experience of life has Lady Windermere drawn that remark? She is twenty-one. Until her marriage at the age of eighteen, she had had a strict and secluded life with her stern Aunt Julia who, we may feel certain, allowed no bad men to approach her. Soon after her twentieth year she becomes a mother. Her marriage and her maternity have not, we may believe, left her much time in which to survey the world and form reliable opinions about it. And if we have difficulty in believing that she could have said, "How weak bad men are!" shall we not find it impossible to believe that she could have spoken those lines in the second act which have been cited in the extract on page 205: "London is full of women who trust their husbands. One can always recognise them. They look so thoroughly unhappy." Can anyone with an ear for characteristic speech accept these lines later in the second act when Lady Windermere, referring to her husband, soliloquises thus: "It is he who has broken the bond of marriage—not I. I only break its bondage"? Or these from the fourth act:

> "Actions are the first tragedy in life, words are the second. Words are perhaps the worst. Words are merciless."

Never in this or any other world could this commonplace, callow girl of twenty-one have spoken those lines. Her mind was incapable of conceiving them. She could never have uttered them because she could never have thought them. We are as bewildered by them, spoken by her, as we are by Miranda's statement that "good wombs have borne bad sons". How does she know who, when she spoke those words, had seen no other people since she was three than Caliban and Prospero? Ariel is a sexless sprite.

39

THE comedy now runs rapidly down the steep place to mindless melodrama. Lady Windermere strides through the scene like one of the Erinyes in a state of nervous collapse. "Oh, the house is tainted", she tells Lord Darlington. "I am degraded in my own eyes!" Darlington, elated by her statement, decides that this is the opportunity for which he has long been seeking; and, in language that might have been lifted from Ouida, pleads with her to fly with him that very night.

LORD DARLINGTON: I offer you my life.

LADY WINDERMERE: Lord Darlington!

LORD DARLINGTON: My life—my whole life. Take it, and do with it what you will. . . . I love you—love you as I have never loved any living thing. From the moment I met you I loved you, loved you blindly, adoringly, madly! You did not know it then—you know it now! Leave this house to-night. I won't tell you that this world matters nothing, or the world's voice, or the voice of society. They matter a great deal. They matter far too much. But there are moments when one has to choose between living one's own life, fully, entirely, completely—or dragging out some false, shallow, degrading existence that the world in its hypocrisy demands. You have the moment now. Choose! Oh, my love, choose!

LADY WINDERMERE (*moving slowly away from him, and looking at him with startled eyes*): I have not the courage.

LORD DARLINGTON (*following her*): Yes; you have the courage. There may be six months of pain, of disgrace even, but when you no longer bear his name, when you bear mine, all will be well. Margaret, my love, my wife that shall be some day—yes, my wife! You know it! What are you now? This woman has the place that belongs by right to you. Oh, go—go out of this house, with head erect, with a smile upon your lips, with courage in your eyes. All London will know why you did it; and who will blame you? No one. If they do, what matter? Wrong? What is wrong? It's wrong for a man to abandon his wife for a shameless woman. It is wrong for a wife to remain with a man who so dishonours her. You said once you would make no compromise with things. Make none now. Be brave! Be yourself!

LADY WINDERMERE: I am afraid of being myself. Let me think! Let me wait! My husband may return to me. (*Sits down on sofa.*)

LORD DARLINGTON: And you would take him back? You are not what I thought you were. You are just the same as every other woman. You would stand anything rather than face the censure of a world, whose praise you would despise. In a week you will be driving with this woman in the Park. She will be your constant guest—your dearest friend. You would endure anything rather than break with one blow this monstrous tie. You are right. You have no courage; none!

Lady Windermere: Ah! give me time to think. I cannot answer you now. (*Passes her hand nervously over her brow.*)

Lord Darlington: It must be now or not at all.

Lady Windermere (*rising from the sofa*): Then, not at all! (*A pause.*)

Lord Darlington: You break my heart!

Lady Windermere: Mine is already broken. (*A pause.*)

Lord Darlington: To-morrow I leave England. This is the last time I shall ever look on you. You will never see me again. For one moment our lives met—our souls touched. They must never meet or touch again. Good-bye, Margaret. (*He goes out.*)

Lady Windermere: How alone I am in life! How terribly alone!

Lord Darlington, it will be observed in this scene, is expert in the arts and devices of seduction. As he goes out, he is probably chuckling to himself, "But I shall get you yet, my girl".

How inferior this clap-trap appears when it is compared with the beautiful scene in Somerset Maugham's cynical comedy, *The Circle*, a play similar in many respects to Wilde's, in which Edward Luton persuades Elizabeth Champion-Cheney to elope:

Elizabeth: I'm afraid.

Teddie (*in a whisper*): Elizabeth.

Elizabeth: I can't face it. It's asking too much of me. Let's say good-bye to one another, Teddie. It's the only thing to do. And have pity on me. I'm giving up all my hopes of happiness.

He goes up to her and looks into her eyes.

Teddie: But I wasn't offering you happiness. I don't think my sort of love tends to happiness. I'm jealous. I'm not a very easy man to get on with. I'm often out of temper and irritable. I should be fed to the teeth with you sometimes, and so would you with me. I daresay we'd fight like cat and dog, and sometimes we'd hate each other. Often you'd be wretched and bored stiff and lonely, and often you'd be frightfully homesick, and then you'd regret all you'd lost. Stupid women would be rude to you because we'd run away together. And some of them would cut you. I don't offer you peace and quietness. I offer you unrest and anxiety. I don't offer you happiness. I offer you love.

It reminds us of Garibaldi offering his recruits wounds and death, and gaining a host of serving soldiers. Elizabeth stretches her arms out to Luton. "You hateful creature," she cries, "I absolutely adore you", and off they bolt.

Soon after the scene with Darlington has ended, Lady Windermere overhears Mrs. Erlynne bargaining with Windermere for an allowance of £2000 a year; and she decides to leave her husband and go to Darlington that night. But she pauses long enough to write a letter stating what she has done, and why. A few moments after she has departed, Mrs. Erlynne enters and asks Parker where his mistress is. "Her ladyship has just gone out of the house", the butler replies nonchalantly, as if the departure of a lady from her home at a late hour of the night were a common occurrence. Lady Windermere, he adds, has "left a letter for his lordship on the table". Parker, we fear, was not familiar with the literature of the servants' hall, for if he had been, that letter would certainly have made him feel suspicious.

MRS. ERLYNNE: A letter for Lord Windermere?

PARKER: Yes, madam.

MRS. ERLYNNE: Thank you. (*Exit* PARKER. *The music in the ballroom stops.*) Gone out of the house! A letter addressed to her husband! (*Goes over to the bureau and looks at letter. Takes it up and lays it down again with a shudder of fear.*) No, no! It would be impossible. Life doesn't repeat its tragedies like that! Oh, why does this horrible fancy come across me? Why do I remember now the one moment of my life I wish most to forget? Does life repeat its tragedies? (*Tears letter open and reads it, then sinks down into a chair with a gesture of anguish.*) Oh how terrible! The same words that twenty years ago I wrote to her father! And how bitterly I have been punished for it! No; my punishment, my real punishment, is to-night, is now!

Lord Windermere enters and, picking up the letter which Mrs. Erlynne, in her agitation, has dropped, discovers that it is written by his wife, but is fobbed off by Mrs. Erlynne from investigating the matter further. She gets him out of the room, and orders Lord Augustus Lorton, who enters opportunely, to take him to his club and keep him there as long as possible. Then the act quietly closes. But this quiet close was Alexander's idea, not Wilde's. He had wanted a "tornado" finish to the second act.

40

THE third act opens with Lady Windermere soliloquising lengthily and rhetorically in Lord Darlington's rooms. To suit her author's convenience at the end of the act, she has considerately brought her fan with her—the last thing she was likely to do. How she obtained admission does not transpire. Darlington presumably has a manservant, but there is no sign of him in the play, and his presence would have prevented the sensational situation at the end of the act; for the servant would have informed Lord Darlington that no less than two ladies were awaiting him! Wilde, after the fashion of melodramatists, ignores awkward facts. We will return to this small but important point later in the section. The state of Lady Windermere's mind is evident from her opening words. Standing by the fireplace, she harangues herself. "Why doesn't he come? This waiting is horrible. He should be here. Why is he not here, to wake by passionate words some fire within me. I am cold—cold as a loveless thing." These remarks sound as if they had been snatched from the works of Mrs. Amanda McKittrick Ros. She moralises on men and their wayward and wicked habits. "If a woman wants to hold a man, she has merely to appeal to the worst in him. We make gods of men and they leave us. Others make brutes of them and they fawn and are faithful. How hideous life is! . . .

Oh! it was mad of me to come here, horribly mad. And yet, which is the worst, I wonder, to be at the mercy of a man who loves one, or the wife of a man who in one's own house dishonours one? What woman knows? What woman in the whole world? But will he love me always, this man to whom I am giving my life? What do I bring him? Lips that have lost the note of joy, eyes that are blinded by tears, chill hands and icy heart. I must go back—no; I can't go back, my letter has put me in their power! . . .

There is more of this stuff, unnatural on those lips, for Lady Windermere is now a very rhetorical woman and accustomed to bouts of eloquence; but it is mercifully interrupted by the entrance of Mrs. Erlynne, whose arrival completely nonplusses the delinquent lady. Wilde is as silent about Mrs. Erlynne's means of admission as he is about Lady Windermere's. It almost appears as if any person who happens to be passing by Lord Darlington's rooms, even in the middle of the night, can enter them without the slightest difficulty. If ever a man keeps open house, he does.

Mrs. Erlynne, belatedly maternal, has come to plead with her daughter to return to Lord Windermere. But Lady Windermere flies into a fury at her interference, in which she sees only the effort of an unscrupulous woman to obtain a screen for her own iniquities. "My husband sent you to lure me back that I might serve as a blind to whatever relations exist between you and him", she cries. "Go back to my husband, Mrs. Erlynne. He belongs to you and not to me. I suppose he is afraid of a scandal. Men are such cowards. They outrage every law of the world, are afraid of the world's tongue. But he had better prepare himself. He shall have a scandal. He shall have the worst scandal there has been in London for years. He shall see his name in every vile paper, mine on every hideous placard! . . ." There is a great deal more in this strain, ending with the assertion, "Women like you have no hearts. Heart is not in you. You are bought and sold."

Then it is Mrs. Erlynne's turn, and she holds forth with immense eloquence in which a bitter note is sometimes sounded:

"I have wrecked my own life, but I will not let you wreck yours. You—why, you are a mere girl, you would be lost. You haven't got the kind of brains that enable a woman to get back. You have neither the wit nor the courage. You couldn't stand dishonour! No! Go back, Lady Windermere, to the husband who loves you, whom you love. You have a child, Lady Windermere. Go back to that child who even now, in pain or in joy, may be calling you. God gave you that child. He will require from you that you make his life fine, that you watch over him. What answer will you make to God if his life is ruined through you? Back to your house, Lady Windermere—your husband loves you! He has never swerved for a moment from the love he bears you. But even if he had a thousand loves, you must stay with your child. If he was harsh to you, you must stay with your child. If he ill-treated you, you must stay with your child. If he abandoned you, your place is with your child."

Lady Windermere bursts into tears and moans plaintively, "Take me home. Take me home."

But it is too late, for voices are heard on the stairs. One of the voices is Lord Windermere's. The bewildered and frightened women flutter round the room like flustered hens. Mrs. Erlynne bids Lady Windermere hide behind a curtain. "The first chance you have, slip out, if you ever get a chance!" "But you?" Lady Windermere replies, "Oh, never mind me. I'll face them." Lady Windermere conceals herself behind the curtain, and Mrs. Erlynne stands in the middle of the room waiting for the men to enter. But she hears Lorton's voice, and herself becomes afraid. "Lord Augustus! Then it is I who am lost!" For Mrs. Erlynne has cast Augustus for the part of her husband. She dives through a door which leads to another room, and the stage is left empty for a few moments.

Lord Darlington, Mr. Dumby, Lord Windermere, Lord Augustus Lorton and Mr. Cecil Graham enter. The time is 2 A.M.

For about a quarter of an hour, the five men converse in epigrams. This is the best part of the play, containing some of Wilde's wittiest remarks, such as the definition of a cynic: a man who knows the price of everything and the value of nothing. The scene has been criticised on the ground that it is irrelevant to the theme and might fit any comedy as easily as this one. But the criticism is captious, for although the wit does not spring out of the nature of the play and its people, it is so pleasantly turned that its intrusion is pardonable even when it resembles an invasion more than an intrusion. It has, however, dramatic value at this point, for it provides a quiet time between the bouts of "tornado". Mrs. Erlynne and Lady Windermere have had their scene. Another is about to take place. The spell of quiet epigram enables the audience to recover its breath after the first and in preparation for the second. It can be contended with warrant that this epigrammatic interlude, seemingly irrelevant, is the most brilliant piece of construction in the play.

Cecil Graham, one of those monkey-minded men who spend their lives devising mischief, finds Lady Windermere's fan lying on the sofa, and, calling Lorton aside, remarks, "Come over here.

I want you particularly. (*Aside*) Darlington has been moralising and talking about the purity of love, and that sort of thing, and he has got some woman in his rooms all the time. . . . Here is her fan." Then he calls Windermere.

LORD WINDERMERE (*walking over*): Well, what is it?

CECIL GRAHAM: Darlington has got a woman in his rooms. Here is her fan. Amusing, isn't it? (*A pause.*)

LORD WINDERMERE: Good God! (*Seizes the fan.* DUMBY *rises.*)

CECIL GRAHAM: What is the matter?

LORD WINDERMERE: Lord Darlington!

LORD DARLINGTON (*turning round*): Yes!

LORD WINDERMERE: What is my wife's fan doing in your rooms? Hands off, Cecil. Don't touch me.

LORD DARLINGTON: Your wife's fan?

LORD WINDERMERE: Yes, here it is!

LORD DARLINGTON (*walking towards him*): I don't know!

LORD WINDERMERE: You must know. I demand an explanation! Don't hold me, you fool. (*To* CECIL GRAHAM.)

LORD DARLINGTON (*aside*): She is here after all!

LORD WINDERMERE: Speak, sir! Why is my wife's fan here? Answer me! By God, I'll search your rooms, and if my wife's here, I'll—(*Moves.*)

LORD DARLINGTON: You shall not search my rooms. You have no right to do so. I forbid you!

LORD WINDERMERE: You scoundrel! I'll not leave your room till I have searched every corner of it! What moves behind that curtain? (*Rushes towards the curtain at the window.*)

MRS. ERLYNNE (*enters from right door*): Lord Windermere!

LORD WINDERMERE: Mrs. Erlynne!

Everyone starts and turns round. LADY WINDERMERE *slips out from behind the curtain and glides from the room, to left.*

MRS. ERLYNNE: I am afraid I took your wife's fan in mistake for my own, when I was leaving your house to-night. I am so sorry.

Takes fan from him. LORD WINDERMERE *looks at her in contempt.* LORD DARLINGTON *in mingled astonishment and anger.* LORD AUGUSTUS *turns away. The other men smile at each other.*

CURTAIN

Mention has already been made of the similarity between this scene and the screen scene in *The School for Scandal*, but how inferior is Wilde's to Sheridan's! Lady Teazle's appearance in the rooms of Joseph Surface is naturally arranged, as are the arrival there of Sir Peter Teazle and Charles Surface and the discovery of Lady Teazle. It is, indeed, absurd to compare Wilde's melodramatic claptrap with Sheridan's robust and superbly-constructed scene: one of the great pieces of dramatic construction in our drama. The end to this act is transparently improbable, and part of it is impossible. The device by which the men are brought to Darlington's rooms is silly in itself. They have been turned out of Lorton's club because it is closed at or about two in the morning, and so they adjourn to Darlington's rooms to utter epigrams. This is improbable. Windermere would almost certainly have gone home, and we cannot believe that Darlington, who intends to leave England in a few hours and has letters to write, letters which are, indeed, written during the session of epigrams, would have invited four men to spend the rest of the night with him. But if we allow Wilde this licence, can we allow him any more? Who can believe that Lady Windermere would so carefully have brought the fan to Darlington's rooms? There are several reasons why she would not have taken it there, only one of which need be named, the fact that it is a gift from her husband whom she believes to have been unfaithful to her. Windermere's passion on finding it is out of his nature. Men of his sort do not instantly fly into ungovernable rage.

There is worse to come. These improbabilities might be overlooked even by the censorious, but is it possible to overlook Lady Windermere's escape from the room without a single person present in it observing her? If we visualise the room—one of a set of bachelor's chambers such as might be found in Half Moon Street or Mount Street—we cannot fail to perceive that it would not be possible for anyone, certainly not for a frightened young woman, to come from behind window-curtains and walk out of a small room in which five men are standing, without being seen by any of them. Nothing in this act or the entire comedy corresponds to probability, nor do its situations develop naturally. One scene does not naturally follow or arise out of another. Had Lady Windermere not carefully carried her fan to Darlington's rooms, she would not have run the risk of discovery. We are not suggesting that accidents and irrational acts shall be debarred from drama. They occur too often and bring about too many decisive situations for them to be debarred. But when an author accumulates accidents and irrational acts, and is scrupulous to exclude probability and reasonable behaviour from his play, he ceases to be a writer of comedy or tragedy and becomes a writer of common-minded melodrama.

The last act is the worst of the four. Probability is here abandoned, and the principal characters entirely deteriorate. They lose any reason they may have possessed and are no longer ordinarily decent. We find Lady Windermere at home again, and oracularly soliloquising. "How securely one thinks one lives—out of reach of temptation, sin, folly. And then suddenly—Oh! life is terrible. It rules us, we do not rule it." A minute later she is uttering Wilde remarks. "Actions are the first tragedy in life, words are the second. Words are perhaps the worst. Words are merciless! . . ." One fears that the habit of soliloquising in this fashion will grow upon her, that presently she will begin to moralise aloud, and that her receptions will resemble those afternoons in Tite Street when Oscar took the floor and held forth on Beauty! . . .

But the situation in regard to the Windermeres and Mrs. Erlynne is changed. Lady Windermere is now her champion; Lord Windermere is vehemently her enemy. "She is bad—bad as any woman can be", he says, but his wife repudiates his statement. "I don't think now that people can be divided into the good and the bad as though they were two separate races or creations. What are called good women may have terrible things in them, mad moods of recklessness, assertion, jealousy, sin. Bad women, as they are termed, may have in them sorrow, repentance, pity, sacrifice. And I don't think Mrs. Erlynne a bad woman—I know she's not." But Windermere, who might have enquired how she knows, will have none of this stuff. "My dear child," he declares downrightly, "the woman's impossible. No matter what harm she tries to do us, you must never see her again. She is inadmissible anywhere." The Windermeres, it will be observed, judge people and events superficially and without the slightest effort to probe into motives or compulsions, or to understand why this is done or that. "Margaret," Windermere exclaims, "if you knew where Mrs. Erlynne went last night, after she left this house, you would not sit in the same room with her. It was absolutely shameless, the whole thing." This is too much for his wife. "Arthur, I can't bear it any longer. I must tell you. Last night! . . ."

But she does not tell him, nor does he press her to do so. In the customary Wilde manner, revelation is interrupted by someone's arrival. Mrs. Erlynne, who has called on a flimsy pretext, is announced. Is it credible that Lady Windermere would not have made her revelation, that Lord Windermere would not have felt inquisitive about the confession his wife had just told him she must make? There was ample time between the announcement of Mrs. Erlynne's visit and her appearance in the morning-room for the revelation to be made, but Wilde dodges the necessity. Mrs. Erlynne has come to return the fan which she had stupidly taken in mistake for her own! . . . She has also come to say good-bye. The English climate does not suit her. She intends to live abroad. Can she have one of Lady Windermere's photographs . . .? This is a device to get Lady Windermere out of the room so that Mrs. Erlynne and Lord Windermere can have a recriminatory conversation; during which Windermere talks as the Earl of Shaftesbury might have done had he known that he was about to be commemorated by the statue of Eros in Piccadilly Circus. At the end of the tirade, Lady Windermere returns with a photograph of herself and her son. There is a sentimental passage, when Lady Windermere informs Mrs. Erlynne that her mother is her ideal and is told that ideals are dangerous. "Realities are better." "If I lose my ideals," Lady Windermere declares, "I should lose everything." "Everything?" "Yes."

Mrs. Erlynne: Did your father often speak to you of your mother?
Lady Windermere: No, it gave him too much pain. He told me how my mother had died a few months after I was born. His eyes filled with tears as he spoke. Then he begged me never to mention her name again. It made him suffer even to hear it. My father—my father really died of a broken heart. His was the most ruined life I know.

This statement makes Mrs. Erlynne feel extremely uncomfortable, and she rises to go, but Lady Windermere has still to thank her for her rescue work a few hours earlier, and she gets rid of her husband by the simple device of sending him to enquire if Mrs. Erlynne's carriage has returned when she might have rung the bell to ask the butler to do so. Windermere goes out, and Lady Windermere immediately gives profuse thanks to Mrs. Erlynne, who exhorts her, however, not to breathe a word of what had happened to her husband. "I owe you everything", Lady Windermere replies. "Then pay your debt with silence", Mrs. Erlynne says. She begs to be allowed to keep the fan, and off she goes, accompanied by Lord Augustus Lorton who has arrived for no obvious reason. A few minutes later, Lorton, full of elation, returns to tell the Windermeres that Mrs. Erlynne has explained everything, and that he and she are to be married and will live abroad. "It was entirely for my sake she went to Darlington's rooms. Called at the Club first—fact is, wanted to put me out of suspense—and being told I had gone on—followed—naturally frightened when she heard a lot of us coming in—retired to another room—I assure you, most gratifying to me, the whole thing." Augustus is manifestly a dolt. But even he must have wondered how Mrs. Erlynne got to Darlington's rooms in advance of the party which had left the club before she reached it! . . .

In the meantime, however, the Windermeres have had a very uplifting conversation which ends with their decision to go to their country house. "Let us go to Selby. In the rose garden at Selby the roses are red and white." Following this decision, comes Lorton's re-entrance and his announcement of his impending marriage to Mrs. Erlynne.

LORD WINDERMERE: Well, you are certainly marrying a very clever woman!

LADY WINDERMERE (*taking her husband's hand*): Ah, you're marrying a very good woman.

This is the end of the play, and how ridiculous it is! Lady Windermere, that model of integrity, does not tell her husband the truth about the situation in Darlington's rooms. She allows Mrs. Erlynne to remain under suspicion of being Darlington's mistress. Can we doubt that the monkey-minded Mr. Cecil Graham and his friend, Mr. Dumby, hastened from luncheon-party to dinner-party, from club to drawing-room, from receptions in Mayfair to week-ends in country houses, spreading the news that Mrs. Erlynne had been detected in Darlington's rooms, with embellishments which would leave auditors in the belief that the lady was discovered stark naked in Darlington's bed? What, we may well wonder, did Darlington do? He was the most mystified man of the five. Is it likely that he departed from London that afternoon without seeking some explanation from Mrs. Erlynne —or Lady Windermere? What happened in Darlington's rooms after Mrs. Erlynne had said she was so sorry to have taken Lady Windermere's fan in mistake for her own? There she is, surrounded by mystified or cynically amused men, all avid for explanations, but not one word is vouchsafed to the audience of what Mrs. Erlynne said to Lord Darlington or he said to her! How did she get out of the house without accounting for her presence in it? No man, finding a lady known to him only in a notorious manner, occupying his rooms in a way which suggests that he and she are intimate, will allow her to depart without accounting for her presence. Any other behaviour would be dissonant with common sense.

This sensational scene in the third act is an assault on reason. It conforms to no human conduct that is intelligent. Lord Augustus Lorton is in love with Mrs. Erlynne and eventually marries her. Had he no questions to ask? Apparently not, for it is not until the fourth act, some hours after the scene in Darlington's rooms, that he receives an explanation which, very surprisingly, satisfies him. Does Windermere believe the explanation Mrs. Erlynne gives Lorton? Will not his scepticism betray itself in his private conversations with his wife when he hears her holding forth on that lady's goodness and nobility? He is an obtuse man, but even he, thick though he is, must sometimes wonder what had caused Lady Windermere to change her mind about Mrs. Erlynne's character. At one moment, Mrs. Erlynne is a degraded creature whose very presence poisons the air for Lady Windermere. At the next moment, Mrs. Erlynne is "a very good woman", and Lorton is lucky to marry her! Something, manifestly, must have happened to make that abrupt alteration of mind, and the something, whatever it was, must have happened in the early hours of the morning, about the time when Windermere was in Darlington's rooms. What was it? Was there someone behind that curtain, as Windermere had imagined, at the moment when Mrs. Erlynne stepped out of the other room and ostentatiously and needlessly discovered herself to the five men? Was it not odd that Mrs. Erlynne should mistake Lady Windermere's fan for her own and carry it to Darlington's rooms? Why had she gone to his rooms? Darlington, obviously, was astonished to find her there. He had expected to see some other woman. Who was this other woman? Men as stupid as Windermere are persistent in their interrogatories, especially those they raise in their thoughts. Many doubts must have come into his head while he smelt the roses at Selby! . . .

Lady Windermere, too, while rusticating, will have questions to put to herself. Why had Windermere made so many visits to Curzon Street? Why had he paid Mrs. Erlynne those large sums of money in less than six months? There must have been something between him and her. What? How long is she likely to remain ignorant that Mrs. Erlynne is her mother? So far as the play is concerned, the revelation is not made. At the end of it, we are back at the beginning. All that furore for nothing! . . . We are left with two exceptionally stupid people who will presently, we feel certain, torment themselves and each other with their unlulled suspicions. There will not always be red and white roses at Selby.

41

THE play is a poor, incredible piece, but it was an immediate success; and Wilde, who had sneered at plays by Pinero which were immeasurably superior to this rubbish, no longer lived from hand to mouth. The critics had been unkind, but the public was indulgent. Wilde reconsidered his decision to become a French citizen. The critics have, of course, been heavily denounced for their imperception about the play. Frank Harris is invincibly fatuous about them and about the play's quality. He describes a conversation he had at the end of the first act with Joseph Knight, a well-known critic of the time. Knight was scornful of the play, but Harris, pontificating like a pompous prig, declares it to be "surely the best comedy in English, the most brilliant". Knight, not unnaturally, was astounded by this statement. Was *Lady Windermere's Fan* better than any comedy by Shakespeare? he demanded in derision. Yes, Harris, who had the courage of his stupidity, replied: "Wittier and more humorous than *As You Like It* or *Much Ado*. Strange to say, too, it is on a higher intellectual level. I can only compare it to the best of Congreve, and I think it's better." This judgement, made at the end of the first act, sufficiently indicates the quality of Harris's mind.

That was a stirring time in the English theatre. On the 13th of March 1891 an obscure play-producing society, grandiloquently entitled The Independent Theatre, and founded by J. T. Grein, a Dutchman domiciled in London, had shaken the town to its core by producing Ibsen's *Ghosts* at the Royalty Theatre. The hysteria with which it was received by the dramatic critics in particular and the press in general is now nearly incredible. Venerable men, seemingly in possession of some self-control, fell out of one fit into another, as if they were doomed to spend the rest of their lives in horrible convulsions. In the following year, 1892, Wilde's first play, and Barrie's first notable piece, *Walker, London*, were performed. That was in February. Towards the end of that year, The Independent Theatre, which had not produced a play since *Ghosts*, announced the forthcoming performance of "a didactic realistic drama" by Bernard Shaw. It was *Widowers' Houses* which was acted for the first time at the Royalty Theatre on the 9th of December. The second performance was the last of the season. This Irishman, despite his diabolonian cleverness, was unlikely, it seemed, to disturb his rival's sleep. William Archer, indeed, bluntly told him that he had no "more specific talent for the drama than he had for painting and sculpture". Two years later, a season of plays, financed by Miss A. E. F. Horniman, began at the Avenue Theatre. The first piece, *A Comedy of Sighs*, by Dr. John Todhunter, was an immediate failure, and Shaw was besought to let *Widowers' Houses* be revived. He refused, preferring to have a new piece produced. This was *Arms and the Man* and was performed for the first time on the 21st of April 1894. It was withdrawn on the 7th of July, having been acted for eleven weeks. The receipts for the entire season were £1777, and the loss was about £4000. By that time, Wilde was in high feather. He had had two plays produced by eminent actor-managers, and each of them had been a success. In the year following the production of *Arms and the Man*, he was to have two highly successful comedies produced in a month, *An Ideal Husband* and *The Importance of Being Earnest*. By 1898, after productions in London, New York and elsewhere, *Arms and the Man* had earned about £800 for its author. The theatre had not opened its arms to Shaw as it had opened them to Wilde and Barrie.

In September 1894 Frank Harris bought *The Saturday Review*, and on the 5th of January 1895 Shaw, who had previously earned a small salary, first as a critic of pictures and then as a critic of music, commenced dramatic critic in that paper at a salary of six pounds a week: a higher sum than he had previously earned. He was then thirty-eight, two years younger than Wilde and four years older than Barrie. Success in the theatre came to him in his middle age. He was approaching fifty before he obtained production in the regular habit of the theatre, and he had then endured disappointments that would have permanently embittered almost any other man. In 1897, for example, when he was in his forty-first year, he suffered two humiliating disappointments in one week, but faced them with superb courage and unquenchable gaiety of spirit. Henry Irving, the leading English actor, and one of the leading actors of the world, suddenly decided about the 17th of April that he would not produce *The Man of Destiny*. About a week later, *You Never Can Tell*, which was to have been performed at the principal comedy theatre in London, the Haymarket, with Cyril Maude and Winifred Emery in the principal parts, was withdrawn after a fortnight's rehearsal. Two of the players had thrown up their parts, and the rest of the company found the play incomprehensible. Nine years were to pass before it was publicly performed. If ever a man had to fight for his life in the theatre, Shaw was the man. And he fought.

But Wilde had only to lift his finger to have theatre doors flung open for him. Herbert Beerbohm Tree, immediately after the success of *Lady Windermere's Fan*, came hurrying to him to beg for a play, and was received in a very hoity-toity manner. Tree might do well as Herod in *Salomé*, but as an English peer! . . . Yet it was as an English peer in *A Woman of No Importance* that Tree was cast; and very good he is said to have been in the part. Wilde could be rude to an actor-manager, but not to the extent of having his play withdrawn. He went to Lady Mount Temple's house at Babbacombe, Torquay, in the summer of 1892 to write the comedy which was produced at the Haymarket on the 19th of April 1893, and withdrawn seventeen weeks later, on the 16th of August. It is almost as foolish as *Lady Windermere's Fan*, but not quite so foolish as *An Ideal Husband*. Despite his sudden good fortune, however, hints and even definite statements of perversion were now being whispered or boldly uttered. A blackmailing pederast had sent a copy of a letter, written by Wilde to Alfred Douglas, to Tree during the rehearsals of *A Woman of No Importance*, and Tree had shown it to Wilde who had waived it aside. It was that appalling "prose poem", as Wilde called it:

> MY OWN BOY,—Your sonnet is quite lovely, and it is a marvel that those red rose-leaf lips of yours should be made no less for the madness of music and song than for the madness of kissing. Your slim-gilt soul walks between passion and poetry. I am sure Hyacinthus whom Apollo loved so madly was you in Greek days. Why are you alone in London, and when do you go to Salisbury? Do go there and cool your hands in the grey twilight of Gothic things. Come here when ever you like. It is a lovely place and only lacks you. Do go to Salisbury first. Always with undying love,
>
> Yours, OSCAR

How Wilde's reputation for sensitive style survived the publication of this stuff is one of the mysteries of the world of letters. That adjective *slim-gilt*! . . . Hysteria seems to start out of every line, the hysteria, not of Shelley, but of Shelley's first wife after she had been reading *Vathek* and *The Mysteries of Udolpho*, and had got them thoroughly mixed in her mind. Even if Wilde had not been dishonest about the letter when under cross-examination by Sir Edward Carson in the witness-box during his action against Queensberry, even if he had admitted that he was a sodomite in ardent pursuit of an uncommonly good-looking youth of aristocratic birth as a relief from the disgusting stable-boys and ostlers with whom he was now frequently cohabiting in the back streets of Westminster, even if he had vaunted and justified his sodomy, this "prose poem" would still be what it unmistakably is, nauseating twaddle, the sort of stuff that might be imagined by an overwrought factory-girl who has lost her self-control after seeing a film-star in the flesh.

Douglas, with imbecile carelessness, had left this letter in a pocket of a suit of old clothes which he had given to a degenerate clerk, called Alfred Wood, whom he had befriended at Oxford, and it was stolen from him, Wood alleged, by a blackmailer named Allen who called at Tite Street and demanded £60 for it. Wilde handled this rascal with great skill, although he garnished his conversation with nonsense about his "beautiful" poem, which, he declared, was about to be published. "I'll send you a copy of it", he said to the staggered Allen: and, indeed, a French version of the "prose poem", made by Pierre Louÿs in the form of a sonnet, appeared in *The Spirit Lamp*, an undergraduate magazine edited by Lord Alfred Douglas, in May 1892. This was, perhaps, a precautionary publication. He gave Allen half a sovereign and ushered him into the street. A few minutes later, the door-bell rang again. A second blackmailer, one Clibborn, now stood on the step. He had come, however, not to blackmail but to return the letter. Allen, it appeared, had developed compunction and declined to "rent" Wilde any longer. Wilde took the incriminating document from Clibborn, to whom he gave ten shillings, and shut the door. He must have felt exceedingly relieved. He had recovered the "prose poem" for a pound! . . .

Unluckily, a copy of the letter had been sent to Lord Queensberry, who suddenly developed a feeling of paternal solicitude for an erring son whose existence he had hitherto scarcely noticed, whose legitimacy he would presently pretend to doubt. Queensberry had become aware of Wilde some months earlier, and had professed horror that a son of his should even be acquainted with such a person; but, coming one day on them both in the Café Royal, had been induced to join them at luncheon and, like many men who were temperamentally antipathetic to Wilde, had been fascinated by him and his conversation. One of the several remarkable facts about Wilde was this power he had of entrancing nearly all those who normally disliked him. This meeting occurred towards the end of 1892 and lasted for several hours. Lord Alfred, indeed, left Wilde and his father to continue a stimulating conversation on atheism and Christianity! . . . A few days later, Lord Queensberry wrote to his son to retract all he had previously written about Wilde, who was, he declared, as clever as he was charming. But he soon retracted his retraction, and wrote highly abusive letters to his son, threatening to stop his allowance if his friendship with Wilde were not instantly ended. A long series of quarrels and reproaches and threats of all sorts, from disinheritance to murder, ensued.

But here we are anticipating the march of events, and must return to Wilde's second production, *A Woman of No Importance*, at the Haymarket Theatre.

42

THE play opens on the lawns of Hunstanton Chase, the country house of the widowed Lady Hunstanton, a prattling, inconsequent and nearly mindless woman, and the action, like that in *Lady Windermere's Fan* and *An Ideal Husband*, takes place within twenty-four hours. The time is the afternoon, before tea. Among the guests are Lord Illingworth, a dingy edition of Lord Henry Wotton in *The Portrait of Dorian Gray*; Lady Caroline Pontefract and her fourth husband, Sir John; Miss Hester Worsley, an exceptionally priggish American girl, who, though she is only eighteen, seems to be wandering about Europe alone; Mrs. Allenby, detached from her husband and no better than she ought to be;

and a member of Parliament, Mr. Kelvil, whose purpose in the play, apart from filling up space, never becomes apparent. Lady Caroline is a variation of Lady Hunstanton. They are both addicted to drivelling and irrelevant remarks, the sort of woman Wilde delighted to draw. But Lady Caroline is unlike Lady Hunstanton in this respect, that she has no kindness in her composition: she is a malicious and insolent woman whose manner is almost habitually rude. The opening conversation, between her and Miss Worsley, is a sample of her general habit of speech, and is sufficient in itself to have justified Miss Worsley in slapping her face:

LADY CAROLINE: I believe this is the first English country house you have stayed at, Miss Worsley.

HESTER: Yes, Lady Caroline.

LADY CAROLINE: You have no country houses, I am told, in America.

HESTER: We have not many.

LADY CAROLINE: Have you any country? What we should call country?

HESTER (*smiling*): We have the largest country in the world, Lady Caroline. They used to tell us at school that some of our states are as big as France and England put together.

LADY CAROLINE: Ah! You must find it very draughty, I should fancy.

Yet this conversation, so nicely calculated to put at her ease a young foreign girl in a strange house where she is surrounded by people she scarcely knows, is almost amiable in comparison with Lady Caroline's charming conversation throughout the remainder of the play, though it is not more offensive than Miss Worsley's turns out to be.

Among the persons assembled on the lawn on this afternoon is a young man of about nineteen, Gerald Arbuthnot, whose inclusion is neither explained nor easily explicable. He is a bank clerk and the only child of a reclusive widow, living in the near-by small town or large village. The reader is reminded that the period of the play is 1893. It is improbable that obscure young bank clerks with morose mothers, even in these times, are accustomed to frequent such country houses as are left, or to associate on familiar terms with ambassadors, actual or potential, but they most certainly were not accustomed to do so in 1893; a fact which must have been well within Wilde's knowledge. Yet he requires us to believe that Arbuthnot, who has no distinction of mind or manner to justify this strain on our credulity, is on terms of such intimacy with Lady Hunstanton that a casual visitor to her house might imagine him to be her close relation. Lord Illingworth, on slight acquaintance, offers him the post of private secretary, and proposes to carry him off to India forthwith. Lads of nineteen, employed as junior clerks in small country branches of banks at a salary of a hundred pounds a year—even the amount of the salary is excessively stated—are unlikely, after the briefest encounter, to be given a post which demands from the man who is to occupy it much wider experience than Gerald possessed.

These are not carping complaints. The smallest of them—the complaint that Wilde over-states the amount of Gerald's salary—denotes that Wilde was ignorant of the facts of the situation he had chosen for his theme or that he wilfully disregarded them in favour of a grossly melodramatic plot. The position of Arbuthnot bears no more relation to life than does the situation of Hester Worsley. Pinero, whom Wilde habitually derided, would have felt ashamed to flout the facts as Wilde flouted them. If an author cannot make a book or a play without falsifying life, he is not worth serious consideration.

Wilde, it is obvious, in writing *A Woman of No Importance*, decided to vary the plot of *Lady Windermere's Fan*. In that play, the heroine, if such a word can be applied to Lady Windermere, turns out to be the daughter of a woman who had deserted her husband and her child and taken to bad ways on the Continent. To rearrange that situation was easy. A man deserts a woman who is left to bear him a bastard son. Mrs. Erlynne returns to the world from which she had fled, with the intention of blackmailing her daughter's wealthy husband. Lord Illingworth, however, is not a male Mrs. Erlynne, though he has the potentialities of one; and he is ignorant of his relationship to Gerald when they meet. No one in Lady Hunstanton's house-party seems to feel any surprise at Gerald's presence. Even Lady Caroline makes no comment, acid or otherwise. There is enquiry about Hester and her origin, but none about Gerald. Our assumption that Wilde's puritanical young women characters may have been based on the elementary evangelical piety of his wife is supported by the re-appearance of Lady Windermere as Hester, who is not less emphatic than that vehement lady on the punishment that should be meted out to sinners. Augustine or Calvin could not have been more severe than Lady Windermere, but Hester Worsley could. This incredible girl, almost the least credible character in the whole Wilde drama, rants like an overwrought Torquemada in her denunciation of delinquents and dissenters. The slight suggestion of reason in her rhetorical arguments is that the male sinner's punishment shall be equal to the woman's; but the punishment is to be harsh for both sexes and, apparently, permanent. Pardon or remission of sentence is not to be thought of by Miss Worsley, the sage of eighteen. The guilty women "are outcasts. They are nameless. If you met them in the street you would turn your head away. I don't complain of their punishment. Let all women who have sinned be punished. . . . It is right that they should be punished, but don't let them be the only ones to suffer. If a man and a woman have sinned, let them both go forth into the desert to love or loathe each other there! . . ." This is the sort of chatty conversation in which Miss Worsley is accustomed to indulge over tea and coffee cups. The vindictive doctrine is elaborated in the third act during a conversation between Hester and Mrs. Arbuthnot who had overheard the speech cited above. A woman who has sinned should not, Hester asserts, be "allowed to come into the society of good men and women", and her children, if she has any, should have her sins visited upon them. "Yes, it is right that the sins of the parents should be visited on the children", the adolescent saint assures the sinner of thirty-eight. "It is a just law. It is God's law."

It is a gross slur on divinity to suggest that because God informs His creatures that their folly may have terrible consequences for their children, He craves these consequences and would feel affronted if they were not severely suffered. Is God, when He reminds us that men who contract venereal disease may infect their children with fearful infirmities, proving Himself a sadist who is determined to gratify His cruel lust by causing babies to be born blind or physically enfeebled? A man is not longing for his country's defeat in battle when he warns his countrymen of the danger of neglecting its defence. Is my neighbour a firebug, longing for incineration, because he warns me that if I smoke in bed or leave my flues unswept, I may have my house burnt about my head? Far too many ruthless people are inclined to make God in their own image. Miss Worsley, we may believe, with the arrogance of her unpleasant species, is endowing the Almighty with the vicious propensities she herself possesses. Wilde is not here doing what an author is entitled to do; portraying a character for whom he feels no sympathy: Miss Worsley, if she is not the first heroine of the comedy, is certainly the second. We are expected to like and admire her. If Wilde detests this sadistic female prig, he dissembles his dislike in a very remarkable manner, for he leaves those who see *A Woman of No Importance* in the belief that he esteems her highly. But surely a young person of eighteen who habitually addresses her hostess and her fellow-guests as Miss Worsley does in the second act, would be told, and rightly told, the time at which the next train leaves for London.

"We [that is to say the Americans] are trying to build up life, Lady Hunstanton, on a better, truer, purer basis than life rests on here. This sounds strange to you all, no doubt. How could it sound other than strange? You rich people in England, you don't know how you are living. How could you know? You shut out from your society the gentle and the good. You laugh at the simple and the pure. Living, as you all do, on others and by them, you sneer at self-sacrifice, and if you throw bread to the poor it is merely to keep them quiet for a season. With all your pomp and wealth and art you don't know how to live—you don't even know that. You love the beauty you can see and touch and handle, the beauty that you can destroy, but of the unseen beauty of life, of the unseen beauty of a higher life, you know nothing. You have lost life's secret. Oh, your English society seems to me shallow, selfish, foolish. It has blinded its eyes, and stopped its ears. It lies like a leper in purple. It sits like a dead thing smeared with gold. It is all wrong, all wrong."

This Marble Arch oratory seems out of place in a house where a totally uninteresting junior clerk in a small town branch of a bank is familiarly received and, without displaying any qualifications for the post, is given the job of private secretary to a man presumably distinguished and destined to occupy important posts. What, one may well wonder, is Miss Worsley doing in society she so heartily despises? Was there not a single house in the whole of Great Britain she could have visited more congenially than Hunstanton Chase? Lady Hunstanton is a silly woman, but she scarcely deserves to be called a leper in purple, nor does she sit about like a dead thing smeared with gold. She certainly is not a snob. It is not she who refuses to frequent Mrs. Arbuthnot's house, but Mrs. Arbuthnot who refuses to frequent hers. Archdeacon Daubeny is not the most exhilarating person one could wish to have in one's house, but Lady Hunstanton does not despise him, and is almost eager for the society of his decrepit wife, whose company in the play, however, the audience is mercifully spared. Are we not justified in saying that this young American bears no resemblance to a human being: that she is a badly manufactured piece of shoddy rhetoric? We can easily imagine what would be the reaction of Americans to a British girl who was stupid enough and sufficiently ill-bred to harangue them in the Worsley manner.

After an outburst of virago rage about one Lord Henry Weston whose name is casually mentioned, in which he is described as "a man with a hideous smile and a hideous past", Miss Worsley concludes her soap-box sermon with the assertion that "you are unjust to women in England. And till you count what is a shame in a woman to be an infamy in a man, you will always be unjust, and Right, that pillar of fire, and Wrong, that pillar of cloud, will be made dim in your eyes, or be not seen at all, or if seen, not regarded." Lord Henry Weston, it turns out, is Lady Caroline Pontefract's brother, a discovery which, surprisingly, disconcerts Miss Worsley, though Lady Caroline feels no resentment against her; indeed, agrees with her. "I regard Henry as infamous, absolutely infamous", she says. One feels that Wilde wrote this extraordinary scene with an eye on the American box-office and for the fun of embarrassing Miss Worsley with the revelation of Lord Henry's relationship to Lady Caroline: both of them motives that are not impressive.

Lord Illingworth's innate vulgarity and, incidentally, Wilde's are revealed by a scene in this act between him and Mrs. Allenby, in which the lady, deeply galled by the fact that she has not yet succeeded in becoming Illingworth's leman, dares him to attempt the little Puritan's virtue. He wagers that he will undo the girl with a single kiss. She shall be subdued by his embraces in a shrubbery, and if she be not ripe for seduction immediately thereafter, he will be a very surprised and nonplussed person! Our complaint here is not that he proposes to undo the girl, for undoing is obviously what she needs, but that he makes bets about it with a woman who has ceased to be exciting and is envious of the virgin. Miss Worsley is an unpleasant young person, but she should not be treated as if she were a greyhound or a horse, with Lord Illingworth as a reckless punter and Mrs. Allenby as an off-the-course bookie. Wilde is here preparing us for a grotesque "curtain" to the third act.

It is during Miss Worsley's tirade that Mrs. Arbuthnot first appears in the play. She steals into the drawing-room, a veiled and mysterious figure, in time to hear the concluding part of Miss Worsley's fervid oration. The words "let all women who have sinned be punished" cause her to give a convulsive start. "It is right that they should be punished, but don't let them be the only ones to suffer." Mrs. Arbuthnot is disconcerted to find a house-party at the Chase, a disconcertion which is difficult to understand, since her son must surely have told her something about it. The recluse has come out only because Lady Hunstanton has asked her to rejoice over Gerald's good fortune in being appointed Lord Illingworth's secretary. In reply to Lady Hunstanton's enquiry, "You don't know Lord Illingworth, I believe, dear?" Mrs. Arbuthnot answers, "I have never met him", but adds that she remembers to have heard "years ago of an old Lord Illingworth who lived in Yorkshire, I think". Gradually there emerges from the chatter which follows, the fact that Mrs. Arbuthnot is very familiar, indeed, with George Harford, who had succeeded unexpectedly to the Illingworth peerage, and she becomes deeply agitated by the knowledge that he is so friendly with her son. When, a few moments later, the men join the ladies, and she and Lord Illingworth have recognised each other, she upsets Gerald by raising objections to his appointment, objections which Illingworth waves aside. Everybody but Illingworth and Mrs. Arbuthnot is then manœuvred on to the terrace so that he and she may talk *tête à tête*, and he opens the conversation with the remark, "So that is our son, Rachel! Well, I am very proud of him. He is a Harford, every inch of him. By the way, why Arbuthnot, Rachel?" "One name", she replies, "is as good as another, when one has no right to any name."

Then follows a scene of bitter recrimination in which Mrs. Arbuthnot's determination that her son shall not associate in any way with his father is made plain. Why should Illingworth, after twenty years of disgraceful neglect, imagine that he can deprive her of her one joy? "You are so rich in other things", she says. "Leave me the little vineyard of my life: leave me the walled-in garden and the well of water; the ewe-lamb God sent me, in pity or in wrath, oh, leave me that! George, don't take Gerald from me." This pseudo-literary fudge leaves Illingworth unmoved, as, indeed, it would leave better men than him. "Rachel," he answers insolently, "at the present moment, you are not necessary to Gerald's career: I am. There is nothing more to be said on the subject."

During this recriminatory conversation, intended by Wilde to be full of pathos, but full of faked emotion, we learn that Illingworth, then George Harford and with no expectation of succeeding to the peerage, was twenty-one when he first met Rachel in her father's, a country clergyman's, garden. She was "little more than eighteen". His wooing was so swift and impetuous that she bore him a son within a year of this encounter. Despite her entreaties, despite, too, his father's disapproval of his conduct, he refused to marry her on the ground that he "had no expectations", and would be hampered as a careerist by a wife and child. As, however, his mother, who supported him in this refusal, offered to allow Rachel £600 a year, an offer Rachel declined to accept, his excuse seems feeble. A lady who can afford to make so large an allowance must have had a substantial fortune, and could have supported her son's wife as easily as she wished to support his discarded mistress. Harford's desertion of Rachel was plainly due to his callous and caddish character, a character which is abundantly revealed throughout the play. When Rachel realises that Harford will not make an honest woman of her, she disappears from his knowledge. For twenty years he neither knows nor seeks to know anything of her and her infant. How she maintained herself during this period, we are not told. Her father, who died of her disgrace, may have left her enough to live on, but country clergymen are seldom affluent men, and we may doubt if he had much to leave her, even if she were an only child. Occupations for women, except as teachers, were few and ill-paid in 1873, the year in which Gerald was born, and it is improbable that a young person of nineteen, with no scholastic training, and encumbered by a baby for which she could not plausibly account, would obtain employment in any school. What honourable occupation, apart perhaps from needlework or domestic service with unparticular people, was open to Rachel then?

Are we niggling when we raise these points? Not in the least. A dramatist who sets out to reveal life should reveal life and not fanciful fiction. It is his business to know his characters so well that he can answer any question about them. Ibsen knew the pet name by which Nora, in *A Doll's House*, was known to her family, and he was able to tell those who were interested what sort of little girl she was: a greedy, wilful infant. Characters do not enter their author's head for the first time when the play begins, nor do they leave it when the curtain falls on the last act. His duty is to make us understand his people, and he neglects his duty when he sends us out of the theatre raising notes of interrogation. It ought not to be possible to wonder how Mrs. Arbuthnot kept herself and her son during the twenty years which followed on her seduction. When the play begins, she is living very comfortably in a well-furnished house with a garden in the country town of Wrockley. But she has no occupation of which we are aware, and her son's salary, a hundred pounds a year, is scarcely sufficient for his own support, and he cannot, therefore, contribute much, if anything, to hers.

These are not the only questions which Wilde leaves unanswered. How, we wonder, did Rachel reply to Gerald when, in his childhood and in his youth, he enquired about his father? An orphan is always inquisitive about the parent he has never seen or does not remember. He must sometimes have asked her if she had no portraits of his father, and have thought it odd that she had not. There were surely times when he questioned her about his paternal grandparents? Had he no uncles or aunts or cousins? Where was his father born? Why did his people never visit them? There must have been some awkwardness about Gerald's birth certificate when he became a candidate for a clerkship in a bank? Many embarrassing discussions must have been held between Rachel and her son, and the boy, unless he were mindless, could hardly have failed to find a mystery in his own and his mother's life. It is difficult to believe that he was content to be mystified. The play, in its conception, has little relation to reality. It has less in its execution.

43

MRS. ARBUTHNOT's determination that she shall not be deprived of her son soon peters out. She has no strength of purpose, neither the strength of a woman of firm character nor of a woman made firm by bitter experience. At the end of the scene in which she pleads with Illingworth to leave her alone with the ewe-lamb God, in pity or in wrath, had sent her, Gerald enters the room. Here is an opportunity for Wilde to display some originality, but, just as he had funked it in *Lady Windermere's Fan*, so he funks it in *A Woman of No Importance*. Gerald asks why she objects to his taking the post Lord Illingworth has offered him, but she does not answer, "He is your father. He refused to marry me and made you a bastard. He deserted us and never, in twenty years, made the slightest effort to find out what had become of us." The boy's reaction to this revelation would have been profoundly interesting.

But Mrs. Arbuthnot does not make this reasonable answer. She weakly murmurs that she "didn't know you were so eager to leave me". As if every son is not eager at the earliest opportunity to leave his home, especially when it is inhabited by an over-doting mother. This answer rightly shocks Gerald, and she tries to amplify it. "I do not think you would be suitable as a private secretary to Lord Illingworth. You have no qualifications." Illingworth is more adroit than Mrs. Arbuthnot. He volunteers to leave mother and son alone so that she may reveal her objections more freely than she can in his presence. "You may have some other reason you don't wish me to hear." "I have no other reason", she replies, and the scene ends, with Gerald, naturally enough, feeling that his mother has made a considerable fool of herself. Wilde has lost his chance to make a notable comedy out of a commonplace melodrama.

The third act is dreadful stuff. It opens with Lord Illingworth delivering himself of a number of sententious and shallow remarks on life in general and English society in particular. The play, like all Wilde's work, is full of witticisms. One sometimes feels that when he was stuck, he sent round to the Army and Navy Stores for a parcel of assorted epigrams and put them into the play as they fell out of the brown paper in which they were enclosed. Some of the epigrams in *A Woman of No Importance* are good, some are pretentious, and some are empty. One of them, in the second act, was so much to his liking that he repeated it in the first act of *The Importance of Being Earnest*. Lord Illingworth, in conversation with Mrs. Allenby, remarks, "All women become like their mothers. That is their tragedy", to which Mrs. Allenby ripostes, "No man does. That is his." Algernon Moncrieff annexes the two speeches and makes them one. "All women become like their mothers. That is their tragedy. No man does. That is his." His retort to John Worthing, who asks if that is clever, is a fair one. "It is perfectly phrased", he replies, much better phrased, he might have added, than it was when Lord Illingworth and Mrs. Allenby divided it between them. If epigrams could save a play, they might have saved *A Woman of No Importance*, but epigrams, like patriotism, are not enough. The dramatist who described fox-hunting as the pursuit of the uneatable by the unspeakable, could excite hope by his wit, but he was too ready to dissipate it by "tornado" curtains. The worst of these "tornado" curtains ends the third act of this play. We are teased for a short time by a scene in which Mrs. Arbuthnot begins, obliquely, to tell Gerald about herself and Illingworth. Gerald is so obtuse that he does not guess that his mother is telling her own history, though a small power of perception must have made the fact plain to him:

"Gerald, there was a girl once, she was very young, she was little over eighteen at the time. George Harford—that was Lord Illingworth's name then—George Harford met her. She knew nothing about life. He—knew everything! . . ."

We interrupt her to remind the reader that he was twenty-one when he met Rachel and "knew everything".

"He made this girl love him so much that she left her father's house with him one morning. She loved him so much, and he had promised to marry her. He had solemnly promised to marry her, and she believed him. She was very young—and ignorant of what life really is. But he put marriage off from week to week, and month to month. She trusted in him all the while. She loved him. Before her child was born—for she had a child—she implored him for the child's sake to marry her, that the child might have a name, that her sin might not be visited on the child, who was innocent. He refused. After the child was born she left him, taking the child away, and her life was ruined, and her soul ruined, and all that was sweet and good and pure in her ruined also. She suffered terribly—she suffers now. She will always suffer. For her there is no joy, no peace, no atonement. She is a woman who drags a chain like a guilty thing. She is a woman who wears a mask, like a thing that is a leper. The fire cannot purify her. The waters cannot quench her anguish. Nothing can heal her! No anodyne can give her sleep, no poppies forgetfulness! She is lost! She is a lost soul! That is why I call Lord Illingworth a bad man. That is why I don't want my boy to be with him."

It is incredible that even such a numskull as Gerald manifestly is, should fail to realise that his mother is describing herself. Mrs. Arbuthnot, it will be noticed, is a highly rhetorical and morbid woman and cannot refrain from expressing herself like an over-ripe undergraduate who writes intense articles for an aesthetic magazine at Oxford. Gerald's obtusity may have been due to his impatience with her highfaluting language or the fact that she bored him so profoundly that he failed to perceive the point she was trying to make plain. His reply is very cool—a fact which we shall do well to remember when we come to the end of the act. It deprives her of any hope she may have had that she can influence him to refuse Lord Illingworth's offer. "My dear mother," he says, "it all sounds very tragic, of course. But I daresay the girl was just as much to blame as Lord Illingworth was. After all, would a really nice girl with any nice feelings at all, go away from her home with a man to whom she was not married, and live with him as his wife? No nice girl would." That remark, one well in the Harford tradition, stuns Mrs. Arbuthnot. She has no more to say in opposition to his desire. "Gerald," she murmurs, "I withdraw all my objections. You are at liberty to go away with Lord Illingworth, when and where you choose." She feels, perhaps, that it will not be long before he is following in his father's footsteps! . . .

Immediately after this scene we have one of the "tornado" curtains Wilde always wanted: a "curtain" lifted off the stage of the Elephant and Castle Theatre or the Standard in the Mile End Road. Hester is heard outside, screaming in terror. She rushes in and flings herself in Gerald's arms:

HESTER: Oh! save me—save me from him!
GERALD: From whom?
HESTER: He has insulted me! Horribly insulted me! save me!
GERALD: Who? Who has dared—?

LORD ILLINGWORTH *enters back of stage.* HESTER *breaks from* GERALD'S *arms, and points to him.*

GERALD (*he is quite beside himself with rage and indignation*): Lord Illingworth, you have insulted the purest thing on God's earth, a thing as pure as my own mother. You have insulted the woman I love most in the world with my own mother. As there is a God in heaven, I will kill you!

One feels that Gerald, who took the story told by his mother so coolly, could hardly feel more enraged if Illingworth, instead of attempting to snatch a kiss, had raped Hester. The American girl, we feel certain, has changed a good deal since Hester's day, and is not driven almost frantic when she is kissed in a picture-gallery. Life would be intolerable if even our Lord Illingworths were in danger of destruction every time they sought a girl's lips. Nicholas Nickleby seldom opens his mouth without indulging in such rhodomontade as Gerald's, but he has associated so long with the Crummles' family that melodramatic language has become his natural speech. Gerald, however, is a bank clerk in a country branch, and accustomed to sober statements and the careful perusal of ledgers and sedate and unemotional entries in pass-books. Is he the sort of young man who will spout stuff that might abash the Infant Phenomenon, and rant before high heaven about the purest thing on earth, and swear by his faith in God's existence that he will put an end to Lord Illingworth's when he does not yet know what offence Illingworth has committed? Apparently he is. But his mother prevents him from committing parricide.

MRS. ARBUTHNOT (*rushing across and catching hold of him*): No! No!

GERALD (*thrusting her back*): Don't hold me, mother. Don't hold me—I'll kill him!

MRS. ARBUTHNOT: Gerald!

GERALD: Let me go, I say!

MRS. ARBUTHNOT: Stop, Gerald, stop! He is your own father!

GERALD *clutches his mother's hands, and looks into her face. She sinks slowly on the ground in shame.* HESTER *steals towards the door.* LORD ILLINGWORTH *frowns and bites his lips. After a time,* GERALD *raises his mother up, puts his arms round her, and leads her from the room.*

leaving Lord Illingworth still frowning and biting his lips as the curtain falls on one of the shoddiest scenes in dramatic literature.

On the following morning Gerald is found in his mother's sitting-room at Wrockley, writing a letter. His duties at the bank by which he is employed seem not to be exacting. He can neglect them with ease and composure. He had spent the previous day at Hunstanton Chase, and is spending this morning at home. Either there is no thrift in Wrockley's inhabitants or they are not rich enough to need bank accounts. Gerald does not now intend to be Lord Illingworth's secretary. The letter he is writing demands that his father shall marry his mother forthwith. It orders him to visit Wrockley that afternoon to make the requisite arrangements! . . . Gerald, it will be noticed, is an arbitrary numskull. He has not yet informed his mother of the way in which he intends to dispose of her, and is extremely shocked when, a few minutes after the act opens, he finds her revolted by his proposal. "I will not marry him", she declares passionately.

"But you don't understand. It is for your sake I am talking, not mine. This marriage, this necessary marriage, this marriage which for obvious reasons must inevitably take place, will not help me, will not give me a name that will be really, rightly mine to bear. But surely it will be something for you, that you, my mother, should, however late, become the wife of the man who is my father. Will not that be something?"

Gerald, as fine a specimen of the prig as ever stepped the earth, has inherited some of his mother's flatulent oratory. He does not, indeed, orate like an aesthetic undergraduate, but he does orate like a politician who has read too many leading articles. While he and his mother are haranguing each other with great vigour, Hester Worsley steals into the room, but, although it is of ordinary size and is occupied by two people, neither of whom is blind or short-sighted, she stands in a conspicuous position for about ten minutes without being observed by either of them. Mrs. Arbuthnot utters a speech which must take about four minutes to deliver effectively—and how an emotional actress must enjoy uttering it! —but does not observe that her audience has been increased by "that girl", who, "last night, good though she is, fled from the room as if I were a tainted thing"! The speech concludes with the declaration that her love for her son is greater than normal mother love because of her dishonour and disgrace. "It is the price I paid for you—the price of soul and body—that makes me love you as I do. Oh, don't ask me to do this horrible thing. Child of my shame, be still the child of my shame." She might be the mother of Little Willie in *East Lynne*.

Her appeal leaves Gerald implacable. "You must become my father's wife. You must marry him. It is your duty."

This is too much even for Miss Worsley who rushes into the middle of the room and embraces Mrs. Arbuthnot:

HESTER: No, no, you shall not. That would be real dishonour, the first you have ever known. That would be real disgrace: the first to touch you. Leave him and come with me. There are other countries than England. . . . Oh, other countries over sea, better, wiser, and less unjust lands. The world is very wide and very big.

MRS. ARBUTHNOT: No, not for me. For me the world is shrivelled to a palm's breadth; and where I walk there are thorns.

HESTER: It shall not be so. We shall somewhere find green valleys and fresh waters, and if we weep, well, we shall weep together. . . .

The temptation to believe that Wilde foresaw his fate and revealed his vision in his work is very great. This harping on tainted life and the need for purity is almost pathological, so frequently is it performed. The final sentence in Hester's speech in the passage just cited has a curious resemblance to the famous ending of *De Profundis*:

"All trials are trials for one's life, just as all sentences are sentences of death . . ."

a statement which, we interrupt him to say, is, like many other assertions in this self-pitying production, entirely false.

". . . and three times have I been tried. The first time I left the box to be arrested, the second time to be led back to the house of detention, the third time to pass into a prison for two years. Society, as we have constituted it, will have no place for me, has none to offer; but Nature, whose sweet rains fall on just and unjust alike, will have clefts in rocks where I may hide, and secret valleys in whose silence I may weep undisturbed. She will hang the night with stars so that I may walk abroad in the darkness without stumbling, and send the wind over my footprints so that none may track me to my hurt; she will cleanse me in great waters, and with bitter herbs make me whole."

This is a handsome tribute to Nature from one who formerly despised her and thought her a servile imitator of Art. Shall we run the risk of being called cynical and callous by suggesting that his prose was more pleasing to its author than the consolation he expected to find in rocky clefts and silent valleys? It was not there that he went from Reading, but to Paris, to ogle conscripts and cadge fivers from his friends. Wilde almost incessantly dramatised himself. The only person in the world for whom he felt pity was

Oscar Wilde. He wept when he thought of himself, not in shame, but in compassion.

Hester declares her love for Gerald, announcing at the same time her conversion from Augustinian and Calvinistic views. She no longer believes it to be God's law that the sins of the fathers shall be visited upon the children. "I was wrong," she says, "God's law is only Love." How soon these sternly strict people change their creed when it presses upon themselves and their belongings. God's law must be amended or abrogated when it touches Miss Worsley. The Creator Himself must be taught that He cannot go about the universe upsetting her! . . . Gerald, transported by his good fortune in winning, with the minimum of effort, the hand of a very wealthy young woman, leads her to the garden, leaving his mother alone. A moment or two later Lord Illingworth enters, to renew and amplify his offer to be a dutiful father to Gerald. He even offers Mrs. Arbuthnot marriage. All his offers are rejected, and, irritated by their refusal, he drops his mask of culture and gentility and becomes what he truly is: a coarse and vulgar man. He begins to sneer at Rachel and his son. "You were the prettiest of playthings," he says to her, "the most fascinating of small romances." He pulls out his watch:

> "Quarter to two! Must be strolling back to Hunstanton. Don't suppose I shall see you there again. I'm sorry, I am really. It's been an amusing experience to have met amongst people of one's own rank, and treated quite seriously, too, one's mistress and one's . . .!"

But he does not complete his sentence. Mrs. Arbuthnot picks up one of his gloves which he has laid on a convenient table and strikes him across the face. The blow startles him: "*He is dazed by the insult of his punishment. Then he controls himself, and goes to the window and looks out at his son. Sighs and leaves the room.*" As he goes out, Mrs. Arbuthnot subsides on the sofa, moaning. "He would have said it. He would have said it." The reader wonders whether the vulgarity was in Illingworth or Wilde. A wilful and perverse author can malign and falsify a character, especially when he spends his life in writing for artificial effect.

A moment or two after Illingworth has departed, Hester and

Gerald return from the garden, full of their happiness, and Gerald picks up Lord Illingworth's glove:

GERALD: Hallo, mother, whose glove is this? You have had a visitor. Who was it?

MRS. ARBUTHNOT (*turning round*): Oh, no one. No one in particular. A man of no importance.

There the play ends. It has no veracity in it from start to finish. There is not a single person in the play who bears a recognisable resemblance to a human being. It is a common play, written by a man who has submerged his genius in the gutter. Even the small strokes of character with which Wilde invests his people are fakes —verbal tricks, not characteristics at all. Lady Hunstanton, for example, can never remember what happened. "I was in hopes he would have married Lady Kelso. But I believe he said her family was too large. Or was it her feet." Saying that Lady Belton had eloped with Lord Fethersdale, she adds, "Poor Lord Belton died three days afterwards of joy, or gout. I forget which."

Archdeacon Daubeny is another contrivance, fashioned to look like a man, but no more than a puppet which utters routine remarks when it is squeezed. When Lady Hunstanton condoles with him about his wife's inability to dine at the Chase that night, he tells her that Mrs. Daubeny is a perfect martyr to headaches. "But she is happiest alone. She is happiest alone." All his conversation is in that strain. Mrs. Daubeny's hearing is slightly defective, says Lady Hunstanton. "Her deafness is a great deprivation to her. She can't even hear my sermons now. She reads them at home. But she has many resources in herself, many resources", the Archdeacon replies. "She reads a good deal, I suppose?" "Just the very largest print. The eyesight is rapidly going. But she's never morbid, never morbid." The humour rapidly becomes mechanical. We know what Dr. Daubeny will reply to any remark Lady Hunstanton may make. "Mrs. Daubeny embroiders a little, too, doesn't she?" Lady Hunstanton enquires. It is always she who speaks to him. No one else does. "She was very deft with her needle once, quite a Dorcas. But the gout has crippled her fingers a good deal. She has not touched the tambour frame for nine or ten years. But she has many amusements. She is very much interested in her own health." When his carriage is announced, Lady Hunstanton says she has told her butler to put a brace of partridges into it. "Mrs. Daubeny may fancy them." The Archdeacon's answer as he departs, never, luckily, to return, is, "It is very kind of you, but Mrs. Daubeny never touches solids now. Lives entirely on jellies. But she is wonderfully cheerful, wonderfully cheerful. She has nothing to complain of."

Except, perhaps, that she seems to be falling to pieces.

44

IT was now high summer for Wilde. *A Woman of No Importance* was almost as successful as *Lady Windermere's Fan* had been, and its success, he felt certain, could easily and continually be repeated. His invention was fertile, and he could compose a story almost without thinking about it. "Tell me a story", his importunate brother would say, and he would instantly tell one, composing it as he went along and with no notion of how it would end. Money poured upon him, and he cultivated extravagant habits. Like many Irishmen, he had several sharply contrasting characteristics: he was humourless, but witty; he could be generous and surprisingly mean, he could be cruel and kind; he was full of exalted ideas, yet he was callous; he was intensely vain and ungrateful, and he hated to hear other people praised, yet he could be charming to those who were least in sympathy with him, and he surprised even his intimates by sudden bursts of tenderness and humility. His nature, after a too common Irish fashion, was florid and ostentatious. He was the master exhibitionist. He liked to be lavish, not because he was generous, but because display pleased him. There was always luncheon at the Café Royal at one, as he told A. E. W. Mason, not because he was prompt to share his good fortune with his friends or even with those who were bare acquaintances, but because a court of sycophants and adulators was essential to his self-satisfaction. There were times when he looked a very vulgar man, and there were times when he behaved like one. An uncultured man of low origin who flings his money about and bestows benefit on all who will gather round and applaud him, is regarded with contempt. How much more to be despised is a man of education and family who behaves like a rich and mindless boor.

The legend of the high-minded, noble-hearted and entirely generous Irishman is a myth. There are *gombeen* men as well as saints in Ireland. If we had Bishop Doyle and Father Mathew and Bishop Berkeley and Vere Foster and Lord George Hill and Horace Plunkett, we had Richard Pigott, the forger of the Parnell Letters, and Joe Brady, the callous cut-throat who slew Lord Charles Cavendish and Mr. Burke in Phoenix Park, and, in our own times, men of such unsavoury character that the very earth is defiled by their presence on it. Showing-off is a common fault in Ireland. Wilde had it in an extraordinary degree. Like his father, he gave banquets to spongers when, despite his large income, he had not enough money to pay the bills, and the bailiffs were about to ring the bell. In 1894 he was so hard up that when George Alexander asked him for another play, he had to beg an immediate advance of £150 on account of royalties. "I am so pressed for money", he wrote to "my dear Aleck", "that I don't know what to do. Of course I am extravagant—you have always been a good wise friend to me—so think what you can do." And, indeed, he was infantilely and vulgarly extravagant. He might have been a coal-heaver who had won a fortune in a football pool, so puerile was his spending. His horde of sycophantic cronies had to be fed and paid and presented with cigarette-cases and tie-pins in return for their shameless flatteries; and the poor fool, becoming more and more obese, more and more in need of adulation, unstintingly paid. He flashed about the town in costly cabs, driving from one expensive hotel to another. In February 1895, shortly before calamity befell him, Wilde entertained Alfred Douglas and a friend of Douglas at the Avondale Hotel, Piccadilly, for ten days. The bill amounted to £140, but Wilde, who had two plays in performance in London at that time, could not pay it. The hotel proprietor refused to let him take his luggage away until the debt was discharged.

Douglas has been accused, especially by Wilde himself, of leading his friend into these extravagances, but Wilde required no leading. He was all too eager to go. It probably did not occur to Bosie that these expensive entertainments might be financially embarrassing to Oscar. Why should he feel any compunction about accepting his friend's offer of hospitality? So far as he knew, Wilde was well off, and a guest does not ask to see his host's bank-book to assure himself that the hospitality can be afforded.

The testimony of nearly all his friends at this time is agreed that success and prosperity were coarsening Wilde's fibre. He had become bloated as well as vain. He ate and drank greedily. He would take a hansom cab from one end of a short street to another, so averse was he from physical exercise. He lay in bed for most of the morning, rising only to drive to the Café Royal to over-feed himself and his sponging friends. He mentioned sums of money loudly and often, and was accustomed to state the cost of all he possessed, especially if it were large: as if he were a bookie who had done well at Ascot and better at Epsom, or a butcher who had suddenly come into a fortune through a lucky speculation in pork. David Low, the New Zealand cartoonist, used, at one time, to depict a rich politician as a vulgar man in a loud check suit, holding a cigar in each corner of his mouth. He might have found his model in Oscar Wilde in 1893 and 1894. Orbicular and gross and scarcely able to breathe because of his obesity, he moved uneasily about the town like a man in mental and physical distress. The minimum poet had contracted a galloping consumption of food and drink and tobacco, and his sallow skin turned greasy and grey and green. He bragged and boasted of his success, and demanded that his sycophants should boast and brag of it too. He sneered at rivals, and belittled those who produced and performed his plays. They were unworthy of him. There was always a derogatory word on his lips for someone, a word dipped in acid and intended not only to wound but to mortify. To dispute his arguments and assertions was to court displeasure, and might result in loss of luncheon at the Café Royal at one! . . . Other writers must be mentioned, if mentioned at all, only in derision. Lazarus, holding out his hands for the rich crumbs falling from this table, was pleasing only in so far as he was able to make himself a successful stooge: providing the big, bloated Dives of literature and drama with ample opportunities to utter spiteful wit! . . .

This was the time when he was most often to be found at dinner-tables in great houses. Guests were invited to meet Mr. Oscar Wilde. The Prince of Wales, who felt sympathy for him in his worst days, liked him and was glad to be seen in his company. A restless mood took hold of him, and drove him across the Channel and back again, so that he was almost as often in Paris as he was in London. Wherever he was, in France or Germany or at home, he spent more money than he earned. His wife saw less of him in these three halcyon years than she had in the previous eight of her marriage.

But this florid life was not the whole of his existence. There were the pseudo-aesthetic, heavily-curtained rooms, smelling of stale incense, in the back streets of Westminster, where mincing stable-boys were waiting to be visited. In the week in which *Lady Windermere's Fan* was produced for the first time, Wilde took the youth, Edward Shelley, to the Albemarle Hotel, but, in the witness-box three years later, denied that there had been any impropriety. Rumours about his peculiar companions began to run round the town, and owners of hotels and restaurants openly wished he would not patronise them. The proprietors of the Savoy Hotel objected to the presence there of Lord Alfred Douglas! . . . And somewhere behind the scenes, the mad Marquess was ferreting around, infuriating himself and everyone he met! . . .

In June 1893 Wilde rented a cottage at Goring-on-Thames as a holiday house for himself and his family: and here he began to write *An Ideal Husband*, which he finished in a farmhouse at Cromer. It was heavy going. The earlier plays, once he had started on them, were quickly, too quickly written, but this one lumbered off his pen as if it were loth to come to life, nor, indeed, did it ever come to life. It still loiters in a state of suspended animation. Wilde, always unwilling to work, ever ready to be distracted from a task, was idler in 1893 and 1894 than he had ever been before. Luncheon and dinner parties, and visits to Cairo and Paris, interfered with the composition of the new play and, worse still, prevented him from thinking it out. The thought he did give it made no demand upon his mind. How restless he was is shown by the fact that he rented chambers in St. James's Place so that he might complete it. Tite Street was seldom frequented, and he seems to have given up all attempts to work there. His mind was disturbed. Constance, eyeing him with apprehension, again wondered if he was sane.

During the stay at Goring, Alfred Douglas was his guest; and in the distortions of gossip, he, with Wilde, were the only occupants of the cottage. The Marquess of Queensberry became uncommonly paternal when he heard this rumour. Lady Queensberry, who had been friendly with Wilde, now began to distrust and fear his influence on Bosie—the familiar name by which her son was known: a corruption of Boysie—and she sought to separate them. He had been sent abroad, first to France, then to Algiers and later to Italy; but Wilde had followed him to Florence. Lady Queensberry then persuaded Lord and Lady Cromer to ask him to stay with them in Cairo; and he went to Egypt in December 1893.

It was during this visit that he met Robert Hichens and E. F. Benson, each of whom was his senior, the first by six years, the second by three. Hichens and Benson were both the sons of Anglican parsons, but parsons in very different degrees, for Benson's father was Archbishop of Canterbury, while Hichens's was a country clergyman who would later become a canon. They were also novelists, with Benson again in a superior degree, though Hichens, in a comparatively short time, was to challenge and change that order. In 1893, however, Hichens, in his own expression, was "nobody". He had published a novel, entitled *The Coastguard's Secret*, when he was seventeen, but it had caused no sensation; and he had supported himself since its issue by writing short stories and paragraphs for the papers. Benson, one of several moderately brilliant brothers, had, however, recently published a novel, entitled *Dodo*, which had been highly successful and sensational: for it was reputed to be based on a remarkable young woman with an incautious tongue and a hatchet face, Miss Margot Tennant, daughter of a Scottish millionaire and destined to become Mrs. H. H. Asquith, hostess at 10 Downing Street, and, later on, Countess of Oxford and Asquith. Benson had spent three or four years in archaeological work in Athens and was now working in Egypt for the Hellenic Society. A friendship quickly developed between the three young men and Benson's sister. Douglas, in addition to being a peer's son and exceedingly handsome, was a friend of the most-talked-of man in London, and his conversation, largely about Wilde, was especially interesting to Hichens, who confesses,[1] with engaging charm, that he envied Benson's success and was eager to surpass it.

Douglas promised to introduce Hichens to Wilde, and, soon afterwards, in London, did so. They met four times, and we may surmise, despite the kindliness with which Hichens remembers Wilde, that they were not congenial to each other. Out of these brief encounters came, in September 1894, a short novel, *The Green Carnation.* It was published anonymously, because Heinemann, the publisher, thought it would sell better if its authorship gave cause for guessing; but both Wilde and Douglas, who figure in it so transparently that Hichens, instead of naming them Esmé Amarinth and Lord Reggie Hastings, might as well have given them their lawful names, realised at once who had written it.

Hichens's innocent desire to become as successful as E. F. Benson was instantly fulfilled. *The Green Carnation* was a very considerable success. Douglas professed to be pleased with its satire, perhaps because he was more kindly treated in it than Wilde was. Wilde, indeed, was not only made to seem absurd, but was depicted in a way which indicated dislike of him and his work. The novel does not, even obliquely, suggest sodomy, but sodomy was read into it by those who were familiar with the rumours which were now spreading more and more widely through the town, and it undoubtedly did Wilde much harm, a fact of which he became well aware. It increased Queensberry's wrath, and made him more resolved than before to punish his son and Wilde. New editions of the novel, now bearing Hichens's name as the author, appeared, and each one inflamed Queensberry still further.

Wilde's sense of humour, never strong, weakened under *The*

[1] In the preface to a new edition of *The Green Carnation*, published by Martin Secker of the Unicorn Press in 1949.

Green Carnation. He took criticism badly, and, prompt to deride others, deeply resented derision of himself. He sneered at Hichens's novel as "a middle-class and mediocre book", although he confessed to some of his friends that it was a cleverer novel than he had thought Hichens capable of writing. The meaning of *middle-class* as a term of abuse and condemnation is seldom apparent. It meant nothing on the lips of Wilde, who was himself essentially middle-class in his social outlook and aspirations and his origin. He hoped, perhaps, to damage the book by using against it an expression which causes middle-class people to recoil from themselves in horror! . . . *The Green Carnation* is a cleverish short story, but not more than that. Its interest now is archaic rather than artistic. Hichens, who is a born story-teller, did skilfully what he had set out to do: to write a topical tale. He reproduced, juvenilely perhaps, the obvious characteristics of Wilde, the follies and absurdities and extravagant expressions, but did not give a hint of the genius that Wilde, even at his worst, never failed to drop. The clown was shown, but that was all. Hichens, drawing his portraits with so much exactitude, lets himself occasionally become tasteless. He refers to Esmé Amarinth's wife several times in a barbarous style, putting words into Amarinth's mouth that Wilde would never have used about Constance. We may believe that Hichens had no intention of humiliating or wounding Mrs. Wilde, had, indeed, ceased, when he mentioned Mrs. Amarinth, to draw on fact and was drawing solely on imagination; but when an author is so particular as Hichens was to make manifest who his originals are, he cannot be excused if his readers find originals where he had put only inventions.

We have here slightly over-run time in this reference to *The Green Carnation*, but it has been necessary to over-run it because the novel helped to precipitate calamity, though that was very far from its author's intentions; as his subsequent behaviour, which will be reported in its proper place, made plain. Most of the raw material for the novel was gathered from Douglas on the banks of the Nile. Hichens had listened very carefully, so carefully that he might have been making verbatim notes of all he had heard! . . .

Bosie's mother disliked his infatuation with Wilde intensely, and she made great efforts to end it. Diplomacy, she thought, was the career her beautiful boy should follow, though no man that is born of woman was less suited to it than her irresponsible and talkative child, whose only test of truth was his personal convenience; and would have thought a war a small price to pay for a bright remark. Accordingly, she persuaded Lord Currie, our ambassador in Turkey, to take him to Constantinople as an honorary attaché. Douglas started from Cairo to Constantinople, via Paris, where he met Wilde, spending a week with him, and London, where he paid a visit to his mother! Lord Currie had not been asked for leave, nor had he been informed of Bosie's intentions, so he cancelled the singular diplomat's appointment; an act which seemed to Douglas a piece of impertinence on the part of one who, compared with the Douglas family, was a common upstart. He was the first peer in his house. There were hundreds of peers in Bosie's! . . . That was the end of his diplomatic career. He did not get as far as Constantinople. Lady Queensberry's scheme for her son's redemption had gone awry.

The Marquess now took a hand in the redemptive task. The friendship between his son and this fellow Wilde must end. Bosie's allowance would cease if it did not. On Sunday the 1st of April 1894 Lord Queensberry sent the following letter [1] to his son from Carter's Hotel, in Albemarle Street:

Alfred,—It is extremely painful for me to have to write to you in the strain I must; but please understand that I decline to receive any answers from you in writing in return. After your recent hysterical impertinent ones I refuse to be annoyed with such, and I decline to read any more letters. If you have anything to say, do come here and say it in person. Firstly, am I to understand that, having left Oxford as you did, with discredit to yourself, the reasons for which were fully explained to me by your tutor, you now intend to loaf and loll about and do nothing? All the time you were wasting at Oxford I was put off with an assurance that you were eventually to go into the Civil Service or to the Foreign Office, and then I was put off with the assurance that you were going to the Bar. It appears to me that you intend

[1] It and the rest of the correspondence will be found in Montgomery Hyde's *Trials of Oscar Wilde*, pp. 152-6.

to do nothing. I utterly decline, however, to just supply you with sufficient funds to enable you to loaf about. You are preparing a wretched future for yourself, and it would be most cruel and wrong for me to encourage you in this. Secondly, I come to the more painful part of this letter—your intimacy with this man Wilde. It must either cease or I will disown you and stop all money supplies. I am not going to try and analyse this intimacy, and I make no charge; but to my mind to pose as a thing is as bad as to be it. With my own eyes I saw you both in the most loathsome and disgusting relationship as expressed by your manner and expression. Never in my experience have I seen such a sight as that in your horrible features. No wonder people are talking as they are. Also I now hear on good authority, but this may be false, that his wife is petitioning to divorce him for sodomy and other crimes. Is this true, or do you not know of it? If I thought the actual thing was true, and it became public property, I should be quite justified in shooting him at sight. These Christian English cowards and men, as they call themselves, want waking up. Your disgusted so-called father, QUEENSBERRY.

Lord Alfred's reply to this singular letter was a telegram:

What a funny little man you are. ALFRED DOUGLAS.[1]

The fury into which it flung the Marquess is understandable. "You impertinent young jackanapes", he wrote on the 3rd of April:

I request that you will not send such messages to me by telegraph. If you send me any more such telegrams, or come with any impertinence, I will give you the thrashing you deserve. Your only excuse is that you must be crazy. I hear from a man at Oxford that you were thought crazy there, and that accounts for a good deal that has happened. If I catch you again with that man I will make a public scandal in a way you little dream of; if it is already a suppressed one. I prefer an open one, and at any rate I shall not be blamed for allowing such a state of things to go on. Unless this acquaintance ceases I shall carry out my threat and stop all supplies, and if you are not going to make any attempt to do something I shall certainly cut you down to a mere pittance, so you know what to expect.

He was in a highly epistolary state then, writing his mind to everyone he knew. Among the recipients of his ill-spelt, ungrammatical

[1] Hichens quotes this telegram in the first chapter of *The Green Carnation*, thus making the identification of his characters with Wilde and Douglas plainer. Douglas seems to have told the story of it to everybody he met.

and vitriolic letters was Alfred Montgomery, the father of his first wife, to whom he wrote from Skindle's Hotel at Maidenhead on the 6th of July:

Sir, I have changed my mind, and as I am not at all well, having been very much upset by what has happened the last ten days, I do not see why I should come dancing attendance upon you. Your daughter is the person who is supporting my son to defy me. She won't write, but she is now telegraphing on the subject to me. Last night, after hearing from you, I received a very quibbling, prevaricating message from her, saying the boy denied having been at the Savoy for the last year; but why send the telegram unless he could deny that he had been there with Oscar Wilde at all? As a matter of fact he did, and there has been a stinking scandal. I am told they were warned off, but the proprietor would not admit this. This hideous scandal has been going on for years. Your daughter must be mad by the way she is behaving. She evidently wants to make out that I want to make out a case against my son. It is nothing of the kind. I have made out a case against Oscar Wilde and I have to his face accused him of it. If I was certain of the thing I would shoot the fellow on sight, but I can only accuse him of posing. It now lies in the hands of the two whether they will further defy me. He plainly showed the white feather the other day when I tackled him—damned cur and coward of the Rosebery type. As for this so-called son of mine, he is no son of mine, and I will have nothing to do with him. He may starve as far as I am concerned after his behaviour to me. His mother may support him, but she shan't do that here in London with this awful scandal going on. But your daughter's conduct is outrageous, and I am now fully convinced that the Rosebery-Gladstone-Royal insult that came to me through my other son, that she worked that—I thought it was you. I saw Drumlanrig here on the river, which much upset me. It shall be known some day by all that Rosebery not only insulted me by lying to the Queen, which makes her as bad as him and Gladstone, but also has made a lifelong quarrel between my son and I.

The reference to Rosebery and Gladstone and the Queen need not detain us here. They refer to an obscure grievance Queensberry felt against Rosebery in connexion with his son, Drumlanrig's, elevation to the peerage: a matter in which Rosebery had been careful to consult Queensberry and to obtain his cordial consent. Soon after Drumlanrig was made a peer in his own right, his father developed a belief that the whole affair had been arranged by Rosebery, in collusion with Gladstone and the Queen, to annoy him for being an atheist and some sort of republican.

On a date not stated, Lord Alfred dispatched a postcard—he had the vulgar habit of writing his abuse on postcards so that it might be read by other people than the addressee—to his father at Carter's Hotel, from whence it was sent on to an address in Scotland:

As you return my letters unopened I am obliged to write on a postcard. I write to inform you that I treat your absurd threats with absolute indifference. Ever since your exhibition at O.W.'s house [1] I have made a point of appearing with him at many public restaurants, such as the Berkeley, Willis's Rooms, the Café Royal, &c., and I shall continue to go to any of these places whenever I choose and with whom I choose. I am of age and my own master. You have disowned me at least a dozen times and have meanly deprived me of my money. You have therefore no right over me either legal or moral. If O.W. was to prosecute you in the Criminal Court for libel you would get seven years' penal servitude for your outrageous libels. Much as I detest you I am anxious to avoid this for the sake of the family; but if you try to assault me I shall defend myself with a loaded revolver which I always carry; and if I shoot you or he shoots you, we should be completely justified, as we should be acting in self-defence against a violent and dangerous rough, and I think if you were dead not many people would miss you. A. D.

This postcard roused his father to furious response. On the 21st of August 1894 Queensberry wrote to his son from Scotland:

I have received your postcard, which I presume is from you, but as the writing is utterly unreadable to me, have been unable to make out hardly one sentence. My object of receiving no written communication from you is therefore kept intact. All future cards will go into the fire unread. I presume these are the "hyerogliphics" [*sic*] of the O.W. posing-club, of which you have the reputation of being such a shining light. I congratulate you on your autography; it is beautiful, and should help you to get a living. I don't know what at, but, say crossing-sweeping. My friend I am staying with has made out some of your letter, and wished to read it to me, but I declined to hear a word. However, according to his advice I shall keep it as a specimen, and also as a protection

[1] This is the visit referred to on page 78.

in case I ever feel tempted to give you the thrashing you deserve. You reptile. You are no son of mine and I never thought you were. QUEENSBERRY.

Queensberry had now convinced himself that Lady Queensberry had made a cuckold of him, and that Alfred was her lover's son. The belief was as false as it was foul, and was odd in the mind of a man who had proposed to his wife that he should bring his mistress to live with her. The fury with which he held to this delusion is manifested in the following letter, dated the 25th of August 1894, and addressed to his son from 26 Portland Place:

You miserable creature, I received your telegram by post from Carter's and have requested them not to forward any more, but just to tear any up, as I did yours, without reading it, directly I was aware from whom it came. You must be flush of money to waste it on such rubbish. I have learned, thank goodness, to turn the keenest pangs to peacefulness. What could be keener pain than to have such a son as yourself fathered upon one? However, there is always a bright side to every cloud, and whatever is is light [*sic*]. If you are my son, it is only confirming proof to me, if I needed any, how right I was to face every horror and misery I have done rather than run the risk of bringing more creatures into the world like yourself, and that was the entire and only reason of my breaking with your mother as a wife, so intensely was I dissatisfied with her as the mother of you children; and particularly yourself, whom, when quite a baby I cried over you the bitterest tears a man ever shed, that I had brought such a creature into the world, and unwittingly had committed such a crime. If you are not my son, and in this Christian country with these hypocrites 'tis a wise father who knows his own child and no wonder on the principles they intermarry on, but to be fore-warned is to be fore-armed. No wonder you have fallen a prey to this horrible brute. I am only sorry for you as a human creature. You must gang your ain gait. Well, it would be rather a satisfaction to me, because the crime then is not to me. As you see, I am philosophical and take comfort from anything; but, really, I am sorry for you. You must be demented; there is madness on your mother's side and indeed few families in this Christian country are without it, if you look into them. But please cease annoying me, for I will not correspond with you, nor receive nor answer letters, and as for money, you sent me a lawyer's letter to say you would take none from me, but anyhow until you change your life I should refuse any; it depends on yourself whether I will ever recognise you at all again after your behaviour. I will make allowance; I think you are demented, and I am very sorry for you. QUEENSBERRY.

As one reads the history of these nervous degenerates, contempt turns to pity. If it was hard on Wilde to be the son of his father and mother, it was hard on Alfred Douglas to be the son of the Marquess of Queensberry. But where shall we put a point to our pity? Was it not hard on Sir William and Lady Wilde and on the Marquess that they were themselves?

45

IN the midst of these excursions and alarms Wilde wrote *An Ideal Husband*. His congenital troubles were now becoming acute. There was the open scandal with Lord Alfred Douglas, and there was the hidden scandal of the male brothel in Little College Street. Mingled with his triumphs on the stage and at high dinner and luncheon tables were the embarrassments and dangers of the slimy world he haunted. Douglas had shown him the letters from the Marquess, and he seems not to have made much effort to restrain the young man's ebullience. It is unlikely that Douglas failed to mention the telegram, "What a funny little man you are". It was the sort of undergraduate insolence in which Wilde delighted, though he professes in *De Profundis* to have thought it vulgar. But his delight was now turning to anxiety. Queensberry had not contented himself with writing letters: he had visited the hotels and restaurants frequented by Wilde and Douglas, and had informed their owners or managers that if he caught the pair of them there he would not only thrash them both, but would wreck the hotel or restaurant. He was likely to fulfil one of his threats. Queensberry's behaviour could not be regarded entirely as the acts of a lunatic. Wilde *knew* what truth was in his charges; knew how much more there was to be discovered than was dreamt of even by the mad Marquess. But he could not justly be charged with corrupting Bosie, whose corruption had begun long before

Wilde and he had met. Douglas was a notorious sodomite while he was at Magdalen, and was accustomed to say that he had been one at Winchester. Wilde, indeed, soon after their acquaintance had begun, had paid £100 to blackmailers who were threatening him with exposure. He was eventually sent down. The letters which are published in *Oscar Wilde and the Black Marquess* by the present Marquess of Queensberry in collaboration with Percy Colson, prove beyond doubt that Bosie became Wilde's "boy". Bosie boasted of the fact, as Mr. Robert Baldwin Ross had done. He, too, had a strong strain of madness, for he frequently fell into sudden rages that were as berserker as any that afflicted his father or Wilde. There was an occasion when, entering a house where Ross was also a guest, Douglas made a terrific scene. Ross, a timorous little fellow, quivered like a mild-mannered rabbit which has unexpectedly encountered a stoat; and Douglas, roaring with rage, pursued him, despite the barrier of a large table behind which Ross crouched. Had it not been for intervention, he would undoubtedly have mauled Ross severely. The little man, thereafter, was careful to keep out of his way. It cannot be said that Wilde's association with his "darling boy" improved his literary style. His letters to him are ill-written and maudlin stuff, such as might be composed by a pretentious and incontinent haberdasher or dentist who has conceived an unlawful passion for a voluptuous barmaid. They are full of phrases such as "purple valleys of despair" that smell of cheap scent.

But although Wilde was not the original corrupter of Douglas, he was the continuing corrupter, if, that is to say, Douglas needed any corrupting; and he was in an awkward situation when the "mad Marquess" began to bellow. He consulted his solicitors, Messrs. C. O. Humphreys, Son & Kershaw, whom he misled; and they, believing him to be innocent, wrote to Lord Queensberry on the 11th of July, demanding that "the assertions and insinuations" in his letters to his son should be retracted and an apology for making them made. Action would be entered against him if this were not done. Queensberry promptly replied, refusing to make any apology. He went further, in a second letter: he threatened that if the friendship between Wilde and his son were not instantly ended, he would lodge an information with the police at Scotland Yard. . . .

A man has difficulty in composing a comedy in such conditions as these. Nevertheless, *An Ideal Husband* was written, and on the 3rd of January 1895 it was produced at the Haymarket Theatre with Mr. Lewis Waller and Miss Julia Neilson in the principal parts. The Prince of Wales, afterwards Edward the Seventh, was present in a box and, according to Pearson, full of praise and compliments. When Wilde confessed that some of the dialogue could be cut, the Prince, whose authority as a critic of literature was not high, protested. "Pray do not take out a single word", he said. That was more than a plea to Wilde. It was a royal command which he had not the effrontery to disobey.

The cast was, perhaps, the best all-round one that had yet appeared in a Wilde play, though Bernard Shaw thought little of it. It included two actors, Charles Hawtrey and C. H. Brookfield, who were notably antipathetic to Wilde. Brookfield was to become and, for the rest of his life, remain his most bitter enemy; a man without the excuse Queensberry had, first, of being the father of Alfred Douglas, and, second, of being mentally deranged. Hawtrey's attitude to Wilde was probably no more than that of a man, essentially masculine, to whom homosexuality was repulsive. He seems not to have shown any venom towards Wilde, although he was a promoter of the complimentary dinner given in honour of Queensberry when Wilde lost his action for libel; nor did he behave as Brookfield did, by hounding, so far as he could, a broken man.

There are several sorry figures in this ignominious matter. None of them is sorrier than Brookfield, a sour-minded man of small talent and bitter tongue who, even if he was unaware of the fact, was envious of the ease with which Wilde won success in a world that Brookfield sought in vain to overcome and conquer. This man, who played the part of a lackey in *An Ideal Husband*, behaved to Wilde during the rehearsals with an insolence that would not have been tolerated by any other dramatist than Wilde. Waller should have dismissed him from the company. He was unfit, either by his ability or his behaviour, to be a member of it.

As a dramatist, he was of no account. His most notable play was an adaptation of a French farce which, under the title of *Dear Old Charlie*, was produced by Hawtrey. It is significant of the frivolity with which statesmen in Britain sometimes behave that when the post of Reader of Plays in the Lord Chamberlain's Office became vacant, Brookfield received it. No more scandalous appointment had been made since the post was given to George Colman the Younger in 1824. The frivolity was on a par with that of the ponderous and cynical Marquess of Salisbury when he made Alfred Austin Poet Laureate.

In this play we are presented again with the familiar Wilde situation: the husband with a secret in his life, in this case a shameful secret; and the stiffly upright and unbending, puritanical wife who is considerably younger than her husband. Out of the middle of Europe comes a blackmailer! . . . Mrs. Erlynne is now named Mrs. Cheveley. Wilde's situation must have been more in his mind than he imagined while he was composing *An Ideal Husband*. There was, as we have already noted, ample room why it should be. The Marquess of Queensberry was taking considerable care to fix it there. There is a passage of dialogue in the beginning of the second act, in which Sir Robert Chiltern discusses his plight with Lord Goring, a human version of Lord Henry Wotton and Lord Darlington and Lord Illingworth, one of the few human characters in the whole Wilde drama; and it is cited here, out of its place in the examination of the play, so that the point shall be emphasised by it. Chiltern, in grave danger of public exposure and ruin, consults his friend Goring. Goring asks him why he did not confess his crime to his wife before their marriage:

SIR ROBERT CHILTERN: When? When we were engaged? Do you think she would have married me if she had known that the origin of my fortune is such as it is, the basis of my career such as it is, and that I had done a thing that I suppose most men would call shameful and dishonourable?

LORD GORING (*slowly*): Yes; most men would call it ugly names. There is no doubt of that.

SIR ROBERT CHILTERN (*bitterly*): Men who every day do something of the same kind themselves. Men who, each of them, have worse secrets in their own lives.

LORD GORING: That is the reason why they are so pleased to find out other people's secrets. It distracts public attention from their own.

SIR ROBERT CHILTERN: And, after all, whom did I wrong by what I did? No one.

That is the question Wilde's supporters asked during and after his trial, the question some of them still, and very unwarrantably, ask about Wilde. Goring gives one answer to it. "Except yourself, Robert", he says.

As we seek for signs of Wilde's troubles in the play, we come on odd examples of the way in which his affairs seem to be mixed up with it. A few speeches after those cited above, Chiltern asserts that his offence was committed "nearly eighteen years ago". The dates denote that this should be "nearly twenty years ago". Wilde always gave his age as two years less than it was. The celebrated cross-examination by Sir Edward Carson opens with the production of his birth certificate, showing that he was born, not in 1856, as he had just stated he was, but in 1854. The point is small, but it is significant. The ham actor was dramatising himself. There in Tite Street was the beautiful and upright Constance, still adoring her brilliant Oscar, but perturbed about him too; and here was Oscar with his shameful secret in imminent danger of discovery! . . . That was his one play. He gave the theatre four variations of it.

46

SIR ROBERT CHILTERN, BART., who is Under-Secretary for Foreign Affairs, and his wife, Gertrude, are holding a reception in the Octagon Room of their house in Grosvenor Square. He is forty and she is twenty-seven. As the curtain rises on the first act, she is seen, "a woman of grave Greek beauty", such as Wilde had striven to discern in Constance, standing at the top of the staircase to receive her guests as they come up. Behind her is "a large eighteenth-century French tapestry—representing the Triumph of Love, from a design by Boucher". The year is 1895, the year of Wilde's disaster, and the rooms are crowded with the "beautiful idiots and brilliant lunatics" who now, according to Sir Robert's sister, Mabel, compose London society. One of the guests, Lady Markby, brings a friend with her, a Mrs. Cheveley, who turns out to have been a school-fellow of Lady Chiltern: a very disreputable school-fellow. "She was untruthful," Lady Chiltern later in the evening tells her husband, "dishonest, an evil influence on everyone whose trust or friendship she could win. I hated, I despised her. She stole things, she was a thief. She was sent away for being a thief. . . ." This woman Cheveley has spent a large part of her life abroad, chiefly in Vienna, where she deals in underground finance and probably adds to her income by living with any rich man who will keep her. Chiltern, during this revelation, endeavours, as Lord Windermere endeavoured in the case of Mrs. Erlynne, to say some kind words about Mrs. Cheveley. She may, he suggests, have changed her character. "No one should be entirely judged by their past", he tells his wife, who promptly and decisively replies, "One's past is what one is. It is the only way by which people should be judged." This is Miss Hester Worsley speaking with an English accent, just as Miss Hester Worsley was Lady Windermere speaking with an American accent.

Mrs. Cheveley has come to London and to the Chiltern reception for a specific purpose; and she very quickly reveals that purpose to Sir Robert. She wants him to do something for her, and she mentions one Baron Arnheim very significantly. The name causes Chiltern to start. An interruption by guests defers the revelation until a little later in the evening. Chiltern asks her how long she means to remain: "My stay in England really depends on you, Sir Robert", she replies.

Sir Robert Chiltern (*taking a seat beside her*): Seriously?

Mrs. Cheveley: Quite seriously. I want to talk to you about a great political and financial scheme, this Argentine Canal Company, in fact.

Sir Robert Chiltern: What a tedious, practical subject for you to talk about, Mrs. Cheveley.

Mrs. Cheveley: Oh, I like tedious, practical subjects. What I don't like are tedious, practical people. There is a wide difference. Besides, you are interested, I know, in International Canal Schemes. You were Lord Radley's secretary, weren't you, when the Government bought the Suez Canal shares?

The quotation is interrupted so that the reader may be reminded that the Suez Canal shares were bought by Disraeli in 1875. The date has point. With it, the reader should remember that the time of the play is 1895, in which year Chiltern is forty. He was, therefore, twenty when the Suez Canal shares were bought, an age at which, we may believe, he was still an undergraduate or had only recently come down from his college. It is unlikely that he would, at twenty, have been private secretary to a prominent politician. This point has importance in our argument. The quotation is resumed:

SIR ROBERT CHILTERN: Yes. But the Suez Canal was a very great and splendid undertaking. It gave us our direct route to India. It had imperial value. It was necessary that we should have control. This Argentine scheme is a commonplace Stock Exchange swindle.

MRS. CHEVELEY: A speculation, Sir Robert! A brilliant, daring speculation.

SIR ROBERT CHILTERN: Believe me, Mrs. Cheveley, it is a swindle. Let us call things by their proper names. It makes matters simpler. In fact, I sent out a special Commission to enquire into the matter privately, and they report that the works are hardly begun, and as for the money already subscribed, no one seems to know what has become of it. The whole thing is a second Panama, and with not a quarter of the chance of success that miserable affair had. I hope you have not invested in it. I am sure you are far too clever to have done that.

MRS. CHEVELEY: I have invested very largely in it.

SIR ROBERT CHILTERN: Who could have advised you to do such a foolish thing?

MRS. CHEVELEY: Your old friend—and mine.

SIR ROBERT CHILTERN: Who?

MRS. CHEVELEY: Baron Arnheim.

This is a good piece of theatrical writing. The curiosity of the audience is aroused and skilful preparation is made for the blackmailing scene which immediately follows. There are a few false statements to be noted, but they need not detain us at the moment.

Mrs. Cheveley's mention of Baron Arnheim's name manifestly disturbs Chiltern, who now tries to break off their intimate conversation. He suggests that he should show her his Corot pictures, but she is in no mood "for silver twilights, or rose pink dawns". She "wants to talk business". Chiltern becomes severe.

He has no advice to give Mrs. Cheveley, except that she should interest herself in something less dangerous than Canal shares. "The success of the Canal depends, of course, on the attitude of England, and I am going to lay the report of the Commissioners before the House to-morrow night." It is at this point that the play, which has already shown some signals of distress as a piece of verisimilitude, begins to be plainly foolish. Mrs. Cheveley speaks bluntly. "That you must not do", she replies. "In your own interests, Sir Robert, to say nothing of mine, you must not do that."

SIR ROBERT CHILTERN (*looking at her in wonder*): In my own interests? My dear Mrs. Cheveley, what do you mean? (*Sits down beside her.*)

MRS. CHEVELEY: Sir Robert, I will be quite frank with you. I want you to withdraw the report that you had intended to lay before the House, on the ground that you have reason to believe that the Commissioners have been prejudiced or misinformed or something. Then I want you to say a few words to the effect that the Government is going to reconsider the question, and that you have reason to believe that the Canal, if completed, will be of great international value. You know the sort of thing Ministers say in cases of this kind. A few ordinary platitudes will do. In modern life nothing produces such an effect as a good platitude. It makes the whole world kin. Will you do that for me?

SIR ROBERT CHILTERN: Mrs. Cheveley, you cannot be serious in making me such a proposition!

MRS. CHEVELEY: I am quite serious.

SIR ROBERT CHILTERN (*coldly*): Pray allow me to believe that you are not.

MRS. CHEVELEY (*speaking with great deliberation and emphasis*): Ah, but I am. And if you do what I ask you, I . . . will pay you very handsomely!

SIR ROBERT CHILTERN: Pay me!

MRS. CHEVELEY: Yes.

SIR ROBERT CHILTERN: I am afraid I don't quite understand what you mean.

MRS. CHEVELEY (*leaning back on the sofa and looking at him*): How very disappointing! And I have come all the way from Vienna in order that you should thoroughly understand me.

SIR ROBERT CHILTERN: I fear I don't.

MRS. CHEVELEY (*in her most nonchalant manner*): My dear Sir Robert, you are a man of the world, and you have your price, I suppose. Everybody has nowadays. The drawback is that most people are so dreadfully expensive. I know I am. I hope you will be more reasonable in your terms.

SIR ROBERT CHILTERN (*rising indignantly*): If you will allow me, I will call your carriage for you. You have lived so long abroad, Mrs. Cheveley, that you seem to be unable to realise that you are talking to an English gentleman.

Then Mrs. Cheveley delivers her blow. "I realise", she says, "that I am talking to a man who laid the foundations of his fortune by selling to a Stock Exchange speculator a Cabinet secret. . . . I know the real origin of your wealth and your career, and I have the letter . . . the letter you wrote to Baron Arnheim, when you were Lord Radley's secretary, telling the Baron to buy Suez Canal shares—a letter written three days before the Government announced its purchase." Following the blow, she delivers a long speech which ends with the demand that he shall promise "to suppress your report, and to speak in the House in favour of this scheme". If he will not do this, she will drive down to some newspaper office "and give them this scandal and the proofs of it". What would have happened if Chiltern had recklessly replied, "All right! Drive down!" does not seem to have been considered by her. If he had taken the heroic course, her Argentine Canal would have been laid in ruins.

But he does not play the heroic part. Having weakly asserted that her proposal is impossible, he first offers her a bribe, and then pleads for time to think. His bribe is scornfully declined and his request for time refused. Mrs. Cheveley must telegraph to Vienna that very night. He then collapses. "I consent", he says. "The report shall be withdrawn. I will arrange for a question to be put to me on the subject."

47

NOW if this were common, back-street melodrama, written for the entertainment of simple-minded people whose demand is for excitement and not for verisimilitude, no one could offer objection to it. It is skilfully composed. The scene is certainly exciting. Interest and suspense are well sustained. But *An Ideal Husband* is not intended to be a commonplace, back-street melodrama for unexacting people: it is high comedy, reflecting life, and is designed for the entertainment of intelligent and informed people. Our judgement of it, therefore, must be based on different principles from those we should use in assessing the value of *The Worst Woman in London*. The law to be observed here was laid down by the Canon of Toledo when he and the priest of La Mancha discoursed together on the high-road concerning the romantic delusions of Don Quixote. "It may be that . . . works of invention should not be criticised for inaccuracy: but I say that fiction should be probable, and that in proportion as it is so, it is pleasing. Fables should not be composed to outrage the understanding; but by making the wonderful appear possible, and creating in the mind a pleasing interest, they may both surprise and entertain: which cannot be affected where no regard is paid to probability." Wilde's play fails to pass this test.

48

ATTENTION has already been drawn to an elementary mistake made by Wilde in the matter of dates. The time of the play is 1895. The sale of the Suez Canal shares took place in 1875. Chiltern, now forty, was twenty when the sale occurred. If he were not still at Oxford or Cambridge in his twentieth year, he would probably have been receiving specialised instruction from a crammer to enable him to pass an entrance examination for the Foreign Office. Even if he had already passed this examination, at that early age, he would have attained no higher office than that of a junior clerk. He certainly would not have been appointed private secretary to a Cabinet Minister and allowed access to Cabinet secrets. We are not here disputing the possibility that a Cabinet secret, even one so vital as the purchase of the Suez Canal shares, may be divulged.

In recent years we have had cause to know not only of leakages of information, even in war-time, from Ministers and their wives, but of a leakage made by a Cabinet Minister while a Chancellor of the Exchequer was reporting his scheme of taxation to his colleagues. We have heard of ignominious "presents" being accepted by minor Ministers, and we are not, therefore, inclined to feel sceptical when a dramatist asks us to believe that eminent politicians are bribable. But he must make the wonderful appear probable. He must not ask us to accept as facts inventions which could not possibly, in the circumstances he describes, ever have been facts. High comedy should not outrage the understanding. If our author cannot obtain his effect otherwise than by creating a situation which would not be possible in the life and conditions he depicts, then he must refrain from obtaining effect and seek other employment than that of a serious author. Wilde could, of course, have evaded our charge in respect of Chiltern's age at the time the Suez Canal shares were sold, by omitting or altering dates: but he, so vague about dates as a rule, is precise about them here. We may wonder, too, whether Chiltern would have been so foolish as to give Baron Arnheim incriminating information *in a letter*. Its danger to himself was surely apparent? He seems never to have tried to secure its destruction. Almost blithely he dropped it from his memory, though its existence must have been a continual menace to his happiness and position. The price paid for the secret by Baron Arnheim was £110,000. Chiltern, who was known to be very poor, immediately resigned his position as private secretary to Lord Radley and entered Parliament. Can we believe that no one wondered where he, a young man of twenty, had so suddenly obtained his large fortune and was enabled to become a politician? Did it not transpire that Arnheim had bought very large holdings in the Canal? One might, perhaps, disregard such questions as these and overlook the slips as small errors to which authors are liable, or as demands that they sometimes make on our credulity. A work of imagination is not to be held too strictly to fact: a general appearance of verisimilitude should suffice.

But these are not the only questions we feel compelled to ask.

There are others, and much more important ones, which demand answers. Chiltern is not the Foreign Secretary: he is only the *Under*-Secretary; that is to say, a minor Minister. Decisions of importance, therefore, are not made by him. This particular decision would not be made by the Foreign Secretary on his own responsibility, but in close conference with his Cabinet colleagues. Under-Secretaries do not send out Commissions. These are appointed by the Government. Such Commissions do not make their reports to minor Ministers. They make them to senior Ministers or the Cabinet. Mrs. Cheveley, if she were the astute woman of the world she professed to be, must have known that Chiltern, however willing he might have been to grant her request, was incapable of doing so. He had no more power to suppress the report of the Commissioners on the Argentine Canal than was possessed by a porter at the Foreign Office door. If his life had depended on his granting her request, he could not have saved it. Wilde asks his audience to believe that this Under-Secretary could not only suppress a Commission's report, although the report must have been known to the Foreign Secretary and his staff, and probably to every member of the Cabinet, but that he could, without even mentioning the matter to his chief, agree, in response to a prompted question in the House of Commons, to reverse a Cabinet decision! This is a grotesque situation. It bears no relation to reality. What, we may wonder, would have happened on the Government Front Bench had Chiltern acted as Mrs. Cheveley demanded he should, as he had agreed to do? Would not the Leader of the Opposition have had something surprising to say? Would not the Commissioners, treated in this cavalier fashion, have made complaint? What would have appeared in the Press on the following morning?

Wilde, having landed his principal in a situation into which he could never have got himself, now has to get him out of it. His first effort in this direction is to make Lord Goring and Mabel Chiltern, another charming and human figure in the play, find a diamond brooch lying on a sofa. This brooch interests Goring very much. He calls it a bracelet, and, when Mabel insists that it is a brooch, remarks, "It can be used as a bracelet". He puts it in a letter-case and asks her to say nothing about it, a request which, naturally, surprises her. "Well, you see," Lord Goring says, "I gave this brooch to somebody once, years ago."

The second effort to extricate Chiltern from his hole is made by Lady Chiltern, in a way that seems certain to push him further into it. Mrs. Cheveley makes a gaffe which, one feels certain, a woman so adroit as she is reputed to be, would not have made. She vaunts herself before Lady Chiltern, saying as she departs that she had found Sir Robert very "susceptible to reason. I converted him in ten minutes." Chiltern is going to support the Argentine Canal Scheme in the Commons! . . . "But, of course, for the next twenty-four hours, the whole thing is a dead secret."

LADY CHILTERN (*gently*): A secret? Between whom?
MRS. CHEVELEY (*with a flash of amusement in her eyes*): Between your husband and me.

That was stupid of Mrs. Cheveley, as she should have had the wit to realise.

The act ends with a scene between Chiltern and his wife, in which she reproaches him for his proposed action. She has heard him describe the Argentine Canal Scheme as "the most dishonest and fraudulent scheme there has ever been in political life", to which, "biting his lip", he fatuously retorts, "I was mistaken in the view I took. We all make mistakes." "But you told me yesterday", Lady Chiltern insists, "that you had received the report from the Commission, and that it entirely condemned the whole thing." His rejoinder is, "I have reasons now to believe that the Commission was prejudiced, or, at any rate, misinformed". She does not ask, as she might reasonably have done, what had transpired in his ten minutes' casual conversation with Mrs. Cheveley to make him change his mind so drastically and abruptly. Lady Chiltern, like all the Wilde women of high moral tone, is addicted to grandiose eloquence. "All your life ", she tells her husband, "you have stood apart from others. You have never let the world soil you. To the world, as to myself, you have been an ideal always. Oh, be that ideal still. That great inheritance throw not away—that tower of ivory do not destroy. Robert, men can love what is beneath them—things unworthy, stained, dishonoured. We women worship when we love; and when we lose our worship, we lose everything. Oh, don't kill my love for you, don't do that!" She forces him, late as the hour is, to write a note to Mrs. Cheveley, withdrawing his promise to support the Argentine Canal Scheme, and has it sent round to Claridge's Hotel at once. She then embraces him, telling him that we needs must love the highest when we see it, and goes to bed. Left alone, Chiltern, in a state of agitation, buries his head in his hands. Mason, his butler, enters to lower the lights. Chiltern looks up, and exclaims, "Put out the lights, Mason, put out the lights!" which Mason does. "*The room becomes almost dark. The only light there is comes from the great chandelier that hangs over the staircase and illuminates the tapestry of the Triumph of Love*"; a nice piece of symbolism which was, one hopes, apparent to an audience whose familiarity with Boucher was not, perhaps, profound.

49

THE second act opens with the consultation between Chiltern and Lord Goring which is mentioned in section 45. During this consultation it transpires that Goring was once engaged to be married to Mrs. Cheveley. The engagement lasted for three days. Goring's advice is not very helpful. It amounts only to the proposal that Chiltern shall fight Mrs. Cheveley, advice about as useful as a suggestion that an unarmed man whose hands are tied, should fight a man with a tommy-gun. Later in the act, Mrs. Cheveley calls to enquire if she had dropped a diamond brooch on the previous evening; and during this visit Lady Chiltern tells her very bluntly that if she had known who she was, she would not have allowed her into her house. "I see that after all these years you have not changed a bit, Gertrude", Mrs. Cheveley replies. "I never change", Lady Chiltern retorts. "Then life has taught you nothing?"

LADY CHILTERN: It has taught me that a person who has once been guilty of a dishonest and dishonourable action may be guilty of it a second time, and should be shunned.

MRS. CHEVELEY: Would you apply that rule to everyone?

LADY CHILTERN: Yes, to everyone, without exception.

MRS. CHEVELEY: Then I am sorry for you, Gertrude, very sorry for you.

Lady Chiltern, it will be noticed, has the same hard attitude to sinners that Lady Windermere and Miss Hester Worsley have. There is no pardon in her, no belief in redemption, no likelihood in her world that the penitent shall be permitted to work out his sentence and try to make amends. While she is dispensing her stern principles, she reveals the fact that it was she who persuaded Chiltern to send Mrs. Cheveley the letter withdrawing his promise to support the Argentine Canal Scheme. This revelation infuriates Mrs. Cheveley, who tells her that her husband is not the model of propriety she imagines him to be. "In this world like meets with like. It is because your husband is himself fraudulent and dishonest that we pair so well together. Between you and him are chasms. He and I are closer friends. We are enemies linked together. The same sin binds us." Lady Chiltern orders her out of the house, and as she does so, Chiltern enters and overhears his wife's order. *He grows deadly pale*:

MRS. CHEVELEY: Your house! A house bought with the price of dishonour. A house, everything in which has been paid for by fraud. (*Turns round and sees* SIR ROBERT CHILTERN.) Ask him what the origin of his fortune is! Get him to tell you how he sold to a stockbroker a Cabinet secret. Learn from him to what you owe your position.

LADY CHILTERN: It is not true! Robert! It is not true!

MRS. CHEVELEY (*pointing at him with outstretched finger*): Look at him! Can he deny it! Does he dare to!

SIR ROBERT CHILTERN: Go! Go at once! You have done your worst now.

MRS. CHEVELEY: My worst? I have not yet finished with you, with neither of you. I give you both till to-morrow at noon. If by then you don't do what I bid you to do, the whole world shall know the origin of Sir Robert Chiltern.

[SIR ROBERT CHILTERN *strikes the bell.* MASON *enters.*

SIR ROBERT CHILTERN: Show Mrs. Cheveley out.

This scene is followed by one of recrimination between husband and wife, with the husband accusing women in general of ruining men by making idols of them. Having delivered this tirade, Sir Robert rushes from the room, leaving his wife in tears, and the curtain falls.

The third act occurs in the library of Lord Goring's house. Among his letters, he finds one from Lady Chiltern. It contains words as brief and frantic as those written to Lord Darlington by Lady Windermere. "I want you. I trust you. I am coming to you. Gertrude." These foolish words, which might almost have been written with the intention of misleading any unauthorised person who might read them, do not puzzle Goring, who realises that Lady Chiltern must have discovered her husband's sin. He decides not to go out, as he had intended to do, but to await her arrival. Unluckily his father, another excellent and natural character, enters, and Goring has difficulty in getting him out of the library into the adjoining smoking-room. But he succeeds.

As he goes to join his father there, he tells his servant that he is expecting a visit from a lady. "Show her into the drawing-room when she arrives. . . . It is a matter of the gravest importance, Phipps." No name is mentioned. A ring is heard at the door, and Goring, saying that this must be the lady, decides to wait for her entrance, but his father makes a nuisance of himself and has to be returned to the smoking-room. While Goring is doing this, a footman, who, of course, has been told nothing, shows the lady in. But she is not Lady Chiltern. She is Mrs. Cheveley. Phipps, mistaking her for the lady Goring expects, tells her that she is to be taken to the drawing-room, a statement which surprises her, for she has come without warning of her visit. Left alone for a few moments, she noses round in the hope of learning who Lord Goring's visitor may be. She picks up his letters and begins to read them. Lady Chiltern's is soon found. "I trust you. I want you. I am coming to you. Gertrude." Such a note is meat and drink to Mrs. Cheveley, who is about to steal it when Phipps re-enters. She slips it under a large silver-cased blotting-book on the table, intending to take it when she is free of Phipps's presence. But when she returns for that purpose, she is frightened away by the entrance of Lord Goring and his father, who is about to leave. When Goring re-enters the library, having seen his father off, he is accompanied by Chiltern, who has come to him for consolation. Goring whispers to Phipps that if the lady, meaning Lady Chiltern, should arrive, he is to tell her that Lord Goring is out of town, but Phipps, who does not know what lady is expected, replies that she has already arrived.

Chiltern, in a state of great agitation, bemoans his unfortunate lot to Goring, and while he is pitying himself, a chair is heard to fall in the drawing-room. He is convinced that someone has been listening to his confession, and refuses to listen when he is told that no one is in the drawing-room. He rushes out, and, a moment or two later, returns. Goring, of course, imagines that he has seen his wife, and begins an assurance that her presence in his house at that hour is entirely innocent. But Chiltern, who has just seen Mrs. Cheveley in the room, assumes that she and Goring are lovers. This is the Erlynne-Lady Windermere scene in Darlington's rooms again, and Chiltern, denouncing his friend, departs. Then, to Goring's amazement, Mrs. Cheveley appears. A scene follows in which she offers to give him Chiltern's letter if he will marry her. Goring, however, is not so self-sacrificing as that, especially as he is deeply in love with Chiltern's sister, Mabel. He declines the offer of the lady's soiled hand. "For the privilege of being your wife," Mrs. Cheveley says, "I was ready to surrender a great prize, the climax of my diplomatic career. You declined. Very well. If Sir Robert doesn't uphold my Argentine scheme, I expose him. *Voilà tout.*" A scathing comment on her conduct by Goring provokes her, almost accidentally, to remark that her single object in going to the Chilterns' house after their reception, had been to learn if she had dropped her brooch there. Goring tells her that he has it. "This is the brooch, isn't it?"

Mrs. Cheveley: Yes. I am so glad to get it back. It was . . . a present.

Lord Goring: Won't you wear it?

Mrs. Cheveley: Certainly, if you pin it on. (Lord Goring *suddenly clasps it on her arm.*) Why do you put it on as a bracelet? I never knew it could be worn as a bracelet.

LORD GORING: Really?

MRS. CHEVELEY (*holding out her handsome arm*): No, but it looks very well on me as a bracelet, doesn't it?

LORD GORING: Yes: much better than it did when I saw it last.

MRS. CHEVELEY: When did you see it last?

LORD GORING (*calmly*): Oh, ten years ago, on Lady Berkshire, from whom you stole it.

MRS. CHEVELEY (*starting*): What do you mean?

LORD GORING: I mean that you stole that ornament from my cousin, Mary Berkshire, to whom I gave it when she was married. Suspicion fell on a wretched servant, who was sent away in disgrace. I recognised it last night. I determined to say nothing about it till I had found the thief. I have found the thief now, and I have her own confession.

MRS. CHEVELEY (*tossing her head*): It is not true.

LORD GORING: You know it is true. Why, thief is written across your face at this moment.

MRS. CHEVELEY: I will deny the whole affair from beginning to end. I will say that I have never seen the wretched thing, that it was never in my possession.

But she cannot remove it from her arm. She does not know where the spring is, and without this knowledge the bracelet is irremovable. He then tells her that he will send for the police immediately, and that she will be prosecuted for theft. This threat overthrows her, and when he demands Chiltern's incriminating letter, she gives it to him, after a little pretence that it is not in her possession. She is not, however, resourceless. Affecting to feel faint, she asks for a glass of water, and while he is getting it she takes Lady Chiltern's letter from beneath the blotting-book, and in a skilfully-contrived scene she tells Goring that she has it, and escapes with it.

The last act is perfunctory: a clearing up of mess. Goring becomes engaged to Mabel; we learn that Chiltern has made the speech of his life in denouncing the Argentine Canal Scheme in the Commons; and Lady Chiltern is told that Mrs. Cheveley has her silly little emotional letter and will make unscrupulous use of it. Goring sensibly proposes that he shall tell Chiltern the truth, but Lady Chiltern, that stern moralist when other people's conduct is in review, shrinks from such an ordeal. The situation, despite its sweeping-up character, is adroitly handled. Chiltern comes into the room, carrying his wife's letter to Goring. He reads its contents aloud. "I want you. I trust you. I am coming to you. Gertrude." He does not know it was posted to him by Mrs. Cheveley, who, with singular stupidity in a malignant woman reputed to be clever, has failed to enclose any explanation of it in the envelope. There is nothing in the letter itself to show to whom it was addressed. The envelope had been thrown away by Chiltern's secretary, who had opened it in error!

Chiltern, we may note in parenthesis, keeps two private secretaries in his own home, a little excessively, surely, for a minor Minister who had, presumably, all the secretaries he needed at the Foreign Office. But Wilde never paid any regard to probabilities. He makes Lord Caversham come in carrying a letter from the Prime Minister, offering Chiltern the vacant seat in the Cabinet. Even arbitrary Premiers do not treat elder statesmen as errand-boys or postmen. "And you well deserve it", Lord Caversham says. "You have got what we want so much in political life to-day—high character, high moral tone, high principles", a curious statement, it must seem, not only to Chiltern himself, but to Goring, who enters while it is being made: for Chiltern, during that consultation with Goring in the second act, had professed no penitence for his youthful crime, had, indeed, justified it on the ground that men rise to power by such means. Bernard Shaw, in a Nietzschean mood, applauded this spirit in Chiltern. "The modern note", he told the readers of *The Saturday Review*, "is struck in Sir Robert's assertion of the individuality and courage of his wrong-doing as against the mechanical idealism of his stupidly good wife, and in his bitter criticism of a love that is only the reward of merit." This, surely, is a strange doctrine for a Socialist to preach. Sidney Webb might have listened to it with patience, but would Beatrice Webb have done so? We perceive in those sentences the mood which compelled Shaw, forty years later, to give three hearty cheers for Hitler and Mussolini. Why the Prime Minister should feel so overcome by Chiltern's denunciation of the Argentine Canal Scheme is hard to understand, since its rejection must have been due to the decision of the Foreign Secretary after consultation with the Cabinet. Wilde suggests that the rejection was made entirely on Chiltern's initiative and on his own responsibility: an absurd misunderstanding of a minor Minister's position and authority.

The offer of a seat in the Cabinet dazzles Chiltern, but a momentary qualm, in which we do not for a second believe, makes him say that he cannot accept it. He intends, he says, to retire from public life: a decision which his wife, the puling prig, approves. Her acquiescence is less pleasing to Chiltern than she might have expected it to be. Goring, however, settles this matter as he has settled the others, and he persuades her to believe that they are both wrong. When Chiltern shows her the draft of his letter refusing the Prime Minister's offer, she tears it up. Goring has taught her to know better. Chiltern is effusive in his thanks to Goring, who has twice put him deeply in his debt. Then the play takes a peculiar and stupid turn. Goring announces his engagement to Mabel, whereupon Chiltern, who, a few moments earlier, was effusively thanking him for his invaluable services and has himself narrowly escaped public exposure for an atrocious crime, draws himself up and becomes as sternly moral as his wife. His sister must not marry a man who keeps a mistress! . . . He had discovered Mrs. Cheveley in Goring's rooms, and like Windermere, when he found Mrs. Erlynne in Darlington's chambers, believes instantly that her presence must be for improper purposes. However, Lady Chiltern clears up the misunderstanding, confessing that her letter had been addressed, not to Chiltern, but to Goring, and explaining how it had come to be written. The play concludes with general felicity. Mrs. Cheveley is heard of no more.

50

AN IDEAL HUSBAND was, and still is, the least successful of the four plays Wilde wrote in those three years. John Hare, alleging that there were too many entrances and exits in the last act, a very unsatisfactory finish to a serious comedy, declined it; and its run, when it was produced by Lewis Waller, was the shortest of the four. It was outrun by *The Importance of Being Earnest*, despite Wilde's arrest and conviction. Its withdrawal had, indeed, been decided on before the arrest was made. Mention has already been made of the fact that Alexander lost £2000 on its revival in 1914. Pearson states that it was an instantaneous success when it was first performed, but those who have practical knowledge of the theatre are well aware of the number of managers who have been ruined by "instantaneous successes", and are not impressed by his opinion. Wilde's mind was essentially melodramatic, even, as Shaw said, sentimental. He was not the son of Speranza, that female dancing dervish, for nothing; and he spoke the truth about himself when, after he had read the last act of *A Woman of No Importance* to some of his friends, he remarked, "I took that situation from *The Family Herald*". Those who thought he was jesting when he made this statement understood him far less than he understood himself. He had taken nearly all his situations from the same source. He took none from life. If his wit had been less and his sense of humour larger, he would have been a more important dramatist. As it was, his talent would have been more suitable to Drury Lane than the Haymarket, had it not been marred by his addiction to epigrams.

The failure of the play was due, no doubt, to public intuition. The critics, apparently, had no perception of the false foundation on which it rested, but it is reasonable to believe that the general audience, even when it was unable to express its belief, was well aware of the play's fundamental flaw. In one of his letters, Keats says that "axioms in philosophy are not axioms until they are proved upon our pulses", and we do ourselves disservice when we disregard the doubts of uncritical people. A man's objections are not to be dismissed with contempt because he cannot explain them. Glibness is not a synonym for wisdom. Even Bernard Shaw, now commencing critic and not yet known, outside a very small circle, as a dramatist or an author of any sort, failed, very surprisingly in a Fabian, to detect the supreme defect in *An Ideal Husband*. Or was he careful not to incur reproach as an envious rival? He was quick to detect the clumsy device by which Wilde makes Sir Robert aware of Mrs. Cheveley's presence in Goring's drawing-room. "Why on earth", he demanded in his second contribution to *The Saturday Review*, "should Mrs. Cheveley, hiding in Lord Goring's room, knock down a chair?" Why, indeed, except that Wilde wanted to call her to Chiltern's attention, and, presumably, did not think that if she were to break a window the audience would feel properly impressed. "That", however, was G. B. S.'s "sole criticism".

51

WHILE Wilde was consulting solicitors and writing *An Ideal Husband*, Walter Pater died. On the 30th of July 1894 he collapsed on the staircase of his house and died in his sister's arms. Wilde, occupied with lawyers and duns, seems not to have noticed his death. Yet it was Pater who inspired him, more even than Ruskin and Carlyle, in his Oxford days. "Mr. Pater's essays became to me 'the golden book of spirit and sense, the holy writ of beauty'." Frank Harris tells a grotesque story of them in *Oscar Wilde*, but whether Harris or Wilde is the liar is hard to tell; for Wilde, it must be remembered, lied as ardently as Harris, with this difference, that his lies were better told and more plausible. Harris, indeed, suggests that the story, told ten years after the incident it describes had occurred, may have "ripened" in Wilde's imagination. Wilde, reminiscing about those who had influenced his youth, remarked that "Pater meant everything to me. He was a sort of silent, sympathetic elder brother. . . . Pater was a very great man. Dear Pater!

"I remember once talking to him when we were seated together under some trees in Oxford. I had been watching the students bathing in the river: the beautiful white figures all grace and ease and virile strength. I had been pointing out how Christianity had flowered into romance, and how the crude Hebraic materialism and all the later formalities of an established creed had fallen away from the tree of life and left us the exquisite ideals of the new paganism. . . . The pale Christ had been outlived: his renunciations and his sympathies were mere weaknesses: we were moving to a synthesis of art where the enchanting perfume of romance should be wedded to the severe beauty of classic form. I really talked as if inspired, and when I paused, Pater—the stiff, quiet, silent Pater—suddenly slipped from his seat and knelt down by me and kissed my hand. I cried: 'You must not, you really must not. What would people think if they saw you?' He got up with a white strained face. 'I had to,' he muttered, glancing about him fearfully, 'I had to—once.' . . ."

We cannot be certain that this story is false or tell whether Wilde or Harris was the liar. Emotional aesthetes, like Habakkuk, are capable of all; and the queer Anglo-Dutchman may have behaved in that puerile manner.

Wilde, in his day of glory, a day soon to be dreadfully and irreparably dimmed and diminished, had no time or thought for the dead Pater. The scarlet Marquess was on his heels, and he was deep in debt, and had a play to write. It is notorious that Pater was cold to him, speaking of him in private with evident distaste. His review of *The Picture of Dorian Gray* was an evasion of a definite opinion. He struggled hard to avoid praising or dispraising the novel, but could not conceal his aversion from it. Masters are sometimes repelled by disciples. Jesus may have felt relieved when Judas betrayed Him.

52

IN the same year that *An Ideal Husband* was written, Wilde, being pressed for money despite his large earnings, began to write a farce at Worthing, whither he had taken his family in September. He wrote it in a month, and it is by far his best work: the only play he wrote which is worth preserving. It was originally named *Lady Lancing*, but this title was tentative, and was abandoned for *The Importance of Being Earnest.* Wilde, who was said to have been shrewd in his judgements, although those who make this assertion offer no proof of it, misjudged actors remarkably. He thought Tree unsuitable for the part of Lord Illingworth in *A Woman of No Importance*, yet Tree was excellent in it. He misjudged again in regard to *The Importance of Being Earnest.*

Alexander, who had paid him £150 for an option on it without seeing it, was not, he told him, likely to be happy in the principal part. "Of course", he wrote, "the play is not suitable to you at all. You are a romantic actor: the people in it want actors like Wyndham and Hawtrey." It is hard to understand why Wilde did not perceive the plain fact that it was because Alexander was a romantic actor that he was exactly suited to play John Worthing. Neither Wyndham nor Hawtrey, both of them light comedians, could have performed the part with that air of sincerity which Alexander brought to it, which increased the humour and absurdity of the character and the play. Had it been acted by a comedian with his tongue, however slightly, in his cheek, its effect would have been greatly diminished, if not lost.

The history of the first transactions between Alexander and Wilde is unknown. Pearson asserts that Alexander "decided that it was not in his line", but Mason, who had access to all Alexander's papers, cannot express an opinion: "either Alexander thought the play too slight or Wilde thought the actor too serious". Alexander may have been influenced by Wilde's disbelief in his fitness to be Worthing. An actor is likely to lose faith in himself in a part if the author of the play has no faith in him. This, however, is surmise, and unimportant, except as proof, if any be required, of the chances which affect the fortunes of any play. We know that Alexander, in a friendly spirit, sent the script, as Wilde had suggested he should do, to Charles Wyndham, who received it round about Christmas 1894. Alexander thereupon busied himself with the production of an eighteenth-century comedy by Henry James, the most unsuitable author to write a play that was ever born on this earth. Its title was *Guy Domville*, and it was utterly and irredeemably a failure. James had a delicate and finicky old-maidish manner which caused him to elaborate and explain and refine his unimpressive opinions and beliefs until they disappeared in a thick fog of "literary" verbiage. His delicacy became clumsiness. He fussed and nattered! . . . In the manner of an over-bred old maid he drew himself up, reminding himself of what a lady he was. Henry James was born expatriate: ill at ease everywhere. Young men with lank hair and damp hands, and young women with lanker hair and damper hands, are addicted to his work. Alexander, who was eager to draw men of quality to the drama, must have suppressed his sense of the theatre when he accepted *Guy Domville*. A single conversation with its author should have convinced him that whatever else James might be, a dramatist he was not and never could be. The letter which accompanied the script of the first act and the scenarios of the second and third should have warned him. James, always heaviest when he was trying to be light, informed Alexander, as Mason reports, that he was well aware "of the lacunae which real treatment of the subject must make good (and will); all the transitions it will smooth over, all the insufficiently explained things it will vivify, all the expression and colour, all the lucidity and atmosphere, and superiority I shall undertake to supply". Mason's comment on this absurd and pompous stuff is apt and sufficient. "So what with remembering all these things and acting at night, Alexander must have had a pretty busy time of it."

The pit and the gallery were less patient than the actor when, on Saturday the 5th of January 1895, *Guy Domville* was performed at St. James's Theatre, for the first time. The play, Mason says, "received . . . an unmannerly and derisive greeting from the cheaper parts of the house". Audiences, after a night of boredom, sometimes display a sadistic desire for vengeance. The author of their distress is inveigled into taking a curtain and is then publicly tortured. "When the curtain fell" on the last act, Mason says, "there were vociferous cries of 'Author! Author!' Behind the scenes the call was misunderstood. Somehow a blunder was made. The curtain was raised again and Alexander led on Henry James to such an explosion of cat-calls and boos and hisses as was seldom heard even in those days when first-night disturbances were not uncommon. H. G. Wells was present as the dramatic critic of the *Pall Mall Gazette*, and he has given in the second volume of his Autobiography a vivid description of the scene." James, dazed and half stunned, was led from the stage, to which he never returned. His play had cost a great deal of money as well as artistic loss. It was expensive to encourage men of quality to dare the drama.

Alexander's mind, naturally enough, reverted at once to Wilde, who, whatever his faults might be, had some sense of the theatre and was incapable, it seemed, of writing a play which would not draw an audience. Wyndham had already accepted *The Importance of Being Earnest*, but was in no hurry to produce it, since the play in which he was then appearing was successful. Alexander wondered, therefore, if Wyndham would return it to him, if, that is to say, Wilde were willing. The people of the theatre are exceptionally magnanimous and generous-minded and very prompt to give help to others more than to themselves; and Wyndham readily agreed to release the play. Wilde, in need of money, consented to transfer it. Rehearsals were at once begun, with a very capable cast which, in addition to Alexander, included Allan Aynesworth as Algernon Moncrieff, and Irene Vanbrugh as Gwendolen Fairfax. Wilde was again on the crest of a wave. Two plays by him were staged in London in six weeks. *An Ideal Husband* was produced two nights before *Guy Domville*; and six weeks later, *Guy Domville* was replaced by *The Importance of Being Earnest.* Six weeks after Wilde's previous production, another play was performed for the first time, but in conditions far less brilliant. At 11.30 A.M. on the 30th of March 1895, a single performance of *Candida* by George Bernard Shaw was given at the Theatre Royal, South Shields, a town not previously, nor since, renowned in theatrical history.

In those days, a dramatist could not secure the copyright in his work unless his play were given some sort of a public performance, before some sort of an audience which had paid for admission. It was the custom, therefore, for a touring company to rehearse, without much care, a work which the manager of the company wished to protect for its author. The performance was advertised in the press, the price of admission to any part of the theatre being one guinea. A person was appointed to buy a single seat for this sum! . . . A. E. Drinkwater, father of the poet, John, who many years later was to become famous for his play, *Abraham Lincoln*, had taken *Arms and the Man* "on the road", and it was during this tour that a copyright performance of *Candida* was given at South Shields. Nine years passed before this charming comedy was produced in London. The temptation to contrast the drab circumstances in which Shaw's first plays were performed with those in which Wilde's appeared, and to compare the subsequent history of the two dramatists, is great, but there is no necessity to yield to it. Merely to state the simple fact is sufficient.

53

THE rehearsals of *The Importance of Being Earnest* were unpleasant. Wilde was exceedingly troublesome, interfering irritably in the production and upsetting the players who were struggling to fix their movements and remember their words. Tempers began to fray. As the day of the first performance approached, Alexander, infinitely patient with his perverse and tantalising author, realised that there would be a dangerous shindy between some members of the cast and the dramatist if Wilde were not induced to go home and remain there until the night of the first performance. So he led him aside and spoke to him persuasively, but plainly: "We know now everything you want," he said, "and if you'll leave us alone to get on with the rehearsals, we shall try our best to give it to you. But if you don't, we shall never be ready. So I'll send you a box for the first night and see you again after the performance." Mason reports that Wilde was taken aback by this remark, as indeed he well might be, for he was, in effect, being ordered out of the theatre. But he took the ultimatum with good sense. He must have realised that he was in no state of mind to be helpful to players who were already sufficiently rattled by the normal trials of last rehearsals. It is harder to act a feathery play, such as *The Importance of Being Earnest*, than it is to act a tragedy, such as *Hamlet*. Shakespeare's play almost acts itself, but a farce or a comedy of any sort requires exceptional skill in those who perform it. Heavy acting or wrongly-delivered lines will ruin light dialogue. Actors, therefore, must be more careful to catch the proper mood for a farce or light comedy than for a serious comedy or a tragedy. In their anxiety not to miss easily-lost effects, their nervous nature is likely to become more sensitive than it ordinarily is, and a tactless or whimsical author may do great injury to them and his play by his untimely interruptions. He will do well to reserve his comments until the end of the rehearsal of the act when the strain is relaxed and the points can be calmly discussed. Even when he feels that he must interrupt immediately, he should do so through the producer or, as he is called in America, director, and not address himself to the players.

Wilde was in an abnormal state of mind. Apart from the trouble he was enduring from Queensberry, he was now in a pathological condition of mind and body which made him difficult to deal with. The taint in his blood, whether it was inherited or acquired, had corrupted him to such an extent that he was now scarcely responsible for himself. He had become a megalomaniac, incapable of brooking any criticism, demanding and buying gross flattery. His adolescent nature made him more susceptible than adult-minded men to the temptations of popularity. Popularity, more perhaps than anything else, was his ruin. Constance, who, despite her devotion to him, still kept possession of her head, offended him by criticism which he considered carping. A wife should praise her husband. It was not her place to find fault with him. If she would not wear beautiful Greek costumes and stand about in lovely attitudes, admiring Oscar, then he would go where at least he could find dutiful people, ready to cry out their admiration of one so witty and unusually wise! . . . Here he was, the most widely discussed dramatist of his day, with two plays about to be performed simultaneously in the West End of London, and all the most eminent ladies in Society clamouring for his presence at their dinner tables, and there was Constance, complaining of neglect and even uttering derogatory remarks about the soundness of his opinions and the morality of his beliefs! . . . He would go to the Café Royal, where there was always lunch at one! . . .

He was on the top of the world, yet a fear haunted him that it would suddenly spin round and hurl him into the void. In his state then, he was unfit to conduct rehearsals of any play, least of all was he fit to conduct rehearsals of so delicate a piece as *The Importance of Being Earnest*. A realisation of the sanity of Alexander must have pierced his mind at that moment when the actor spoke of him so frankly. "My dear Aleck," he replied, "I have still one more thing to say to you and to Aynesworth. So if you will both come and have supper with me to-night at the Albemarle Club, I shall not trouble you again."

Mason may be left to tell the rest of the story:

"It sounded portentous and alarming. Both Alexander and Aynesworth, tired with a long evening's rehearsal, walked up St. James's Street a little anxious and worried. What further alteration could Wilde want at this time of day? Of what did he now complain? They were met in the hall of the club by Wilde in full evening dress. He laid one friendly hand on Alexander's shoulder, the other upon Aynesworth's. 'My dear Aleck,' he said, 'and my dear Tony, I have only one thing to say to you. You are neither of you my favourite actor. We will now go into supper.' He then left the company to its own efforts and was interviewed before the production by a reporter who asked him whether he thought the play would be a success. 'My dear fellow,' Wilde expostulated, 'you have got it wrong. The play *is* a success. The only question is whether the first night's audience will be one.' "

He omitted to tell Alexander and Aynesworth that his favourite actor was Oscar Wilde, but perhaps he realised that they were both well aware of the fact. His remark to the two players, tired after a long and exhausting rehearsal, is always mentioned by his admirers as if it were a piece of superb wit. But it isn't. It is a twaddling remark. How poor a thing it is in comparison with his reply to the reporter who had asked him if he thought *The Importance of Being Earnest* would be a success. But it is almost impossible to persuade a Wildeite to believe that any remark by Wilde, however banal, is not unmatchably brilliant. The first-night audience was an enormous success, and the charming and delightful farce seemed well set for a long and prosperous run. And it would undoubtedly have enjoyed one had not Wilde's megalomania caused him, at a critical moment of his career, to lose his head. But before we come to that fatal event, we must examine the farce which preceded the tragedy.

54

HOW is a bubble to be described and analysed? It may burst before you have done more than observed its rainbow lights and perceived how beautifully round it is. Bernard Shaw, criticising the delicious farce, found singular fault with it, and he betrayed his surprising lack, on occasions, of a sense of humour. His embarrassed admirers have not forgotten their blushes when he said that Brieux was "incomparably the greatest writer France has produced since Molière", and that "after the death of Ibsen, Brieux confronted Europe as the most important dramatist west of Europe". Shaw had forgotten himself. He had done worse than that: he had forgotten Victor Hugo. Shaw's faculty for fun, despite happy displays of it from time to time, was limited. A play about main drainage or the rate of infantile mortality in South Wales was more to his liking than a play in which whim prevailed: and he was ill at ease with Wilde's piece. He suggested "with some confidence" that it had been written under the influence of Henry Arthur Jones, basing his belief on no better evidence than the fact that Jones had written a play called *The Case of Rebellious Susan* and that Wilde had followed it with a play called *The Importance of Being Earnest*. Each play had five words in its title! . . . The maps of the world, as Fluellen told Captain Gower, show that in the comparisons between Macedon and Monmouth, "the situations, look you, is both alike. There is a river in Macedon; and there is also moreover a river at Monmouth." G. B. S. felt certain that even if Wilde had "retouched" his farce "immediately before its production, it must certainly have been written before *Lady Windermere's Fan*. I do not suppose it to be Mr. Wilde's first play: he is too susceptible to fine art to have begun otherwise than with a strenuous imitation of a great dramatic poem, Greek or Shakespearian; but it was perhaps the first which he designed for practical commercial use at the West End theatres."

I cannot say that I greatly cared for *The Importance of Being Earnest.* It amused me, of course; but unless comedy touches me as well as amuses me, it leaves me with a sense of having wasted my evening. I go to the theatre to be moved to laughter, not to be tickled or hustled into it; and that is why, though I laugh as much as anybody at a farcical comedy, I am out of spirits before the end of the second act, and out of temper before the end of the third, my miserable mechanical laughter intensifying these symptoms at every outburst. If the public ever becomes intelligent enough to know when it really is enjoying itself and when it is not, there will be an end of farcical comedy. . . .

The thought here is thinner than his readers have every right to expect from Shaw. His criticism amounts to no more than the fact that he does not laugh with much, if any spontaneity, but must first be argued into laughing. "Tell me why I should laugh, and I'll laugh." "Prove to me that this joke is funny. Go on. Prove it to me. And when you've proved it, I'll roar my head off." Shaw had gone to St. James's Theatre as he would have gone to a meeting of the Fabian Society, to listen to Sidney Webb reciting statistics; but Wilde was no statistician and had no head for mathematics. "On the whole," Shaw, who thought little of the acting, concluded, "I must decline to accept *The Importance of Being Earnest* as a day less than ten years old." Here he was reasonable enough, for he perceived the fact that Wilde's mind lacked originality, that it was a hackneyed mind, brilliantly decorated and lit by powerful lights, but essentially an old-fashioned, melodramatic and routine mind. Its conventionality, however, did not prevent it from being entertaining. Its conventionality, indeed, helped it to be entertaining, for the audience was able to enjoy the fun without fussing itself about the thought. Notes of interrogation do not rise up to interrupt the laughter in *The Importance of Being Earnest.* The farce has its faults, but they were not detected by Shaw, who was accustomed to regard the theatre programme as if it were a Fabian agenda. He was liable at any moment to spring to his feet and move a resolution or second an amendment! . . .

The play begins with pleasing and inconsequent gaiety in Algernon Moncrieff's "luxuriously and artistically-furnished" flat in Half Moon Street. Algernon is playing the piano when his manservant, Lane, enters:

ALGERNON: Did you hear what I was playing, Lane?

LANE: I didn't think it polite to listen, sir.

ALGERNON: I'm sorry for that, for your sake. I don't play accurately—anyone can play accurately—but I play with wonderful expression. As far as the piano is concerned, sentiment is my forte. I keep science for Life.

LANE: Yes, sir.

ALGERNON: And speaking of the science of Life, have you got the cucumber sandwiches out for Lady Bracknell?

LANE: Yes, sir. (*Hands them on a salver.*)

ALGERNON (*inspects them, takes two, and sits down on the sofa*): Oh! . . . by the way, Lane, I see from your book that on Thursday night, when Lord Shoreman and Mr. Worthing were dining with me, eight bottles of champagne are entered as having been consumed.

LANE: Yes, sir, eight bottles and a pint.

ALGERNON: Why is it that at a bachelor's establishment the servants invariably drink the champagne? I ask merely for information.

LANE: I attribute it to the superior quality of the wine, sir. I have often observed that in married households the champagne is rarely of a first-rate brand.

ALGERNON: Good heavens! Is marriage so demoralising as that?

LANE: I believe it *is* a very pleasant state, sir. I have had very little experience of it myself up to the present. I have only been married once. That was in consequence of a misunderstanding between myself and the young person.

ALGERNON (*languidly*): I don't know that I am much interested in your family life, Lane.

LANE: No, sir; it is not a very interesting subject. I never think of it myself.

ALGERNON: Very natural, I am sure. That will do, Lane, thank you.

LANE: Thank you, sir.

LANE *goes out.*

ALGERNON: Lane's views on marriage seem somewhat lax. Really, if the lower orders don't set us a good example, what on earth is the use of them? They seem, as a class, to have absolutely no sense of moral responsibility.

This is good fun, but it is fun in an old and well-established style. Molière knew the vein, and used it. But is it any the worse for that? Wilde makes it appear to be fresh. The two men speak to each other frankly and dispassionately. They accept the facts of life, and do not become ill-tempered about them. When Algernon remarks on the excessive consumption of champagne by his servants, Lane does not stand upon his dignity and give in his notice. It is a fact that servants are accustomed to help themselves lavishly to their employers' food and drink, almost an honourable tradition of service, and Lane does not waste time in stupid denials of habits which have been sanctified by time. He respects Algernon's eagerness for information, and promptly gives it. This charming and unimpassioned frankness is the main feature of the play in which there is no ill-temper, no pretence of offended dignity, no serious lying or deceit. Lane acknowledges that a good deal of champagne has been drunk in the kitchen. It is a tradition of service; and civilised people, whether they be masters or men, do not quarrel about customs which have been made honourable by age. The final speech by Algernon in the passage cited above loses none of its entertaining quality because it is obvious padding, put in to fill up the time between Lane's exit and his re-entrance to announce Mr. Ernest Worthing. Another author would have made Algernon wander round the room, straightening a picture which had gone askew, or fussing with cushions, or picking up a book and turning its pages for a moment or two; but Wilde had a better trick than that for filling a gap: and he gives us this amusing interjection.

It is here that one realises how impossible it is to describe and analyse *The Importance of Being Earnest*, and resolves, very sensibly, to abandon a task which should never have been begun. To sit down like a man in a laboratory and inspect this play through a magnifying glass is to deprive it of its charm and stamp oneself as a humourless fool. Analysed, it no longer exists. Impale a butterfly on a pin and there's no butterfly—only a specimen of lepidoptera, or scaly-winged flies, which have knobbed antennae, a definition which is satisfying to a lexicographer, but abolishes beauty. The play is a piece of pure frivolity. Shaw, trying to find evidence that it preceded *Lady Windermere's Fan* in order of composition and derived from the works of Henry Arthur Jones, asserts with scorn that it has a plot! This fact, he declares, proves what old-fashioned stuff it is. But what is the plot? He would be daring and audacious who set out to describe it. There is about as much plot in *The Importance of Being Earnest* as there is in the

Pickwick Papers. The dialogue runs along inconsequently, one speech manifestly following, erratically, almost irresponsibly, any hare that might have been started in the speech to which it responds. An air of spontaneity is created by the fact that Wilde, as he wrote his dialogue, clearly had not the slightest idea of what his characters would say next. He put down the first things that came into their heads, careless whether it led anywhere or nowhere; and when he had filled a fair number of pages with irrelevant remarks, he concluded an act. The fact that he produced an uncommonly entertaining farce by this means does not alter the fact that he permitted his pen to write what it liked, exactly as Sterne did in the *Sentimental Journey*. Had he been asked what his play was *about*, he could not have given an answer. When, for instance, Algernon, explaining Bunbury to Worthing, incidentally remarks that "in married life three is company and two is none", a hare at once starts up and bolts with the explanation. Worthing, whose Christian name, we have just learnt, is John and not Ernest, replies sententiously to Algernon:

JACK: That, my dear young friend, is the theory that the corrupt French drama has been propounding for the last fifty years.

ALGERNON: Yes; and that the happy English home has proved in half the time.

JACK: For heaven's sake, don't try to be cynical. It's perfectly easy to be cynical.

ALGERNON: My dear fellow, it isn't easy to be anything nowadays. There's such a lot of beastly competition about. . . .

Bunburyism is momentarily forgotten.

The fluent irrelevance of the dialogue brilliantly conceals the skill with which it is composed. Wilde, despite, or perhaps because of his melodramatic propensities, was a born dramatist in the sense that he could handle a play superbly. He knew the tricks of the trade instinctively, and had no need to read manuals on stagecraft. Nowhere in his work is his skill so well displayed as in the character of Lady Bracknell who enters the play soon after the passage of dialogue just cited has been spoken. Here we have the silly, inconsequent woman we have met in the previous plays, but there is a difference between her and Lady Hunstanton and

Lady Caroline Pontefract in *A Woman of No Importance.* Lady Hunstanton is unaffectedly a silly-minded piece. So, despite her acerbity, is Lady Caroline. But Lady Bracknell is a serious-minded fool. Her most drivelling remark is delivered in a portentous manner, as if she were a sententious bishop addressing nervous ordinands. Throughout the play, but especially in the first act, she behaves as if she were Mrs. Sidney Webb disguised as Mrs. Humphry Ward. Her most absurd statements are uttered with a solemnity that could not be surpassed by Labour M.P.s at a banquet given by Sir Stafford Cripps.

How well Wilde conducts her interview with Worthing after she has caught him in the act of proposing to her daughter! Her first remark, as she finds Worthing on his knees, has a comic severity that is delicious. "Rise, sir, from this semi-recumbent posture. It is most indecorous." Her reply to Gwendolen, who tells her that she and Worthing are engaged to be married, is matchless in its ludicrous sobriety: "Pardon me, you are not engaged to anyone. When you do become engaged to someone, I, or your father, should his health permit him, will inform you of the fact. An engagement should come on a young girl as a surprise, pleasant or unpleasant, as the case may be. It is hardly a matter that she could be allowed to arrange for herself. . . ." Her examination of Worthing is a piece of writing that any dramatist might envy. Worthing confesses to her that he smokes. "I am glad to hear it", she says. "A man should always have an occupation of some kind. There are far too many idle men in London as it is." She is relieved to hear that Worthing knows nothing. "I do not approve of anything that tampers with natural ignorance. . . . Fortunately in England, at any rate, education produces no effect whatsoever." Her solemnity reaches its funniest point when Worthing tells her that he has lost both his parents and that he does not know who they were:

LADY BRACKNELL: . . . Are your parents living?

JACK: I have lost both my parents.

LADY BRACKNELL: To lose one parent, Mr. Worthing, may be regarded as a misfortune; to lose both looks like carelessness. Who was your father? He was evidently a man of some wealth. Was he born in what the Radical papers call the purple of commerce, or did he rise from the ranks of the aristocracy?

JACK: I'm afraid I really don't know. The fact is, Lady Bracknell, I said I had lost my parents. It would be nearer the truth to say that my parents seem to have lost me. . . . I don't actually know who I am by birth. I was . . . well, I was found.

LADY BRACKNELL: Found!

JACK: The late Mr. Thomas Cardew, an old gentleman of a very charitable and kindly disposition, found me, and gave me the name of Worthing because he happened to have a first-class ticket for Worthing in his pocket at the time. Worthing is a place in Sussex. It is a seaside resort.

LADY BRACKNELL: Where did the charitable gentleman who had a first-class ticket for this seaside resort find you?

JACK (*gravely*): In a handbag.

LADY BRACKNELL: A handbag?

JACK (*very seriously*): Yes, Lady Bracknell. It was in a handbag—a somewhat large, black leather handbag, with handles to it—an ordinary handbag, in fact.

LADY BRACKNELL: In what locality did this Mr. James, or Thomas Cardew come across this ordinary handbag?

JACK: In the cloak-room at Victoria Station. It was given him in mistake for his own.

LADY BRACKNELL: The cloak-room at Victoria Station?

JACK: Yes. The Brighton line.

LADY BRACKNELL: The line is immaterial. Mr. Worthing, I confess I feel somewhat bewildered by what you have just told me. To be born, or at any rate bred, in a handbag, whether it has handles or not, seems to me to display a contempt for the ordinary decencies of family life that reminds one of the worst excesses of the French Revolution. And I presume you know what that unfortunate movement led to? As for the particular locality in which the handbag was found, a cloak-room at a railway station might serve to conceal a social indiscretion—has, probably, been used for that purpose before now—but it could hardly be regarded as an assured basis for a recognised position in good society.

JACK: May I ask you what you would advise me to do? I need hardly say I would do anything in the world to ensure Gwendolen's happiness.

LADY BRACKNELL: I would strongly advise you, Mr. Worthing, to try and acquire some relations as soon as possible, and to make a definite effort to produce at any rate one parent, of either sex, before the season is quite over.

JACK: Well, I don't see how I could possibly manage to do that. I can produce the handbag at any moment. It is in my dressing-room at home. I really think that should satisfy you, Lady Bracknell.

LADY BRACKNELL: Me, sir! What has it to do with me? You can hardly imagine that I and Lord Bracknell would dream of allowing our only daughter—a girl brought up with the utmost care—to marry into a cloak-room, and form an alliance with a parcel? Good morning, Mr. Worthing.

That, surely, is comic dialogue at its highest pitch? It may be matched, but can it be surpassed? And is it so far removed from the substantial facts? Is it not a strictly reasonable satire on worldly women with daughters to settle?

The two girls in the play, Gwendolen Fairfax and Cecil Cardew, are original characters, without a trace of conventionality about them. Miss Prism and Canon Chasuble retain the lineaments of credible characters even in their most absurd situations. The ends of the acts are untidy, but untidiness in conclusion is the mark of light comedy and farce; and Wilde's ends are far less untidy than Noel Coward's whose curtains are left flopping in the air as if their author had forgotten how to pull them down. Wilde, at his worst, would never have ended a play as *Design for Living* is ended. He never imagined that a badly constructed charade was a play. *The Importance of Being Earnest* marked a point of definite development in his career as a dramatist. There should have been much more thereafter. But, alas, he had bitter enemies, of whom the worst was Oscar Wilde, and they were all assembling for his ruin. The scarlet Marquess was rampaging round the town. He had applied for tickets for the first performance of *The Importance of Being Earnest*, with the intention of causing uproar, but his application was refused. He, therefore, sought admission for himself and his pugilistic attendant in an unreserved part of the theatre. But unluckily for his intention, he talked too much, and Wilde became aware of it. Carrying a monstrous bouquet of the grosser vegetables, he turned up, accompanied by the prize-fighter, but was repelled by the police. At the end of three hours' vain effort to gain admission to the theatre, he departed, chattering like a demented ape. A subtler means of destroying Wilde must be found. In this search he was entirely successful.

55

WILDE's situation in the spring of 1895 was this: he had two plays simultaneously in performance in the West End of London, the second produced six weeks after the first; and his prospects seemed extraordinarily brilliant. The first of the two plays was a moderate success: the second bore the signs of light genius and was likely to become very popular. Four days after the first performance of *The Importance of Being Earnest*, the Marquess of Queensberry, baulked of his opportunity to make a demonstration in the theatre, opened the attack which ended in Wilde's ruin. He walked into the Albemarle Club, of which Wilde and his wife were members, and left his card with the hall porter, Sidney Wright, requesting that it should be handed to Wilde immediately on his arrival. On this card he had scrawled: "To Oscar Wilde posing as a somdomite", the last word being misspelt either because he was semi-illiterate or in such a towering rage that he could not see what he was writing. Wright took the card and glanced at it without, as he subsequently testified, understanding the meaning of the words written on it. He placed it in an envelope and, a fortnight later, gave it to Wilde. Technically a libel had been uttered, but, in effect, there had been none. Apart from Queensberry and Wilde, no one had seen the card except Wright, and he had not understood its message. Is a man libelled when the libel is casually scanned by someone who does not apprehend it? The libel was uttered by Wilde himself, when he showed the card to Ross that night and to Lord Alfred Douglas on the following day. His letter to Ross, sent from the Hotel Avondale in Piccadilly, is full of the nauseous self-pity and "literary" verbiage which were seldom out of Wilde's mind:

DEAREST ROBBIE, Since I saw you something has happened. Bosie's father has left a card at my club with hideous words on it. I don't see anything but a criminal prosecution. My whole life seems ruined by this man. The tower of ivory is assailed by the foul thing. On the sand is my life spilt. I don't know what to do. If you could come here at 11.30 do so to-night. I mar your life by trespassing ever on your love and kindness. I have asked Bosie to come to-morrow.

Yrs,
OSCAR

Ross went to the Avondale as requested, and, once again, gave him bad advice. The small, obsequious sodomite was always prompt with misdirection. Wilde must see his solicitor immediately and instruct him to apply for a warrant for the Marquess of Queensberry's arrest. On the next day, Douglas arrived and, presumably, supported Ross, for the three men went at once to consult Mr. C. O. Humphreys, who asked him, on his solemn oath, if there was any truth in Queensberry's accusation. Wilde solemnly swore that there was none. It was on the strength of this assurance, Montgomery Hyde asserts, that Humphreys agreed to apply for a warrant. There was a discussion of expense. Wilde, despite his success in the theatre, was deeply in debt and could not raise the large sum which the proceedings would cost. This trouble, however, was quickly settled by the rash and impetuous Bosie who was panting for vengeance on his father. His family, he said, "would be only too delighted to pay the necessary costs". Montgomery Hyde makes some illuminating remarks on this matter. Wilde, in his reproaches to Douglas, written from Reading Gaol eighteen months later, accused his dear boy, Bosie, of rushing him into the courts and then allowing him to be bankrupted by the costs. He had a very convenient memory. It reminded him, not of what had happened, but of what he wished had happened. Douglas scraped up some £360 there and then to pay for immediate expenses: a fact which Wilde had forgotten or did not care to recall; and his bankruptcy proceedings involved a larger sum than the costs he incurred over the Queensberry trial. There were times when these odd people behaved capriciously to each other, but there is little or no evidence that Douglas was ever ungenerous to Wilde in money matters or that he failed to relieve his distress when he had the means to relieve it. The disservice he and Ross rendered him was to give him their advice. If Wilde had ignored Queensberry's card, he might have avoided disaster. The scarlet Marquess seems not to have made any move during the fortnight that elapsed between the date on which he left his card at the Albemarle and the date on which it was delivered. He might have continued inactive if Wilde, as he had intended to do, had gone abroad. The man was mad, and ideas dart out of a lunatic's head as quickly as they dart into it.

But Wilde was inflated with megalomania, and his inflation was assisted by Ross and Douglas. It seems as certain as anything in an uncertain world can be that the trouble which brought ruin on Wilde was precipitated, if it was not actually caused, by the decision the three men took on the 1st of March 1895, when Douglas joined Ross in urging Wilde to have Queensberry arrested. The decision became fatal when Wilde lied to Humphreys, swearing that he was innocent of sodomy when he and Ross and Douglas knew well how guilty he was, how guilty they all were. It is immaterial to our argument that pederasts are now regarded as pathological cases. They were not so regarded then. Even if they had been, sodomy was, in law, a crime. All three knew this to be the fact. Had Humphreys been told the truth, that Wilde was a sodomite, that he had committed sodomy with Ross and with Douglas, he would not have applied for a warrant for Queensberry's arrest, but would have advised Wilde to leave England as soon as possible and for as long as possible. Wilde sentenced himself when he lied to his lawyer. His friends imprisoned him when they counselled him to have the law on Bosie's father. Wilde not only assured Humphreys that he was innocent of the charge made against him, but assured Sir Edward Clarke that it was "absolutely false and groundless". Had Clarke not received this solemn assurance, he would not have accepted his brief.

56

FORTIFIED by his client's assurance of his innocence, Humphreys applied for a warrant for the arrest of the Marquess of Queensberry, who was taken from Carter's Hotel in Albemarle

Street on Saturday morning the 2nd of March, and formally charged at Vine Street police station. From Vine Street he was removed at once to Great Marlborough Street Court and brought before the presiding magistrate, an irritable old man called Robert Milner Newton, who remanded him, on bail, for a week. It may here be noted that the single piece of good advice Wilde received at this time was given to him by Lord Alfred Douglas. It was that Sir George Lewis, a famous solicitor of the time, should be employed in preference to Humphreys, and it was rejected. Montgomery Hyde says that Lewis knew far more about Wilde's habits at the period than Humphreys knew, and that he would probably have advised him to tear up the visiting card and do no more about it. Lewis, in the event, was employed by the Marquess. On such lightly made decisions as these, men's lives are determined. But Lewis did not long continue to act for the Marquess. He returned his instructions, and was replaced by Charles Russell, of Messrs. Day and Russell, the second son of the Lord Russell of Killowen who had made himself famous over Parnell's action against *The Times*. Russell briefed Edward Carson, but not without long effort, for Carson remembered that he and Wilde had been undergraduates together at Trinity College, Dublin, and was, at first, unwilling to appear against him. How reluctant he was to accept his brief is made plain by the fact that he consulted Lord Halsbury before he consented to take it. There can seldom have been a case in which so many people were reluctant to appear as this one. Our feeling that the farce would never have become a tragedy had it not been for the perversity of its principal victim and his infatuated companions is strengthened. Wilde may almost be said to have broken into Reading Gaol.

He had now convinced himself, by what process of ratiocination it is impossible to imagine, that the trial would end in a magnificent triumph for him and utter disgrace for Queensberry. He did not know how busy Queensberry's enquiry agents were, nor did he know that Charles Brookfield, who was playing the part of the flunkey in *An Ideal Husband*, was presently to be the most persistent sleuth of all, bringing to the search for evidence against him almost the passion of a religious fanatic. Hatred inspires devotion no less than love; and Brookfield loathed and detested Wilde as only an impotent rival can hate anybody.

> Envy's a sharper spur than pay,
> No author ever spar'd a brother,
> Wits are gamecocks to one another,

said John Gay, and he was right. We do well when we pray in the Litany to be delivered from envy, hatred and malice, and all uncharitableness. No man needed to make that prayer more fervently than Charles Brookfield.

So certain was Wilde of victory over his enemy that, on the day the case was resumed in the Magistrate's Court, he swaggered to the Court in a carriage and pair, accompanied by Queensberry's sons, Lord Alfred Douglas and Lord Douglas of Hawick. The small Court was crowded, and Wilde and his friends had difficulty in finding seats. Exquisite and disdainful youths with sibilant voices were profusely present, assuring each other of the rich entertainment they would receive when Oscar stepped into the witness-box to utter epigrams and make an exhibition of these lawyer fellows. They had not the slightest apprehension that in a few days some of them would cross the Channel in great haste. When Queensberry's name was called, he entered the dock, but, a few moments later, was accommodated with a seat in front of it. The magistrate, catching sight of Lord Alfred Douglas, who was the point of contention in the case, ordered him to leave the Court, which he did. Wilde then went into the box and began to show off. He was quietly and properly rebuked by the magistrate. Queensberry, when his turn to answer questions came, was asked what he had to say in reply to the charge against him, and, very adroitly, he took up the position of an anxious and distressed father seeking to save his son from corruption. He was committed for trial, bail being allowed, at the next Old Bailey Sessions, less than three weeks later.

57

THE three trials have been described so often that any further description is unnecessary, especially since the publication of

Montgomery Hyde's book in the Notable British Trials Series. The salient facts which emerge from the evidence are:

(*a*) That Wilde should not have taken action against Queensberry;
(*b*) that he ruined himself by his incurable exhibitionism;
(*c*) that he was guilty of what he knew to be legally a crime; and
(*d*) that he misled his solicitor and his counsel, whose advice, had they known the truth, would have been very different from what it was.

Wilde's behaviour in the witness-box, apart from his showing-off, was skilful enough, and on at least one occasion he reached a high point of eloquence. Had he restrained his passion for applause and display, he might have won his case. But temptation, as he once made a character remark, was the one thing he could not resist; and his case was lost and himself ruined when, yielding to it, he made the famous slip in his cross-examination by Carson to which reference has already been made. Even Wilde realised what a mortal hurt he had done himself with that flippant reply.

It will be sufficient if we cite the pertinent dates, which are taken from Hyde's book. Queensberry was arrested on the 2nd of March 1895, and brought before the magistrate at Great Marlborough Street Court on that day. The proceedings were formal, and the case was adjourned for a week, until the 9th of March, when Queensberry was committed for trial. On the 18th of March the Grand Jury returned a true bill against the Marquess, who filed an amended plea of justification on the 30th March. This amendment was made as a result of the damning evidence against Wilde which had been collected by Brookfield and Queensberry's detective. Four days later, on the 3rd of April, the trial opened at the Central Criminal Court, Old Bailey, before Mr. Justice Collins. How confident of victory Wilde felt is proved by the fact that he took Lord Alfred Douglas to Monaco between the date of Lord Queensberry's committal for trial and the date on which the trial began. The fact was used against Douglas in *De Profundis* a few years later, when Wilde, pitying himself profoundly after his fashion, complained that he was forced to make holiday on the Mediterranean, so that Bosie could indulge his insatiable passion for gambling, when he should have been in London taking wise counsel. During this holiday, rumours of the evidence that had been gathered against him spread through the West End and frightened his friends, who, on his return to London, besought him to go back to France. The pleas sobered him, but he was not daunted: his overweening confidence forbade him to listen to them. Putting a flower in his best frock-coat, he entered the Court like a prima donna taking a warm curtain at the end of an opera.

But, soon after his cross-examination by Carson began, he received a set-back over his age, which he, with infantile vanity, had under-stated by two years: a small set-back, but enough to prejudice the jury against him. Nevertheless, he held his own brilliantly in his conflict with Carson until the latter began to question him about certain youths and boys to whom Wilde, very oddly, had made expensive gifts. The epigrams were not now so numerous nor so brilliant; and on the following day, when he re-entered the witness-box, he was a more chastened man than he had been the day before. It was on this day that Wilde made the famous slip. It led him down the road to Reading.

If bad had gone before, worse remained behind. At the end of the day Carson announced that he would call certain youths into the witness-box on the next morning. Clarke, who had grown more and more anxious as the cross-examination proceeded, pulled a very long face when he heard the news. It was becoming crystal clear that his client would lose his case. What else he would lose, Clarke scarcely dared to think. Reflection during the night and in the morning made him advise Wilde, at a consultation held on Thursday, before the Court reopened, to withdraw the prosecution and consent "to a verdict as regards the charge of 'posing'. By thus admitting the lesser charge, which in fact had not been made out by the defence", he "hoped to prevent the intervention of the Public Prosecutor, a development which might lead to Wilde's arrest in open Court if the case were allowed to continue". So Hyde reports. Wilde, entirely sobered now, accepted his counsel's advice. Clarke told him there was no need for him to be in the Court while the announcement was made. "I hoped and expected that he would take the opportunity of escaping from the country, and I believe he would have found no difficulty in doing so."

Ten minutes after Clarke had made his announcement, the jury returned a verdict of Not Guilty, and a burst of cheers broke out in Court. In the street outside the cheering was repeated, while several pimps and prostitutes, whose number has been grossly exaggerated by some of Wilde's admirers, danced with delight. On leaving the Court, the triumphant Queensberry sent a message to Wilde: "If the country allows you to leave, all the better for the country: but if you take my son with you, I will follow you, wherever you go, and shoot you".

58

THAT evening, Friday the 5th of April, in the Cadogan Hotel, in Sloane Street, Wilde was arrested. Round the corner, in Tite Street, Constance, bewildered and dazed, wept while Ross told her what had happened.

59

THAT is as far as we shall go in discussing the long-drawn-out proceedings. Wilde, and a pederast called Taylor, who conducted himself with some dignity throughout the trials, were charged together at Bow Street Police Court on Saturday the 6th of April, and remanded in custody. Bail was, surprisingly, refused. On the 19th of April the two men were committed for trial. True bills were returned against them by the Grand Jury on the 23rd, and the trial at the Old Bailey opened before Mr. Justice Charles on the 26th. On the 1st of May the jury disagreed, and Wilde was released on bail on the 7th, pending a retrial. Why the matter was not allowed to drop is a mystery to those who are unskilled in legal practice. The tide of hate had, perhaps, risen too high. On the 21st of May the second trial began, before Mr. Justice Wills.

Four days later, on the 25th, Wilde and Taylor, who had been tried separately, were found guilty and sentenced to two years' imprisonment, with hard labour. The verdict and sentence surprised and severely shocked Wilde, who had dramatised himself throughout the several hearings as if he were the suffering servant in the Book of Isaiah. His friends, attempting to account for his refusal to take flight when it was evident to everybody that he must be condemned, offer this explanation. Despite his knowledge of his guilt, he saw himself as a man about to be martyred, yet capable of saving himself from the final penalty by his brilliant self-defence. At the penultimate moment, Wilde, with a superb effort of epigrammatic eloquence, would overthrow his enemies and step out of the dock a public hero, universally acclaimed. This belief is strained, in *De Profundis*, to the point at which he is nobly bearing another man's guilt—but whose, is not plain, though there is a vague suggestion that it was Alfred Douglas's:

The sins of another were being placed to my account. Had I so chosen, I could on either trial have saved myself at his expense, not from shame indeed, but from imprisonment. Had I cared to show that the Crown witnesses—the three most important—had been carefully coached by your father and his solicitors, not in reticences merely, but in assertions, in the absolute transference, deliberate, plotted and rehearsed, of the actions and doings of someone else on to me, I could have had each one of them dismissed from the box by the judge, more summarily than even wretched perjured Atkins was. I could have walked out of Court with my tongue in my cheek, and my hands in my pockets, a free man. The strongest pressure was put upon me to do so. I was earnestly advised, begged, entreated to do so by people whose sole interest was my welfare, and the welfare of my house. But I refused. I did not choose to do so. I have never regretted my decision for a single moment, not even in the most bitter periods of my imprisonment. Such a course of action would have been beneath me. Sins of the flesh are nothing. They are maladies for physicians to cure, if they should be cured. Sins of the soul alone are shameful. To have secured my acquittal by such means would have been a lifelong torture to me. But do you really think that you were worthy of the love I was showing you then, or that for a single moment I thought you were?

This is exalted stuff, and no doubt Wilde, who had a remarkable capacity for convincing himself of his own nobility and genius, believed every word of it. But is there any obligation on any human being to sacrifice himself and his wife and children for someone who is worthless as well as guilty? If Wilde was the general genius he claimed to be—"penning comedies that were to beat Congreve for brilliancy, and Dumas *fils* for philosophy, and I suppose everybody else for every other quality"—what right had he to fling away his gifts so that a useless and insatiable parasite should be held immune from punishment and public exposure? Mawkishly self-righteous, he laid claim to high-souled conduct when he had no jot or tittle of right to it. He had illuded himself, and not for the first time, with the belief that he was a superman, exempt from the moral obligations of ordinary men, and he fully expected to be hailed as a hero whose eloquence and high spirit had delivered him from his ignoble enemies and made him the protagonist of all suffering artists in a world of mean-minded savages. As he heard the judge's sentence pronounced, however, his illusion ended. Taylor, his companion in crime, betrayed no sign of emotion, but Wilde staggered slightly and caught at the rail of the dock to steady himself. The greasy, grey-green face flushed with fear and dismay, and his eyes filled with horror. There were no epigrams now on his lips, no brilliant rejoinders to lawyer fellows. "And I, may I say nothing, my lord?" he muttered in a thick and almost inarticulate tone. The judge did not reply, but silently signalled the warders to remove the prisoners from the dock. They touched Wilde on the shoulder and, gazing in agony round the court where he had scintillated, so he thought, with such conviction that he must be not only discharged but applauded, he was led down the stairs: the most broken man in all the world that day. On the following evening Brookfield and Charles Hawtrey gave a dinner in honour of Queensberry, which was attended by forty gentlemen of high distinction! . . .

On the 26th of August Wilde was adjudicated a bankrupt, and on the 12th of November he was brought from Wandsworth Prison to be publicly examined in the bankruptcy court. On the next day, the 13th, he was removed from Wandsworth to Reading, where he remained for the whole of the remaining period of his sentence.

60

IT was during his removal from Wandsworth to Reading that an incident is alleged to have occurred at Clapham Junction which has been described with indignation and deep emotion by all who have written about Wilde's life. It excited compassion even in those who were antagonistic to him. No one seems to have wondered if there was any truth in the story. Wilde is the single authority for it, and he first told the story in *De Profundis*, but told it many times after his release from Reading, and always with embellishments, especially when his demoralisation was nearly complete. He was addicted to telling tales at that time, tales in which he could indulge his passion for self-pity. Sherard prints the story in *Oscar Wilde: the Story of an Unhappy Friendship* which was published in 1902, but he omits it from the *Life* which appeared in 1906. Harris alleges in *Oscar Wilde* that he heard it from Wilde himself.

The fact that Sherard omits it from his formal *Life*, suggests that he no longer believed it. Nevertheless it continues to be told, and Pearson prints it in his book, which was issued in 1946. Here it is as Sherard tells it:

It was during this subterranean journey that I heard he had been removed to Reading Gaol, which, it appears, is a healthier prison than Wandsworth. I felt sorry to reflect on the reminiscences of his sunny youth, and the glorious and triumphant days of Oxford, which must have filled his mind when the chain-gang alighted at Reading, but I had no conception of the cruel outrage which had lent the bitterness of death to that journey. It appears that whilst the gang of prisoners to whom he was chained were waiting for their train at Wandsworth Road station, exposed in their ignominy on the general platform—the Prison Authorities feel that they owe an occasional spectacle to the ratepayers—a British elector, who had been feasting his eyes on the faces, garb, and chains of the shivering crew, recognised among the prisoners one to whom all England owed a little gaiety, cried out, proud of his superior knowledge, and for the benefit of the other lookers-on, "By God, that's Oscar Wilde!" and spat in his face. And my friend's chains and gyves held him inert and passive under outrage so sanguinary.

Harris, flamboyant as ever, reports the story in a detailed account of long conversations which he purports to have had with Wilde in Paris. Harris was the world's wonder as a recording angel. He never forgot a word, no matter how long the speech!...

"I never told you the worst thing that befell me," he makes Wilde say. "When they took me from Wandsworth to Reading, we had to stop at Clapham Junction. We were nearly an hour waiting for the train. There we sat on the platform. I was in the hideous prison clothes, handcuffed between two warders. You know how the trains come in every minute. Almost at once I was recognised, and there passed before me a continual stream of men and boys, and one after the other offered some foul sneer or gibe or scoff. They stood before me, Frank, calling me names and spitting on the ground—an eternity of torture."

Finally, we have Pearson's version, taken from *De Profundis*:

On November 13th, 1895, I was brought down here from London. From two o'clock till half-past two on that day I had to stand on the centre platform of Clapham Junction in convict dress, and handcuffed, for the world to look at. I had been taken out of the hospital ward without a moment's notice being given to me. Of all possible objects I was the most grotesque. When people saw me they laughed. Each train as it came up swelled the audience. Nothing could exceed their amusement. That was, of course, before they knew who I was. As soon as they had been informed they laughed still more. For half an hour I stood there in the grey November rain surrounded by a jeering mob. For a year after that was done to me I wept every day at the same hour and for the same space of time.

The last sentence is, obviously, a piece of literary adornment to the tale. There is considerable discrepancy in the details of the three versions of the story, but these discrepancies, in themselves, do not disprove the essential part of the story, that Wilde, while standing on Clapham Junction station, was derided by the passing mob. A story, when repeated by several persons, is certain to be changed in detail. It is likely to vary even when it is told several times, especially over a period of time, by the same person. Wilde's stories "evolved" and were radically different at the tenth telling from what they had been at the first. The fact that, according to Sherard, he was "chained" to a "gang of prisoners", but, according to Harris, was "handcuffed between two warders", and, according to Pearson, was merely "handcuffed", gives no ground for disbelieving the substance of the story, nor need we disconcert ourselves with other discrepancies in the several versions. It will be sufficient to consider the probabilities and the facts of such a situation that are within our general knowledge. Clapham Junction is not a station at which people normally alight in any number, especially between two and two-thirty in the afternoon; it is one at which trains branch off a main line to go to the City or to Victoria or to Waterloo. The probability, therefore, of crowds of passengers assembling on the centre platform to jeer at convicts is slight. The number of passengers with business to transact or changes of compartment to make at Clapham Junction could not have been large, and any such passengers that there were would not have wasted from thirty to sixty minutes in idle derision of handcuffed men. Trains do not arrive at any platform, except possibly on underground systems, "every minute", whatever Wilde may have meant by that loose expression, and we need not misuse our minds by giving credit to his assertion in *De Profundis* that "each train as it came up swelled the audience". What a congestion there would have been on the central platform that bleak and dripping November afternoon had this statement been even approximately true. Suburban railway platforms are not places where people feel inclined to loiter, even when rain is not falling; and the fun to be extracted from the spectacle of fettered convicts shivering in November murk and drizzle is limited.

Moreover, it was not the habit then, whatever may have been the habit in any earlier age, nor is it the habit now for people of this nation to mock and deride the misery of hapless men in handcuffs; nor was it the habit of the prison authorities in 1895 to expose prisoners to public mockery and derision. One sometimes sees convicts of good conduct working to-day in towns and cities, just as one has long been accustomed to see convicts working in the fields round Dartmoor, but it is rare for passers-by to do more than glance at them casually, for no one feels inclined to embarrass the unfortunate and captive by peeping and prying. I have known people to speak to prisoners engaged in such work, but the conversation was not derisory or even moralistic: it was no more than might have been said to ordinary workmen. A person who spat on Wilde, as Sherard alleges "a British elector" did, would surely have been rebuked, if not arrested, for this assault on a bound and helpless man? Are we to believe that the warders, between whom, according to Harris, he was handcuffed, sat indifferent to the treatment of their prisoner? Were they not themselves, thus fettered, in some danger of suffering from the coarser insults alleged to have been offered to him? Were there no porters and railway policemen to disperse the jeering mob, if there was a mob to disperse? Surely the congestion and inconvenience caused on a narrow platform by crowds which were reinforced "every minute", was excuse enough for their dispersal, even if common decency were not?

The detail in the story which excites the greatest doubt of its veracity relates to the hour at which the incident is said to have happened: between two and two-thirty in the afternoon. Workmen and business men, who must have made up the majority of the travellers on any railway in 1895, were seldom seen in railway stations at that time of the day. They were about their work, and unlikely to be in trains unless it obliged them to be there, in which event they would have lost no time in mocking convicts. The most likely passengers to have been at Clapham at that hour would have been women, bent on shopping, and how many of them would have been tempted to travel on such a drizzling day in November, or would, had they fallen to temptation, have cluttered like clucking hens round Wilde and his companions? The emotion of pity is wider and deeper than we are sometimes tempted, and tempted with justice, to believe it is, wider and deeper, too, than this story suggests, and we may be pardoned for thinking that it was invented by Wilde to win compassion from those to whom he told it. It is an incredible tale, told by an unhappy man who had fallen from a high place to one in which he was dependent on people's pity. He is the sole authority for it. It is neither confirmed nor denied by any witness. There is no record of it anywhere, in official documents or in reminiscences or in newspaper reports. And how strange a thing that is. Here is a renowned figure, recently the centre of sensational trials, publicly humiliated by large crowds of jeering and expectorating passengers on the central platform of Clapham Junction, but not one person in all that huge throng made any comment on it that has been recorded—no one, save the object of the derision himself, who made it in circumstances almost calling for incredulity and disbelief.

61

WHILE he was in prison Wilde endured a good deal of distress, as was inevitable in a man of his social habits; and this distress was increased by the behaviour of the Governor of Reading Gaol, a Colonel H. Isaacson, under whom he was first imprisoned there: a man of severe disposition, whose normal severity was probably increased by his natural aversion from sodomites. He was inclined to confuse sadistic desires with moral principles, and to imagine himself a reforming influence when he was indulging his passion for misusing those of whom he disapproved. Wilde was not a good prisoner, partly because he was new to prisons, but mainly because a man of his temperament is almost certain to violate regulations, not wilfully, but inadvertently. Old lags are excellent prisoners, having learnt from long experience that life in gaol is likely to be more comfortable for those who observe the rules than it is for those who break them. Wilde infringed the regulations without being aware that he was infringing them. He took a long time to become accustomed to a way of life in which he could not do what he liked. The change from the baked meats of the Café Royal to the skilly and ill-cooked bits of fat and gristle in Wandsworth and Reading was too abrupt for a man who had been accustomed to take a hansom cab to cross the street. He was constantly in trouble, and Isaacson punished him heavily even for trivial offences, venting on him not only his official wrath at the violation of a prison rule, but his personal wrath at the crime for which he had been imprisoned. A more imaginative man would have averted his eyes from most of them.

But this harsh and unimaginative Governor was under observation, and remonstrance was made to the Home Office, where sympathy for Wilde was sufficient to cause Isaacson to be removed, in July 1896, from Reading to Lewes. The new Governor, Major J. O. Nelson, was a man of humaner type than his predecessor, and he relieved Wilde's distresses in so far as they were capable of being relieved. Note has already been made of the significant fact that his health, as his friends observed on his release, had greatly improved during his incarceration. Prisons are not recommended as health resorts, but Wilde was a far fitter man when he left Reading Gaol than he was when he fared sumptuously at the Savoy or staggered in dismay from the dock of the Central Criminal Court. The strength he gained in prison was dissipated in Paris.

It was in Nelson's time that he was allowed a greater range of books and permitted to use pens and ink and paper. He now began the long letter to Lord Alfred Douglas which, under the title of *De Profundis*, was published in part in 1905, and in full in 1949. Time has modified opinion on this work. It is not now considered to be the small masterpiece it once was. Compassion gave it a spurious reputation when it first appeared, but the decline of emotion, one way or the other, about its author has allowed reason to assert itself. *De Profundis*, despite some felicities of style, is a dreadful production, almost nauseating in its reproaches, most of them now known to be undeserved, and its self-pity and its transparent insincerity. Its defects are more apparent in the full edition than they were in the edition carefully edited by Ross.

Wilde, who had read the Bible, even when he was at Portora School, oftener than it is read by conventionally devout people, studied it in prison, in default of other books, with closer care than he had ever read it before, reading it in Greek as well as in English; and, in his morbidly pathological state, began to perceive himself as a betrayed man, a saviour brought to Calvary by a false disciple. In lucid intervals, he realised that he had only himself to blame, if we exclude his heredity, for his misfortune; but those lucid intervals grew fewer and fainter, and he believed himself to be another Christ, but more cruelly betrayed. It was as if Our Lord had been kissed, not by Judas, but by John. Alfred Douglas was the beloved disciple, turned traitor; and Wilde, now convinced of his own identity with Jesus, filled sheet after sheet of prison paper with bitter reproach. In his self-righteous wrath he failed to notice two facts which, apart from all else, destroyed his argument: first, that Our Lord, after the kiss of betrayal, mentioned Judas no more, and, second and more important, that Jesus would have walked every inch of the way to Calvary by His own deliberate act even if Judas had never existed. The Stations of the Cross began before the Last Supper and the anguish in the Garden. That swift and fierce invasion of the Temple when the money-changers were flagellated and their tables overturned, was an act as deliberate as the defiance with which the questions asked by Annas, the High Priest, were answered: a defiance which seemed to the policeman standing by the prisoner in the dock to be intolerably insolent. This worthy man, sincerely deferential to his superiors, was so shocked and enraged by Our Lord's bold replies that, St. John reports, he slapped His face. How this policeman must shudder with shame when he remembers that he struck the Son of God! Did Wilde detect a second resemblance to himself in Jesus when he read this story in the Fourth Gospel? Did he recall the central platform at Clapham Junction and see himself, another bound and fettered man, insulted as Our Saviour was? We cannot doubt that he did. But in his haste to identify himself with Jesus, he did not stop to note that Our Lord's arrest and condemnation were sought, and his was not. The journey to the hill outside the city wall was not the result of whim or miscalculation or mischance. Jesus was not imprisoned after He had sought to have another man imprisoned. There were no reproachful letters indited in gaol to Judas. The march to Calvary was a triumphal march, planned and deliberated, made in the hope of trial and execution and ultimate vindication. It was Wilde's failure to perceive this vital difference between his suffering and Our Lord's which brought him to the final blasphemy of casting the blame for it on his disciple, himself exonerated and deeply pitied, and his part condoned. If there was a Judas in this sorry imitation of the supreme sacrifice, Ross was the traitor: the discarded mistress whispering evil of the favourite, and demonstrating his own fidelity and worth by his solicitude for the betrayed master. Wilde, eager to find consolation for his fall, listened with avidity when the little man, magnanimously repaying unkindness with superb devotion, came to visit him in Reading, to tell him tales of Bosie's indifference to his fate, and how he was luxuriating by the Mediterranean Sea while poor Oscar was eating vile food and enduring harsh treatment in a provincial prison! . . .

The pen flew across the paper, as reproach was added to reproach, and the heartless jade was accused of causing his master's ruin. The money Wilde had spent on the greedy boy, the tantrums and exactions he had patiently borne, the submission he had made to foolish whims and unreasonable demands! . . . He, the lord of language, had subjected himself to the dominion of a wilful and indisciplined youth whom he had devotedly loved and indulged—with what reward? He had been betrayed and publicly condemned and humiliated and ruined; and now, while he languished in prison, the capricious creature was diverting himself in expensive hotels, and eating sumptuous food.

Occasionally, he forgets his anger against Douglas and follows an idea which has fluttered through his head like a bewildered butterfly, but resentment soon returns. At moments, too, he rises to heights when he seems transported, and the reader is momentarily transported too. There is a beautiful passage in the letter in which he says that he has become suffused by a spirit in prison which has changed his attitude towards his punishment and life. For the first year of his imprisonment, he could only wring his hands and moan over his fate. "What an ending, what an appalling ending!" to a life. But "now I try to say to myself, and sometimes when I am not torturing myself do really and sincerely say, 'What a beginning, what a wonderful beginning!' " He would go out of Reading Gaol remembering "great kindness that I have received here from almost everybody, and on the day of my release I shall give many thanks to many people, and ask to be remembered by them in turn". Then follows a passage of noble prose which any man might be proud to have written:

> If after I am free a friend of mine gave a feast, and did not invite me to it, I should not mind a bit. I can be perfectly happy by myself. With freedom, flowers, books, and the moon, who could not be perfectly happy? Besides, feasts are not for me any more. That side of life is over for me, very fortunately, I daresay. But if after I am free a friend of mine had a sorrow and refused to allow me to share it, I should feel most bitterly. If he shut the doors of the house of mourning against me, I would come back again and again and beg to be admitted, so that I might share in what I was entitled to share in. If he thought me unworthy, unfit to weep with him, I should feel it as the most poignant humiliation, as the most terrible mode in which disgrace could be inflicted on me. But that could not be. I have a right to share in sorrow, and he who can look at the loveliness of the world and share its sorrow, and realise something of the wonder of both, is in immediate contact with divine things, and has got as near to God's secret as any one can get. . . .

The mood was not maintained, and he sought his consolations, not in freedom, flowers, books and the moon, but on the pavements of Paris, where he readily attended any feast that was provided; but it was a fine mood while it lasted, and we may profit by it, if he did not.

Ross was aware that the letter was being composed, and the little man with a wizened soul was full of joy. At last the cast-off mistress was about to regain his Oscar and be installed again as head of the harem, while the flaunting and selfish favourite was condemned and discarded. He was told to have the letter carefully copied several times on a typewriter. He should be Wilde's literary executor, with full control over all his works. Dear Robbie, so dull and devoted, so devoted and insinuating, always willing and always there! . . . "The very books in my cell are paid for by Robbie out of his pocket-money; from the same source are to come clothes for me when I am released." How different dear Robbie, so faithful and attentive, was from the proud and callous beauty, Bosie, who had not written a single letter to his imprisoned and betrayed and generous friend!

On the day Wilde was discharged from Pentonville—the 19th

of May 1897—to which he was taken from Reading because a prisoner can only be discharged from the gaol to which he was first committed—a curious piece of pedantry—he handed the manuscript of a long letter to Ross, who was to deliver it to Douglas. But Ross, who was an astute man of business, perceived that it had immense value as a social document, apart from any value it had as a piece of literature, and he kept it to himself. Vyvyan Holland, in a preface to the full edition of *De Profundis*, gives an account of this transaction which suffers from two defects: it is derived from Ross in whose favour Holland is naturally and rightly biassed, and it is inadequately dated. He says that Ross sent a copy of the letter to Douglas, and seems to suggest that it was sent immediately after the original was received from Wilde. But no date is given; an omission of some importance, since Douglas denied that he had any knowledge of the letter until 1905, about five years after the date of Wilde's death. He was not aware, he said, that the letter was addressed to him until it was read in Court during the trial of his libel action against Arthur Ransome. That was in 1913, about sixteen years after the original letter had been handed to Ross. It is impossible to form a trustworthy opinion on the subject because all the principals, Ross, Wilde and Douglas, were habitual and incorrigible liars, as all pederasts are, except when they wish to wound. The original manuscript, written on folio sheets of blue prison paper, was deposited in the British Museum by Ross in 1909, to remain there, under seal, for sixty years. It was, however, unsealed in Court during the Douglas-Ransome trial, and long passages from it were read and reported in the press. Thereafter, it was returned to the Museum where it remains.

Wilde, within a year of his release, became reconciled to Douglas, but with a duplicity which is difficult to pardon, even if, in his state of moral degeneration, it is easy to understand, concealed the fact that the bitter reproach had been written and that Ross possessed it. He must have known that Douglas was ignorant of its existence, that Ross still had it, yet he made no effort to retrieve it and destroy it, although he was living on Bosie's bounty. Douglas and he parted in the end, because Lady Queensberry had threatened to withhold her son's allowance unless there was a separation; but the parting was a friendly one, and it was made pleasant by a parting gift from Douglas of £200 that he could ill afford. Less than a fortnight later, Wilde was again writing to Ross, denouncing the Judas! . . .

In the lapse of time, however, *De Profundis* has done Wilde's reputation more harm than good. None of his friends, not even Harris, has defended it. Despite passages of fine and even lyrical prose, it produces to-day, particularly in the full edition, a sense of disappointment that quickly turns to deep disgust. This man, one perceives, was not, as he claimed to have been, purged by suffering: he was confirmed in self-admiration, polluted by self-pity. He was a blear-eyed, corrupted Narcissus, fondly imagining himself to be kneeling by a crystal brook when he was wallowing in a pestilential drain.

62

BUT there was a short space of time in Reading Gaol when he forgot himself and was moved by pity and compassion for another person; and the recollection of it enabled him to write the single work of any value which he produced after his release on the 19th of May 1897. A young guardsman, Charles Thomas Wooldridge, a trooper in the Blues or Royal Horse Guards, whose age was thirty, was hanged in Reading Gaol on the 7th of July 1896, for the murder of his wife, Laura Ellen, on the night of Sunday, the 29th of March. The girl—her age was twenty-three—was flighty and, perhaps, unfaithful, and she provoked her husband to deep wrath which was not diminished by his discovery that she passed as an unmarried woman, under her maiden name of Glendell, in the post office at Eton where she was employed. Meeting her on the road between the Great Western Railway station at Windsor and the village of Clewer, and stung to jealous rage, he cut her throat. Such is the poor and pitiful story. The sight of the young soldier, about to die an ignominious death, stirred an emotion in Wilde which he had seldom felt in his life;

and in the summer of 1897, while he was staying in the Chalet Bourgeat, Berneval, near Dieppe, he began to write *The Ballad*. Tranquillity was not a mood in which Wilde was often found, and there was little in his life then, but in such tranquillity as he was capable of feeling, the recollection of Trooper Charles Thomas Wooldridge returned to his mind, and in the Chalet Bourgeat he could, in his imagination, see him exercising in the prison yard:

He did not wear his scarlet coat,
  For blood and wine are red,
And blood and wine were on his hands
  When they found him with the dead,
The poor dead woman whom he loved,
  And murdered in her bed.

He walked among the Trial Men,
  In a suit of shabby grey;
A cricket cap was on his head,
  And his step seemed light and gay;
But I never saw a man who looked
  So wistfully at the day.

I never saw a man who looked
  With such a wistful eye
Upon that little tent of blue
  Which prisoners call the sky.
And at every drifting cloud that went
  With sails of silver by.

It was a different Wilde who wrote this opening to *The Ballad of Reading Gaol* from the Wilde who wrote *De Profundis*; a finer, nobler-natured man than the author of that witty essay, *Pen, Pencil and Poison*. There are some lines in *The Ballad* which shock the moved reader, lines recalling the Wilde we wish were dead, but they are few and need not be remembered except in sorrow:

And all men kill the thing they love,
  By all let this be heard,
Some do it with a bitter look,
  Some with a flattering word,
The coward does it with a kiss,
  The brave man with a sword!

So *The Ballad* ends—with a lie on its lips, a lie which none of Wilde's admirers, not even the ecstatic Sherard, could believe. The whole of the fifth section of the poem, in which Wilde denounces Law, is rife with puerile pity for the law-breaker and wrongdoer.

> But this I know, that every Law
> That men have made for Man,
> Since first Man took his brother's life,
> And the sad world began,
> But straws the wheat and saves the chaff,
> With a most evil fan.
>
> This, too, I know—and wise it were
> If each could know the same—
> That every prison that men build
> Is built with bricks of shame,
> And bound with bars lest Christ should see
> How men their brothers maim.

Whose shame? The gaoler's or the law-breaker's? If there had been any reason in Wilde's head when he wrote this section of *The Ballad*, if he had not been full of self-pity, he would have realised that these lines forbid us to make any attempt to civilise ourselves, since all our efforts at reform and discipline and control of unruly elements have failed. We have struggled up from slime to what we are, but how useless our struggle, according to Wilde, has been. We have only worsened what we sought to improve. The fact that we have too often been at fault does not justify this pessimism. We are as God made us, and cannot justly be blamed if, with our defective minds, we fail instantly to perceive the right and proper course to follow; but such as we are, we have sought for the better way and we have sometimes found it. In Wilde's verse, we may have sought it, though he seems unsure of this, but have never found it; and he leaves us with the discouraging thought that it will never be found.

> The vilest deeds like poison weeds,
> Bloom well in prison air;
> It is only what is good in Man
> That wastes and withers there:

Pale Anguish keeps the heavy gate,
And the Warder is Despair.

What, then, must we do? Abandon hope? Must we sit down at our ease like the gods in his poem, *Panthea*, strewing with leaves of rose our scented wine, or sleep beneath the rocking trees where asphodel and yellow lotus twine,

Mourning the old glad days before they knew
What evil things the heart of man could dream, and dreaming do.

and, after we have gazed in contempt and pity on the crowd of little men, turn back to our lotus-haunts to kiss each other's mouths and mix more deep the poppy-seeded draught which brings soft purple-lidded sleep? Wilde has no other counsel to give us than that.

Yet *The Ballad* has beauty and it stirs our hearts, even when it sometimes appals our thoughts. His compassion for the condemned soldier was not free of self-pity, but at least the compassion was felt, and it is communicated. For a short time in his life of self-indulgence, Wilde forgot Wilde; and this fact overcomes all our complaint about it. The skill with which it is composed is remarkable, convincing us that prison had at least improved his style, almost compelling us to believe that had he remained in Reading a year or two longer and been given more facilities for writing, he might have enriched us with finer work than any he did. If Mr. Robert Baldwin Ross, who is accused by some of his friends of having tempted him back to sodomy, had died of heart failure long before he did, Wilde might have lived in better health for longer than a year after his release. Unlike Lady Macbeth, Ross should have died sooner.

How effectively Wilde uses repetition and internal rhymes in this Ballad! The third verse in the first section, which is printed here on page 313, is repeated three times, and is most effectively varied in the final repetition, where the wistful glances at the sky are given, not by the condemned soldier, but by his fellow-prisoners after his execution.

Out into God's sweet air we went,
But not in wonted way,

For this man's face was white with fear,
 And that man's face was grey,
And I never saw sad men who looked
 So wistfully at the day.

I never saw sad men who looked
 With such a wistful eye
Upon that little tent of blue
 We prisoners call the sky,
And at every careless cloud that passed
 In happy freedom by.

The form, no doubt, is familiar, and the style is not original, but originality is granted to few, and most of us must follow form as best we can. Wilde was not a man of supreme or even great genius: he was a man of considerable talent who might have been a man of greater talent had he kept himself in closer discipline than he did. It is idle, therefore, to complain that his work is not equal to Shakespeare's or that he failed to reach the lyric heights of Keats and Shelley, though we may justly rebuke those who seek to place him on their level. The man was Wilde and he probably did as much as Wilde was capable of doing, despite our belief that he might, with a stricter control of himself, have done a little better than he did. It may be that the physical and mental deterioration which brought him untimely to the grave could never, in any conditions of life, have been averted, and that he was a doomed man from his mother's womb. In that event, he did what he could, and a little of it was worth doing. *The Ballad* was his last communication with his kind, and it showed him at his best. There is no profundity of mind in it, but there is profundity of feeling; the feeling a man has for other people more than he has for himself. How moving is his description of his emotion when, at exercise in the prison yard, he sees a new prisoner and idly wonders who he is and what he has done:

I walked with other souls in pain,
 Within another ring,
And was wondering if the man had done
 A great or little thing,
When a voice behind me whispered low,
 "*That fellow's got to swing.*"

Dear Christ! the very prison walls
Suddenly seemed to reel,
And the sky above my head became
Like a casque of scorching steel:
And though I was a soul in pain,
My pain I could not feel.

Is it any wonder that those who read *The Ballad* on its first appearance in print hoped that Wilde had begun a new life, and that out of the ashes of the fire in which his old, decaying body had been consumed, a new and burnished body would arise? For the first time in his life, since his sister Isola had died, Wilde had forgotten himself.

Timorously published, on the 13th February 1898, by a rapscallion, Leonard Smithers, who, like some other rapscallions, had a keen sense of fine prose, it quickly became a fairly popular success: a fact which greatly surprised Smithers, who could not believe that, after a life spent on the verge of the Bankruptcy Court, he had at last published a book that the public wished to buy, and, therefore, had not the nerve to venture on editions of more than a thousand copies. He was, indeed, dismayed by his first experience of a best-seller, and seemed to tremble with apprehension every time he signed an order to the printers for another thousand. His fears, perhaps, were stimulated by the fact that he could not persuade any editor in America to offer more than £20 for the serial rights of the poem, and few were willing to pay so much. The first edition, now worth considerably more than £20, was 800 copies at half a crown, and 30 copies on Japanese vellum at a guinea. Within a few days of their issue, the whole of the 800 copies and 20 of the 30 were sold, and Smithers, feeling terribly audacious, ordered a second edition of 1000 copies. By the date of Wilde's death 7000 had been sold, a number that might have been increased had a less impecunious and frightened publisher been employed. Harris, with characteristic extravagance, informs his readers that "in a few weeks it ran through dozens of editions in England and America, and translations appeared in almost every European language". Reviews at first were few, but among the earliest and most enthusiastic was one which must have astonished

Wilde as much as it probably pleased him. It appeared in *The War Cry*, the official organ of the Salvation Army, and it was signed with the initials of William Bramwell Booth, the eldest child of the Founder and himself the second General. Its title, *A Prison Agony*, sufficiently indicates its sympathetic character. But when the reviewers perceived the public interest in the book, they not only plucked up enough courage to mention both it and its author, but went beyond reason in their praise. "One reviewer", Harris says, "compared it with the best of Sophocles", a statement which may mean much or mean little, for Harris does not tell us how the comparison was drawn; "another", he continues, "said that 'nothing like it has appeared in our time' ", another statement which scarcely entitled Harris to state that the "enthusiasm" for *The Ballad* "in England was astounding". A critic is not to be regarded as saying that a poem is an immortal work because he says that "nothing like it has appeared in our time". He may mean no more than he says, that it is the only work of its kind to have been written in a specified period. A man who runs a race by himself is not to be treated as the equal of a man who wins a race against twenty competitors. The muddle which Harris called his mind is sufficiently revealed in his statement that *The Ballad* "is beyond all comparison the greatest ballad in English: one of the noblest poems in the language. That is what prison did for Oscar Wilde." The reader with the first part of this passage in his mind, may well wish that Wilde had been sent to prison sooner, and deplore the fact that he was not kept there for the rest of his life if "that" was "what prison did for" him. To turn a minimum poet and a mediocre dramatist into the author of the greatest ballad in English and one of the noblest poems in the language was a feat so tremendous that one wonders our prisons are not so crowded with people ambitious to be great writers that there is no room in them for criminals.

63

THE prophet Isaiah, in a great chapter, describes himself as an anointed man, moved by the spirit of the Lord God to proclaim liberty to the captives, and the opening of the prison to them that are bound, to comfort all that mourn and give them beauty for ashes. Wilde, for a few months, seemed as if he might be moved as Isaiah was moved, that he had come out of Reading Gaol, purged and purified, bearing beauty for ashes and ready to repair the waste cities and the desolations of many generations. But the hope was delusive. Self-pity repossessed him, and the brief compassion he had felt for Trooper Wooldridge faded and died. The rest of the story is a dreary tale of dismal descent. The fire sometimes sent out flashes of bright flame, but these times were few. Wilde, who had been a lord of language, became a drunken shuffler on barren pavements, cadging and sponging, a lath painted to look like a lath. He whined about his poverty, though he was not poor, and complained of his friends who had helped him to their own distress. He was wilful as only weak men are wilful, and fawned on those he had secretly traduced. His ear was too attentive to the smooth whispers of little Mr. Robert Baldwin Ross, and soon he was deep in the mire again, a leering old bouser, though his age was only forty-three, selling a plot for a play to this one and that one, until a group of people could claim rights in it, and busy buying a bicycle for a mindless conscript he had picked up in Paris. He lived on Douglas, but did not tell him that Mr. Robert Baldwin Ross had a long letter about him, full of bitter reproach. When, at last, he and Douglas parted, he clutched at any hand he could grasp . . . and bit it.

Once, in this reel to the steep place, anguish came upon him again. Constance, tried beyond her strength, had died; a most unhappy woman, no more than forty. There had been no meeting between them since the day when she had come from Genoa to tell him in prison of his mother's death because she could not bear the thought that he should hear the news from any lips but hers.

The love formerly felt for her had perished in the fens and bogs of Sodom and Gomorrah. On the 7th of April 1898, less than a year after his release from Reading, she died. Alfred Douglas, according to Pearson, was told by Wilde that on the night before her death, he dreamt that she came to see him, "and I kept on saying, 'Go away, go away, leave me in peace' ". A telegram told him the next day that she was dead in Genoa. He was almost kinless now. The posturing old woman, his mother, had died on the 3rd of February 1896, while he was still in prison. Then, after the death of Constance, his scallywag brother, Willie, died at 9 Cheltenham Terrace, Chelsea, on the 13th of March 1899. The two little boys, Cyril and Vyvyan Oscar Wilde, no longer Wilde but Holland, were in the guard of their mother's relations. They had not seen their father since his arrest.

Solitude, despite his praise of it in *De Profundis*, was uncongenial to him. He needed company, and since he could not find it in the circles he had once frequented, he sought it in back-street cafés and wine-shops. "Incapable of writing a line, with atrophied brain, he had only as listeners men who haunted the restaurants and stood him drinks. . . . There only remained to him his musical voice, and his large, blue childish eyes." So Joseph Renaud wrote of him in *La Grande Revue*, early in 1905, about the time when *De Profundis* first appeared, some five years after Wilde's death. There had been a brief period of humane writing, when a couple of articles on harsh prison regulations had appeared in *The Daily Chronicle* and were followed by *The Ballad*. But that was all. The will to write was failing fast. Dare we believe that he might have spent the rest of his life in peace if he had returned to Constance, if these two unhappy people had not been beset by counsellors who bewildered and angered them with tales of each other's arbitrary demands? Douglas has been cruelly maligned for insisting that Wilde should join him at Naples, yet it is true that it would have been far better for Wilde if they had never met again, and better, too, if Mr. Robert Baldwin Ross had played the part of the benevolent solicitor in a strictly professional fashion. One person in this world might have saved what was good and fine in Wilde, his wife, but the poor lady, now near her end, was distracted by the wisdom of the wise when all that was needed was the wisdom of the foolish. When she died, any hope he had died too.

There is a moving story in Pearson's book which confirms the belief that Wilde might have been realised some happiness in reunion with his wife. It seems that while he was living at La Napoule on the calculated bounty of Frank Harris, the industrious note-taker, a man called Harold Mellor had become acquainted with him. This eccentric person had a house at Gland on Lake Geneva, to which he invited Wilde for an unspecified period. The visit was a failure, and Wilde, who had begun by liking Mellor, ended by detesting him. Our concern, however, is not with Mellor, but with an incident which occurred during Wilde's journey from La Napoule to Gland. He broke his journey at Genoa, so that he might visit his wife's grave. "It was very tragic", he subsequently wrote, "seeing her name carved on a tomb . . . my name not mentioned, of course. . . . I brought some flowers—I was deeply affected—with a sense, also, of the uselessness of all regrets. Nothing could have been otherwise—and life is a very terrible thing." We need not dwell on the despair of the final, deterministic sentence, one that is common on the lips and pen of any man who has made a mess of his life and is reluctant to take the responsibility for his misfortune. But we may note as important to our argument, the description of the visit given by Pearson, who remarks that Wilde "drove out to the cemetery from Genoa in a little ramshackle green cab", and "gave way to a paroxysm of grief and remorse at the graveside, where he sobbed and prayed, and strewed crimson roses on the earth, and vowed eternal fidelity to the memory of Constance, his strongest emotion having been expressed by himself in a youthful ballade:

> O mother, you know I loved her true!
> O mother, hath one grave room for two?

Utterly overcome by his feelings, exhausted and weeping, he drove away! . . ." It does not diminish his grief that later in the day he caroused at "a small inn on the quay, Albergo di Firenze". The depth of his sorrow may, indeed, be denoted by the extent of his carousal. As he stood by the lonely grave of the young Irish girl he had married, and remembered her beauty and her bewilderment and her love, and thought of the wreck he had made of his brilliant life, a deep disgust with his own existence may have swept through his mind and heart and filled him with a self-loathing that was as deep as the self-pity, deeper, indeed, than that which he too often displayed. He had written a charming little lyric in her honour, "from a poet to a poem", when he gave her a copy of his *Poems*:

For if of these fallen petals
  One to you seem fair,
Love will waft it till it settles
  On your hair,

And when the wind and winter harden
  All the loveless land,
It will whisper of the garden,
  You will understand.

"I have no power to do anything but just love you", she told him in one of the letters she wrote before their marriage, "my whole life is yours to do as you will with it. . . . Do believe that I love you most passionately with all the strength of my heart and mind." And again, in another letter, "When I have you for my husband, I will hold you fast with chains of love and devotion so that you shall never leave me, or love anyone as long as I can love and comfort". Alas, alas, that this devoted girl should have lost her lover in the stews of Westminster, in the shoddy incense-reeking brothel full of stable-boys and ostlers and decaying clerks, that this lovely lily should have been cast aside when little Mr. Robert Baldwin Ross, the furtive pussy-cat of foul, unlawful lust, came mincing by. As Wilde, stricken with grief, stood by the sepulchre of his wife, she was, for a little while, his darling once again. The air was sweet with the honey of a man's love for a woman, and there was no defilement by the lonely grave.

64

HIS time is short now, and he makes the least of it. Back in Paris, he drops deeper and deeper into the mire. In debt to one hotel-keeper, he moves to the house of another, and is soon expelled for unsettled bills. A third hotelier evicts him, and he is found in the street without a home or money by Jean Dupoirer, the landlord of the Hôtel d'Alsace, in the rue des Beaux Arts, to whom he owed a heavy sum. Dupoirer, overcome by his distress, discharged his debt at the hotel from which he had just been evicted and, recovering his small effects, took him to his own. There was a little interlude in the spring of 1900 when Mellor appeared again, and, after a short stay at Gland, carried him off to Italy. In Rome, he toyed with the thought of conversion to Roman Catholicism: a thought that had occurred to him before: but he did not then yield to the temptation. The theology of Rome made no appeal to him: its ceremonial did. He took no interest in its creed, but was profoundly moved by its ritual. But not, at that date, moved enough to become a convert.

Stuart Mason, in his *Bibliography*, asserts, on page 118, that Wilde "declared more than once to intimate friends that he had a distinct recollection as a child of being christened in a Catholic church", and this recollection was corroborated by a statement published in 1905, by the Rev. Lawrence Charles Prideaux Fox, a priest of the Oblates of Mary Immaculate, who was a convert from the Society of Friends. Formerly a dentist, he had been received into the Church of Rome in the early fifties. Father Fox contributed a number of articles, under the general title of *People I Have Met*, to a Boston paper, *Donahoe's Magazine*. In the April number, vol. 53, No. 4, page 397, there was a portrait of Lady Wilde with the inscription, "Whose son, Oscar, I baptized". Mason also reports that in the following issue, the May number, page 472, these particulars were printed:

When stationed at the reformatory [St. Kevin's, Glencree, about fifteen miles from Dublin] I sometimes called on Sir William Wilde, who was reported to be one of the cleverest oculists of his time. He was bitterly opposed to reformatories, and made no secret of his animosity; not so, however, his talented and patriotic wife, Lady Wilde, who was better known by her *nom de plume*, Speranza. She used to take lodgings every summer for herself and her children at a farmhouse, at the foot of Glencree, belonging to a worthy family of the name of Evans, intimate friends of mine. On my calling there one day, she asked my permission to bring her children to our chapel to assist at Mass on Sundays. As we had a tribune in the chapel from which the boys and the altar could be seen without actual communication I readily acceded to her request, and after the Mass was over, I enjoyed many a pleasant hour with this excellent lady. I am not sure whether she ever became a Catholic herself, but it was not long before she asked me to instruct two of her children, one of them being that future erratic genius, Oscar Wilde. After a few weeks I baptized these two children, Lady Wilde herself being present on the occasion. At her request, I called on their father, and told him what I had done, his sole remark being that he did not care what they were so long as they became as good as their mother. I presume I must have removed from Glencree soon after that time, as I never met any of the family again.

The date of this singular baptism, according to Mason, "was probably 1862 or 1863, at which time Oscar Wilde was eight or nine years old".

The story told by Father Fox has an air of verisimilitude, especially when it is read immediately after Mason's assertion that Wilde had declared "more than once to intimate friends that he had a distinct recollection as a child of being christened in a Catholic church", but reflection causes doubt. Why is it that none of his friends, in their numerous books about him, mention this story? Why did Lady Wilde, so eager for the salvation of two of her children, not have the third baptized? Why did she not seek her own salvation on the day that Oscar and the other child were baptized? Why did Wilde, when he toyed on several occasions with the idea of conversion to Rome, not recall the fact that he was already a Roman Catholic? He is known to have had interviews with priests at the Oratory of St. Philip Neri at Brompton in 1878. It would, surely, have been natural for him to mention this remarkable baptism. The priests would soon have enlightened him on his spiritual relations if he had. How, too, did it come about that Wilde, as Mason himself reports, was stated in *The Tablet*, of the 8th of December 1900, to "have attributed his catastrophe to the fact that his father would not allow him, when he was a youth, to submit himself to the discipline of the Catholic Church", when, two pages later, Mason is citing Father Fox's account of the baptism at Glencree and reporting Sir William's indifference to it?[1]

If this baptism ever took place, the Wildes seem to have been very slightly affected by it. Apart from purely emotional or aesthetic interest in the Roman Catholic Church, Wilde never in his life betrayed any concern about it as an institution to which he owed a duty. His marriage was celebrated in an Anglican church, and his children were baptized as Anglicans. He must have concealed his baptism from Ross, although Ross was a Roman Catholic, for had Ross known of it, he would not have arranged for Wilde to receive conditional baptism and absolution from Father Cuthbert Dunne on the 30th of November 1900, a few days before his death. Father Dunne, as was his duty, asked Wilde the customary questions that are put to persons seeking reception into the Church of Rome. One of these questions must have been about his baptism, but Wilde does not appear to have mentioned that curious ceremony at Glencree. He was, it is true, almost moribund and may have forgotten it or been too near his death to be able to talk about it. But he never mentioned it to anybody. Father Fox's story cannot be dismissed as the romantic delusion of a priest in his dotage unless we dismiss also Mason's story of Wilde's declaration that he remembered being baptized; but we shall need better authority for it than we have if we are to give it credence. Fox must have been a very old man when he published his reminiscences in *Donahoe's Magazine* in 1905. We are told by Mason that he was in his early fifties when he was received into the Roman Catholic Church. He cannot have been ordained immediately on his reception, but even if he had been, he must have been over sixty when he is alleged to have baptized

[1] The Marquess of Queensberry in his book, *Oscar Wilde and the Black Douglas*, asserts that Sir William's will contained a clause depriving Oscar of his Irish property if he should have become a Roman Catholic.

Oscar Wilde at Glencree. In 1905, when his reminiscences were published, that is to say, more than forty years later, he must have been a centenarian! . . .

Here we have an example of the myth that is now so closely woven with the facts of Wilde's life that it is almost impossible to separate one from the other. Bedevilment is increased by the readiness of his biographers to accept or reject any story that pleases or displeases them. Pearson dismisses as "quite untrue" a story told by Dame Nellie Melba, presumably in *Memories and Melodies*, of an occasion when Wilde lurched round a corner in Paris and asked her for money. Pearson's comment on this story is infantile. It cannot be true, Melba must have lied, because Wilde "did not borrow money from" women! . . . But he had borrowed money, in his young manhood, from his impoverished mother,[1] and he had lived on his wife's bounty though he had stinted her of money when she had bitter need of it. How does Pearson, who was thirteen years old when Wilde died, know that he never borrowed or begged money from women? Is it not obvious that a man in the state of moral and physical collapse that Wilde was in during the last two years of his life, would have borrowed money from anybody, male or female, rich or poor, young or old, friend or foe? Pearson is almost maudlin in his emotion about Wilde. Mary Anderson ought to have given him four thousand dollars for the worthless *Duchess of Padua*, which she could have "shelved! . . ." The landlord of the Hôtel Marsollier in Paris "had the chance of immortalising himself by giving Wilde reasonable credit", but "he had the soul of a tradesman, bartered his immortality for a hundred francs, and forced Wilde to leave". This is mawkish sentimentality, unworthy of an adult man. The landlord of the Hôtel Marsollier was not seeking immortality: he was seeking his livelihood.

How ready Pearson is to charge anyone with lying who is not fulsome about Wilde appears from his statement that a story told by Edward Marjoribanks in *The Life of Lord Carson* is "quite as

[1] He repaid her out of the money he earned in America, but this fulfilment of obligations does not alter the fact that he, who might have been expected at the age he then was to be earning his living, was willing to sponge on his mother who had been left badly off by his father.

untrue" as that told by Melba, "with a touch of burlesque to make it more piquant". Carson, it appears, was about to cross a street in Paris one day when he was almost run down by a cab. "Stepping back quickly to the pavement, he knocked someone down, turned to apologise and recognised 'the haggard, painted features of Oscar Wilde', who was obligingly lying in the gutter. Carson begged his pardon, and, we are to assume, left him in the gutter."

Why we are to assume this, Pearson does not pause to explain. Only a brutal boor or a callous lorry-driver would knock a man down, accidentally or carelessly, and depart without rendering any aid. Pearson may not, but he certainly ought to, have known that Carson was reluctant to accept a brief against Wilde because they had been contemporaries at Trinity College, Dublin, and it was only when the nature of the charge against Wilde was fully revealed to him, and he was persuaded to believe that it was his duty in the public interest to accept the brief, that he agreed to do so. Can a biographer be considered responsible when he writes such a sentence as "Carson begged his pardon, and, we are to assume, left him in the gutter"?

"Whether this is Carson's invention or not", Pearson continues, "will probably remain a mystery, but everyone knows what happens when a motor-car collides with a tank. Wilde was the tank. Apart from that, it can confidently be stated that Wilde never put paint on his face, except when he was lecturing in America, never had a hunted nor a haggard look, was never shabbily dressed, did not shuffle, could carry his drink without staggering, and would have stood firm against the shock of anything short of a bull." This is shallow-minded stuff. Any man, even one as robust as Wilde was in his prime, can be capsized by the impact of unexpected collision. Wilde's face may not have been painted, but we have no proof that Carson ever said it was. The reference to paint may have been an embellishment by Marjoribanks. A well-made and powerful motor in good condition could certainly damage an exhausted tank and might even, in certain circumstances, overthrow it. We have the testimony of some of his friends that Wilde was often helplessly drunk in Paris in the last two years of his life, to the extent, sometimes, of having to be carried to a cab. This is not inconsistent with an appearance of sobriety, any more than occasional displays of fine raiment are inconsistent with frequent displays of shabbiness and squalor. Wilde's temperament was such that he was likely to look, on occasions, a shuffling sot and, on other occasions, a man of fashion. He was notorious at Portora for slovenliness, and equally notorious at Oxford for eccentric clothes. In one year he was affecting the languid aesthete, and in the next, affecting the fop. There is no discrepancy between the dissimilar accounts of his last years: a man who saw him being carried out of a back-street wine-shop in Paris might seem a liar to a man who met him only in a fashionable restaurant, enthralling his companions with his charming conversation, but the latter must also seem a liar to the former.

We have to deal with probabilities in a man of his character in his condition. His moods changed extremely and rapidly. New from weeping at his wife's grave in Genoa, he soon caroused with immense gusto and verve in the nearest inn. His periods of solitude in Paris were longer than his periods of companionship; and in these periods he, who had no love of solitude, desponded. Drink was his comfort. His constant sense of lost position, the feeling he had of a furtive alien in France—for the French, especially those in authority, were no kinder in their attitude to him than were the British [1]—and that he might at any moment find himself cut by a countryman—all these must have combined to lower his intellectual and spiritual vitality; and when he returned again to drink and debauchery, his physical vitality was soon sapped. We are now dealing, not with a man in the full flush of his strength, but with a man whose strength has been steadily reduced, a reduction made swifter by intellectual despair and loose living. The Wilde of the last two years was a Wilde in an advanced state of degeneracy. He was now a rabid hunter of small boys and simple-

[1] Harris states that Jean Lorrain, "the wittiest talker I have ever heard in France, and a most brilliant journalist", brutally and publicly insulted Wilde at a reception in Paris. Lorrain, whose "life was as abandoned as it could well be; in fact, he made a parade of strange vices", had "always pretended to be a friend and admirer" of Wilde "in the days of Oscar's supremacy", but when Wilde, catching sight of him at the reception, advanced "with outstretched hands" to greet his friend, as he supposed him to be, saying "Delighted to see you, Jean", Lorrain "folded his arms theatrically and replied, 'I regret I cannot say as much: I can no longer be one of your friends, Mr. Wilde' ". See *Oscar Wilde*, page 289.

minded conscripts, and his body and his mind had deteriorated terribly. None of this contradicts the fact that some of his friends found him as brilliant in conversation as ever he had been. The man dying of consumption is certain of recovery when he is on the point of death. Wilde found congenial companions infectious, and he could muster a night's brilliance for their entertainment. But he was a doomed and dying man, no longer capable of any sustained effort; and when he crept back to his small hotel, squalid in comparison with his former haunts, tides of despair would sweep across his heart and drag him down to depths of self-abasement, until he could cry out, as Satan cried in *Paradise Lost*,

> which way shall I fly
> Infinite wrath, and infinite despair?
> Which way I fly is Hell; myself am Hell;
> And in the lowest deep a lower deep
> Still threatening to devour me opens wide,
> To which the Hell I suffer seems a Heaven.

Any writing now was too hard a task for him to accomplish. He had squandered in Paris the strength he had recovered in prison, and was a sheer hulk about to perish and be broken up. The man who could drink the Colorado miners under the table when he was still in the vigour of his berserker youth, could only drink himself under it when he had flattered young poets in Paris with his enchanting talk.

65

HE is racked with pain. His head hurts him horribly, so that he clutches it in his hands and, like Job, curses the day wherein he was born. There is a frightful ache in his ear, and he must have an operation to ease it. But there is only one operation now that will bring ease to Wilde; an operation which can be performed only by that sinister surgeon, the dark angel of death. His sudden alternations of mood even at this time deceive his friends. Insisting that his agony is unbearable, he makes them rollick with laughter as he pokes fun at his doctors. How can he be distracted with pain, his friends say to themselves, who is so gay? Ross, in October 1900, did not believe that Wilde was as ill as he made himself out to be, but in November it was plain that his debt to Death was due and must soon be paid. It was not a peaceful death, but one of dreadful pain. "He was dying", Pearson says, "of cerebral meningitis, probably complicated by syphilis." But when the complication was started no man can say. The stories of infection at Oxford are less convincing than those who tell them seem to think, nor is there much conviction in the tale that he had ceased to live with Constance in the way of marriage because he was horrified to discover that the disease, of which he had thought himself cured, had broken out again. Why, even if that were true, should it have compelled him to become a pederast? We may more easily believe that this complication, if it existed, was the result of the underground life he led in Paris after his release from Reading. It is idle to speculate on these things, since no man can say what another man's life is, and is seldom sure of his own. It must be enough to say that Wilde died dreadfully. All that splendour and applause in great mansions and famous theatres and places where people talk long and well, had fallen down to this shabby room in a poor apartment-hotel in a back street in Paris where a stricken man in exile held his tormented head in his hands and blasphemed against himself and God. The wages of sin are hard wages, but they must be paid; and Wilde had to pay. His inexorable debtor, Death, screwed his last penny from him, and gave him no relief until it was paid.

Collapse came swiftly, the one mercy Wilde was granted then. On the 29th of November, Ross, summoned from Nice, returned in time to find him conscious, but inarticulate, and asked him if he wished a priest to be called. Wilde made a sign that he did, and the Passionist Father, Dunne, was called to his bed. His routine questions were answered by signs. The lord of language, so brilliant in his discourse on mundane matters, was silent in the hour of his most high decision: his tongue was tied in the presence of his Lord God. He was baptized and given extreme unction, but not the sacrament, which he was now physically unfit to take. He lingered, only just alive, until the following day, the

30th of November 1900. About two o'clock in the afternoon, he began to struggle for breath, and Dupoirer, the landlord of his hotel, lifted him in his arms, holding him up for a few minutes, and in that kind embrace, Wilde, with a sigh of relief, relaxed and died. Eleven months earlier, in January, his implacable enemy, the ninth Marquess of Queensberry, had predeceased him, dying in the delusion that he was a pauper. But Wilde, if he ever heard of the death of the scarlet Marquess, appears to have made no comment on it.

66

HE preached the doctrine of art for art's sake, insisting that moral judgements were none of the artist's business; and he proudly told his critics that he had put his genius into his life and conversation and only his talent into his work. But those who listened to the doctrine felt unimpressed. A faith that led a man to Reading Gaol and a squalid end in France, is one to be avoided, not embraced, a faith unworthy of a martyr.

What he meant by his argument was never made apparent. His doctrine bears little or no relation to his work. What evidence of art for art's sake is to be found in *An Ideal Husband*? Is there any sign of it in *Lady Windermere's Fan* or *A Woman of No Importance*? *Salomé* is full of severe and even morbid puritan passion. He was excessively moved by whim and brief emotion, and he said and wrote the first thing that came into his head. None of it had any relation to a *considered* belief about life. Wilde talked about art for art's sake, but did not practise it. Anyone who tries to relate *The Importance of Being Earnest* to a philosophic argument will have a hard and heavy task. He found fault with *The Ballad* and his articles in *The Daily Chronicle*, in which he exposed harshness in prison regulations, because they were not "pure" art, but were alloyed with counterfeit emotion. But that will not do. How can we explain the fact that *The Ballad*, which he, perhaps in a moment of flippancy, belittled as an exercise in humanitarianism, an "impure" form of art, a piece of propaganda, has been acclaimed, and is still acclaimed by some, as the greatest ballad in English and one of the noblest poems in our language? Can we believe that the emotion which moved Wilde when he remembered the young soldier who was hanged in Reading Gaol was a false emotion, rising from no spirit of fine art, but only from a party feeling? If we can, may we not wonder why Wilde was never able to produce a greater work for art's sake than *The Ballad* he wrote in a moral mood? An artist has a view of life. It is absurd to think that his vision is unbiassed by belief. The choice of a subject is in itself the result of complicated ideas of which he may not be fully aware, if, indeed, he is aware of them at all. Why did Shaw choose to write about St. Joan and not about Saint Catherine of Siena? It is not enough to say that the Maid had more appeal. Why did she appeal at all, and why more than, say, Savonarola? Joan, establishing the idea of nationality in a world in which a primitive conception of a united Western Europe was forming, might seem certain to alienate rather than attract Shaw. Yet it was to this rebellious child that he turned, and not to Catherine or Teresa.

Wilde was a neo-Epicurean, an extreme individualist, who demanded the right to live as he liked, and insisted that he should not be subjected to the restrictions of small, frightened men who mistake their fears for principles and are determined to have us all made in one mould or kept to one level lest some should grow to greater heights than others. There is no tyranny more ruthless than that of little men, who seek incessantly to bind the giant, Gulliver, on the ground. Wilde perceived this fact in *The Soul of Man Under Socialism*, and warned us to beware. If art for art's sake means anything, it means that a man shall have the right to tell us what he sees, and shall not be forbidden because it clashes with local and ephemeral codes. The sage and the seer, like the rest of us, are subject to delusions and may deceive themselves and us, but we have judgement here and can settle how much credence we can give to their apocalypse. The community has weapons of defence against those who seek to change its mind: it can ignore them and their message. But it will forbid them to announce it at its peril. For no man knows who his saviour may be.

It will be well, then, to forget for a moment that Wilde went down the drain, and endeavour instead to discover what value there is in his argument that art is separate from morals and superior to them. This is an age in which it is specially desirable to make this enquiry. Governments deliberately circumscribe the range of individual thoughts and are ready to maim minds and bodies. The supine and fatalistic masses of the world, the great witless herds which infest the eastern plains, are eager to corrupt the daring and aspiring spirit of the western man and reduce him to their own level of inert and bound dependence, their pathetic acceptance of a fate they fear to change or challenge. For these are not free men who submit themselves to an authority which they can overthrow, but slave-minded men who have never learnt to disobey.

Wilde, despite his brief abasement in *De Profundis*, seems never to have known that he was, directly in his argument about art for art's sake, and indirectly in his downfall, pointing a moral as strictly and severely as a priest or arbitrary politician; and any hope he might have had of spreading his belief was destroyed when, after his release from Reading, he reverted to his sewer life in Paris. Yet his argument calls for a reply, and a world almost overwhelmed by materialism must think of an answer, if it is not to perish of cogs and wheels and little men in power.

Two men, one of genius, one of talent, came out of Ireland at the same time to change the face of England. They differed from each other deeply and irreconcilably. Wilde, pleading for individual liberty, fell into the Slough of Despond and could not extricate himself, but Shaw, pleading for supreme power of the State, rose slowly from obscurity and disregard to such authority that he became venerable even in the eyes of conservative people. Are we sure that Shaw was right and Wilde was wrong? That long, lean abstainer with laughing light-blue eyes and kindly heart, whose favourite reading was the tables of mortality and Blue Books and State statistics, could fling up his hat for Mussolini and withhold his pity from Ethiopian Bedouins whose bodies were disrupted by Italian bombs. He had a word to say in praise of Hitler and shook the heavens with his cheers for Stalin. Any dictator would do for Shaw, no matter what uniform he wore. These sinister and evil men, like those evil men, Augustine, Calvin and Karl Marx, would have seemed ominous and full of dread to Wilde, a tall, fat man with a greasy, grey-green face and an unaccountable and unlawful lust. Shall we, then, in making audit of our time's account, decide that Wilde deserved the drain and Shaw the starry sky? Or turn from both and seek another sage?

The mind of Shaw soared far above the mind of Wilde, and none who had the happiness to come under that gracious influence can feel otherwise than grateful for the experience. But Wilde, too, had a thing to say, and he, too, had friends who loved him though he tried them hard. Despite his insincere and selfish heart and his lack of any deep affection, there were those who, though he wronged them and flayed them with his pen, were glad that they had known him and heard him speak. How strange it is that this man, Wilde, whose art was slight and his achievements few and his defilement deep, should have kept his hold on men's attention all these years! He comes before us in his poverty, an unsightly sinner, offensive with the stench of a foul and festered life, and holds out his small bundle of plays and poems and asks for our applause; and, amazingly, we give it. Do we cheer because we feel that what he had to say, but did not adequately say, was something we had need to hear? Or are we only sorry for a man who lost his soul but did not gain the world?

How shall we decide between these two: the moral Shaw, the a-moral Wilde? Was each in his way right or each in his way wrong? What is man to do, confused by his guides? Where are we to look for help who see menace everywhere, and are bewildered by the clamant cries and contradictions of contending prophets? We look into the heavens, but see no sign. We look down at the earth, but see no sign. We are beset. Shall we do as the Venerable Bede did when the bird flew into the hall from the darkness outside and fluttered for a few moments in the flare of the fires before it flew back to the darkness, forget the darkness and remember only the beauty of the bird's wings and flight?

That poet of genius, Elizabeth Barrett Browning, was right when, in *Aurora Leigh*, she wrote these various passages:

. . . a twofold world
Must go to a perfect cosmos. Natural things
And spiritual,—who separates those two
In art, in morals, or the social drift,
Tears up the bond of nature and brings death,
Paints futile pictures, writes unreal verse,
Leads vulgar days, deals ignorantly with men,
Is wrong, in short, at all points.

. . . . .

Ay, Carrington
Is glad of such a creed: an artist must,
Who paints a tree, a leaf, a common stone,
With just his hand, and finds it suddenly
A-piece with and conterminous to his soul.
Why else do these things move him, leaf or stone?
The bird's not moved that pecks at a spring-shoot;
Nor yet the horse, before a quarry a-graze;
But man, the twofold creature, apprehends
The twofold manner, in and outwardly,
And nothing in the world comes singly to him,
A mere itself, cup, column or candlestick,
All patterns of what shall be in the Mount;
The whole temporal show related royally,
And built up to aeterne significance
Through the open arms of God.

. . . . .

Earth's crammed with heaven,
And every common bush afire with God;
But only he who sees, takes off his shoes—
The rest sit round it and pluck blackberries,
And daub their natural faces unaware
More and more from the first similitude.

. . . . .

Art's the witness of what Is
Behind this show. If this world's show were all,
Then imitation would be all in Art.

. . . . .

Art itself,
We've called the larger life, must feel the soul
Live past it. For more's felt than is perceived,
And more's perceived than can be interpreted,
And Love strikes higher with his lambent flame
Than Art can pile the faggots.

Wilde came into the world with a small talent and made little of it. He did worse than that. He denied his principles by his practice. He cast such pearls as he had before swine, and then wallowed with the swine at the troughs in the sty. He was a flippant man who turned high matters to bibblers' jests, and would not forgo a witticism to spare a friend a wound. A brawler in the temple may be sincerely affirming a faith, but a man who titters in the temple and is flippant about his faith is a recusant who denies without any affirmation in the denial. The steward who hid his talent in a napkin was cursed and condemned, but what punishment is fitting for the man who takes his gift from God and drops it in the mire? That was the sin committed by Oscar Wilde. It was the sin against the Holy Ghost.